DISCARD

D1273192

Renaissance Culture in Poland

RENAISSANCE CULTURE IN POLAND:

The Rise of Humanism, 1470–1543

Harold B. Segel

Cornell University Press

Ithaca and London

DK
4252
.S44
1989

Copyright © 1989 by Cornell University

All rights reserved. Except for brief quotations in a review, this book, or parts
thereof, must not be reproduced in any form without permission in writing from
the publisher. For information, address Cornell University Press, 124 Roberts Place,
Ithaca, New York 14850.

First published 1989 by Cornell University Press.

International Standard Book Number 0-8014-2286-8
Library of Congress Catalog Card Number 89-30788
Printed in the United States of America
Librarians: Library of Congress cataloging information
appears on the last page of the book.

The paper in this book is acid-free and meets the guidelines for
permanence and durability of the Committee on Production Guidelines
for Book Longevity of the Council on Library Resources.

FEB 1 3 1990

IN MEMORIAM LAUDEMQUE VICTORIS WEINTRAUB
HIC LIBER DEDICATUR

Vir magnae sapientiae, praeceptor et amicus,
qui in cordibus nostris vivit.
Utinam ea res voluptati sit.

Contents

Acknowledgments

I am deeply grateful to the late Wiktor Weintraub of Harvard University for volunteering to read the manuscript and for offering many helpful suggestions at a time when grave illness surely made this a difficult task, and to the National Endowment for the Humanities for their generous support in the form of a research fellowship when this study was first launched and for their exemplary encouragement of East European studies.

H.B.S.

New York City

Guide to Polish Pronunciation

This guide is intended solely as an aid to readers who know no Polish. It makes no claim to any scientific exactness.

Accent: All Polish words are stressed on the next-to-last syllable.

Vowels: a, e, i, o, u are pronounced as in most European languages (a as in *father;* e as in *met;* i as in *machine;* o as in *more;* u like the double o in *proof;* ó is pronounced the same as u. There are also two nasal vowels in Polish: ą *(on)* and ę *(en)*.

Consonants: Those different from English are:

    c = ts
 ć (or ci) = like ch in *chime* (soft ch)
    ch = kh (like German ch)
    cz = like tch in *patch* (hard ch)
    h = never silent in Polish
    j = y
    l = like l in *lure* (soft l)
    ł = like English w (hard l)
 ń (or ni) = ny, as in *canyon* (soft n)
    rz, ż = zh, as in *rouge,* or sh after p, t, k (hard zh)
 ś (or si) = sh, as in *sure* (soft sh)
    w = v
 ź (or zi) = zh, as in *leisure* (soft zh)

Renaissance Culture in Poland

Introduction

In the West the Renaissance is commonly regarded as pertaining almost exclusively to the people of western Europe. To most of us, the Renaissance arose in Italy and spread from there to northern Europe, principally France, Germany, and England. But students of eastern Europe—in this case primarily Bohemia, Dalmatia (that part of Croatia lying along the Adriatic, with the city of Dubrovnik as its cultural center), Hungary and Poland—know that in its diffusion throughout Europe the Renaissance did not halt at some arbitrary boundary dividing Europe into western and eastern halves. To be sure, in the West Renaissance studies by specialists on eastern Europe are fairly recent and rare, so that Renaissance scholarship in general has not yet had to digest new learning or change its perspective to any appreciable degree. The Renaissance is still studied and taught as a Western movement.

The political division of Europe into two competitive and conflicting blocs since the end of World War II has certainly not helped matters. Eastern Europe is perceived as a Soviet sphere of influence or as within the orbit of Soviet power. In a sense, then, eastern Europe becomes part of the new Russian empire; the longer the political status quo remains and the longer Europe stays divided into two blocs, the more natural the tendency to project the present political realities onto the past—to relegate eastern Europe to a kind of Russian vassalage over a much longer period than has actually been the case. Related to this perception, and far worse, is the common confusion of political and cultural realities. By this I mean the tendency to assume that since the east European states are part of the Soviet bloc their cultures, like their societies, must be similar to Russia's. Because all of eastern Europe—except Hungary and Romania—is Slavic, as is Russia, this line of reasoning is all the more inviting.

The fact is that the present division of Europe dates only from the end of World War II—from 1945. Although most of the east European peoples are Slavs, their cultures and political institutions developed along divergent lines and resemble each other no more than they do the Russian, which followed its own evolutionary path. This is especially true of Poland, the largest Slavic state after Russia, which was divided among Russia, Prussia, and Austria by the partitions of 1772, 1793, and 1795 and regained its national independence only after World War I.

The cultural evolution of the east European peoples, Slavs and non-Slavs, took place largely within the context of the West. This is not to say that foreign conquest, by both Turks and Russians, and calamitous upheavals such as the Hussite wars, the Thirty Years War, and the partitions of Poland did not create periods of relative isolation and stagnation. But however uneven the development of the east European cultures compared with those of the West, there is no denying their rightful place within the Western orbit. This is also more readily appreciated, I believe, when we consider that with the exception of the Romanians (who like the Serbs and Russians are Orthodox) the east Europeans were part of the Western church until the Reformation—which also had a considerable influence on Bohemia, Hungary, and Poland both politically and culturally—and hence shared in the universality of Latin.

Because of its profound significance for the development of Western civilization—its reunion with Greco-Roman antiquity, its new belief in the importance of man, its liberation of the human spirit, its learning and scientific achievements, its impact on Christianity, its great sense of discovery—the Renaissance is a splendid frame within which to examine the *Europeanness* of the east Europeans in light of their participation in it. And in speaking of participation, I cannot emphasize enough that I am not referring to marginal or peripheral societies belatedly responding to Western cultural and intellectual stimuli and then haphazardly assimilating them over time. The notion that the east European cultures are derivative must be set aside. We are not dealing with massive cultural indebtedness, with the simple matter of an eastward flow of Western cultural products. We have to recognize that in a period such as the Renaissance it is best to regard Europe as a whole and not to allow geography to determine cultural judgments. Since the Renaissance began in Italy and then spread elsewhere, the east European embrace of it should not be regarded as any more derivative than, let us say, the German, French, English, Spanish, or Portuguese. To be sure, social and cultural differences modified Italian forms wherever the Renaissance spread, but any particularities of the east European response should be looked upon as no more indicative of indebtedness, of culture "lag," than other European variations.

The humanism that is the subject of this book was that early and, to my mind, exciting phase of the Renaissance—in northern Europe coming for the most part in the late fifteenth and early sixteenth centuries—in which scholars and poets sought to recover the long-forgotten, maligned, or imperfectly known treasures of classical Greek and Roman culture and thought, reveled in a liberating epicureanism, or conversely sought to reconcile their Christian beliefs and the pagan culture they now admired (hence the term "Christian humanism"). In these pursuits they shared, whatever their national origins, a common literary language—Latin.

Because of this universality of Latin the humanists could—and indeed did—feel they were members of a single elite community. They all wrote and often spoke the same language, they all affected latinized names, they all were steeped in classical antiquity, which became a living presence to them in an extraordinary collapsing of historical time, and they tended to share the same worldview. In light of this, it is easy to understand that for the humanists national boundaries were minor inconveniences. They took much pleasure in traveling from country to country, city to city, university to university in search of each other; they delighted in learned discourse, in sharing literary and philological achievements, and in cultivating the pleasures of earthly existence. Coming together in salonlike circles within academies, sodalities, or symposia or in royal, aristocratic, or ecclesiastical courts— where itinerant humanists were always welcome—they dined and drank in an atmosphere of conviviality and spoke of new editions and interpretations of classical works, of problems of language, of philosophical issues, and of difficulties with the Scholastics, who were suspicious of their secular enthusiasms and their passion for pagan antiquity and fought them tooth and nail wherever and whenever they had the chance.

Humanism developed significantly in eastern Europe, principally among the Poles, Hungarians, Dalmatians, and Czechs. It was nourished from the same sources as the west European movement and shared the same sense of cosmopolitanism and universality. Whenever possible, east European humanists made the same intellectual pilgrimages to the leading Italian universities of the time—Bologna and Padua—and they traveled as widely as their west European counterparts and for the same purposes: to establish contact with their spiritual compatriots and to attend lectures by the most distinguished exponents of the new learning. Humanist circles, at courts and elsewhere, sprang up in eastern Europe and played host to Western humanists, who sought out such cities as Budapest, Cracow, and Prague with as much eagerness and curiosity as the east Europeans brought to the Western shrines of the movement. The humanists' sense of membership in an elite community of like-minded people who had a common tongue blunted national differences (and dislikes), though it by no means eradicated them.

The coming of the Reformation and the ascendancy of the European vernacular languages in the sixteenth century ended the hegemony of humanism. By now the Renaissance was in full flower, and the cultural, intellectual, and scientific achievements made possible by the new learning of humanism had already begun to manifest themselves. The schism in the church, the waning of Latin, and the cultivation of the national languages obviously undermined the cohesion of a humanist Europe. National cultural as well as the more obvious social and political differences became sharper and more visible. But the experience of sharing in the great adventure of the spirit that was the Renaissance informed the consciousness of west and east European alike and helped maintain the essential sense of a single Europe. It has been this perception of an integral, organic place in the shaping of Western culture—as opposed to a provincial or marginal status—that has sustained the east Europeans in later ages when for political reasons artificial barriers were created to impede, if not cut off altogether, the normal free flow of ideas across the length and breadth of Europe.

My concentration on the emergence of Renaissance humanism in Poland has been motivated by one major consideration—the conviction, which I am not alone in holding, that the humanist movement that developed within the Polish commonwealth during the Renaissance, when Poland experienced its golden age, must be regarded as the most impressive of any in eastern Europe. To me it is also the most appealing.

Poland was at the height of its prestige as a nation in the late fifteenth and sixteenth centuries, when humanism and the Renaissance developed there.[1] This enormous state, the largest in Europe after Muscovy and European Turkey, was politically and militarily powerful and widely respected. The dynastic union in 1386 with the grand duchy of Lithuania, then ruled by the pagan prince Iogaila (1348–1434;

Jagiełło in Polish, subsequently Christianized as Władysław, Latin Ladislaus), brought to the kingdom of Poland a line of strong, able rulers whose Jagiellonian dynasty—which died out in 1572—was one of the most esteemed in Europe. The combined Polish-Lithuanian state, in which Poland was politically and culturally dominant, became the formidable and extraordinarily interesting commonwealth (Rzeczpospolita, in Polish). It was that commonwealth that endured until Poland itself was erased from the map of Europe by the calamitous partitions of 1772, 1793, and 1795.

The dynastic union of Poland and Lithuania made possible the stunning defeat of the Teutonic Order of the Knights of the Cross at the battle of Grunwald in 1410 and assured the hegemony of Poland over the Prussian states (royal and ducal) until the eighteenth century. The relationship was put on a still firmer footing when the dynastic union of 1386 was supplanted by the formal political union of 1569.

The stability and power of the Polish state prepared a fertile field for the expansion of Polish culture. The university in Cracow, which was then a thriving city as well as the royal capital, was established by King Kazimierz Wielki (Casimir the Great, 1310–70) in 1364, some two decades before the union between Poland and Lithuania.[2] The oldest university in eastern Europe after the University of Prague, which was founded in 1348, it antedates the University of Vienna by a year.

After the death of Casimir in 1370, the University of Cracow (also commonly known as the Jagiellonian University) entered a period of decline that was finally arrested by reforms instituted in 1400 on the initiative of King Władysław (Jagiełło) and especially Queen Jadwiga. Cognizant of the need to strengthen the principal seat of learning in Poland in order to carry forward the immense task of Christianization in the grand duchy of Lithuania and to serve the administrative needs of the new commonwealth, the royal court took a keen interest in the well-being of the university. This support enabled it to become a distinguished academic center in the fifteenth century; its faculties had a number of eminent professors, and students and scholars from throughout Europe, including Italy and England, were attracted to it.

Among the prominent men of learning in Cracow before the advent of humanism were such theologians as Master Jędrzej Gałka of Dobczyn, an ardent supporter of the Hussite movement (who eventually had to flee Cracow because of his beliefs); Mateusz of Cracow, who came from Heidelberg to organize the university's new faculty of theology (Pope Boniface IX had consented to its creation in 1397); Jakub of Paradyż; the Silesian Jan Elgot, who became rector of the university in 1427; Tomasz Strzempiński, rector of the university in 1432 and widely known for his advocacy of conciliarism in the church. There were also such legal scholars as Stanisław of Skalbmierz, first rector of the reorganized university and architect of the doctrine of "just wars" (de bellis iustis) in 1411, and Paweł Włodkowic (best known by his latinized name Paulus Vladimiri), who attracted considerable attention at the Council of Constance in 1414–15 when in defending the Polish position against the Teutonic Order of the Knights of the Cross he forcefully argued (in his treatise *De potestate papae et imperatoris respectu infidelium*) the right of pagans to their own land, of which neither the pope nor the Holy Roman Emperor could deprive them.[3] The disciplines of astronomy and mathematics were especially well represented in Cracow in the second half of the fifteenth century by Marcin Król of Żurawica, Jan of Głogów, a philosopher as well as an astronomer, and Albert Blar (or in the Polish versions of his name, Wojciech of Brudzewo or Wojciech Brudzewski), an outstanding mathematician with whom Copernicus studied from 1491 to 1495. Besides Copernicus, the University of Cracow counted among its distinguished graduates one of the foremost statesmen of the fifteenth century, Zbigniew Cardinal Oleśnicki, and Poland's first historiographer, Jan Długosz, author of a twelve-volume history of Poland from legendary times to 1480.

How and when humanism first came to Poland cannot be established with any great precision. Because its faculty of theology had a strong commitment to Scholasticism, the University of Cracow was not a particularly hospitable environment for humanist learning, at least until the late fifteenth century and the beginning of the sixteenth. Latin, of course, was the language of instruction at the university and the only one regarded as worthy of serious writing. But the study of Latin and Latin-language authors was still medieval in character, and the curriculum was controlled by theologians who for the most part were not only unsympathetic toward humanism but openly hostile.

Extensive Polish-Italian ecclesiastical and mercantile contact in the fourteenth century as well as study by Poles in Italian universities such as Bologna and Padua in the late fourteenth and early fifteenth centuries undoubtedly provided a conduit for information about the new learning.[4] But there is so little evidence about how such contacts influenced the emergence of humanism in Poland that the issue remains speculative at best.

Polish participation in the great church councils of the early fifteenth century offers a more fruitful path of inquiry. The first was the Council of Constance of 1414–18, convened to address two great areas of conflict in the Western church—the schism of 1387 that created rival popes in Rome and Avignon and the "heresies" of the Englishman John Wyclif and the Czech Jan Hus. Poland was represented at the council by a large delegation in part because of the continuing conflict between the Poles and the Teutonic Order, which both sides came prepared to pursue. The principal spokesman for the Polish delegation was the legal scholar Paulus Vladimiri, and it is quite likely that contacts between Paulus and his colleagues and members of the Italian delegation such as Cardinal Zabarella and the humanist Pietro Paolo Vergerio (1370–1440)—who was passionately committed to pedagogical reform and the secularization of learning—opened the way to Polish interest in humanism. The Council of Basel, which lasted from 1431 to 1449 and at which the Poles were also well represented, provided a still broader range of such contacts. That they must have been fruitful is evidenced in the exchange soon afterward of literary correspondence between Cardinal Oleśnicki (1369–1455) and the outstanding Italian humanist Aeneas Sylvius Piccolomini (1405–64; later Pope Pius II). It is also reflected in the lecture in praise of oratory given at the University of Cracow in 1440 (*De oratoriae facultatis laudibus oratio*) by the medical doctor Jan z Ludziska (John of Ludzisko), who drew heavily on Italian humanist sources and became, in effect, the university's first orator in the new humanist style;[5] in the historian Długosz's desire to write a great history of Poland on the model of the Roman Livy; and in the humanist-inspired anti-Vatican treatises of Poland's first major political writer, Jan Ostroróg (1436–1501), palatine of Poznań.

Whatever role the church councils might have played in stimulating Polish interest in humanism, the greatest initial impetus clearly came from the appearance in Cracow in the late fifteenth century of two outstanding Western humanists. One was the Italian renegade Filippo Buonaccorsi (widely known by his assumed name of Callimachus, 1437–96), who arrived in Poland as a fugitive from the papal police and remained there the rest of his life, rising to great prominence both as a statesman and as a humanist writer. The other was the major German Renaissance Neo-latin poet Conrad Celtis (1459–1508), who spent two years in Cracow and organized the first humanist society of letters in the Slavic world.

Before the arrival of Callimachus and Celtis, Polish humanism was represented principally by one figure, Grzegorz z Sanoka (Gregory of Sanok, 1406–77). When this worldly churchman became archbishop of Lwów (Lvov; then in eastern Poland, now the Ukrainian city of Lviv), he had a small town built around his residence near the Dunajec

River, called, appropriately, Dunajów. It was at the archbishop's palace there that something resembling a humanist salon came into being; the first of its type in Poland. Sadly, so little of Gregory of Sanok's own literary legacy has been preserved that it is difficult to reconstruct his career in any detail. Although Polish scholarly interest in him has been high for many years, it is symptomatic of the paucity of primary source material that studies on him still take as their point of departure the Latin account of Filippo Buonaccorsi. When the Italian first arrived in Poland in 1470, a few steps ahead of Vatican representatives demanding his extradition to Rome for leading a foiled plot to assassinate Pope Paul II in 1468, Gregory welcomed him at his court in Dunajów and became, in effect, his first Polish patron.

It is, then, with the career of the first significant pioneer of humanism in Poland—Gregory of Sanok—that this book begins. The critical contributions made to the Polish humanist movement by Filippo Buonaccorsi and Conrad Celtis are examined next. The rest of the book traces the subsequent course of Renaissance humanism in Poland through the achievements of several outstanding representatives. These include the first disciples of Buonaccorsi and Celtis, the Silesian Laurentius Corvinus and Paweł z Krosna (Paul of Krosno, Paulus Crosnensis), also important in the history of humanism in Hungary; Jan z Wiślicy (John of Wiślica, Ioannes Visliciensis), a student of Paul of Krosno and the first major Polish Neo-Latin poet, whose principal work is an epic celebrating the Polish-Lithuanian defeat of the Teutonic Order at the battle of Grunwald in 1410; the great scientist Mikołaj Kopernik (Nicolaus Copernicus), who began his literary career in typical humanist fashion with a Latin translation of an ancient Greek text; and Mikołaj Hussowczyk (Nicolaus Hussovianus), author of a remarkable poetic work about the bison of the eastern Polish forests, commissioned for the hunt-loving Pope Leo X. There was also Jan Dantyszek (John of Gdańsk, Ioannes Dantiscus), foremost Polish diplomat of the Renaissance, who spent many years at the courts of the Holy Roman Emperors, above all Charles V, and was a friend of Erasmus; Andrzej Krzycki (Andreas Cricius), whose career progressed from membership in a hard-drinking and womanizing circle of hell-raisers to the royal court, where his venemously satirical pen earned him a formidable if dubious reputation, and eventually to the highest church office in the land, primate of Poland; Klemens Janicjusz (Clemens Ianicius), the best of the Polish humanist poets, whose poetry owed much to the inspiration of the Italy he loved so dearly and whose fragile health terminated his life at age twenty-seven; and finally, Jan Kochanowski (Ioannes Cochanovius), the first great poet in the Polish vernacular, the greatest of Polish Renaissance poets, and a bilingual writer whose sizable Latin oeuvre exemplifies, above all, the twilight of humanism in Poland. With Kochanowski's death in 1584, humanism—in the chronologically delimited sense in which the term is used here—can be seen as reaching its definitive end in Poland.

In presenting this first comprehensive view of Renaissance humanism in Poland, I feel it essential to point out what it is and what it is not. Because my own interests lie principally in the field of literature, and because I believe that the highest achievement of Polish humanist literary creativity was in poetry, my focus is primarily on the Polish Neo-Latin poets. But as I have already indicated, rare indeed was the Polish humanist for whom poetry was more than a welcome respite from concerns of church and state, politics and diplomacy, science and learning. Of necessity, therefore, this book while highlighting the poetic achievement of the Polish humanists, makes every effort to situate that achievement within the larger context of their careers. Its emphasis on the literary notwithstanding, it also devotes appropriate space to the careers of men whose importance to the development of humanism in Poland lay almost wholly in other spheres, such as the prominent churchman Gregory of Sanok, the political thinker Filippo Buonaccorsi, and the scientist Nicolaus Copernicus.

In the sphere of Renaissance political thought, Poland produced one of the outstanding minds of the age, Andrzej Frycz Modrzewski (Andreas Fricius Modrevius, 1503–72).[6] His most admired and influential work, the five-book *Commentariorum de Republica emendanda libri quinque* (Commentary on the Reform of the Commonwealth, in Five Books), was printed for the first time in its entirety in Basel, Switzerland, in 1554 and became widely known throughout Europe. Although a separate chapter on Frycz Modrzewski might seem in order, it has been omitted for two reasons. First, his most influential work falls into the second half of the sixteenth century and belongs more to the history of the Renaissance proper in Poland than to its earlier phase, represented by humanism. Second, Modrzewski's political writings form part of a much larger and more complex picture—the transformation of Poland into a gentry, or noble, republic in the sixteenth century and the emergence of a sizable body of political and polemical literature engendered by that transformation. The study of Polish Renaissance political literature cannot be severed from a study of the politics of the age; to do justice to it as well as to the importance of Frycz Modrzewski's proposed reforms would require a separate book. By way of balance I have dealt substantially with the career of the Italian renegade Filippo Buonaccorsi, whose contribution to Polish

Renaissance political thought was considerable. Many of the reforms advocated by Frycz Modrzewski—above all strengthening the monarchy at the expense of noble privilege—were anticipated by Buonaccorsi. Since Buonaccorsi is also a more central figure in the development of Polish Renaissance humanism, the emphasis on him seems reasonable.

Although Renaissance Poland lacked philosophical and theological thinkers of the stature of the Dutchman Erasmus of Rotterdam, the Germans Nicholas of Cusa and Philipp Melanchthon, and the Spaniard Luis Vives, its contributions to both the Reformation and the Counter-Reformation have hardly gone unnoticed.[7] Remarkably free of the strife and bloodshed that accompanied the challenge of Protestantism elsewhere in Europe, Poland became a major arena of Catholic-Protestant conflict in the sixteenth and seventeenth centuries. This conflict, which for a time threatened the hegemony of the Roman Catholic church in the country, produced its share of energetic and imposing figures.

On the Protestant side, clearly the most outstanding was Jan Łaski (1499–1560), a nephew of the Polish primate of the same name.[8] Widely known in the West as Ioannes à Lasco, or John à Lasco, Łaski earned the admiration of his fellow reformers by his organizational skills and his tireless efforts to bring about a union of the various Protestant groups. Although very much a product of humanism—his contacts with Erasmus and Swiss theologians in Basel early in his career played a pivotal role in his eventual decision to embrace Protestantism—Łaski has been omitted from more extensive discussion here because he spent much of his adult life and activities as a Protestant organizer outside Poland, primarily in East Frisia and England. It may legitimately be claimed that it was the English period of his career—from 1548 to 1553—that laid the foundation of his fame as a theologian and church organizer. Łaski returned to Poland for good in 1556 to take an active part in ending the fragmentation of the Protestant community there, but he died only four years later. Łaski's place in history was determined far more by his career as a Protestant reformer in the West than by his contribution to the diffusion of humanism in Poland.[9]

If John à Lasco (as he is best known in the English-speaking world) had a Catholic counterpart in Poland, it was Stanisław Hozjusz (Stanislaus Hosius, 1504–79).[10] Steeped in humanist learning like John à Lasco, Hosius rose from the bishoprics of Chełm and Warmia to be named a cardinal in 1561. An astute political thinker, Hosius became an indefatigable defender of Roman Catholicism and one of the leading figures in the post-Tridentine Counter-Reformation, not only in Poland. It was he who introduced the Society of Jesus (Jesuits) into Poland in 1565, and his major theological treatise, *Confessio catholicae fidei christiana* (A Christian Confession of the Catholic Faith), first printed as a whole in Mainz in 1557, reprinted many times, and translated into several languages, became immensely popular in Catholic circles and secured Hosius's position as one of the foremost Catholic thinkers of his time.

If we add the names of Frycz Modrzewski, John à Lasco, and Hosius to those of the Polish humanists who form the substance of this book, we gain a sense of the range, complexity, and distinction of Polish humanism. Although their greatest achievements relate primarily to sixteenth-century Polish political and ecclesiastical reform, the influence of humanism on their outlook and writings is well established. They remain among the most illustrious representatives of the Renaissance in Poland, and if they are not dealt with here to the extent they deserve it is only because they belong more properly to the full flowering of the Renaissance in Poland in the second half of the sixteenth century.

The Polish humanists who constitute the dramatis personae of this book either studied in the West at some point in their careers or sojourned there, sometimes for substantial periods of time, as academic travelers, members of church entourages, or diplomats. Their knowledge of the West was good, and their contacts with Western humanists, both in and out of Poland, were extensive. They were always aware that they were Poles and that their distant northern land still tended to be regarded as remote, exotic, and even barbarian in western Europe. But because of the reputation the Poles enjoyed throughout Europe for their knowledge of Latin,[11] their pride in the coming of age of Polish learning as represented above all by the University of Cracow, and their sense of the greatness of the Polish commonwealth and its institutions, they carried no baggage of either cultural or national inferiority. For all their "strangeness" as Poles (or Sarmatians, from a Latin term for Poland, Sarmatia), they did not see themselves as second-class citizens in the elite community of humanism. In this regard their sense of being European superseded their Polishness. If their particular genius discharged itself in poetry rather than in philosophical or theological inquiry, no one thought less of them for it. The art of poetry was held in highest esteem among the humanists, who dreamed of becoming successors of Vergil, Horace, Ovid, Juvenal, Tibullus, and Propertius. This privileged place of poetry in early Renaissance Europe was accorded formal recognition, in fact, in the public crowning of a poet with a ceremonial laurel wreath (hence the title *poeta laureatus*), particularly by the Holy Roman Emperor. Two of the Polish poets discussed in this book were so honored. If the distinction bore no greater practical import than the "poet laureate" title of England does today, its symbolic value and the visibility it represented for poetry should not be underestimated.

How much a part of Europe the Polish humanists felt themselves, and how close were their relations with their Western counterparts can be seen—to take one significant example—in the case of Erasmus. Although the great Dutch humanist's fame reached Poland before any of his works did, the first lectures on him were given at the University of Cracow in 1519 by an itinerant English humanist named Leonard Coxe (d. 1549).[12] A devoted admirer of Erasmus and one of the Dutchman's legion of foreign correspondents, Coxe lectured there in 1518–19 and 1525–27; the rest of his time in eastern Europe was spent teaching in secondary schools in Hungary. During his stay in Cracow, apart from lectures on the classics (Coxe had a certain reputation as a Ciceronist), he conducted readings from Erasmus, mostly informal sessions in the students' residence, the Bursa Jerozolimska (Jerusalem College), where he lived. Before long a lively circle of Polish Erasmians came into being. Within a few years Polish interest had grown to such an extent that in 1522 Coxe was invited to give the first public lecture on Erasmus, an explication of the Dutchman's *De duplici copia verborum ac rerum* (On the Twofold Abundance of Words and Things.).

As Erasmus's reputation grew in Poland, his many admirers in that country lost little time joining the ranks of the Dutchman's epistolary contacts. Always attentive to correspondence, Erasmus answered in due course. Apart from his personal pleasure in maintaining literary relationships with worshipful humanists and other admirers throughout Europe, the new contact with Poles opened up to Erasmus a part of the Continent of which he had no great knowledge, and his interest grew with his correspondents there. How Erasmus viewed Poland when he had learned more about it is evident from a letter to Jodok (or Jostus) Ludovicus Decius (real name Dietz, ca. 1485–1545). This historian and economist was also a Cracow town councilman, secretary to King Sigismund I, and Leonard Coxe's patron during the Englishman's early years in Poland. An Alsatian by origin, Decius had met Erasmus in Basel in 1522 and began a correspondence with him upon his return to Poland. In a letter to Decius dated October 24, 1523, Erasmus had high praise for Poland and her cultural attainments though in terms we might regard as a backhanded compliment:

Genti gratulor, quae quum olim ab barbariem male audierit, nunc et
literis et legibus et moribus et religione, et se quid aliud est quod a
barbariei probro vindicet, sic floreat ut cum praecipuis ac laudatissimis
nationibus certare possit.[13]

(I congratulate a people who, though formerly ill regarded as barbarian,
now so blossoms in letters, laws, customs, religion, and in whatever else
may spare it the reproach of uncouthness, that it can vie with the most
distinguished and praised of nations.)

Besides Decius, Erasmus's other Polish correspondents included
Piotr Tomicki (1464–1535), bishop of Cracow, vice-chancellor of the
Polish Crown, and the principal architect of Polish foreign policy in
the time of Sigismund I; Krzysztof Sydłowiecki (1467–1532), great
chancellor of the Crown and castellan of Cracow; Piotr Kmita (1477–
1533), great marshal of the Crown and well known for his patronage
of humanists; Andrzej Krzycki (Andreas Cricius, 1482–1537), primate
of Poland and an outstanding humanist poet; the great Polish diplomat
of the age, Jan Dantyszek (Ioannes Dantiscus, 1485–1548), who came
to know Erasmus personally and enjoyed a warm relationship with
him; Seweryn Boner (1486–1549), a leading member of the Cracow
town patriciate; Andrzej Zebrzydowski (ca. 1496–1560), one of Leonard Coxe's Erasmian circle and later a bishop and chancellor of the
University of Cracow; Jan Antonin (Ioannes Antoninus, 1499–1543),
court physician of King Sigismund I, who lived for a few months in
Erasmus's home in Basel in 1524; Cardinal Hosius, whom we have
already met as the most vigorous champion of the Counter-Reformation in Poland, and the historian Marcin Kromer (ca. 1512–89). Jan
Łaski (John à Lasco), the distinguished Polish Reformation organizer—who had once lived with Erasmus in Basel—as an act of admiration bought his library in 1525 with the understanding that Erasmus
would have the use of it for the rest of his life. After the Dutch
humanist's death in 1536 the library was transported to Poland; the
Pole who came to Switzerland on Łaski's behalf to arrange the transfer
was the political writer and reformist Andrzej Frycz Modrzewski, himself an Erasmian enthusiast. Andrzej Krzycki, then archbishop of Cracow, and his powerful uncle, Piotr Tomicki, had the idea in 1525 of
bringing Erasmus to Poland both to enhance national prestige and to
breathe new life into the University of Cracow. The project also had
the backing of King Sigismund I, with whom Erasmus corresponded.
But despite his new interest in Poland and his personal esteem for
Krzycki, whom he regarded as one of the most illustrious poets in

Europe, Erasmus was not quite ready to exchange Basel or Freiburg for Cracow; not did he, in fact, ever visit Poland.

The immense popularity of Erasmus in Poland obviously cannot be explained just in terms of the Dutchman's great reputation throughout Europe as a whole. Special circumstances in sixteenth-century Poland paved the way for the warm reception accorded Erasmian ideas. In the struggle to contain the political ascendancy of the nobility, which threatened both the monarchy and the burgher class, Polish reformist politics, epitomized by the writings of Frycz Modrzewski, placed great emphasis on the need to improve public morals and ethics. Arrogance and avarice were the sins of the Polish landowning class most frequently decried in progressive Polish Renaissance political literature from Callimachus through Frycz Modrzewski, Łukasz Górnicki (1527–1603), and Piotr Skarga (1536–1612). In light of this, Erasmian thought, with its strong moral and ethical dimension, would have been irresistible.

The spread of Lutheranism in Poland, beginning in Royal Prussia, followed by the cohesion of a strong Calvinist community and the emergence of a variety of reformist sects, also greatly encouraged the diffusion of Erasmian ideas. The primacy of the Bible and of the inner religious life in Erasmus's writings held great appeal for the more radical reformist sects, chief among them the culturally important Polish Brethren (otherwise known as Antitrinitarians, Socinians or, more commonly Arians).

But Erasmus was not only an inspiration to political and religious reformers in Poland; the most vigorous and intellectually gifted exponent of the Counter-Reformation in the country, Cardinal Hosius, was no stranger to Erasmian thought. Traces of the Dutchman's immensely popular *Enchiridion militi christiani* (Handbook of the Christian Knight, 1503) can be found in his own influential *Confessio fidei catholicae christiana* (Christian Confession of the Catholic Faith, 1553) and *De expresso Dei verbo . . . libellus* (On the Clear Word of God, 1558). Before the sharpening tensions of religious dissension turned Hosius into a militant in more than just faith, he had come to Erasmus's attention principally through John à Lasco. So highly did Erasmus regard Hosius that in a letter to Lasco in early December 1527 he expressed his willingness to be of any service he could to the future cardinal.[14]

Primate Krzycki, whose epistolary relationship with Erasmus was one of the warmest among the Dutchman's many Polish correspondents, also became an implacable foe of Protestantism in Poland, concentrating his wrath primarily on the Lutherans. When Erasmus mentioned in one of his letters to Krzycki that he had been given a copy of his anti-Luther diatribe entitled *Encomia Lutheri* (In Praise of Luther, published in Cracow and Rome in 1524), Krzycki lost no time in writing to soften Erasmus's judgment, saying that the book—of which he makes light in his letter—was published against his will and that though he could agree with some of Luther's arguments he took strong exception to the insults heaped on bishops like himself by Luther and his followers. As Krzycki was to discover from subsequent correspondence with Erasmus, the Dutch humanist had his own grievances against Luther, which he was not loath to share.

When the full range of Erasmian influence in Renaissance Poland is brought clearly into view, it seems incontrovertible that the Dutchman's impact on sixteenth-century Polish political and religious thought overshadowed that of any other contemporary Western thinker. If unaware of this at the time, Erasmus nevertheless relished his personal contacts and epistolary exchanges with Poles, and he closely followed events in Poland, now happily freed from its earlier "barbarian" stigma.

Renaissance humanism in general and particularly in a country such as Poland, whose culture is still not well known in the West, may conjure up the image of an arid scholarly landscape—dust-laden manuscripts, an ancient tongue, pallid imitations of classical authors. But the contributions of humanism, that harbinger of the Renaissance, were of incalculable value to the development of Western civilization, and studying them is an exhilarating journey of the mind that does not dim once we cross the borders of the old Polish commonwealth. The rise of humanism in Poland is the story of colorful, sometimes engrossing figures with a zest for life, great curiosity about the world, a predilection for concreteness as opposed to abstraction, for action as opposed to contemplation, and a sensitivity to the complexities of court and state politics that reflects the society of the huge multiethnic Polish commonwealth on the threshold of its greatness as a European power. If they are not yet familiar figures, they are anything but dull.

By enlarging our field of vision to encompass the nature of the humanist enterprise in the largest—and politically and culturally most important—state in east central Europe during the Renaissance, we can understand far better the extent to which humanism and the Renaissance were diffused throughout Europe. In that way we can appreciate the essential oneness of Western civilization and the absurd artificiality of the walls, concrete or otherwise, now dividing Europe into two antagonistic camps. If this book makes even a modest contribution to our understanding of the common heritage of western and eastern Europe and, above all, to the way the Renaissance is viewed and studied, I will be immensely gratified.

Now a few words about some technical aspects of this book. Since it is mainly about writers who chose to express themselves exclusively in Latin, I have thought it best to include as many excerpts from their works as feasible. No historical survey or criticism, whose principal task is to provide a context of understanding, can ever take the place of a direct meeting with the words and thoughts of the writers themselves. Since interest in the Renaissance and in Neo-Latin literature is widespread, most excerpts appear both in the original Latin and in English translation; all translations from Latin are my own. In a number of instances, to conserve space, the Latin excerpt is shortened to give readers who can read the language some sense of the original without placing an undue burden on those who do not know Latin. Some excerpts are given only in English, partly to save space and partly because it seemed little was to be gained by including the Latin text.

On the matter of Polish names, two concessions to the nonspecialist reader have been made. First, a rudimentary guide to the pronunciation of Polish appears in the prefatory materials. Second, following a common practice in scholarship, the names of all non-English rulers and members of their families, including the Polish, are anglicized. For Poles, on the first appearance of a name the original Polish form is given, with the English version in parentheses. Thereafter only the anglicized forms are used. With the Polish humanists consistency was harder to achieve and in fact was not attained. In general, all names appear first in their Polish forms. But the actual family names of some humanists, such as Mikołaj Hussowczyk and Klemens Janicki, are not known. Both Hussowczyk and Janicki are later attributions. In both instances I felt more comfortable using the latinized names by which they were best known in their own time—Hussovianus and Ianicius—although Polish scholars frequently use the name Janicjusz, which is just a polonized form of the Latin Ianicius. As the more logical choice in a book in English, I also prefer the Latin Hosius to the Polish form Hozjusz. With figures whose names are actually place-names—for example, Grzegorz z Sanoka, Paweł z Krosna, and Jan z Wiślicy—I give the original Polish forms first, followed in parentheses by the translations. After the first appearance of a name, the anglicized form is used exclusively; hence Gregory of Sanok, Paul of Krosno, and John of Wiślica. The one exception to this formula is Jan Dantyszek, as he is best known in Poland. The English version of the name would be John of Gdańsk, but since this greatest of Polish Renaissance diplomats was widely known throughout Europe under his humanist latinized name Dantiscus, I prefer that name here. My one serious breach in the relative consistency of these patterns concerns Andrzej Krzycki. Although he wrote exclusively in Latin and was known in Poland and beyond as Andreas Cricius, Polish scholarly literature almost always uses his Polish name. Without having a strong conviction in the matter, and because the Latin Cricius seems further graphically from the Polish Krzycki than the latinized forms of other Polish humanists' names, I have generally used Krzycki in the chapter devoted to him. The names of all other Polish figures mentioned appear only in their Polish forms.

CHAPTER 1

Gregory of Sanok,
the Freethinking Archbishop

Although foreigners were undeniably important in the early development of humanism in Poland in the late fifteenth century—notably the German Conrad Celtis and the Italian Filippo Buonaccorsi (best known by his non de plume Callimachus)—indigenous Polish humanism already had an exceptional representative in Grzegorz z Sanoka (Gregory of Sanok, 1406–77). Yet despite his significance, there is such a dearth of primary source material relating to him that writing about Gregory remains something of an exercise in futility. A small body of scholarly literature, including a monograph by Andrzej Nowicki, *Grzegorz z Sanoka, 1406–1477* (1958),[1] does exist in Polish, and as far back as 1882 the prolific Polish historical novelist Ignacy Kraszewski made Gregory of Sanok the subject of his novel *Strzemieńczyk* (The Horseman), but the novel mixes fact and fantasy and in any case covers his life only through the battle of Varna in 1444. For writers of fiction and scholarly works alike the principal source of information about Gregory—over five hundred years after his death—remains the contemporary account of his life written by Buonaccorsi, the *Vita et mores Gregorii Sanocei* (The Life and Times of Gregory of Sanok).[2]

Although Buonaccorsi-Callimachus himself is dealt with at much greater length in chapter 2, some preliminary information about this remarkable figure is essential at this point so we can understand how the *Vita* of Gregory of Sanok came to be written and assess its value as biography.

Unlike the outstanding German humanist Conrad Celtis, who visited Cracow for nearly two years, attracted by the Polish capital's cultural and intellectual life as well as by the German character of its patrician population, Filippo Buonaccorsi was a man on the run, for whom Poland was above all a safe haven. A prominent member of Pomponio Leto's humanist academy in Rome, the Accademia Romana, in 1468 Buonaccorsi became involved in a conspiracy to assassinate Pope Paul II. The plot was foiled before any harm befell its intended victim, but Buonaccorsi could no longer remain in Italy. A relentless pursuit by the papal police forced him to put distance between himself and his homeland. His odyssey brought him to Turkey, where influential friends and relatives harbored him for a while before sending him on to still more remote Poland. Italian merchants were well established in Poland by this time, and Buonaccorsi had distant relatives among them who could look after him. He was still a wanted man, however, and the papal legate's successful appeal to the Polish diet to permit his extradition to Rome for trial meant he needed more protection. Through family connections, the good offices of the respected and influential archbishop of Lwów, Gregory of Sanok, were enlisted, and Buonaccorsi soon found himself settled in at the archbishop's palace at Dunajów. Here, in an atmosphere far more reminiscent of a humanist court than an ecclesiastical residence, the learned Italian fugitive enjoyed greater security from both papal and parliamentary threat.

During his stay at Dunajów, Buonaccorsi and Gregory developed a close relationship. The Italian deeply appreciated the Pole's hospitality and protection, while for Gregory, whose outlook was shaped by humanism and who had a lively curiosity about other cultures, Buonaccorsi's visit was an opportunity for rewarding intellectual companionship with a man who had come out of the most prominent humanist circle in Italy. By the time the Vatican renounced pursuit of Buonaccorsi and granted him amnesty, a bond of friendship existed between the Italian expatriate and his Polish protector and patron. When Buonaccorsi could leave Dunajów without fear of arrest and extradition, and could with impunity return to Italy, he chose to remain in Poland and begin a new life there.

Combining intellectual and literary skills with the support of someone as prominent as Gregory of Sanok, Buonaccorsi advanced rapidly in a career as royal secretary and counselor and in time became one of the most influential statesmen in the Polish kingdom. He never returned to Italy for good, though he visited his homeland briefly on diplomatic assignments for the Polish Crown.

Once had had left Dunajów to make an independent life in Poland, Buonaccorsi expressed his gratitude to Gregory of Sanok by writing his biography in 1476, while the archbishop was still alive (although the literary conventions of the time forced him to write as if his subject had already died). Considering the warm relationship between the two men, it should come as no surprise that the biography is a flattering account of the former patron who shared the Italian expatriate's commitment to humanist goals and ideals. Enough secondary literature about Gregory has appeared by now that it is possible for the most part to sift the objective from the hagiographical in Buonaccorsi's account. But the *Vita et mores Gregorii Sanocei* is still the principal source about the archbishop and is so used here. With the *Vita* of Philippus Callimachus (since that is the name the Italian wrote under) as our guide, then, let us explore the career of Gregory of Sanok and his role in the development of Renaissance humanism in Poland.

According to Callimachus, Gregory was from the gentry (a claim generally disputed now by Polish scholars, who find no evidence to back it up) and at age twelve ran away from home because of harsh parental discipline. He came to Cracow to further his education and begin a career, but he found that doors were closed to him because he knew no German, the language of the city's urban and academic patriciate. Determined to remedy the situation, Gregory crossed the Elbe into Germany. He spent the next five years traveling (where, we do not know for certain) and earning his living by tutoring (what, precisely we are also unsure of). He must have spent considerable time in German-speaking lands, because he is eventually credited with knowing German well. It is also possible that his travels took him as far as Italy.

In 1428, after ten years of a largely itinerant life, Gregory returned to Poland and enrolled in the University of Cracow as a candidate for the bachelor of arts degree. Poland's foremost late medieval historian, Jan Długosz (1415–80), had himself become a student there just a few months before. This was also the period when Jędrzej Gałka of Dobczyn, a leading Hussite ideologue, was giving lectures at the university.[3] Gregory of Sanok's interest in and even apparent sympathy for the Czech Hussites could well have been stimulated by contact with Gałka. Six years after earning his bachelor's degree in 1433, Gregory became a master of arts. Although there is no doubt that thereafter he began giving lectures (which Callimachus describes as immensely popular) on classical Roman poetry, Vergil's *Bucolics* in particular—which he is credited with introducing into Poland—there is disagreement among Polish scholars over his affiliation with the university, if any; that is to say, whether he formally lectured at the university or only gave informal lectures, a common enough practice during the Renaissance.[4] Had Gregory been formally affiliated, the reigning Scholasticism of the institution would have made for an inhospitable environment in view of his own already strong predilection for humanism. As an ardent admirer of Roman poetry, Gregory would naturally have allied himself with the humanist scholars then struggling to replace medieval with classical Latin; this meant ending the hegemony of the *Doctrinale,* or grammar of medieval Latin, which formed the basis of Latin-language pedagogy at the University of Cracow until 1503.[5]

Whatever the nature of his relationship with the University of Cracow after he received his master's degree, it was not in academia that Gregory's career began to develop. After an apparently brief period of lecturing in the royal capital, he accepted a position as tutor to the sons of the master of Tarnów, a city some eighty kilometers east of Cracow and an important center of Renaissance culture in the sixteenth century. Already acknowledged for his talent as a singer, which Callimachus says he exhibited upon his return to Poland from his early years of foreign travel and which was valued in a city like Cracow that emphasized music in religious rites and celebrations, Gregory also seems to have possessed literary gifts. It was while he was in Tarnów that he began to write poetry, becoming known especially for his epitaphs. Unfortunately, virtually none of his original compositions have survived, so while we know of his serious interest in poetics and rhetoric and his fondness for poetry, there are hardly any surviving literary monuments by which to assess the quality of his writing.

From serving as tutor to the sons of the master of Tarnów Gregory passed next to the royal court in Cracow, where he was employed as one of the king's secretaries, having at some point brought his charges to the capital from Tarnów to further their education. Little is known of Gregory's stay in Cracow at this time other than that he became interested in writing a comedy in the style of Plautus, whose plays had recently come into his hands. Whatever opportunities opened up for him at the court in Cracow, Gregory was already determined to become an ecclesiastic. When a church office became available in Wieliczka, site of the famous salt mines just southeast of Cracow, his by now respectable connections in Cracow and at court guaranteed him the post. Not long after accepting it, he set out on the obligatory trip to the Vatican for his official confirmation.

In Italy Gregory made the acquaintance of Pope Eugenius IV, who was then holding court in Florence after his expulsion from Rome. The pope was so favorably impressed that he tried to persuade him to remain in Italy as a member of his own court, but to no avail.

Confirmed in his post as parish priest of Wieliczka, Gregory returned to Poland to assume his new duties.

Although there is every indication that Gregory was an unqualified success in Wieliczka, his stay there was brief, lasting no more than two to two and a half years. What lured him away from a position in which he was clearly both happy and successful was the ascension to the throne of Hungary of his former pupil King Władysław (Ladislaus) III. The new monarch of the Magyars invited Gregory to travel with him to Hungary as his personal confessor, and Gregory accepted without hesitation.

The several years Gregory spent in Hungary were most rewarding for his intellectual and cultural formation. Humanism was already well developed there, owing especially to the encouragement of the influential János Vitéz (1408–72), bishop of Várad, uncle of the outstanding Hungarian humanist poet Janus Pannonius (1434–72) and one of the most potent figures in Hungarian political as well as cultural life at the time. Gregory became a welcome guest at the episcopal court at Várad, which Vitéz was transforming into a true center of humanist culture and which doubtless served as a model for Gregory's own court at Dunajów when he became archbishop of Lwów. It was at Várad that Gregory must have made the acquaintance of the well-known Italian humanist Pietro Paolo Vergerio (Petrus Paulus Vergerius) and the Greek poet Philip Podachatherus. Both enjoyed Vitéz's patronage and were among the first foreign disseminators of humanist learning in Hungary.[6]

Gregory was by no means the only Pole visiting Várad at the time. Bishop Vitéz's pro-Polish political orientation, which culminated in the ill-fated conspiracy he and his nephew Janus Pannonius instigated to unseat King Matthias Corvinus and offer the Hungarian throne to the king of Poland, made the court at Várad particularly hospitable to Poles. One of the more distinguished Polish guests there was Marcin z Przemyśla (Martin of Przemyśl), a doctor and astronomer who may have contributed to the development of Gregory's views on both medicine and astronomy.

The lively intellectual climate at Várad and the close relations the guests enjoyed among themselves and with their host, Bishop Vitéz, made a lasting impression on Gregory and in part compensated for the sad loss of King Ladislaus at Varna in 1444. The battle against the Turks proved a disaster. Ladislaus gave up his life there, and Gregory, who had accompanied him on the campaign, barely escaped. Less fortunate was Giuliano de Cesarini, Pope Eugenius IV's legate to

Hungary and a man with whom Gregory had more than once crossed political and intellectual swords.

After the debacle at Varna, Gregory decided to remain in Hungary at least a few years. His good relations with King János Hunyadi, Matthias Corvinus's father, won him a place at court as tutor to the royal family; the strengthening ties with Bishop Vitéz and the circle at Várad, on the other hand, provided an environment of intellectual and cosmopolitan humanism that made the decision to remain in Hungary after Varna seem all the more correct.

Gregory had come to Hungary in the retinue of King Ladislaus in 1440. After the events at Varna in 1444, he remained among the Hungarians for another six years. What prompted his decision to return to Poland then is difficult to establish. Perhaps after ten years it seemed the time had come to go back. Or perhaps he heard that it was presumed in Poland that he too had fallen at Varna and that King Casimir had placed another cleric in charge of his parish.

Whatever the reason, Gregory made his way back to Poland sometime in 1450 and soon discovered that he had indeed not been forgotten. Within a year of his return, in 1451, he was appointed successor to Archbishop Jan Odrowąż of Lwów, who died in 1450 after a fourteen-year tenure. The appointment showed the esteem in which Gregory was held, for it was made over the strenuous objections of the powerful Zbigniew Cardinal Oleśnicki, who did not share Gregory's enthusiasm for humanism and regarded the former parish priest of Wieliczka as too worldly in his tastes.

The archbishopric he inherited from Jan Odrowąż was in a sad state of neglect, which Gregory lost no time trying to rectify. But resources were meager, and change came only with difficulty. Although he persisted and eventually achieved much, Gregory could not help despairing over the change in his fortunes after leaving Hungary. So discouraged was he at times, reports Callimachus, that he was unable to hold back the tears: "But when he became convinced there was nothing at all there by which he could sustain himself, however wretchedly, with tears in his eyes he fell to deploring his fate, that he had to give up a most flourishing way of life for a poor and hard existence. And from the beginning he thought of abandoning everything and returning to his friends in Hungary. Later, as a man both pious and religious, with his whole heart turned to God, he determined to bear in a manly way whatever burden had been placed upon him as if a splendid opportunity had thus presented itself to him to exercise himself in the vineyard of the Lord."[7]

Gregory's reforms as archbishop of Lwów were aimed at raising the level of his clergy, some of whom were not averse to getting drunk in public inns (these Gregory punished by barring them from celebrating mass for several days) and at improving the archbishopric's finances. Eventually he succeeded on both counts, although the former was in some respects the harder. Gregory had a low opinion of the clergy of his time and consecrated priests only rarely, dissatisfied with most of those who presented themselves to him. He believed, Callimachus relates, that in his own time the clergy had lost much of its former majesty and had become a refuge for men wanting to hide some shameful ignominy or low origins beneath clerical garb or to find in the priesthood a way out of vexing impecuniousness. He praised the custom of the ancients, especially the Hebrews, by which their kings were also their highest priests. Between God and man, he thought, there was nothing higher than the priesthood; therefore it should be entrusted only to those possessing the greatest virtues or the highest rank.

When his financial condition was healthy enough to permit it, Gregory bought a few villages where he settled peasants and built them homes, made the land productive, and thus increased the revenues and prosperity of his parish. His ambition was to build a town alongside the Dunajec River out of the nucleus of these villages. His dream was at last realized, and he named the town Dunajów from the river that flowed by it. When the population was large enough to warrant it, he also built a castle for himself and added fortifications to protect the entire community against the Tatars, who then posed the greatest external threat.

According to Callimachus, Gregory loved the tranquillity of Dunajów, and whenever he could free himself from the cares and concerns of his responsibilities as archbishop of Lwów, he was only too happy to return there and devote his energies to reading and writing. His earlier intellectual passions were poetry and history; theology and ethics followed later.

Although almost nothing of Gregory's poetry remains, there is reason to believe he was well regarded as a poet in his own time. The first great Polish historian, Jan Długosz, wrote enthusiastically of him as a poet (in 1477), and in his Latin history of Poland he quotes the whole 114-line epitaph Gregory wrote on the death of King Ladislaus Jagiełło.[8] The *Chronica Polonorum* (1519)—which has the distinction of being the first printed history of Poland, since it appeared long before Długosz's—by the physician, historian, and geographer Maciej z Miechowa (Maciej Miechowita or Mathias de Michovia in Latin, 1457–

1523), also contains a poem ascribed to Gregory. Since Miechowita rarely quotes poetry in his *Chronica*, this gesture may reflect the regard of the learned community of his time. But Gregory, never without his share of detractors in high places because of his liberal views, was one of the casualties of the confiscation of the first edition of Miechowita's *Chronica*. Angered by remarks it regarded as offensive to members of the Jagiellonian dynasty, the Polish Senate ordered the work seized without giving specific reasons at the time. When permission was granted for a second edition of the *Chronica* in 1521, it was with the understanding that a number of changes would be made. Two of these changes—doubtless demanded by Gregory's antagonists, most notably Zbigniew Oleśnicki—eliminated the poem by Gregory and expunged his name from the index.[9]

What is known of the rest of Gregory's poetic writing suggests, however, that he parted company with both the themes and the style of the Middle Ages and identified much more closely with those of humanism. Besides the epitaph to Ladislaus Jagiełło already mentioned, he also composed love elegies, epigrams, and polemical verses related to political issues, among them a verse reply to a papal nuncio in Hungary who wrote a poem mocking the Poles' lack of success at arms in Silesia in 1474. Gregory is also reported to have written comedies in the manner of Plautus, but there is no evidence and it seems doubtful.

Much of Gregory's energy as archbishop of Lwów was directed toward his efforts to improve the lot of peasants and burghers alike. His enlightened outlook was manifest above all in his solicitous and benevolent treatment of the peasants he settled on his own lands at Dunajów. To enhance the social and economic status of the burghers, Gregory understood he must be a firm advocate of strengthening the Polish cities. To do so, however, meant challenging the privileges of the powerful Polish magnate class, whose own selfish interests precluded removing any of the limitations on town growth, for which the magnates were largely responsible. Gregory was willing, however, to accept such a challenge, aligning himself with those committed to buttressing the power of the monarchy at the expense of the magnates and of the nobility generally.

Gregory's progressive views were also reflected in his attitude toward the church. The thrust of what may be regarded as a distinct current in fifteenth- and sixteenth-century Polish political, social, and ecclesiastical thought was a keen desire to free Poland from papal (read here Roman) policies and politics. Fidelity to the tenets of the Catholic faith was not, of course, the issue; we are not dealing with anything protoheretical in the theological sense. What was involved was the grand design of a papal worldview furthered by policies to which the interests of the Polish state necessarily were subordinate. Polish proponents of anti-Roman views insisted on seeing the papal nuncios and legates as the collective embodiment of the pope's right to interfere in Polish internal affairs and even to intrude on specific aspects of Polish foreign policy. The tension between these spokesmen for papal policy and the Polish champions of the right—indeed the duty—of Poles to pilot their own ship of state was generated by divergent positions on the two predominant Polish political concerns of the age: the final settlement of the relationship with the Teutonic Order of the Knights of the Cross in the Prussian lands and the termination of hostilities with the Turks.

While other considerations understandably shaped his thinking on the subject, one reason for Gregory of Sanok's determined support of a strong monarchy was his conviction that only a monarch with real power would command the resources to bring the Teutonic Order into submission to the Polish Crown. To accomplish this, pressure had to be brought to bear especially on those magnates whose wealth derived from estates in the vast eastern reaches of the kingdom and who were consequently indifferent to the threat posed by the Knights in the Baltic area. Papal support of the magnates and hence of the Knights was motivated primarily by the desire to impose Roman Catholicism on the large Orthodox population in the east (present-day Lithuania, Belorussia, and Ukraine) who were falling under Polish domination with the extension of the magnates' landholdings.

Gregory's campaign against both the magnates and the Knights eventually propelled him into a head-on confrontation with the powerful Cardinal Oleśnicki. Since the highest church positions in Poland were held by magnates, the conservative social and political attitudes of the hierarchy were wholly understandable. Oleśnicki is a case in point. As the son of a palatine, throughout his distinguished career as a churchman he was a spokesman for and an ardent defender of the interests and privileges of the magnate class. His positions were manifest early in his long tenure as bishop of Cracow, a post he came to hold in 1423 at the age of thirty-four without any prior career in the clergy. After the death of Jagiełło in 1434 and the defeat of the Polish Hussites at Grotniki five years later, Oleśnicki was at the height of his power and a truly formidable figure in Polish political as well as ecclesiastical circles.

The conflict with Gregory of Sanok had more than a single facet, but it pivoted on the entwinement of Polish policy toward the Knights of the Cross with the preservation of the magnates' privileges. Because their interests lay elsewhere, most magnates felt no particular urgency about the issue of the Knights, who despite their defeat at the great battle of Grunwald in 1410 still posed a serious threat to Polish interests in the Baltic region. As the leader of a magnate faction that sought accommodation with the Knights (whose grand master and commanders were themselves magnates)—with the approval of the papacy and the Holy Roman Emperor—Oleśnicki soon found himself opposed by Gregory, who as archbishop of Lwów also wielded no small authority. From the viewpoint of contemporary Polish historiography, the conflict between the two high church figures was also a conflict between the new antifeudal outlook of humanism, represented by Gregory, and the vestigial but still influential medieval theological-feudal attitudes held by Oleśnicki and his camp.

The first confrontation between the two men took place early in 1454 when emissaries from Prussia came to King Kazimierz Jagiellończyk (Casimir the Jagiellonian) with a declaration that a union of the gentry and fifty-six Prussian cities and towns desired the return of the Prussian lands to Polish sovereignty. Indicative of Rome's position on the matter was the appearance in the Polish capital of the papal nuncio, the inquisitor Giovanni Capistrano. His purpose was to involve the Poles in a war with the Czechs, with the goal of crushing the Hussite movement (again a policy advocated by Oleśnicki and opposed by Gregory, who counted on an alliance of the Poles, Czechs, and East Slavs to defeat the Knights of the Cross), and to assist Oleśnicki and the magnates in their efforts to reach an accommodation with the Knights. It was in furtherance of this latter goal that Pope Calixtus III (1455–58) pronounced a curse on the Prussian estates for opposing the Knights and for paying tribute to the Polish king. Despite Oleśnicki's support, however, on this occasion the mission of the papal nuncio failed; but as an expression of their anger, the clergy who supported Oleśnicki quickly moved to deny funds to continue the war against the Teutonic Order.

The difficulty posed by the papal nuncios' attempts to shape Polish foreign policy is exemplified by Gregory of Sanok's relationship with Cardinal Cesarini, legate of Pope Eugenius IV, who continued the policies toward Poland of his predecessor, Martin V. In the summer of 1444 the Poles concluded a favorable treaty with the Turks at Sziget under which the Turks were obliged to return a number of cities and towns seized from Poland. Expectations were high that the way to a long and stable peace had at last been found. The papacy viewed the matter differently, however, and Cesarini was entrusted with undoing the new Polish-Turkish accord. Although agreements between the Vatican and the Turks were signed in the fifteenth and sixteenth centuries (treaties in some ways detrimental to the interests of Christian states), the official policy of the Holy See was that Christian nations should not enter into agreements with infidels and heretics, and if they did, they were morally enjoined not to honor them.

On this particular occasion Gregory's warnings were to little avail despite his vehemence. His failure has to be attributed in part to his position at the time. He was thirty-eight years old and still a parish priest. It is highly unlikely that in royal circles—regardless of the esteem in which he might then have been held—his appeals would have carried the weight of arguments put forth by a forceful papal nuncio who was a cardinal of the church. And so Cesarini carried the day: the Poles renewed the war against the Turks and paid a heavy price in the disastrous defeat at the battle of Varna.

The encounter with Cesarini over Polish policy toward the Turks was rancorous and sowed the seeds of later alienation. Gregory's charge that the Vatican was becoming "perfidiae patrona" (the patroness of perfidy) angered Cesarini and was met with the countercharge that Gregory's opposition to Vatican policy was a crime, that Gregory was "religionis inimicus" (an enemy of the faith) and hence worthy of fetters and imprisonment ("minae vinculorum et carceris"). Cesarini's later death, presumably at the hands of thieves, lent itself conveniently to interpretation as just retribution for his role in the "betrayal" of Poland. According to the account in Długosz's history, Cesarini lost his life because of the gold he was carrying when thieves fell on him and stripped him bare. In Callimachus's biography, Gregory comes across the dying papal nuncio by chance and tells him he is dying justly because he dared make the apostolic capital the patroness of perfidy.

The papal policy of attempting to involve the Poles in conflict with the Czechs in order to crush the Hussites, which went back to Pope Martin V and Jagiełło, led to further difficulties between Gregory and the Holy See in the 1460s. The pope now urging the Poles to war with the Czechs was Paul II, and the strategy on this occasion was twofold: to destroy the Hussite movement by means of Polish armed intervention and thus to divert the Poles from their campaign against the Knights of the Cross. The papal nuncio this time was Bishop Rudolf von Rüdesheim, later assisted by the Veronese inquisitor Gabriele Rangoni. On August 1, 1467, Rüdesheim announced two potential papal bulls, one promising peace with the Teutonic Order, the other lifting the excommunication of the Prussian cities and towns. To activate the bulls, all the Polish king Casimir had to do was accept the

Czech crown either personally or on behalf of his son. Toward the end of the month Casimir replied that his decision would be made only after he consulted the secular as well as the ecclesiastical dignitaries of his realm. Gregory of Sanok was one of those consulted, since King Casimir had already determined that if he did not accept the Czech crown himself but sent his son Ladislaus to Bohemia instead, Gregory would accompany him and assume the position of archbishop of Prague. Gregory's answer to the proposal, which we know of from Callimachus's biography, was a letter rejecting the entire plan outright. That this accorded with the king's wishes is shown by the meeting that took place in 1470 between the historian Jan Długosz, whom Casimir had appointed to represent him in the deliberations with Bishop Rüdesheim, and Czech emissaries. The meeting resulted in an accord, drawn up by Długosz and the Czechs, guaranteeing peace between Poles and Czechs. Casimir remained faithful to the accord until the death in 1471 of the Czech ruler George Podiebrady, after which he agreed to the accession of his son Ladislaus to the Czech throne. The coronation took place in Prague on August 21, 1471.

Not content to let the matter rest there, the papal legates Rüdesheim and Rangoni next machinated to foment conflict between Poles and Hungarians and force Ladislaus from the Czech throne. This time they were more successful. War erupted between Bohemia and Hungary, the latter led by King Matthias Corvinus, who, like Ladislaus, had once been a pupil of Gregory of Sanok. The costly conflict dragged on until November 21, 1474, when Corvinus and Ladislaus met to shape an accord. Counting on wounded Polish pride to trigger new conflict with Hungary, the papal nuncio Rangoni wrote verses mocking the Poles for retiring from the siege of Wrocław (Breslau). The verses were answered in kind by Gregory in one of his few surviving literary works. The tone of his reply reflects Gregory's abrasive relations not only with Rangoni, but with other representatives of the Vatican whose primary purpose was to bend Polish policies to the will of Rome:

> Garrula lingua tace, nec sensu nec ratione
> Ulla vales tantum verba pudenda vomis. . . .
> Hoc ibi persuasit pietas, Kasimirus ab urbe
> Ammovit populum pacificusque redit.
> Tu ne fugam fingas regressum hunc et pietatem
> In vicium vertas furcifer ore tuo!
> I nunc et melius discas iam vera fateri,
> Et dedisci pios dedecorare viros.[10]

(Be silent, jabbering tongue, for the infamous words being vomited out
by you so abundantly contain neither sense nor reason. . . . Compassion
caused Casimir to withdraw from the city. Cherishing peace he went away
and took his forces with him. You, you scoundrel, desist from circulating
the story that this withdrawal was a rout and with your yap do not turn
his uprightness into weakness. Be off with you now, and better learn to
speak the truth and unlearn the defamation of men who hold peace dear!)

Between the beginning of Rüdesheim's mission to Poland in 1467
and the coronation of Ladislaus in Prague in 1471, circumstances
provided yet another opportunity for a contest of wills between Gregory and the Holy See. The issue this time involved the fugitive Italian
humanist Filippo Buonaccorsi, who had fled from Rome in 1468 after
being implicated in a conspiracy against the life of Paul Paul II. His
flight carried him to Sicily, Cyprus, Chios, Turkey, and finally Poland.
Wherever he went, he was pursued by emissaries of the pope, who
sought his return to Rome for punishment. Hardly had he reached
Poland when the papal emissary, Alessandro of Forla, arrived to demand his extradition. The matter was referred to a session of the
Polish diet convened in the town of Piotrków, midway between Warsaw
and Cracow, in 1470. Despite Buonaccorsi's pleas that he be permitted
to remain in Poland, the diet agreed to surrender him to the pope. It
was then that Gregory of Sanok and a powerful Polish political figure
of the time, Dersław z Rytwian (Dersław of Rytwiany), stepped forward
in the Italian's defense and thwarted the papal extradition. Though
Gregory may have recognized a kindred spirit in Buonaccorsi, his and
Dersław's defense of the fugitive was motivated mainly by a desire to
use his case to reaffirm Polish sovereignty and not bow submissively
to the wishes of the pope.

Turning from Gregory of Sanok's role in Polish politics to his place
in his country's cultural life, we also find a record of significant achievement. Apart from the humanist "court" he established in Dunajów,
Gregory's principal cultural pursuits were poetry and philosophy.

Callimachus paints the portrait of a widely read liberal intellectual
who held Scholasticism and the Scholastics in low regard, attacked
Aristotle, and advocated relying on one's own intellect, reason, and
judgment rather than the authority of theologians. "Nobody," Buonaccorsi recalls his declaring, "demeans himself more than those people
who, discovering nothing on their own, are absorbed in the defense
of the convictions of others, especially those of Aristotle; so many
volumes have been filled, he used to say, in support of his [Aristotle's]
views that it may seem strange that people do not see how much

falsehood is concealed in these works, which have to be propped up with so many supports lest they fall, while those things that are true remain standing by virtue of their own nature and more effectively obtrude on our cognition than that which has to be confirmed by means of arguments" (64). Needless to say, views like these, as well as Gregory's vigorous defense of Polish national interests, as he understood them, in confrontations with representatives of the Vatican and supporters of Rome's policies in Poland earned him many enemies and eventually caused him to withdraw almost completely from public affairs. The king continued to seek his counsel from time to time, particularly with respect to Poland's Prussian policy, but Gregory's independence and outspokenness on many issues had caused so much animosity that for the sake of his own peace and quiet, and perhaps even his safety, he chose to turn his back on the public arena.

Gregory's philosophical interests inclined to the Stoics in matters of ethics and to the Epicureans in natural matters. He appears to have been conversant with the writings of Lucretius as well as of Lorenzo Valla and is generally regarded as the first Epicurean in Poland. This in part explains his initial defense and later patronage of Filippo Buonaccorsi, for the Roman Academy of Pomponio Leto was a bastion of humanist Epicureanism, and Buonaccorsi himself was a lifelong exponent of the philosophy. The roots of Gregory's hostility toward Scholasticism and his embrace of Epicurean materialism are not difficult to discover. Much of his early life was spent in want, and this clearly contributed to an attitude of realism and tolerance. He was born in a poor village not far from the southeastern Polish city of Sanok and spent his childhood there. When the time came to do something about his schooling his father took him to Sanok, where his formal education began. In 1418, at only twelve years of age, he ran away and traveled from one town to another until he eventually reached Cracow. He spent a few years there and then left for a five-year stay in Germany. When he returned to Cracow in 1428 to enroll at the university, he had behind him ten years of wandering, propelled by the twin hungers of mind and body. What living he earned during this period came from teaching and from copying books for his own pupils.

Perhaps impoverishment and extensive travel bred in Gregory a tolerance of other peoples and cultures that not only shaped his later thinking but also set him at odds with tradition and authority. He was, we know, keenly interested in other religions. His relations with Jews, who were numerous in Cracow and Lwów at the time, were especially good; he also enjoyed the stimulation of discussing religion with Moslems, whom he had occasionally met in Lwów, which lay on a significant East-West trade route. Nowicki also reports that as archbishop of Lwów Gregory is reputed to have given permission for a pagan to marry a Christian woman.[11]

Gregory's personal experience of hardship as well as his own modest background go far to explain his social philosophy. Throughout his adult life he showed a true sense of civic utility, and its absence in Scholasticism further estranged him from that system of thought. A champion of the rights of cities and of the natural, organic development of urban life, Gregory also recognized the need to improve the lot of the peasants. To achieve his social goals and also his political goal of enhancing royal authority, he appreciated the contribution education could make. Hence his interest in schools and pedagogy and his recognition that institutions of learning that still bore the stamp of the Middle Ages were inadequate to cope with social needs in a period of considerable growth and change. In Gregory's view learning had to be socially beneficial to both the monarchy and the cities and useful in resolving conflicts between them for the good of the state as a whole.

The obstacle to realizing Gregory's concept of a socially beneficial learning was the continued submission of scholarship to the authority of religion. If learning was to flourish, to provide answers to questions about man's world, it had to be set free from the fetters of theologians. As time went on this became one of the more passionate campaigns of Gregory's career, inevitably alienating him further from the ecclesiastical conservatives both in his own country and in Rome.

To loosen the theologians' grip on learning, Gregory argued against applying laws of nature to Christian theology "as if we found it necessary," to quote Callimachus, "to confine God within borders that seem to us the natural boundaries of things, although God's activity should, after all, be the norm for nature itself, or as if we were no longer in his debt if he changed something from the usual and natural order of things for us or if he did something in accordance with the demands of nature." (58). Gregory was equally incensed that sermons were based on antiquated theological texts without knowledge of the principles of rhetoric or reliance on the speaker's own judgment. He placed a high value on the need to study rhetoric and poetry and thus distinguished between the homilies of Jerome and Augustine and those of more recent theologians, which he regarded as boring and lifeless. According to Callimachus, Gregory himself was an eloquent speaker whose ability to move audiences, especially when he spoke on matters of faith, owed most to the emphasis he placed on his own powers of persuasion rather than on the authority of theologians.[12]

Gregory's independence of spirit and liberalism, so reflective of the influence of humanism on his thinking, were also apparent in his attitude toward the church's role in domestic life. He lamented for example, that he lacked sufficient freedom to dissolve marriages that were obviously unsuccessful, and he argued that it was wrong to regard as joined by God those husbands and wives who no longer loved each other. When love dies, he believed, a marriage ceases to be pleasing to God. In his view it was both unwise and dangerous to force people who hated each other to live together.

Deeply concerned about civic society and the well-being of the state in general, in line with his secular orientation, Gregory believed in cultivating especially those studies that teach how to protect and preserve the state. He also believed that the behavior of those who guide the state should be based on religion, if not on the authority of theologians or the church. States depended most for their survival, he argued, on the power of the spirit rather than on the power of the flesh. He took a pragmatic approach toward the law, rejecting abstract principles of justice in favor of a flexible legal system tailored to the needs of the individual society. What mattered most was not that laws be just but that they be socially beneficial. As a humanist and a poet, Gregory emphasized the study of poetry, which he considered as necessary to the young as food. According to Callimachus, Gregory likened those who try to undertake other disciplines without the support of poetry to people who want to enter a walled city yet pass by open gates out of contempt. He even believed it was more possible to understand all fields of learning through poetry than for one educated in all other things to master the art of poetry of his own will.[13]

Gregory's individualism revealed itself in other areas as well. Although he was maligned because of it, he saw nothing wrong in his meeting and talking with women and is known to have had women guests at his palace in Dunajów. If we trust Callimachus's account, and there is no reason not to in the matter, then one of the female guests at Dunajów—although we have no idea now long she was there—was Callimachus's own friend Fannia. In recalling Gregory's great reluctance to show his writings to other people, Callimachus mentions as exceptions his account of the ascension of King Ladislaus to the throne of Hungary and of his expeditions against the Turks as well as several epigrams Gregory wrote "for fun and amusement against my Fannia, though elsewhere he confessed that she was the pride and ornament of his town" (72). Gregory was also critical of such popular pastimes of the period as jousting and hunting. Jousting he dismissed as poor preparation for warfare; because the object of the sport was to unseat an opponent rather than kill him, the contests usually ended in falls or slight wounds, since the natural tendency of the jousters was to avoid being badly hurt. Hunting had no redeeming virtues at all in his eyes, and he regarded it as a labor and obligation of slaves. In Callimachus's words, "He regarded as ridiculous those who left work that could be useful to people in order to race around forests in pursuit of animals" (66).

Callimachus closes his interesting and sometimes colorful account of the life and manners of Gregory of Sanok with a description of his subject's personal habits. The archbishop, we learn, cared little for sleep and was so passionate a reader that his bed was always covered with books. Disorder, at least in his private life, was Gregory's style. His bedroom was in constant disarray with books, weapons, food, and all manner of household utensils and other items strewn around shelves and even on the floor in no apparent order. When someone who was troubled by the mess brought it to his attention (Callimachus is undoubtedly speaking about himself at this point), Gregory used to reply that the only people who worry about order are those who have things to sell and so must be able to find them easily; he, however, had nothing for sale. On the grounds that they were incompatible with his nature, Gregory rarely took baths. He fell ill only infrequently, but when he did it was usually very serious and even dangerous; true to his own kind of individualism, however, he never summoned a doctor and insisted on treating himself with juices and herbs. Whenever he traveled—and he was indifferent to the time of day or the weather— he always carried with him a handbook of herbs. Although a warm and gracious man, he was given to fits of anger—which Callimachus ascribes to an enervation of his exhausted mind—in which he would scold his household servants and sometimes take a stick to them. When he was older, Callimachus reports, he would pretend to have lost his reason in order to find out what those around him were thinking and would play the role for days at a time.

Callimachus's *Vita* paints the picture of an exceptional figure whose individualism and independence accorded with the spirit of humanism. There was something of the natural rebel in Gregory. His distaste for tradition and authority and his realism and pragmatism seem to have been inborn. It is less that his consciousness was inclined to these attitudes by the influence of humanist thought than that his nature made him highly receptive to the new learning and philosophy. That these facets came together as they did in an outstanding member of the church hierarchy in fifteenth-century Poland makes Gregory all the more unusual for his time and place.

Based on Callimachus's account alone, there can be no doubt that Gregory of Sanok deserves recognition as Poland's first major humanist. His views on philosophy, theology, secular education, and the classics, his great interest in and concern for civic society, the intellectual climate of his palace at Dunajów, his enthusiastic welcome and patronage of an Italian renegade humanist, and what we know of his reading habits and writings argue convincingly for such recognition. What the paucity of material on Gregory denies us, however, is a better sense of the nature of his contribution to an emerging Polish humanism. Callimachus is so vague on this point that in this respect his *Vita* is almost without value. We are told, for example, that "many learned men came to him daily from Cracow and that he frequently visited that city himself, going where disputations and readings were held and offering his own opinions about the matters under discussion as freely as he heard the arguments of others" (24). Unfortunately, however, we have no specific information on who these "learned men" may have been or on anything related to Gregory's participation in disputations and learned gatherings in Cracow, either at the university or anywhere else in the city. Apart from expressions of admiration and some quotations from his works, the histories of Długosz and Miechowita are also of no great help in a more detailed reconstruction of the milieu in which Gregory moved and the impact he may have had on academic and other cultural circles in Cracow. We are left with the impression of an undeniably exceptional figure who, while acknowledged as the first significant expression of humanism in Poland, cannot be seen as the fount of subsequent developments. Thus we turn now to the careers of two men, both foreigners, whose contributions to the course of humanism in Poland have been amply documented.

From San Gimignano to Cracow: The Extraordinary Career of Filippo Buonaccorsi, Alias Callimachus

Of the foreigners who helped shape an emergent Polish humanism, none was more fascinating or influential than the Italian Filippo Buonaccorsi (1437–96). In time he became better known by the Latin pseudonym Callimachus, the name of one of the most admired Greek poets and scholars of classical antiquity.

A prolific author after he settled in Poland, Buonaccorsi became active principally in politics. Although widely resented as a foreigner because of his prominence at the royal court, he won the confidence of the Polish king Casimir IV, to such an extent that during his reign he became the main architect of Polish foreign policy and the head of several major diplomatic missions.

What brought this multifaceted and talented Italian to permanent exile in Poland constitutes a tale of high intrigue and adventure. A Tuscan like Machiavelli, to whom he is sometimes compared, Buonaccorsi came from that superbly preserved medieval hill town San Gimignano, roughly midway between the great cities of Florence and Siena and long celebrated for its fine location and splendid, once-fortified towers. The Buonaccorsis were a well-off merchant family with wide commercial interests and a taste for politics.[1] In July 1459 Filippo himself, at age twenty-two, was elected *prior populi* of San Gimignano under the name Damianus Pieri Angeli. His brothers Francesco and Ettore later also held political office. Biagio Buonaccorsi, a direct descendant, won a place in history primarily as a close friend and collaborator of Machiavelli. There was also a political skeleton in the Buonaccorsi closet, worth mentioning in view of Filippo's later career:

Giuliano, the son of uncle Antonio, had been condemned to death in 1454 for an attempt on the life of none other than Cosimo de' Medici.

Filippo Buonaccorsi's early years were spent in San Gimignano. It was there between 1450 and 1453 that he studied poetry, for example, with Mattia Lupi (1380–1468), who seems to have had a fondness for young boys, a proclivity hinted to apply to Buonaccorsi as well, at least during his association with Pomponio Leto, founder of the famous humanist center in Rome, the Accademia Romana. Although it is impossible to reconstruct Buonaccorsi's early studies and travels, there is a strong possibility that after leaving San Gimignano he studied for a while in Siena, where his grandmother, Nicoletta Malvolti (the wife of Angelo Malvolti), lived. Lupi had once taught rhetoric there, and it may well have been at Lupi's suggestion that young Filippo continued his studies in Siena.

From 1460 to 1462 Buonaccorsi was in Venice, in the company of his brother Francesco. Venice was an important center of learning, and it is very likely that some of Buonaccorsi's later intellectual interests were formed during this period. Venetian scholarly life during Buonaccorsi's stay included close contact with Greek scholarship and classical studies in Constantinople. Although the presence of Greek scholars grew after Constantinople fell to the Turks in 1453, Venice had established itself as a center of Greek studies even before that cataclysmic event.[2] When the Italian scholar Guarino da Verona visited the Byzantine capital to acquire a knowledge of ancient Greek literature, he was hosted by Emmanuel Chrysoloras (1350–1415), who in 1397 came to Florence, where he initiated the renewal of Greek studies in Italy. In Buonaccorsi's brief Venetian period, no expatriate Greek scholar was more prominent than George of Trebizond (Georgius Trapezuntius, 1395–1484) whom Francesco Barbaro (1390–1454) was instrumental in resettling from Crete.[3] While *podestà* (chief magistrate) of Vicenza, Barbaro secured George's appointment as a teacher of Greek in the school there, and when Barbaro moved on to Venice the expatriate scholar lived for a time in his house. We do not know whether Buonaccorsi ever studied with, or even met, George of Trebizond, but some traces of his influence have been detected in Buonaccorsi's *Rhetorica*. It is also believed that Buonaccorsi's familiarity with so-called esoteric sciences, especially astrology, can be traced to his Venetian experience. He and his brother Francesco lived near the residence of Girolamo Silvano of Prague, onetime confessor of the king of Poland and curator of an important collection of hermetic literature to which Filippo may have had access. But Venice was so much a center of astrology and related subjects in this period that no single source or conduit of information need be posited. There were any number of ways he could have been initiated into the esoteric sciences while in Venice; what matters is that his interest in them remained throughout his life and formed the basis of a certain reputation he had.

From Venice Buonaccorsi traveled to Rome in early 1462, still accompanied by his brother Francesco and possibly also by a friend named Lucio Condulmer. Buonaccorsi was attracted to Rome by the fame of the Accademia Romana. By now wholly committed to humanistic studies, he would naturally have been drawn to the academy, which enjoyed a reputation as the foremost center of humanist erudition in all of Italy. Established by a well-to-do nobleman, Pomponio Leto (the "pontifex maximus" of the academy), the Accademia Romana had a distinctly elitist and hedonistic character.[4] Garbed in ancient Roman dress and using classical Roman names, its members spent most of their time in the rustic mansion on the Esquilino discussing poetry, art, philosophy, philology, and archaeology. A regular feature of their routine was the renewal of ancient Roman religious rites. For example, each year on April 21 they celebrated the birth of the city of Rome itself. No doubt also in the spirit of ancient Rome, an undeniable libertine atmosphere prevailed, permeated with a distinct epicureanism. Women and drink were frequent companions at academy functions, and homosexuality and bisexuality are believed to have been practiced freely both as individual tastes and as an aspect, one assumes, of the elitist classical style.

Buonaccorsi's entry into the Accademia Romana seems to have come about through his friendship with one of its members, Bartolomeo Sacchi (1421–81), who adopted the pseudonym "Platina" and eventually won fame as the author of a history of the popes (*Liber de vitis ac gestis summorum pontificum*)[5] that he dedicated to Pope Sixtus IV, under whom he later served as Vatican librarian. Apart from their common humanist interests—Platina (as I shall henceforth refer to him) had studied Greek in Florence from 1457 to 1461 under John Argyropulos—Platina was well established and in a position to be of help to Buonaccorsi. In 1462 he had accompanied Francesco Cardinal Gonzaga to Rome, where two years later Pope Pius II named him papal *abbreviator*. By the time Buonaccorsi made his acquaintance, Platina was already a member of the Accademia Romana. Besides bringing Buonaccorsi into the academy, Platina also introduced him to high church dignitaries, among them Cardinals Roverella and Ammanati. Roverella took a particular interest in the newcomer, appointing him first his *familiare* and later his secretary.

As a member of the Accademia Romana, Buonaccorsi was called "Caeculus" (the Blind, from Latin *caecus*, "blind"; Caeculus was also the name of the god who caused blindness) because of his myopia. The nickname was probably given him by Platina. He is described this way by Platina in his *De honesta voluptate et valetudine* and by Giovanni Antonio Campano (d. 1477) in the following epigram:

> Callimachi quamvis lippi videantur ocelli,
>   Sitque minor stella pupula Cantaridis.
> Plura videt, quam linx, vigili nec cesserit Argo,
>   Noctem vel media perspicit ille die.
> Clarus erit caelo, quamvis Sol aspicit umbras,
>   Sitque serena dies, tota videt nebulam.
> Cumque alii videant, que sunt tantum modo, suevit
>   Quaeque etiam non sunt, cernere Callimachus.
> Quodque magis stupeas, oculis non spectat apertis,
>   Ut videat, claudit lumina Callimachus.[6]

(Although Callimachus's little eyes seem blind, with pupils smaller than those of a Spanish fly, he sees more than a lynx and yields nothing to the vigilant Argus [the hundred-eyed dog who guarded Io, the beloved of Zeus;] whether midnight or noon, he sees the same. Although the sun beholds shadows the sky will be bright to him, and though the day may be clear he can yet discern a cloud. And when others see only those things that are, Callimachus can see even those things that are not. What may astound you more, Callimachus does not see with his eyes open; in order to see, he shuts his eyes.)

As Campano's epigram also indicates, Buonaccorsi had additionally acquired the pseudonym "Callimachus" while at the academy, a name possibly bestowed by Pomponio Leto himself, though for what reason it is difficult to say.

His association with the Accademia Romana shaped the course of Filippo Buonaccorsi's life and ultimately was responsible for his expatriation to Poland. The incident that set the chain of events in motion was his involvement in a conspiracy to assassinate Pope Paul II in 1468. Determining an exact chronology is impossible, but what evidence there is suggests the conspiracy was probably hatched during the spring and summer of 1467, while Pomponio Leto was out of Rome. After working an entire school year without salary, Leto was feeling a financial pinch reminiscent of his first ten years in Rome, when he had lived in poverty after running away from his affluent family to avoid a pestering stepmother. In 1467 Leto decided to quit Rome for a while and go to Venice, where he hoped to earn money by private tutoring. After the conspiracy against Paul II was crushed and Leto was brought in for interrogation, he wrote a *Defensio* while incarcerated in which he sought to clear himself of any knowledge—to say nothing of complicity—concerning the whole affair. In the *Defensio* he said he went to Venice intending to travel on to the East to study Greek and Arabic. It seems likely, however, that Leto had already caught wind of the conspiracy and wanted to get as far away as possible. In any case Venice proved a mixed blessing for Leto. Although he found two young men to tutor to cover his expenses, it was not long before he was arrested by the Venetian authorities for pederasty. The charge was a serious one in Venice, and Leto had probably already been jailed when in March 1468 an extradition request arrived from Rome implicating him in the conspiracy against Paul II. The Venetians were quick to comply, and Leto was packed off to Rome like, in the words of Platina, "another Jugurtha."[7] Back in Rome, he was imprisoned in the Castel Sant'Angelo along with other accused members of the Accademia Romana, and it was there he wrote his *Defensio*.

As we reconstruct the events leading up to the discovery and suppression of the conspiracy, it now seems apparent that while Pomponio Leto was away from the academy Buonaccorsi quickly came to the fore as leader of the plot.[8] Although Buonaccorsi, Platina, "Glauco" (Buonaccorsi's old friend Lucio Condulmer), and "Petreio" (probably Petreio Marso, a member of the Accademia Romana and secretary to Cardinal Ammanati, bishop of Pavia) are usually identified as the "heads" of the conspiracy, there is some consensus that the true instigator and leader, the mastermind behind it, was Filippo Buonaccorsi.[9] He was so identified by both Pomponio Leto and Platina during the official investigation that began on February 29, 1468. In his *Defensio*, Leto in particular spares no pains to present Buonaccorsi in the worst possible light and to absolve himself of any guilt in the affair: "Callimachus, whom I wish I had never met, when he came to Rome because of his desire to pursue the study of literature was received by me hospitably. From the moment his extravagance and wickedness became known to me, I immediately became an enemy instead of a friend. I began to view him not as a man and to hate his perverse ways, which were so different from my own. I always loved frugality, thriftiness, and sobriety. He, on the contrary, threw himself into gluttony, drunkenness, and intemperance in all things, valuing all people but himself for little."[10]

While in prison, Platina gave testimony that included the following indictment of Buonaccorsi: "I can affirm one thing—speaking above all for myself—with respect to the folly and inebriation of Callimachus, and that is that I hold carelessness in lighter regard than the words of an unsober man; and because I viewed his cloddishness with contempt and especially because he is a bad man and an informer, I had no wish to follow him."[11]

Letters written by Platina to the pope himself during this period express similar sentiments.[12] Later in his career, however, when he had returned to papal favor, Platina reversed his earlier position and maintained that during the interrogations of 1468 he testified that Buonaccorsi had neither the physical and moral qualities nor the material means to head a conspiracy. As he wrote in his life of Paul II in his history of the popes:

> Who ever saw me swearing an oath to Callimachus as our leader? Then, trusting in my innocence, I replied resolutely that I was untroubled by any pangs of conscience. Disheveled and wan, he kept on pressing me to acknowledge the truth, now threatening torture, now death. But when I saw armed men and everything in tumult around me, fearing something more serious would be considered against us out of fear and danger, I stated the reasons why I believed Callimachus incapable of contriving any such thing, much less of planning it, since he was wanting in counsel, persuasion, power, solicitude, accomplishments, supplies, followers, weapons, funds, and, finally, eyes. For Caeculus was more drowsy than P. Lentulus and more sluggish than Lucius Crassus weighted down by his fat.[13]

That the conspiracy of 1468, whether devised and led by Buonaccorsi or not, plotted not only the assassination of Pope Paul II but also that of most members of the Roman curia now seems certain. What real chance of success the conspiracy had is impossible to know. The lid was blown off it before any harm could be done, probably as a result of an indiscretion by one of the conspirators. Wanting to get back into the good graces of his former patron Cardinal Ammanati, Petreio confided in a former factor of Ammanati named Giuliano (or Angelo) dell'Aquila and apparently revealed the conspiracy to him. Dell'Aquila ran off to the cardinal, who reported to the pope, who then moved swiftly to nip the plot in the bud. Once he realized what he had done, Petreio seems to have made an effort to warn Buonaccorsi, but it was already too late.

Before considering the aftermath of the aborted conspiracy and Buonaccorsi's subsequent activities, eventually leading to his flight to Poland, we ought to try to understand what circumstances might have led the young humanist from San Gimignano to become involved in something so bizarre as a plot to kill the pope and members of his curia. There are three plausible explanations. The first has to do with Pope Paul II himself. Born Pietro Barbo in Venice in 1417, Paul II was pope from August 30, 1464, to July 26, 1471.[14] A powerful and ostentatious leader who intensified the struggle against the Turks and encouraged the Hungarian King Matthias Corvinus to depose George Podiebrady as king of Bohemia in order to suppress the Hussites, Paul II earned the disfavor of the humanists because his supposed antipathy toward the movement. The humanists' hostility (if it can be called that) toward the pope was not entirely well founded. To be sure, Paul II was himself not a humanist in the full sense,[15] and he did move swiftly to dissolve the Accademia Romana once the conspiracy against him had been uncovered. Paul had been unhappy about what he regarded as the paganizing atmosphere and activities of the academy and was undoubtedly glad of a pretext to close the place down. But Paul II was also proud to have scholars in his entourage and encouraged the establishment of the first printing shop in Italy at Subiaco in 1465.

Another element in the conception of the conspiracy may well have been what Italian scholars refer to as *catilinarismo* ("Catilinism" in English). Its name derived from the Catiline conspiracy that Cicero helped quell in ancient Rome and that the historian Sallust made the subject of his *Bellum Catilinae* (The War with Catiline). It signifies a kind of anarchic compulsion, an urge to rebel against authority, not only characteristic of society and politics during the Renaissance but deeply imbedded in the Renaissance ethos. Italian history of the period offers ample evidence of it, but that the Catilinian revolt could have served as a model to anyone familiar with the history of ancient Rome seems doubtful. Nevertheless, a myth about the Catilinian conspiracy grew up in postclassical times that transformed the relatively minor and unromantic original event into an archetype of antiestablishment revolt. Dante kept the myth alive in the *Inferno* by reviling the descendants of Catiline in book 15, 68, basing his treatment of the Catilinian conspiracy on the tradition that after fleeing Rome Catiline made his way to Fiesole, just outside Florence, and incited the people to revolt against Rome. According to the tradition, the Florentine nobility descended from the Romans, whereas the descendants of Catiline's followers were commoners and, moreover, envious and avaricious (as indeed Catiline himself appears to have been).

More inspirational conspiracies in ancient Rome were available as models, above all those of Scipio and Brutus, and to the Renaissance mind may have represented essentially the same social and political phenomenon as the Catilinian conspiracy. But the republican ideals that motivated Scipio and Brutus were far more appealing to Renaissance thinkers than the causes underlying the Catilinian revolt, which is why Machiavelli takes pains to present Caesar in a worse light than Catiline in his *Discorsi* (Discourses, first published in 1531):

> Nor should anyone be deceived by Caesar's renown when he finds writers extolling him before others, for those who praise him have either been corrupted by his fortune or overawed by the long continuance of the empire which, since it was ruled under that name, did not permit writers to speak freely of him. If, however, anyone desires to know what writers would have said, had they been free, he has but to look at what they say of Catiline. For Caesar is the more blameworthy of the two, in that he who has done wrong is more blameworthy than he who has but desired to do wrong. Or, again, let him look at the praise bestowed on Brutus: Caesar they could not find fault with on account of his power, so they cry up his enemy.[16]

What Machiavelli condemns in Caesar, above all, is the imposition of tyranny; hence a conspiracy to end the reign of a tyrant and restore republican ideals is laudable. Conspiracy against a republic, on the other hand, is viewed as contemptible and worthy only of the swiftest and most thorough suppression. To the youthful conspirators of Pomponio Leto's Accademia Romana in 1467, ending by force the rule of a pope judged to be excessively authoritarian and unsympathetic to the new learning might well have seemed honorable and in the best tradition of the ancient Rome they admired so much.

Flight

With the conspiracy of 1468 aborted and accusing fingers pointing him out as the principal instigator, Buonaccorsi's first instinct was to go into hiding. He wanted at all costs to avoid falling into the hands of the papal police and being brought to trial. He managed to hide for a short while in Rome itself, but this was far too risky a refuge and so he headed for the small Adriatic port of Trani in the Apulia region just north of Bari. It was not long before the hot breath of the papal pursuers (under the diligent command of Gasparo Chilico) was felt there as well. The only course left was flight from Italy. Where and for how long would have to be settled later. The main thing was to get away as fast as possible.

Buonaccorsi's itinerary, probably determined by chance and circumstance, led to the eastern Mediterranean. We know that after setting sail from Trani he passed to the west of the island of Citera (Cerigo) and made a brief stop at Candos, situated on the northeast coast of Crete and known in modern times as Candia. That he may also have touched Rhodes and perhaps even Egypt seems likely. How long he intended to remain in Cyprus after he disembarked there we have no way of knowing, but his stay was brief because of events he could not have foreseen.

Cyprus at the time was ruled by Jacob II of Lusignano, natural son of John III, who had seized power from his half-sister Carlotta. To legitimize the throne he had usurped, Jacob needed pontifical investiture, and it was for that reason and also to arrange his possible marriage with a daughter of Thomas Paleologus, the last despot of the Peloponnesus, that a papal legate, Atanasio Calceofilo, bishop of Gerace, had come to Cyprus. Calceofilo had arrived before Buonaccorsi and apparently lost little time bringing Jacob up to date on what had been happening in Italy—certainly not least the conspiracy to assassinate Paul II and the ringleader Buonaccorsi's flight from Italy. As soon as the papal legate learned of Buonaccorsi's fortuitous appearance in, of all places, Cyprus, he immediately demanded that the king order his arrest. Jacob's position was awkward. He could not afford to antagonize the bishop of Gerace because he needed pontifical investiture, but he wanted to maintain a certain independence from Rome. For the sake of the former, he declared Buonaccorsi persona non grata; to demonstrate the latter, he ordered the fugitive to leave the island but gave him enough time to get away from the papal authorities.

Matters hardly improved when Buonaccorsi reached Chios at the beginning of summer 1469. The evidence is scant, but it appears that a rendezvous took place on Chios between Buonaccorsi and another member of the Accademia Romana, Marco Franceschini (or Perugini, or Franceschini of Perugia, or Marco Antonio Romano). Other Italian friends seem to have been there as well—Niccolò and Francesco Ugolini, of a well-known Florentine mercantile family with business interests in Chios and Constantinople. As if permanently imbued with a taste for political conspiracy that needed only the slightest encouragement, Pomponio Leto's former charges soon found themselves involved in high adventure on Chios. Buonaccorsi was probably not the originator, but once a plan was hatched to deliver Chios—then a Genoese possession that paid tribute to the Turkish sultan—to an eagerly assembled fleet of some 250 Turkish ships, he threw himself into it with characteristic zest. What reward the little circle of Italians hoped to gain remains a mystery. In any case, as in the conspiracy of 1468, the plot was foiled by carelessness. Letters between Buonaccorsi and Marco Franceschini were intercepted by the police, and the whole affair was stopped before much could happen. Buonaccorsi, now doubly a fugitive, hastened to Pera where he was out of danger. Franceschini was not so fortunate. After being taken by the authorities on Chios, he was tortured into confessing the entire conspiracy and was eventually hanged. Before leaving Pera for the far safer haven of Constantinople, Buonaccorsi composed an elegy about the events on Chios and the fate of his friend Marco, which he titled "In obitu clarissimi viri Marci Antonij Romani" (On the Death of the Most Noble Marco Antonio Romano).

Buonaccorsi had reasons to make for Constantinople besides safety. Francesco Ugolini, whose hospitality Buonaccorsi enjoyed for the nearly nine months he was in the city, probably had encouraged him to come there from Chios whatever the outcome of the plot. Ugolini's Turkish connections were good, and since he seems to have had the most to gain from delivering Chios to the Turks, it is likely that he concocted the island scheme. Buonaccorsi must also have been attracted to the idea of locating in Constantinople because a relative on his mother's side, Jacopo Tedaldi, had long been residing there for commercial reasons and had become a prominent member of the Italian community. After the Ottoman conquest of 1453, Tedaldi proved so adept at dealing with Constantinople's new masters that he became a trusted member of a small circle of advisers around Sultan Mehmed II. Between Ugolini's hospitality and Jacopo Tedaldi's prominence in Constantinople, Buonaccorsi was assured of more protection than he had known since his flight from Rome.

It was during his stay in Constantinople that Buonaccorsi most likely made the contact that paved the way for his lifelong expatriation in Poland. At some point he met another member of the Tedaldi family, Arnolfo, who occasionally came to Turkey on business but who resided in Poland, where he held the by no means inconsequential position of director of the state monopoly of salt mines in Drohobycz, then an important commercial center in the southeastern corner of the country, now part of the Ukrainian Soviet Socialist Republic. Although the notion of a resident Italian businessman in late fifteenth-century Poland may seem surprising, Italian merchants had been ranging far and wide in search of new markets for a very long time, and by the late Middle Ages they constituted a small but thriving community in Poland, especially in towns such as Cracow, Lwów, and Drohobycz that lay on vital trade routes. By the time Buonaccorsi met Arnolfo Tedaldi, Italians had already achieved dominance over the lucrative salt trade in southeastern Poland.

A combination of considerations must have motivated Buonaccorsi to leave Turkey for Poland; Arnolfo Tedaldi's ability to help him make a new life for himself in a Christian country far away from Italy, and the ever-present danger of papal arrest; the existence of a well-off Italian community where he could feel at home while pursuing a career in the vast Polish-Lithuanian state, in which the opportunities for an educated and enterprising foreigner with good connections could not have been negligible; the possibility of further study and even an academic career at the renowned university in Cracow; the hope of patronage—always an important consideration for an itinerant Renaissance man of letters—at the court of the leading Polish humanist at the time, Gregory of Sanok, archbishop of Lwów.

Initially, anyway, the last may have been the deciding factor. Gregory of Sanok had an admirable reputation as a liberal churchman and humanist who was familiar with Italy and whose palace at Dunajów, near Lwów, was the closest thing to a humanist academy that existed in Poland. Besides, Arnolfo Tedaldi enjoyed good relations with the archbishop and could be counted on to intercede on Buonaccorsi's behalf.

In Poland

By the time Buonaccorsi reached Lwów, after traveling a doubtless well-worn merchant route through Moldavia, Arnolfo Tedaldi was already there to greet him and provide a roof. Although it was only a matter of time before Tedaldi would have presented his relative to Gregory of Sanok, the introduction became urgent for a familiar reason. The papal authorities had by no means put Buonaccorsi out of their minds and were as eager as ever to get their hands on him. It seems likely that they had managed to keep tabs on him while he was in Constantinople and apprised themselves of his further plans, for in October 1470 a papal legate to Poland—Alessandro, bishop of Forlì—presented a formal demand for extradition to the Polish diet convened in Piotrków on October 28. After hearing the case for the Vatican, the diet agreed to honor the request. Fearing that Buonaccorsi would be sent back to Italy in chains, Arnolfo Tedaldi turned to Gregory of Sanok for help. The archbishop was more than accommodating; besides promising to do what he could to reverse the diet's decision, he invited Buonaccorsi to settle in his palace in Dunajów in November 1470.

Now that he was again moving in a humanist milieu Buonaccorsi preferred to use his old Latin sobriquet Callimachus, or Callimachus Experiens ("experienced," "active"), in an obvious reference to his adventurous life. He was not one to passively entrust his fate to another, no matter how well intentioned. Thus, when an opportunity presented itself to plead his own case against extradition and for the right to remain in Poland, he drew up a "memorial," or petition, in Latin, addressed to the powerful palatine of Sandomierz, Dersław of Rytwiany, whose opinion was known to carry considerable weight with King Casimir IV Jagiellończyk (the Jagiellonian) and who was not present when the diet agreed to extradite Buonaccorsi. The petition, dated April 15, 1471, and composed at Dunajów, is a fairly lengthy and clever *apologia pro vita sua* that gives ample evidence of the political cunning that was to become the hallmark of the Italian's subsequent career. The "memorial" is well worth quoting in full, but for practical reasons only a brief summary can be given here.

In seeking to make his case—or plead his defense—Buonaccorsi sought first of all to portray himself as a person of little consequence, possessing neither resources nor powerful backing, hence lacking the ability to organize a conspiracy against a pope. Much of the thrust of the "memorial" is an attempt to persuade Dersław of the impossibility of his conspiratorial leadership or initiative. As he writes at one point: "Semper privatus vixerim et in eo statu, ut non modo non timeri a tanta potestate debuerim, sed nequidem inimici mihi multum invidere potuerunt" (I always led a private life, and in such circumstances that there was no cause for me to be feared by such a powerful person [the pope]; but even my enemies had no grounds for envy).[17] And in another place: "Ridebor et aut improbus et impudens, aut levis et inconsideratus censebor, quod eum credi velim statum et condicionem pontificis summi, ut salus sua et rerum suarum columen ab homunculo isto pendeat" (I would be laughed at and regarded as shameless and arrogant, or lightheaded and thoughtless, if I wanted people to believe that the position and condition of the pope, his own welfare and the support of all his affairs, depended on such an inconsequential person as myself [24]).

Having established the absurdity of the idea that he might have plotted against the pope, Buonaccorsi then describes his hiding and his flight as the natural reaction of an innocent man caught up in a nightmare of intrigue and suspicion: "Fateor aliquando invaluisse in urbe fabulam illam, quod contra pontificem coniurassem idque eadem hora mihi atque illi nuntiatum fuisse. Cuius rei novitate et magnitudine territus, ego primum delitui, deinde cum viderem supra opinionem meam rem magni fieri, clanculum in Apuliam me recepi" (I admit that at one time the story began to be spread around the city that I had conspired against the pope and that it was reported to me and to him at the same time. Frightened by the strangeness and magnitude of the affair, I at first went into hiding. But then when I saw that the matter was becoming bigger than I could have imagined, I secretly betook myself to Apulia [27]).

He mentions further that when the papal authorities were unable to apprehend him they took his brother and some friends into custody, along with papers he had hidden. Even though no charges could be brought against those arrested despite lengthy interrogation and torture, they were imprisoned in the Castel Sant'Angelo. They were eventually released, however, and when the charges against Buonaccorsi himself could not be substantiated, his confiscated property was ordered returned to him and official word conveyed to Cyprus, which he had already left for Turkey, that he was free to return to Italy.

Buonaccorsi takes some pains at this point in his "memorial" to show his hoped-for Polish protector that he did not come to Poland as a fugitive from justice, since he could already return to Italy a free man; therefore the extradition demand submitted to the Polish diet was unjustified, probably motivated by a vengeful pope bent on harassing him now because of supposed antipapal and even anti-Christian machinations with the Turks. The reason he gives for traveling to Poland from Turkey is an understandable desire, once so far from his native Italy, to see as many countries as possible on the way home, and especially Poland because "regni huius nomen inter alia non est postremum" (the name of this kingdom is not the least among others [30]).

Buonaccorsi is equally at pains to allay suspicion concerning his activities in Turkey. He was, he assures Dersław of Rytwiany, only too happy to leave Turkey, since "me taedabat maxime et pigebat morum et vitae illorum hominum, quibuscum habere consuetudinem oportebat" (I was greatly annoyed and offended by the customs and way of life of those people whose company was forced upon me by circumstances [30]). Since his persecutors made it impossible for him to find refuge anywhere in the Christian world, he had no choice but to go to Turkey; but as soon as he learned he could return to Italy, he went "to those who are faithful to Christ" (42), meaning, of course, Poland. The very idea, he adds, that a poor, unknown, hunted foreigner, of no resources or important contacts and of a different faith, could possibly conspire with a figure as potent as the sultan of Turkey is as ridiculous as the charge that he had conspired against the pope.

Flattery and an appeal to Polish nationalism were the principal weapons in Buonaccorsi's strategy to convince Dersław to reverse the diet's decision. Since other kings (those of Sicily and Cyprus) had refused to hand him over to his papal pursuers, the Italian asked, how could the king of Poland, who was better known for his compassion and kindness, not do likewise? Indeed, not only had the kings of Sicily and Cyprus protected him, but as he informs Dersław at one particularly hyperbolic point in his petition, "me, quem civitates praestantissimae, principes egregii, reges incliti et denique Deus ipse per tot manifestissima terrae marisque discrimina servavit" (the most illustrious states, distinguished rulers, famous kings, and finally God himself saved me through so many most obvious dangers of land and sea [40]). Furthermore, the reason other kings would not extradite him should be equally valid for the Poles: the desire not to surrender any of their sovereignty to the Vatican. In the spirit of this line of reasoning, Buonaccorsi is not above admonishing Dersław of Rytwiany: "Keep your kingdom the most invincible in war, the most outstanding in the virtue and magnificence of its people, the most sacred in its principles, the most exceptional in its privileges, and free and submissive to no one! You must give great thought to the necessity to leave it to your descendants just as you received it from your forebears, and with all diligence and zeal strive to close even the smallest crack of servitude" (38).

The previous decision of the Polish diet to extradite him obviously pained Buonaccorsi, and he fulminates against it on several occasions in his petition. But well aware of tensions between Poland and the Vatican, particularly over aspects of Polish foreign policy, he sought to place all responsibility for the diet's decision on papal intrigue aimed at using him as the pretext for encroaching on Polish sovereignty. To this end he directed several appeals to Polish national pride and the Poles' need not to compromise their sovereignty to accommodate the pope: "Great things proceed from small beginnings," he says at one point, arguing that honoring the papal demand would establish a dangerous precedent for the future well-being of Polish independence. One concession will lead to another, and heretofore inviolate laws and privileges of the kingdom of Poland will inevitably become subject to even greater provocations. After all, he asks, why does the pope continue to trouble himself over an insignificant exile who has not been proved guilty of any crime and who has been given permission to return to Italy? His answer contains the kernel of his strategy and abandons an earlier pretense of respect and esteem for the papacy: "He [the pope] persists in my affair and exerts himself in order that you may learn to be obedient and gradually become prepared for servitude. Who among mortals that has ever come to know the pope's ambition and desire to rule over all can have any doubt that he would willingly take even an innocent man handed over to him by you not for the sake of him, whoever he may be, but so that other kings might be compelled by your example to submit to [the pope] in foul and ignominious servitude not only in religious matters but in any other? Truly do you bare yourselves too much and expose a defenseless body to blows! Perhaps you do not know with whom you are dealing. It is easier for you to win by resisting than by submitting" (38).

By the time he reaches the end of his "memorial," Buonaccorsi has done a convincing job of equating his extradition with no less than a betrayal of Polish national interests and the integrity of Christendom. What is at stake, he asserts in all modesty, is not his own safety but "the majesty of the entire state, the preservation of royal dignity and greatness" (44). And of equal if not greater importance, a treaty and alliance not only with Italy but with the entire Christian community hangs in the balance, for if indeed the members of the conspiracy of 1468 had designs on the papacy then Buonaccorsi's extradition could bring the secret plans of the conspirators to light; the whole of Christendom might then experience greater dissension than it had ever known.

How moved Dersław of Rytwiany was with the opportunity thus presented him to be the guardian of Polish sovereignty and the savior of Christendom we may never know. But whatever the impact of Buonaccorsi's eloquence and persuasiveness, the influential palatine of Sandomierz was inclined to favor the Italian's cause out of esteem for Gregory of Sanok and because of his friendly relations with Arnolfo Tedaldi, whom he had met through their common interest in the salt trade.[18] Fate intervened, however, before much could be done, and the entire affair was at long last put to rest. Pope Paul II died on March 13, 1471, and was succeeded on August 9 by Sixtus IV, who seemed if anything well disposed toward Buonaccorsi and sufficiently unafraid of humanism to permit the reconstitution of Pomponio Leto's Accademia Romana.

Now that the way was definitely clear for him to return to his native land, Buonaccorsi chose to remain in Poland. The decision could not have been an easy one. But after everything he had experienced—and perhaps still suspicious about Vatican intentions toward him—he may have felt it was prudent to stay where he was, at least for the time being, and begin to make a new life. The advantages were obvious. His case had made him an object of some curiosity, even notoriety, in Poland, and once the stigma of being a fugitive was lifted he no doubt found many doors open to him. He was, after all, a well-educated, intellectually sophisticated Italian who had seen something of the world and whose life held no small adventure. Moreover, he was by this time well connected in Poland. His distant relative Tedaldi had already proved his ability to help, and the patronage and support of such outstanding men as Gregory, archbishop of Lwów, and Dersław of Rytwiany were not to be taken lightly.

Romance may also have played a role in Buonaccorsi's decision to remain in Poland. Unfortunately, little is known about the object of his affection, but that the relationship mattered to him seems highly likely. Her name usually appears as Fannia Swentocha, and she could have been either Franciszka Świętoszanka or Anna Ligęzina. But who she was, whether she was of noble or humble origins, and where and how she and Buonaccorsi met remain mysteries. Buonaccorsi portrays her in his poetry as a tavern maid, which may have been only a literary affectation or a method of concealment, but later attempts to relate her to Leszek Bobrzycki, a famous knight and companion of King Ladislaus III at the disastrous campaign of Varna in 1444 are unconvincing. The Italian was smitten enough to prompt Gregory of Sanok to invite her to Dunajów for a while, for which Buonaccorsi thanked his patron in several panegyric verses. Since Gregory himself was reputed to have enjoyed the company of women at his court, there was nothing really unusual in this. Buonaccorsi's poems of gratitude, with others he wrote during this early period in Poland and dedicated mostly to Fannia, were eventually collected under the title *Fannietum* and offered in 1472 to his benefactor Arnolfo Tedaldi as a token of his indebtedness.

Although Buonaccorsi's "Dunajów poems" are cast in the familiar classical mode, they are more than conventional exercises in humanist poetics. Apart from being the first poetry written in Poland on erotic themes, they are also interesting for loosening the constraints of Neo-Latin poetry and painting a more true-to-life picture of the range and complexity of human emotions and experiences. Needless to say, here too Buonaccorsi introduced something new into Polish literature.

We can appreciate how personal and human a poet Buonaccorsi could be when we consider two of his most important poems to Fannia. The first, mainly describing his flight from Rome, is a lengthy elegy beginning "Scire meos casus, populos gentesque requiris / Et loca, quae vidi fatis agitatus iniquis" (You want to know of my experiences and the nations and peoples I saw as I was pursued by inimical fates).[19] The second, also titled "To Fannia" (Ad Fanniam) or "To Fannia Swentocha" (Ad Fanniam Swentocham) and opening with the line "Quid mihi si pacti potuisti federis horam" (Why, if you were unable to come at the agreed-upon hour)[20] addresses the torments of love and may have been written not long before Buonaccorsi left Dunajów early in 1472 to pursue his fortune in royal Cracow.

The first of these "Fannia poems" is clearly the more interesting. Although it is addressed to Fannia Swentocha, research on the manuscripts[21] and the structure of the poem itself make it clear that Buonaccorsi wrote it before ever meeting Fannia and probably even before he took up residence in Poland. That it was intended originally as a verse account of his flight from Italy and subsequent adventures for one of his Italian friends seems likely. Once he was under the wing of Gregory of Sanok at Dunajów and already in a romantic relationship with Fannia, Buonaccorsi simply reworked the poem to accommodate a new addressee and his new situation. He had done this with other poems, and in this case few changes were necessary. What makes this reconstruction of the genesis of the poem all the more convincing is that apart from Fannia's name and a few general remarks, little information about her is provided; furthermore, with the exception of a reference to his "corpse resting beneath a Sarmatian rock" (funusque quiescat / Sarmatica sub rupe meum),[22] no further details about his stay in Poland are given.

After "reluctantly" agreeing to recall the adventures that befell him after fleeing Rome, Buonaccorsi proceeds to describe his journey from the "Lavinian shores" in an old, small boat. His account is couched in terms of classical mythology, some of it inspired, for obvious reasons, by the *Odyssey*. Circe, Heracles and the Nemean lion, the Hydra, the Styx, Dis (the male god of the underworld in Roman religion), the Fates, and a number of other allusions are worked in not only as part of the conventional literary baggage of the humanist poet but undoubtedly so Buonaccorsi could liken his journey and travail to classical models. The following typical excerpt demonstrates how the poet intertwines the narrative of his own travels with mythological imagery, collapsing the temporal distance between his own time and classical antiquity, as was common among the humanists:

> Directly before me lay the grave of Myrtilus [the treacherous charioteer of Oenomaus, in Greek mythology the king of Pisa and father of Hippodamia] and the steep cliffs and barren slopes of Caria and the gentle coast

of the island of Kos [an island in the Aegean Sea where Hera sent a storm to shipwreck Heracles] and the celebrated murmuring of the water that flows all around and moistens the temple of Juno of Samos. Rhodes was on the right, behind me; on the left was Megista; before the bow of the ship stood the queen of the Cyclades, Ortygia [Delos], who was swimming before the birth of Phoebus and his snow-white sister Diana [Apollo and Artemis, in Greek mythology, both born on Delos]. Now she is rooted in deep shoals and from the distance displays the ruins of venerated shrines that once upon a time inspired undoubted faith in uncertain matters through accounts of the future. Slowly Naxos appeared on the left and craggy Marpesia, the rival of snowy Othrys, when I began from afar to behold the vine-covered hills of Phanae and barely gave voice to my sadness in these words: "O island, sought by so many wayfarers across the sea, if you once joined your shores with the boat of Thoas [king of Lemnos], who was fleeing the wrath of the Lemnians, and you gave the fugitive a hiding place and a home, and if aroused by the tenderness of Ariadne's wailing you judged her complaints just and repaid the deceitful agreements of Theseus with a much better husband [Theseus, king of Athens, abandoned his wife, Ariadne, on the island of Naxos, where Bacchus found her and married her], take me in and give me refuge in my flight and the peace of a deserving man.[23]

That the poem to Fannia Swentocha about his flight from Italy is more than a mythologized poetic travelogue is made evident in those passages where the poet voices his sorrow over his forced separation from homeland, family, and friends. A passage such as the following conveys unmistakable pain and would wrongly be viewed as self-dramatization:

And I grieved that the storms of land and sea, which I had endured before as I was chased about different corners of the globe, could not put an end to my calamities . . . and I was often overcome by such loathing for life that I can swear on the ashes of my mother that have already been buried and on the health of my still living father and brothers that on more than one occasion I wanted to kill myself and placed a ready hand on the hilt of my sword so that I could plunge it into my chest and so be parted from this disgusting world.[24]

The poem ends shortly thereafter with the poet expressing his gratitude to the gods for taking pity on his wretched fate and letting him find a haven in Poland, where Fannia, now his greatest comfort, more than compensates for the loss of his homeland and family.

Since the path of love, of course, is never smooth, Buonaccorsi experienced moments of unhappiness with his beloved that he writes about in his second, much shorter, poem to Fannia Swentocha.[25] The poet is unhappy over Fannia's failure to keep a tryst with him. Comparing such a broken promise to soiling one's hands with someone's blood, Buonaccorsi recalls the stories of Pyramus and Thisbe and of Demophon and Phyllis to lend greater weight to his indictment. After describing the joy he felt anticipating the arrival of his beloved, he then records the despair that overtook him when she failed to appear. The only difference between him and a corpse, he laments, is that he is still capable of feeling pain. But from his experiences, hope has taught him to bear adversity with patience. After all, he consoles himself, if every lover were to die from broken promises, there would not be one left; besides, love has its good and bad sides, and he has to accept that reality and live accordingly. And so he tells Fannia that he is not ashamed to lie again at her feet; but he warns that she must not deceive him a second time. If she does, the gods will surely punish her frightfully. In closing, however, he is so overcome by love for her that he renounces his own threat, saying he would rather let her deceive him constantly than see the awful anger of the gods descend on her because of him.

Callimachus in Polish Politics

To do justice to the political activity of Callimachus (as I shall refer to him primarily from now on) would require a separate book. Here an overview concentrating on highlights will have to suffice. Callimachus's political views lend themselves to fairly easy categorization; they tend to group around particular concerns and to reflect a consistent and largely cohesive program of Polish foreign policy.

One major track of this policy, which was to bring the Italian expatriate into even greater conflict with the Vatican, had to do with the continuing danger posed by the Ottoman Empire. As Callimachus's political vision and sense of what was best for his adopted country took shape, he found himself increasingly at odds with Vatican policy. Part of the explanation undoubtedly is found in his antipathy toward the Holy See, dating back to his Roman period. It is hard to imagine that Callimachus's dislike and distrust of the papacy did not remain with him throughout his life, as reflected in his decision to make Poland his home long after a papal amnesty had cleared the way for his return to Italy. But personal feelings aside, he had a more reasoned and moderate political outlook that simply did not—and could not—share the Vatican's obsession with the "Turkish menace" and the great papal preoccupation with ever more grandiose "holy crusades" against the infidel.

Callimachus's friendship with Gregory of Sanok and his good relations with Zbigniew Oleśnicki, nephew of the cardinal of the same name, who in 1472 became vice-chancellor of Poland, proved of inestimable value to his future career. In 1472, the same year (not coincidentally) Oleśnicki acceded to the vice-chancellorship, Callimachus was appointed secretary to the king. Not much later, in spring 1473, he entered international politics. The chronology is important here, since it sheds light on the consistency of Callimachus's views and his inevitable collision with the Vatican.

As early as 1474, in the first of his political treatises, *Consilium non ineundae societatis cum Italis in bello contra Turcos suscipiendo* (Plan for Not Entering into an Alliance with the Italians in a War against the Turks Then Being Undertaken), he argues cogently against Polish participation in a crusade being urged on the Poles both by the Vatican itself and by representatives of the Venetian republic, insistent advocates of papal policy. During 1474, in fact, the Venetians attempted more than once to convince the Poles to agree to the pope's plan to use Persian and Tatar troops against the Turks, requiring—primarily for the Tatars— passage across Polish territory. That the Poles were not enthusiastic about opening their lands to the armed forces of a people with whom conflict had been frequent and sharp hardly comes as a surprise. Despite the entreaties of the Venetian envoy Ambrogio Contarini, who may have believed that a countryman would certainly be sympathetic to his views, Callimachus saw no merit in the Vatican-Venetian policy and opposed it decisively. His contempt is shown by his return to the subject between 1487 and 1492 when he worked on his treatise *De his quae a Venetis tentata sunt Persis ac Tartaris contra Turcos movendis* (On the Deployment of Persians and Tatars against the Turks Proposed by the Venetians).[26]

Viewing the Turkish threat more rationally than did the Holy See, Callimachus sensed a decline in Ottoman power and, at the same time, saw too much dissension among the Christian states of Europe to permit any truly effective league or crusade against the Turks. Aware, certainly, of the need to restrain Ottoman power, Callimachus placed greater faith in a coalition of Poland, Venice, the Vatican, Hungary, and the Holy Roman Empire, which would be strong enough to deter pressures from the Turkish side, whether military or political.

To gain acceptance of his own plan, Callimachus traveled extensively both to Italy and to Constantinople as a member or as head of Polish diplomatic missions. He participated in the Polish mission to Constantinople in 1476 led by Marcin Wrocimowski, which reached an agreement alleviating Turkish-Moldavian tensions and achieving the liberation of the palatine of Moldavia, Stephen III (the Great), who was at least nominally a vassal of the king of Poland. On January 1, 7, and 10, and again on June 25, 1477, Callimachus presented his case before the Venetian Senate and, we are made to understand, was received with great deference.[27]

Callimachus's diplomatic journey to Italy in 1477 was a long one. After appearing before the Venetian Senate in early January he traveled to Rome, whence he had fled eight years before. Little is known of his five-month stay in the city. The Accademia Romana had been reconstituted, and his old nemesis Platina was now cloaked in pious respectability as superintendent of the Vatican library. It seems highly unlikely, however, that despite the length of his Roman sojourn Callimachus either met with Platina or sought a papal audience. Although Callimachus's visits caused no perceptible changes of thought in Venice or Rome, his policy of ultimate accommodation with the Ottoman Empire was realized when on January 25, 1479, Venice signed a peace treaty with the Turks.

Interlocked with Callimachus's strategy of resisting Vatican and Venetian pressures to bring Poland into another "holy alliance" against the Turks was his fervent championing of the Polish right of succession to the crown of Bohemia. Vatican interests at the time favored the acquisition of the Bohemian crown by the powerful king of Hungary, Matthias Corvinus. The Holy See sought the complete suppression in Bohemia of the Hussite heresy, which it continued to view with alarm, and it regarded Corvinus as a more reliable ally in the campaign than a member of the more tolerant Jagiellonian royal family of Poland. This Vatican preference for Hungarian over Polish claims distressed the Poles for more than one reason. Corvinus's acquisition of the Bohemian crown was seen as adding strength to an already formidable competitor in east central Europe. Moreover, Vatican—and Venetian—aid to the Hungarians (intended, to be sure, for use against the Turks) more often than not found its way into campaigns against both the Poles and the Hapsburg emperor Frederick III.

Callimachus's political interest in the Bohemian succession again assumed diplomatic as well as literary form. Toward the end of 1476 the enterprising Tuscan embarked on a diplomatic mission to Venice to win Venetian and papal recognition of the Polish Jagiellonian prince Ladislaus as the legitimate heir to the throne of Bohemia. If his appearances before the Venetian Senate in early January 1477 were devoted primarily to the Turkish question, his appearance on June 25 was motivated by his desire to urge the Venetians to find some way of pressuring Corvinus into accepting an accord with the Holy Roman Emperor Frederick III as well as with the kings of Poland and Bohemia.

The matter was also delicate for the Venetians. Their close relationship with the Vatican obliged them to aid the Hungarians, however unobtrusively, but their need for Polish help in the conflict with the Turks obliged them to avoid overt measures that might alienate or offend an important ally.

Behind Callimachus's Bohemian policy lay his desire to neutralize a strong Hungary by placing on the Bohemian throne a future claimant to the crown of Hungary. Vehement Vatican opposition to Jagiellonian possession of both the Bohemian and Hungarian crowns was a major stumbling block, however, and thus Callimachus failed to win Venetian approval for the investiture of Ladislaus as king of Bohemia.

When efforts to win the Venetians over proved unproductive, Callimachus was not averse to reaching his goal by another route. Since an alliance between Turkey and Poland—of great advantage in the campaign against Hungary—seemed to be in the making in March 1478, Callimachus threw his wholehearted support behind it, and on May 14 he directed a "memorial" on the subject to Zbigniew Oleśnicki. The treatise points up the consistency and tenacity of Callimachus's political views. Friendship with the papacy in the forseeable future is dismissed on the grounds that the Vatican's fear of the Hussites creates an adversary relationship with the Poles, whom it regards as "soft" on the reform movement. The Venetians are also dismissed as unreliable in view of their collusion with the Holy See to support Corvinus in Hungary. Maintaining hostile relations with the Turks only further disadvantages the Poles. Their desire to constrain an aggressive and competitive Hungary lacks the support of such influential Western powers as the Vatican and the Venetian republic, who not only fail to support the Poles but provide the Hungarians with ample aid. Continued conflict with the Turks, moreover, weakens the Poles on their strategically important eastern flank and ties up forces that could be used against adversaries elsewhere.

Callimachus had no illusions about the Turks, and indeed hostilities were renewed under the sultanship of Bajazet II in 1483. But as a pragmatist anxious to keep Poland from becoming dangerously outmaneuvered and isolated, Callimachus envisaged as wholly realizable and practical a new configuration of political relationships based not on the traditional enmities of the past, but on present realities of power. The only way Poland could contain Hungarian ambition in east central Europe was to establish Jagiellonian (that is, Polish) hegemony over the thrones of both Bohemia and Hungary, and this was predicated on peace with the Turks. The goal was far from easy to achieve, but the logic was unmistakable.

When hostilities again erupted between Poland and Turkey in 1483, the goal became more elusive. To buttress the Polish position against the Ottomans, Callimachus sought the support of the Holy Roman Emperor, leading a diplomatic mission to Vienna and the court of Frederick III in February 1486. The effort proved futile. The emperor was himself warring with Hungary at the time and was more interested in enlisting Polish help against Corvinus than in joining forces with the Poles against the Turks. Attempting to seize the moment and end the threat from Corvinus's Hungary, Callimachus next rushed to Venice, where he sought to draw the Venetians into a common front against Hungary together with Poland and the Holy Roman Empire. The Venetians gave the proposal a cold shoulder, but lest the respected Callimachus leave Venice with empty hands, they did offer to act as mediators between Poland and Turkey. While Callimachus was pleading his case first in Vienna, then in Venice, another Polish diplomatic mission headed by Jan of Targowisko and Rafał of Leszno visited Rome, where on July 5, 1486, they prevailed upon the Vatican to issue a bull calling for a crusade against the Turks.

The various efforts to defuse the Polish-Turkish situation began to bear fruit in 1487. Both sides were willing to enter into direct negotiations. Callimachus took charge, and ultimately they signed a three-year treaty.

Although 1486 and 1487 found Callimachus enmeshed in efforts to end the Polish-Turkish conflict, he managed to find time to write two major literary works, both dealing with the issues to which so much of his energy had been directed—the campaign by the Vatican to subvert Jagiellonian policy in east-central Europe and Poland's relationship with Hungary in the time of Corvinus. The first work completed was the *Historia de rege Vladislao* (History of King Ladislaus), written in 1487 and recounting the ascension to the throne of Hungary of the Polish king Ladislaus III and his death at Varna in 1444.[28] The second work, *Attila*, was begun a year earlier, but was completed after the *Historia de rege Vladislao* and published the following year, becoming one of the few literary efforts by Callimachus to be published in his lifetime.[29] Before publication the manuscript of *Attila* was sent to his old friend Emiliano Cimbriaco, who delivered it to the printer in Pordenone-Tarvisio accompanied by several poems written by Cimbriaco himself. When the work finally appeared in print it bore a dedication to the Holy Roman Emperor Maximilian I.

An accomplished and prodigious writer, at home in several literary forms, Callimachus best demonstrated his skill with his historical biographies. One of his earliest works in prose, the *Vita et mores Gregorii Sanocei* (The Life and Times of Gregory of Sanok, 1476) remains, as we have seen, the basic source on this important figure in early Polish humanism. It was followed four years later by his biography of Zbigniew Cardinal Oleśnicki (*Vita et mores Sbignei Cardinalis*, 1480),[30] his work on King Ladislaus of Hungary (1487), and then the *Attila* of 1486–88. Certainly the most intriguing of his works for the implications that can be drawn from it (if indeed not read into it), the *Attila* registers unmistakably as an allegory. While ostensibly about Attila the Hun, whom Callimachus portrays in a far more sympathetic light than one would expect for the period, the real subject of the biography is King Matthias Corvinus of Hungary. Although it is possible that Callimachus and the Hungarian king had met on the occasion of the Italian's diplomatic mission to Budapest in 1483,[31] and though it is likely that they corresponded, there is no evidence of any direct meeting. Corvinus, however, apparently fascinated Callimachus, though the fascination repelled as much as it attracted. Insufficient primary source material makes it extremely difficult to construct a psychological profile of Filippo Buonaccorsi-Callimachus. Yet certain facets of his personality do emerge from his career and writings: great intelligence, considerable acuity of mind, pragmatism, shrewdness, boldness, an evident relish for the game of politics, and a taste for power. Corvinus was an extraordinarily capable and impressive ruler as well as an adept political strategist, and Callimachus could not help admiring him, however grudgingly. In his biography of Callimachus, the Italian scholar Gioacchino Paparelli speculates,[32] and I believe correctly, that given the way his subject's mind worked, his admiration for Corvinus may have drawn sustenance from an image of the great deeds he himself might accomplish with just such a master. To Callimachus, Corvinus seemed the embodiment of the ideal prince (and this before the *Principe* of his countryman Machiavelli). But his admiration was tempered by the reality of his own position as a *Polish* statesman, a counselor to the kings of Poland, for whom Matthias Corvinus was a dangerous opponent as well as a rival. Callimachus could esteem Corvinus only as the most talented of Poland's enemies, a man worthy of respect but an adversary to be feared and to be dealt with as skillfully as his talents demanded. Perhaps, displaying a hubris not alien to

Callimachus, Corvinus appeared as the one political figure in contemporary Europe best able to challenge the Italian's own talent as strategist and tactician.

The treaty with the Turks, besides providing a welcome respite from conflict, represented at least a partial success for Callimachus's political program. But it was achieved at the cost of a certain erosion of his position in Poland. Already resented by a faction at court because he was a foreigner who wielded considerable authority, Callimachus added to those resenting him by his efforts to reach peace with the Turks. Not that peace was not a common goal, but the Italian's emphasis on the need for an understanding with the sultan even through a policy at odds with the Vatican disconcerted many for whom the Turks were the feared and hated enemy who was to be given no quarter. To those unable or unwilling to view Polish-Turkish relations from any perspective other than the traditional, Callimachus was suspect for his willingness to take risks for the sake of a different concept of Poland's security. When he returned from a diplomatic mission to Constantinople and presented a Turkish delegation to the Polish diet at Piotrków in May 1488, it seemed to his detractors and those now willing to join their ranks that matters had indeed gotten out of hand.

Stung by the aura of scandal hovering about him and annoyed at the carping and behind-the-scenes backstabbing, Callimachus began giving some thought to returning to Italy. Two letters to Lattanzio Tedaldi, one dated simply July 1488, the other September 1, 1488, leave no doubt as to his state of mind. But whatever disappointment, lack of appreciation, and insecurity he may have felt in 1488 eventually evaporated, and with them any serious idea of resettling in Italy. When Callimachus did return to his native land in 1490 it was not as a prodigal son but as personal envoy of King Casimir IV of Poland. He was to represent the Polish side in deliberations then taking place in Rome on the one topic still capable of bringing all the Christian powers together—the formation of an anti-Turkish league and the launching of a "holy crusade" against the infidel. The conference had been convoked by Pope Innocent VIII on March 25, 1490, and it lasted until June 3, when it was officially adjourned.

Callimachus's ideas about the impracticality of such "leagues" and "crusades" remained unchanged through the years, as is made abundantly clear in his treatise *De bello Turcis inferendo* (On Waging War against the Turks), which he probably delivered at the conference and possibly in the presence of the pope himself.[33] If indeed he did deliver the oration during the conference—whether before the pope or not— it was as unlikely to have swayed minds as the conference itself was to achieve anything other than the repetition of pious platitudes and the usual saber rattling. The Poles, however, did not leave empty-handed. One reason for their coming to the conference was to campaign for a cardinal's cap for King Casimir's son Fryderyk (Frederick) who for two years had been serving as bishop of Cracow.

By the time the Polish delegation returned to Cracow with the expectation (ultimately unfulfilled) of a red cap for Frederick,[34] a dynastic crisis had erupted at home in which Callimachus was bound to become embroiled. The crisis was triggered by the death of Matthias Corvinus on April 6, 1490. A struggle for succession to the crown of Hungary ensued almost immediately, the principal claimants being two sons of King Casimir of Poland—Ladislaus, crowned king of Bohemia in 1471 (which Callimachus had helped achieve and had celebrated in verse) and Jan Olbracht (John Albert). When the latter decided to resolve the issue as quickly as possible by leading an army into Hungary, he was accompanied by Callimachus. It was a serious miscalculation. Ladislaus defeated his brother and took him prisoner, while Callimachus, to avoid a like fate and the humiliation that went with it, was forced to flee.

The death of Callimachus's great friend and protector King Casimir caused a further deterioration in the Italian's situation. An interregnum lasted from June 7 until August, when Casimir's son Aleksander (Alexander) announced that according to his late father's wishes John Albert should succeed to the throne of the kingdom of Poland while he himself would become grand duke of Lithuania. It was during this period that the death of the king removed the one major barrier to open expressions of resentment and hostility toward Callimachus, especially among the nobility. So untenable did his position become that, appreciating the difficulty of his remaining in Poland until the succession had been resolved, he repaired to Vienna to wait for a change of climate at home. He did not have to wait long. John Albert's release from prison and his elevation to the throne on September 23, 1492, ended the interregnum and paved the way for his return. Peace, at least for a while, had been restored to Polish domestic politics: John Albert succeeded his father, Casimir IV, as king of Poland; Ladislaus was now king of both Bohemia and Hungary; and their brother Alexander became grand duke of Lithuania.

Even after John Albert's succession to the throne, Callimachus did not rush to reassert his position at court but lingered a few months longer in Vienna. However, the election of John Albert as king could be seen as a vindication, perhaps even a victory, for the politics of Callimachus and those who sided with him in advocating a strong monarchy in Poland at the expense of some of the privileges of the country's numerically large and politically powerful nobility. With admirable timing, Callimachus left Vienna for Cracow and resumed a position of authority and influence at the royal court that he was to enjoy for the last four years of his life (1492–96). How complete Callimachus's return to power was can be judged from a report on the relations between the new king of Poland, John Albert, and Callimachus presented to the Venetian Senate in May 1495 by the official emissary of the Polish king, Jan Pot. Pot had come to Venice at the beginning of the year on the specific orders of Callimachus. Doubtless having heard of Callimachus's flight to Vienna during the Polish interregnum and wondering if his countryman had succeeded in reestablishing himself at the court of the new monarch, Augustino Barbarigo (or Barbadico, reigned 1486–1501), the doge of Venice, presumably inquired of Pot as to Callimachus's present position in Poland and his relations with John Albert. To set the doge's mind at ease that in Poland Callimachus's authority was as before, Pot drew up the report that he presented to the Venetian Senate. The document makes the important point that not only was Callimachus's position at the Polish court virtually unassailable, but the king himself was obedient to him.[35]

Perhaps it was this "obedience" that John Albert's brother Frederick, now cardinal and archbishop of Gniezno, had in mind when, angered by Callimachus's defense of the Jews over some dispute with the Cracow city authorities, he wrote a letter to his brother on September 26, 1495, lamenting that the impertinence of a "foreigner mattered more than the authority and faith of the first citizens of the capital" (plus valere debeat apud Maiestatem Vestram unius hominis peregrini pertinacia et instancia . . . quam istorum virorum auctoritas et fides).[36]

Complaints like this, even from the king's own brother, were insufficient to topple Callimachus once he had returned to power. And to hold that power as well as to maintain the security of the state and avoid a repetition of what happened following the death of Casimir IV, Callimachus worked assiduously to keep peace between the royal brothers John Albert and Ladislaus. This became a matter of real urgency to him when in 1490 the Holy Roman Emperor Maximilian I entered into an alliance with Muscovy against Poland, partially as a way of furthering his own claims to the Hungarian throne. To strengthen the fraternal bonds while drawing Poland, Bohemia, and Hungary into an even closer and more secure relationship, Callimachus helped promote the Treaty of Buda (December 5, 1492), which sanctioned the principle of reciprocal collaboration. A congress convoked in the spring of 1494 ratified and extended the Buda accords, thereby enabling the Jagiellonians to project an image of power—or so the Buda treaty and later accords were interpreted by Antonio Bonfini, a Hungarian humanist of Italian origin, in his *Rerum Ungaricum decades quator cum dimidia* (Four and a Half Decades of Hungarian History).

The accords drawn up on May 5, 1494, may also have contained provisions, not made public, resulting in an armistice between the Polish sovereigns and the Turkish sultan Bajazet II—achieved in June 1495—thus restoring calm to that troubled quarter, and the marriage of the king's brother Alexander, grand duke of Lithuania, to the daughter of Ivan III of Muscovy. The latter event was of particular significance in view of the increasing attacks on the grand duchy of Lithuania by Muscovy, culminating in Alexander's capitulation to Ivan III on February 5, 1494, and the subsequent loss of territory. The conflict between Lithuania and Muscovy was resolved a year later, however, when Alexander married Ivan's daughter Yelena on February 18, 1495. When Alexander succeeded John Albert as king of Poland in 1501 the personal union between Poland and the grand duchy of Lithuania, which was broken when Alexander became grand duke, triggering the conflict with Muscovy, was restored.

A problem of sorts still remained with the last Jagiellonian brother, Sigismund, whom part of the nobility in Lithuania had favored for grand duke instead of Alexander. Sigismund's sympathy toward the nobility ensured the support of many of them. Cognizant of this threat to the stability of the Polish-Lithuanian union, Callimachus made every effort to keep Sigismund as far from Cracow as he could, even suggesting that Sigismund become head of the armed forces of the Venetian republic not only to provide military guidance in the face of a threatened invasion of Italy by Charles VIII of France (who had designs on Naples), but also symbolically to sanction the union of Venetian and Jagiellonian forces. This novel idea was amplified in a letter from Callimachus to the doge of Venice on April 7, 1495.[37]

The scheme to get Sigismund out of harm's way by transferring him to Venice came to naught, however. When the Holy Roman Emperor Maximilian I learned of the French plans for Naples and their reluctance to furnish troops for a fresh campaign against the Turks, he invited Venice to join the anti-Turkish "league." This not only provided the Venetians with a stronger shield against French ambition than Sigismund the Jagiellonian's military prowess alone could offer, but it obviated the Venetians' need to defend themselves against the very states Callimachus was trying so hard to convince them they should fear.

After the plan to pack the troublesome Sigismund off to Venice failed, Callimachus's last political involvement might surely have caused him to end his days in ignominy had not death mercifully intervened. Toward the end of 1495 and in early 1496, Callimachus served as King John Albert's ambassador to his brother Alexander, grand duke of Lithuania, while Alexander dispatched his own envoy to Cracow. At some point during this period apparently an agreement was worked out to wage a joint military campaign against the Tatars and so liberate the Black Sea ports of Kilia and Białogród, which Sultan Bajazet II had occupied in 1484 and which were now in the hands of that restless and uncertain vassal Stephen III of Moldavia.

The expedition to liberate Kilia and Białogród was duly launched in 1497, but it soon turned into a disaster. After an unsuccessful attack on the fortress of Suceava, the Polish cavalry was surprised by Stephen near Cernauti (today Chernovtsy in the USSR) and decimated. Whatever the reasons for the debacle—the poor preparation for the campaign, for which the nobility's indifference toward the undertaking was in part to blame, the hostility of Turkey (and Hungary as well), Callimachus's personal obsession with the liberation of the two Black Sea towns—King John Albert's punishment of those deemed responsible was swift and stern. Although many were only too eager to place responsibility for the disastrous outcome squarely on Callimachus, the fact remains that, whatever his counsel, it was John Albert himself who decided the details of the campaign. The king's loyalty to Callimachus remained steadfast throughout, and no matter what accusing fingers were pointed his way the Italian felt none of his wrath in the grim aftermath of the episode. And then, before any reversal of fortune could occur, Filippo Buonaccorsi died of a hemorrhage on November 1, 1496.

The great funeral procession through the streets of Cracow was as elaborate as one would expect for a dignitary of Callimachus's stature. How elaborate, we know from a detailed description by Callimachus's friend Ottaviano de Guccio de' Calvani, a relative and collaborator of Arnolfo Tedaldi. The account appears in a letter from Calvani to Lattanzio Tedaldi noting that all classes of contemporary Cracovian society were officially represented in the cortege.[38]

After the procession the body of Callimachus was interred in the Church of the Holy Trinity in Cracow, which was maintained by the Dominicans, near that of Arnolfo Tedaldi, who had passed away the year before. A mausoleum was eventually erected over the tomb, and two epitaphs were incised on it. One, in prose, was cut beneath a bas-relief in bronze executed either by the great sculptor Wit Stwosz (Veit

Stoss), who had come originally from Nuremberg and settled in Cracow, where he did some of his best work, or by his son Ladislaus. The relief depicts Callimachus seated at a lectern in his library, affixing his seal to some document. (A reproduction of the bronze bas-relief was donated in 1937 by the city of Cracow to the town of San Gimignano. The reproduction derives, however, from a copper etching made in the eighteenth century from a design not entirely faithful to the original.) The prose epitaph beneath the relief reads:

Philippus Callimachus Experiens Natione Thuscus Vir Doctissimus / Utriusque Fortune Exemplum / Imitandum Atque Omnis Virtutis Cultor / Precipuus Divi Olim Casimiri et Johannis Alberti Polonie Regum / Secretarius Acceptissimus Relictis Ingenii ac Rerum A Se / Gestarum Pluribus Monumentis, Cum Summo Omnium Bo / norum Merore et Regie Domus Atque Huius Reipublice / Incommodo Anno Salutatis Nostre MCCCCLXXXXVI CAL/ENDIS Novembris Vita Decedens Hic Sepultus Est.

(Philippus Callimachus Experiens, Tuscan by Origin, Most Learned Man, / Example of the Ways of Fortune, / Distinguished Venerator of Virtue, / Beloved Secretary in Days Past of the Divine Casimir and John Albert, Kings of Poland, / By the Fruits of His Genius and the Many Monuments of His Deeds / Raised by Merit and Royal Act to the Summit of All Benefices of This Land and Republic, / Taking Leave of Life in the Infelicitous Year of Our Savior 1496, the First of November, / Here Lies Buried.)

The second inscription, in verse, appears on a painted slab that shows Callimachus on his knees before the Madonna with Child. This second epitaph was almost certainly the work of Bernardino Gallo of Zara, secretary of Cardinal Frederick (King John Albert's brother). The Latin verse reads:

Hic iacet heu patria procula regione sepultus
progenitus Thusco sanguine Callimachus.
Quem fatum variis adversum erroribus egit
invictum his tandem constituitque locis.
Illius, ut postquam virtutem regia sensit,
vidit florentem Sarmatis ora virum.
Qui memor hospicii tam mitis, contulit isti
Consiliis regno commoda multa suis,
quod sentit praesens et postera sentiet aetas,
cuius iudicium sanctius esse solet.
Plura quoque aggressum ut quaedam maiora parantem
haud opportuno tempore mors rapuit.

(Alas, here lies buried, in a place far from his native land, Callimachus, born of Tuscan blood, whom adverse fate drove into various wanderings until, unconquered, he settled in these places. Once the Crown discerned his excellence, the land of the Sarmatian came to behold a man in full flower. Grateful for the hospitality shown him and kind by nature, he brought to this kingdom many advantages by means of his *Counsels* of which the present age is aware and the future age, whose judgment will be yet more reverent, will also become aware. More and still greater undertakings were being planned by him when death seized him at an inopportune time.)

Callimachus's Counsels

The *Consilia* (Counsels) referred to in the verse inscription on Callimachus's tomb remains his best-known if most problematic literary legacy. Although artistically and intellectually less significant than several of his other writings, it merits discussion before them because of its fame—or perhaps notoriety. There is no firm date for the composition of the *Consilia*; circumstantial evidence suggests as most likely October 1492, when Callimachus happened to be in Venice, although no special importance attaches to the particular Italian setting in which the work presumably was conceived. That the *Consilia* derives, however, from an Italian Renaissance political philosophy and tradition cannot be doubted.

The perhaps disproportionate interest in the *Consilia* has several sources. To begin with, it lends itself to consideration as a summation of Callimachus's political philosophy, committed to paper just a few years before his death and therefore all the more likely to have been taken as a legacy. In view of the immensely important role Callimachus played in the formation of Polish foreign policy during the reign of King Casimir IV and in the early years of King John Albert, the *Consilia* would naturally come to occupy a central place in the development of Polish Renaissance political theory and practice. The second consideration is that the work is informed with the spirit of Machiavellianism *before* Machiavelli wrote *The Prince*, so the matter of influence understandably has arisen. And third, questions have been raised for some time concerning the authenticity of the *Consilia*, which is easy to understand in light of the loss of the original text and the ultimate publication only of a reconstruction.

A fair amount of scholarship in Poland (Garbacik, Ptaśnik, Estreicher) and in Italy (Agosti, Solimena)[39] in the present century has laid to rest any serious doubts concerning the authenticity of the *Consilia*. At the same time, there is no doubt that the bilingual Latin-

Polish edition of the work published by Romuald Wszetecki in Cracow in 1887 (*Rady Kallimachowe* in Polish)—the first unbowdlerized edition of the *Consilia* ever to be published—incorporates interpolations and textual changes by other hands through the centuries. There is a consensus now that articles 34 and 35 of the *Consilia,* for example—those dealing with the ill-fated campaign against Stephen III of Moldavia—were later additions intended to place full responsibility for the defeat at Suceava on Callimachus and thus discredit him in the eyes of future generations. How truly problematic the entire matter of the *Consilia* becomes is indicated by another transcription of the text in which the same incriminating article 34 makes no mention of the campaign against Stephen III and has an entirely different ring, and by the existence of a notorious seventeenth-century falsification bearing the Polish title *Kalimachowe maksymy infames* (The Infamous Maxims of Callimachus).

The attempt to use the loss of the original text of the *Consilia* to blacken Callimachus's reputation in Poland through "reconstructions" incorporating slanted interpolations and outright falsifications such as the one perpetrated in the seventeenth century is easy to understand given the widespread resentment against him among the Polish nobility during his lifetime.[40] Any foreigner occupying such an important and prestigious political position as Callimachus enjoyed during the reign of Casimir IV was bound to be disliked, envied, and held suspect by the nobility, who developed a prodigious appetite for politics in the late fifteenth and the sixteenth centuries and eventually were to dominate Polish political life down to the loss of independence in 1795. But what made Callimachus particularly odious was his advocacy of a strong centralized power (that is, the monarchy), which could be achieved only by curbing the drive for power of the constituent elements of the noble class, the gentry (*szlachta*) on the one hand, and the uppermost stratum of the nobility, the magnates, on the other. A developing political consciousness among the Polish nobility already was setting the stage for the inevitable showdown with the monarchy as to where true political authority in Poland was to reside. As later developments bear out, the nobles' greed for power could be satisfied only with absolute conquest, and by the end of the sixteenth century the kingship had become reduced to an elective office with the monarch chosen by the nobility. Moreover, another rival power base— the bishops of the Roman Catholic church (who traditionally wielded considerable political clout in the Polish Senate)—was weakened by defections to Protestantism among the nobility so extensive that in the second half of the sixteenth century the unthinkable possibility of Poland's becoming a Protestant country became conceivable.

When the *Consilia* became known the nobility's worst fears concerning Callimachus appeared confirmed, for here in the form of a political testament intended as a guide for present and future Polish monarchs was an outright defense of a strong crown and a rationale for imposing restraints on the power of the gentry and the magnates.

The *Consilia* holds few surprises to anyone familiar with Callimachus's thought. The old antipathy toward the Vatican expresses itself in an advocacy of strict church/state separation colored by unmistakable antipapism. In article 22, for example, Callimachus urges the monarch to be master of his own kingdom and not allow the pope to assume that role: "Sis Dominus in Regno tuo. Ne Papae quidem id concedito." The same article urges that bishops be appointed from among learned men rather than from the old and illustrious families, whose greed for power threatens the state. Article 24 cautions against allowing appeals to Rome lest they impoverish the monarchy, and in article 8 the king is advised to play off the lay senator against the ecclesiastic, the better to control both.

With respect to internal politics, the *Consilia* urges the king to trust only in one or two advisers, a select inner court. Senators are not to be trusted, nor are they to share any confidences with their wives, since "even the most secret things generally fly away from drinkers and women." New statutes, especially those capable of diminishing royal authority, should be prohibited (article 3), while in general provincial diets should not be allowed to convene, since they become breeding grounds for conspiracy (article 4). Threats emanating from the Senate should be disregarded, for as Callimachus notes, the Poles "talk a lot and finally do nothing" (Nam Polonorum est: multa loqui, nihil exsequi; article 7). Similarly confident of his understanding of the Polish mentality in article 6, the Italian urges the king himself to keep the nobility off guard by the annual threat of a levy en masse (that is, general mobilization). As he observes: "The Polish nobility gives the appearance of demanding the levy en masse but actually fears it greatly." Meanwhile, half the money raised in taxes for the levy should be put in the king's treasury, while the other half should be used to hire mercenaries. The employment of mercenaries looms large in Callimachus's thinking, as it did for later Polish political reformers, because of the twofold advantage mercenaries offer the Polish Crown: a regular standing army that would ensure swifter response to threats to national security, and less reliance on the nobility, whose contributions in men and material represented real leverage against the Crown for concessions.

Curbing the power of the magnates is as important a goal of the

Consilia as restraining the gentry. In advising the king to cultivate the illustrious families of Poland, Callimachus advocates granting them palatinates and castellanates because such administrative offices will contribute to their impoverishment (article 9). Power and money are closely intertwined in Callimachus's political philosophy. No office, for example, is to be given away, and the greater offices are to go to the highest bidders. Moreover, Callimachus advises in article 12, funds received from the sale of offices should be held on to carefully. To further strengthen the king's hand financially, the *Consilia* suggests paying no annual stipend to anyone; reducing the number of pages and stewards at court; being attentive to the merchants of the big cities and allowing them access to the king, thus buttressing the Crown's financial position and securing important allies against the nobility, whose policies were inimical to the merchant class and the cities; and granting abbacies only to worthy men, but then levying a tax on each abbacy.

Aware of the inequities in the Polish social system, Callimachus used the *Consilia* to ameliorate the situation, again with an eye toward increasing the power and dignity of the Crown by diminishing sources of internal weakness. In article 25, for example, he urges abolishing the penal immunity enjoyed by members of the nobility guilty of killing commoners, since this is viewed with contempt by foreigners ("Statutum de homicidiis plebejorum, cum derisui sit exteris, abrogato"). Article 26 similarly advocates repealing the statutes governing the murder of noblemen and substituting a penalty "secundum ius divinum" (according to divine law). And finally, in article 27, Callimachus calls for an end to the abuse of the poor by the rich.

The *Consilia* could not have carried weight without specific recommendations on dynastic matters. Accordingly, articles 29 through 33 address the king's relations with his brothers as well as with other rulers. He is advised, for example, to keep his brother Sigismund at a distance and to invest him with the palatinate of Wallachia. Brother Frederick is to be situated in Prussia to keep the Teutonic Order in line. Good relations with the king of Hungary and the grand duke of Lithuania are urged to gain their support against the powerful members of illustrious families who might press claims against the Crown. The dukes of Mazovia in particular are not to be trusted. They are at present "as powerful as you," warns the *Consilia*. They were, moreover, hostile to his election and so must be regarded as enemies. In view of this potential threat, the king is advised to think how best to achieve the status of "unus rex, una lex" (one king, one law).

Callimachus's vision of a healthy Polish state rested on the fundamental belief that Poland could be effectively governed by a strong monarch who would gain strength both by curbing the nobility's privileges and drive for power and by imposing restraints on the Roman Catholic church (represented, above all, by the Polish bishops). The goal was feasible, within limits, but it depended on two forms of relative independence of the monarchy: financial independence from the nobility, to be brought about by improving the economic and political status of the cities and the merchant class, and political and financial independence from Rome, which would then make possible a foreign policy shaped by Polish interests rather than by those of the Vatican. Callimachus also understood fully, as the *Consilia* makes clear, that if the king is to be a strong and effective monarch, rival power centers can no longer be tolerated, nor can there be separate legal systems, one for the privileged (the nobility) and one for ordinary people. In urging the king to be sole ruler in his kingdom, he also sought to make him understand that he would derive additional strength by instituting a unified legal code throughout the country.

Enlightened Polish political thought of the sixteenth-century Renaissance (especially that of the greatest political thinker of the age, Andrzej Frycz Modrzewski) would embrace views similar to those Callimachus espoused in his *Consilia*. But as we know only too well from subsequent Polish history, the goals of a strong monarch, curbed noble power, and a prosperous bourgeoisie were never achieved. The nobles, in fact, succeeded so well in grasping the reins of political power that they effectively destroyed the monarchy and pushed through measures so inhospitable to the interests of the burghers that they stunted the economic growth of the cities for centuries. The nobles thus satisfied their lust for an absolute power of their own definition, and they took great pride in achieving democracy in Poland—a democracy limited, however, to their own class. According to this elitist concept of democracy, all members of the nobility were equal, and Polish political institutions became structured accordingly. The problem was the exclusion of all other classes, and what Callimachus and the Polish political reformers of the Renaissance feared most came to pass: instead of a Polish state based on a strong central authority, the monarchy, a state evolved in which all political power came to rest in the hands of the class the reformers were most intent on curbing. Equality before the law—which was of such fundamental concern to the reformers—was now a reality only for the nobles. The strong middle class reformers such as Callimachus hoped for as a reliable guarantor of monarchic supremacy never came into being in the lifetime of the Polish commonwealth, for the economy of the state, like its politics, came to be totally dominated by a nobility concerned only with its own well-being. The foundation was thus laid not for the future prosperity of Poland as envisaged by Callimachus, or by Frycz Modrzewski, but for its inevitable collapse in the partitions of the late eighteenth century.

Although it may be appealing to think that the far less celebrated *Consilia* of the Italian expatriate Filippo Buonaccorsi served as a source of Machiavelli's renowned *The Prince*, little evidence exists to support such a claim. To begin with, the two works are of different character, despite obvious similarities. That both may ultimately have been bred by the specific intricacies of Renaissance Italian political life seems reasonable. But beyond advocating political expediency divorced from morality and urging national unity within the context of a powerful central authority, the two works have little in common. Callimachus's *Consilia* consists of a set of precepts addressed to a reigning monarch and is based on Polish political conditions of the time. Assuming the work is authentic, it reflects an acute understanding of the nature and deficiencies of the Polish political system and prescribes specific remedies. By the time he came to write the *Consilia*, Callimachus had enough experience of Polish political life to formulate a concrete program of reform for his adopted homeland.

Although he was a very able and prolific writer with sufficient erudition to exchange substantive correspondence with Italian humanists of the stature of Marsilio Ficino (1433–99), Angelo Poliziano (real name, Angelo Ambrogini, 1454–94), and Giovanni Pico della Mirandola (1463–94), as well as with the Florentine poet and author Ugolino Verini (1438–1516), Callimachus was above all a politician. And it is probably in his love of politics and his understanding of the mechanics of power that he most reflects his Italian background. But it is the practical politician rather than the literary artist and humanist scholar that is seen in the *Consilia*. Unlike Machiavelli's *Prince*, Callimachus's work has no pretensions to either literary or philosophical significance. The *Consilia* was written late in Callimachus's life, just a few years before his death and at a time when his career seemed in eclipse. But John Albert's election to the throne restored him to his former position and provided the incentive to draw up a political program for the new king that was intended to strengthen his power, avoid the political chaos that had preceded his elevation to the throne, and at the same time assure Callimachus's own position. Hence the *Consilia* arose out of a specific set of political circumstances and was a response to those circumstances. The work was not conceived as a science of politics like *The Prince*, nor did it appear as the distillation of ideas long in the making about the nature of authority, the uses of power, and the structure of the state. Comparing one major item in the *Consilia* and in *The Prince* demonstrates the different political situations the works addressed. Machiavelli's knowledge of and bad experience with mercenary troops in the Italian city-states completely soured him and led him to an ardent advocacy of a national militia as one means of achieving national unity. With Callimachus it was just the opposite. Taking note of the Polish kings' costly reliance on the nobility for their armed forces in the absence of a standing army, he saw hiring mercenaries as one important way to strengthen Poland's military posture while lessening the king's dependence on the nobility. Yet despite this and greater differences between them, the *Consilia* and *The Prince* share the same point of departure: the recognition that national unity cannot be achieved (as among the Italians) or preserved (as among the Poles) without a strong central authority, and it was to provide the rationale for that authority and show how to attain it that both works came to be written.

Machiavelli could easily have known of Buonaccorsi-Callimachus even though there is no evidence he knew the *Consilia*. *The Prince* was written some twenty years after the *Consilia,* so somewhere along the way it could have come to Machiavelli's attention. But more important, Callimachus was so well known to the leading Italian humanists (and perhaps still remembered for his part in the conspiracy against Pope Paul II) that it is hard to imagine Machiavelli had not heard of him and maybe even taken an interest in his career and writings. The case is strengthened by the many Florentine associations of both writers and by Machiavelli's personal relationship with Biagio Buonaccorsi, who on some occasion must have acquainted him with his family history. When the evidence is weighed, however, there is no escaping its circumstantial nature or the fact that, whatever knowledge Machiavelli may have had of Filippo Buonaccorsi and his career, *The Prince* and the *Consilia* are two quite different works, written for very different audiences, and that nowhere in *The Prince* or in Machiavelli's other writings is there anything pointing to a specific knowledge of Callimachus's *Consilia*. So the case has to close as still speculative, though intriguing—as it has been from the beginning of any interest in the possibility that Callimachus influenced Machiavelli and especially the conception of *The Prince*.

Callimachus and Italian Renaissance
Philosophical Thought

Callimachus's political career in Poland, extraordinary and time-consuming as it was, proved no barrier to his cultivating a literary career of no less interest. Much of this writing grew out of or paralleled his political activity, as his histories and the *Consilia* amply attest. Callimachus was, as I previously characterized him, every inch the politician, and his literary legacy reflects an immense delight in the game of politics. But he was also a well-trained and thoughtful humanist with as much zeal for the philosophical as for the political. If affairs of state left him little time for composing essays and treatises on humanist topics on the order of his political biographies and the *Consilia,* letter writing provided a more than adequate substitute. The high esteem in which the Renaissance held epistolary art invested such writing with considerable respectability. But Callimachus's use of the form was governed by another consideration as well—his desire to maintain close contact with old friends and relatives in Italy.[41] Despite his flight from his native country and his long residence in Poland, he made every effort to keep in touch with Italy and Italians. Until diplomatic assignments on behalf of the Polish Crown made it possible for him to return to Italy and directly reestablish old ties, correspondence became the principal way he maintained contact not only with friends and relatives but with Italian cultural and intellectual developments.

Of particular importance in Callimachus's correspondence are the letters he exchanged with such luminaries of the Italian Renaissance as Marsilio Ficino and Giovanni Pico della Mirandola. It was in these exchanges above all that he demonstrated a continuing commitment to humanist ideals as well as to his own intellectual vitality and sophistication.

An enthusiast of Neoplatonism, Callimachus would inevitably have sought contact with members of the Florentine Accademia Platonica, particularly Ficino, whose fame rested on his renovation and promulgation of Neoplatonic philosophy. That Callimachus was acquainted with Ficino seems certain, though there is no evidence on precisely when the two Platonists may have met or over what period they may have known each other. The possibility exists that Filippo Buonaccorsi may have begun a friendship with Ficino before his flight from Italy, possibly even before he left Tuscany for Rome in the service of Bartolomeo Roverella, cardinal of San Clemente. There is also the possibility that the two men met only much later when Buonaccorsi, already long active in Polish diplomatic service, was on a mission to Venice and Rome on behalf of King Casimir IV. Whatever the time or circumstances of their meeting, however, no correspondence between Callimachus and Ficino apparently antedates the early 1480s.

The earliest letter of Callimachus to "the most outstanding philosopher of all ages" carries no date and is ascribed in Polish sources to "before 1485," meaning not long before 1485. At the very beginning of it, when he mentions that Ficino honors him by calling him a "co-Platonist" (complatonicum),[42] Callimachus leaves no doubt that his letter is a response to Ficino's reply to a now lost effort by Callimachus to establish a correspondence between them. Ficino's flattery may have been prompted in part by embarrassment over taking so long to reply to Callimachus's first letter, which was accompanied by gifts. In any case, Ficino's long-awaited reply was all the encouragement Callimachus needed to write back, in the longest and most thoughtful of the letters addressed to Ficino.

In the nature of a polemic over the issue of demons and demonic possession, Callimachus's letter at once reveals those qualities of mind evident throughout his literary and political career—independence of attitude and judgment, critical skepticism, and willingness to challenge authority. The point of departure with Ficino, with whom Callimachus did not shrink from arguing, was the philosopher's views concerning the classification, nature, number, and hierarchy of demons and angels and his acceptance of the theological position that human souls are guided by demonic custodians.[43] While willing to subscribe to Ficino's classifications and the principle of satanic possession of the soul, Callimachus nevertheless felt compelled to voice serious reservations about the way the evil spirit enters the body and appropriates functions and activities of the soul. While accepting the teaching of religion on the matter as a believer, Callimachus, as a Renaissance thinker of great intellectual independence, also argues for the evidence of nature. That external spirits can enter the body and possess the soul, as religion teaches, he acknowledges as a theological given. But the same teaching that advances this principle is inadequate, from his point of view, in explaining precisely how the act occurs. Callimachus argues that the complete diffusion of the soul throughout the body leaves absolutely no room for the penetration of any spirit from the outside. He also rejects the notion that the animated body may harbor more than one motor (that is, the soul) because an inanimate object is often subject to the action of many motors. Though cognizant of the distinction between corporeal and noncorporeal beings and the possibility that many of the latter may simultaneously occupy the same place, Callimachus wonders how entities whose properties and activities are distinct can indeed fill the same space. After considering the necessity of distinguishing one spirit from another, as Ficino had done, he concludes his argument by advancing—and then rejecting by reference to reason and nature—the hypothetical possibility that an external spirit can enter the body only if the soul sets aside some corner of the body for the entry of an external spirit or if the soul withdraws from the body as the external spirit enters, thereby making room for it.

The significance of Callimachus's letter to Ficino is less in the particular issue addressed than in his refusal to accept theological positions contrary—from his point of view—to reason and nature. As he states at the conclusion of his letter: "I ask you, therefore, to write back and explain to me—not theologically, but by the principles of nature—how you understand this matter to occur. As far as theology is concerned, I am completely unsatisfied. But once you enlighten me as to how two spirits of different substances can exist simultaneously in one body, you will still have to describe to me by what law a spirit entering a body from outside can expel the soul as if from its own possession and then make use of the body according to its own will."[44]

The consistency of Callimachus's thought from the time of the antipapal conspiracy to the twilight of his life is striking. His rejection of the temporal authority of the church was paralleled by his rejection of theological authority, as the letter to Ficino makes abundantly clear. Just as he championed the liberation of state politics from religion, so too did Callimachus predicate true independence of thought and scientific inquiry on the recognition that the authority of theology was limited to matters of religion.

Callimachus's very long letter to Pico della Mirandola on the nature of sin—more an essay than an epistle—dates from 1485 or 1486 and stands as even more eloquent testimony to his uncompromising independence of mind. The letter is a natural outgrowth of the polemic with Ficino, which Callimachus mentions in the very beginning. Recalling the bonds of friendship and intellectual interests between Ficino and Pico della Mirandola, Callimachus declares that perhaps it would be appropriate for him to link them now by the knot of related problems. Having not long before addressed Ficino on the matter of the evil spirit, he will now discuss with Pico the question of sin ("Et qui egerim cum illo paulo ante de daemone, agam nunc tecum de peccatis" [502]).

In raising the fundamental question of how the body and soul relate to each other in sin, Callimachus repeats the request he made to Ficino, asking that Pico have no recourse to the authority of religion. Again, he declares, the subject of his inquiry is the nature of things, not religious mysteries. Displaying his usual caustic attitude toward theologians, Callimachus adds that with respect to religious mysteries the theologians have written a great many books employing the most elaborate arguments to prove things that can be rendered better service if one believes them against one's reason.

Eschewing thus the traditional theological approach and unwilling to suspend reason, Callimachus argues—in contradistinction to Pico's more conservative position—that the body and the soul have their own unique properties and functions, that they are therefore autonomous entities, and that the sins of the mortal and temporal entity known as the body cannot be punishable through all eternity. Furthermore, because of the differences between soul and body, neither can influence the other with respect to sin. A noble soul cannot be depraved by the body, nor can a base soul be uplifted by it. If man sins because he has the power to distinguish good and evil, Callimachus then asks, how can guilt for sin fall on the body, which lacks this faculty? Possessed of the power to reason and judge, the soul alone must bear responsibility for sin. The body can act only in accord with the instincts nature has endowed it with, making impossible the commission of sins punishable through all eternity, in which the finite and perishable body has no existence.

Using the analogy of a ship that cannot be faulted when it runs aground or is wrecked, Callimachus then proceeds to argue that the body is a vessel guided by the soul. Possessing the power of reason and judgment, it is the soul that can lead the body into sin and the soul that must be held accountable and culpable. Among all things that exist Callimachus distinguishes the divine or eternal from the human or mortal. Since the mortal has no influence on the divine, it follows that in the perishable, or mortal, part of his nature man cannot do harm or good to the divine; all man's activities occur within the framework of his mortal nature, within the sphere of the earthly and transient. Transgressions in this sphere concern only laws, customs, and mores and must be punished in compliance with conventions that vary from one society to another.

In sum, Callimachus's concept of sin proceeds from a thoroughgoing humanist vision of man that exceeds Pico della Mirandola's in shedding any remnant of medieval Scholasticism. Man is made up of body and soul. Both entities are unique, with different attributes and functions. The body responds to instincts and sensations derived from nature and in itself is incapable of sin. Transgressions in the terrestrial, transient sphere of man cannot be viewed as more or less than violations of the social order, which men protect by laws that determine punishments for crimes. These punishments cannot be disproportionate to the crimes and hence cannot extend beyond man's earthly sojourn. But the soul, created to recognize and honor God and the source of man's ability to reason and judge toward the realization of that goal, besmirches its own immortal nature when it spurns or turns aside from its fundamental responsibilities. When this happens, the soul must be punished eternally.

In closing his letter essay to Pico, Callimachus exercises the same combination of shrewdness and flattery he reveals on other occasions when dealing with the prominent, especially when disagreement is possible. Hailing Pico as one who knows "all things human and divine better than anyone else" (qui humanorum omnium et divinorum rationem prae omnibus aliis scientissime teneas [124]), Callimachus declares that the many arguments he himself sets forth in defense of his position seem silly even to him, "as if it could even enter your [Pico's] head that any terrestrial and corruptible thing could in any way act in unison with the divine and eternal; for if their power of action were dependent on the nature of impermanent things, then nothing would prevent their being called imperfect, which in no way can I accept" (quasi venire tibi in mentem queat rem quampiam terrenam et corruptibilem posse modo aliquo videri simul agere cum caelestibus et aeternis, quorum si vis agendi penderet ex natura caducorum, nihil obstaret, quin per se imperfecta dicerentur. Quod ita esse nullo modo mihi persuadeo [124]).

Whether convinced, disarmed, or overwhelmed, Pico never replied directly to Callimachus's letter. This was also a busy period for Pico, when he was completing his famous *900 conclusiones* for publication,[45] and he may simply have lacked time to think through Callimachus's arguments and draft an appropriate response. This does not mean, however, that Pico took no heed of the long letter. Two scholars who have studied the Callimachus-Pico relationship—Giorgio Radetti and Jerzy Zathey—agree that the *Conclusiones* demonstrate some accommodation of Callimachus's point of view in Pico's apparent acceptance of the argument that finite, mortal sin is undeserving of infinite (that is, eternal) punishment.[46]

Callimachus's longer letters to Ficino and Pico are the most intellectually substantive of the many he exchanged with his Italian compatriots. And these ought to be regarded as more the exception than the rule, stimulated by his eagerness to maintain his credentials as a writer and thinker in Italian humanist circles despite his long absence from his native country and his obvious susceptibility to intellectual challenge. Matching wits with the likes of Ficino and Pico della Mirandola was too much of a temptation to let pass.

Generally, Callimachus's letters to friends and acquaintances in Italy were of a lighter, more casual nature. One written to Ficino from Sandomierz, dated approximately December 31, 1486, refers to the Florentine Academy, where the visitor had the chance to view at first hand how Ficino, for example, "husbands his time, counting the minutes devoted to morning massages of the head, which he regarded as of such value for the well-being of his health and body."[47] As so often in Callimachus's correspondence, the letter is essentially an apology for a long hiatus in writing, which Callimachus hopes in part to atone for by promising to send Ficino several of his smaller essays for him to read—once, of course, Ficino completes his great work on Plato ("Habeo enim quaestiunculas aliquot dignissima a te discuti, ubi Platoni tuo summam manum imposueris" [128]). In another letter to Ficino sent from Piotrków on May 15, 1488, Callimachus tells him how his house burned and many of his own writings as well as much of his personal library were lost. Among the papers destroyed were several works—possibly those referred to in the earlier letter from Sando-mierz—that Callimachus had dedicated to Ficino; while he modestly characterizes them as "inept and philosophically erroneous," he still would have sent them to Ficino had they not gone up in smoke. The fire also serves as a clever pretext by which Callimachus can scold Ficino for lagging in correspondence and neglecting to send him a copy of his book on Plato. Ficino, he declares, must have foreseen the fire and for that reason did not send him his Plato ("Sed redeo ad incendium, quod futurum te divinasse credo atque ideo Platonem tuum non misisse" [134]). Callimachus closes his letter with the request that Ficino convey his salutations to the other members of the Floren-tine Academy and especially to the Neo-Latin poet Zenobio Acciajuoli, who shared Callimachus's brief sojourn on the island of Chios in 1469 after the flight from Italy, and to the distinguished Florentine humanist Angelo Poliziano.

Callimachus's relationship with Poliziano went back at least to 1485. In a letter to Poliziano from Lwów dated September 29, 1485, Callima-chus refers to an earlier correspondence and an exchange of writings between them. Callimachus has high praise for Poliziano's *Rusticus*, which he might have received personally from its author—"a charming work, full of wisdom and elegance, that truly draws the brightest light from fog" (*Rusticus* tuus sane urbanissimus doctrinaque et elegantia plenus et qui vere ex fumo clarissimun lucem efferat [96])—and he also takes the occasion to thank his correspondent for favorable re-marks about his own "little purses" (locellos).

Callimachus's most extensive letter writing to Italy was directed to his relative and friend Lattanzio Tedaldi, a poet and musician who was also one of Lorenzo de' Medici's secretaries. Although Callimachus did not know Tedaldi personally before his flight from Italy, his friend-ship with and indebtedness to Arnolfo Tedaldi engendered warm feelings for the Tedaldi family. Lattanzio's service at the Medici court and his close contact with the circle of Florentine humanists made him, therefore, an ideal epistolary partner: a member of a family to which Callimachus was related and of which he was especially fond and a resident of Florence well positioned to keep him abreast of the latest developments in Italian thought and art. Callimachus's first letter to Lattanzio from Drohobycz on July 9, 1482, makes specific mention of both his feelings for the Tedaldis and his enthusiasm for Lattanzio's intellectual interests: "But your letters indicate that you are trained in the good arts, a circumstance that would have disposed me kindly to you even if you were not connected by blood to Arnolfo."[48]

Lattanzio may not have realized it at the time, but Callimachus's closing words were to prove anything but platitudes: "You cannot doubt how much say you will have in my affairs, as much as you have in your own, which you will become convinced of if opportunity and desire impel you to try, something that you can do whenever and wherever you care, but preferably there [in Italy] should you so desire. At present there is much that stands in the way of my becoming a Sarmatian instead of an Etruscan [or Tuscan]."

Lattanzio Tedaldi played his role admirably, becoming Callimachus's principal link with contemporary Florentine culture. It was he, for example, who provided Callimachus with his first information about Pico della Mirandola, for which the expatriate thanked him in a letter written in Italian, sent from Lwów on November 11, 1485: "Thank you so much for the conscientious account with which you provided me with information about the illustrious Count della Mirandola. I would write to such a virtuous man on any occasion, to the best of my ability" (98).

Until his return to Italy on diplomatic assignments, which enabled him to reestablish old ties, Callimachus not only depended on correspondence to maintain contact, but also relied on visits to Italy on his behalf by his servant Mikołaj, whom he usually dispatched laden with exotic gifts from Poland for friends and relatives. In his letters to Lattanzio Tedaldi on November 3, 1485, and April 1, 1486, Callimachus recalls Lattanzio's kindness to Mikołaj on one of his visits and mentions the letters that he wrote to him and other Italian friends right after Mikołaj's return to Poland from an Italian trip. A later letter, dated May 15, 1468, apologizes for the demands of a diplomatic career that again resulted in a long hiatus in correspondence and informs Lattanzio that Callimachus had been on the verge of sending Mikołaj on another trip to Italy when plans had to be changed because of a mission to Turkey. Callimachus's trust in Mikołaj was consider-

able—the servant was truly his right-hand man—as the following remark from the same letter makes clear: "Because of my innate negli-
gence and my clumsiness when it comes to taking care of domestic
matters, I understood that it would not be possible for me to undertake
the mission, what with all my many daily cares, without that servant to
whom I long ago entrusted all my domestic matters, so I postponed
his trip to you until some other time and took him along with me"
(130).

With Lattanzio Tedaldi acting as his go-between, Callimachus succeeded in establishing, or reestablishing, close links with the Florentine
humanists. Besides Ficino, Pico della Mirandola, and Poliziano—with
whom he eventually entered into direct correspondence—he was also
in touch through Tedaldi with Alamanno Rinuccino, Lorenzo de'
Medici, Bartolomeo Scala (1430–97), author of the *Apologia contra
vituperatores civitatis Florentiae* (Defense against the Calumniators of the
City of Florence, 1496), the previously mentioned poet and translator
of Greek classics into Latin, Zenobio Acciajuoli, and the poet Ugolino
Verini, who once wrote a poem dedicated to Callimachus under the
title "Ad Callimachum Etruscum, poetam insignem, Pannonii regis
amicum" (To Callimachus the Tuscan, Distinguished Poet, and Friend
of the King of Hungary). Verini was also the author of an epic poem
about Charlemagne, *Carlias,* and he sent his son to deliver a copy to
Callimachus personally in Poland in 1482.

Verini's poem to Callimachus, as well as his sending his son all the
way to Poland to present him with a copy of *Carlias,* suggests that
Callimachus's contacts with his Italian compatriots were not a one-way
street. Given the circumstances in which he left Italy and his life in
faraway Poland, one can assume that renewing ties with Italy, entering
into correspondence with luminaries of the stamp of Ficino and Pico
della Mirandola, even matching wits with them, obviously meant a
great deal to Callimachus, probably more than to his epistolary friends
in Italy. But Callimachus's reputation as a bold, freethinking humanist,
which had begun to develop before he fled Italy, could only have been
enhanced by the events surrounding his life and what must have struck
his Italian compatriots as a romantic and exotic exile to a "Sarmatia"
(Poland) that few had ever visited but about which they had heard
enough to excite their curiosity. When Lattanzio Tedaldi began to
relate stories in Florence about the life in distant Poland of his relative
Filippo Buonaccorsi, now known as Callimachus Experiens, and to
pass on his regards to friends and acquaintances and anyone else he
was interested in establishing contact with, the positive response should
hardly be considered extraordinary. Besides, Callimachus had already

become a celebrity—the expatriate humanist and would-be pope killer who was now a statesman and even adviser to the kings of Poland. If there were any doubts as to his new status, the trips to Italy made by his personal servant and emissary Mikołaj and his generous gifts soon dispelled them. Everyone likes getting presents, and fifteenth-century Italian humanists were no exception. Ficino, for example, received a coat of marten fur, a smaller garment woven of feathers, and a sword whose hilt was made of horn resembling jasper; Bartolomeo Scala was given a large and costly white bearskin along with several smaller skins of white wolves and a leather suit; Ugolino Verini got a purse of Prussian leather of superb fragrance (so we are told); Lattanzio Tedaldi was given a sable coat; and Lorenzo de' Medici received nothing less than a twelve-year-old "Scythian" slave completely attired in Scythian garb complete with a bow, a quiver of arrows, and a small horse.[49] Callimachus's concern over gifts is also reflected in one of his letters to Lattanzio Tedaldi. Apparently written from Venice in July 1486 during his diplomatic mission there, the letter makes a point of reminding Lattanzio of a stone seal for letters that Callimachus had asked be prepared so he could have it made into a ring for Arnolfo Tedaldi.[50]

That Callimachus was well regarded by his Italian friends, apart from their willingness to exchange literary works with him and to seek his opinions and judgments, is seen in their response to the news that his library and personal effects had been lost in a fire. Callimachus first mentioned his loss in a letter to Lattanzio Tedaldi dated May 15, 1488, probably written from Piotrków. Excusing his inability to respond to particular questions raised by his friend in previous correspondence, Callimachus informs him that "last year [1487] my residence and all my belongings including my own books and papers as well as those of my friends were destroyed by fire, so I am unable now to recall everything you wrote about" (131). Callimachus also shared the news of his misfortune with Marsilio Ficino in a letter written the same day as the one to Lattanzio Tedaldi. With Ficino, however—as mentioned previously—Callimachus uses the fire as a pretext for a tongue-in-cheek modesty concerning essays that he had intended to send but that went up in smoke. Perhaps, muses Callimachus, it is better that the essays were lost in the fire, because they were unworthy of being read by the great Platonist Ficino, owing to their ineptness and philosophical shortcomings. In a sense, he declares, it is a case of his writings not so much being destroyed as escaping disrepute ("quantum ad ea, quae scripseram, attinet, non tam illa mihi periisse, quam infamiae esse subtracta" [134]). The lightness of such remarks could scarcely conceal the severity of Callimachus's loss, and as soon as Ficino, Tedaldi, Verini, and other friends in Italy learned what had happened, they lost no time in sending whatever books they could so he could restock his library and remain a part of their common world. This one gesture from fellow Italian humanists for whom he held the highest regard would probably have weighed more in Filippo Buonaccorsi's personal scale of values than the titles and perquisites of high office. For the former fugitive and expatriate, it was as if he had never left home.

CHAPTER 3

The Humanist a-Touring: Celtis among the Sarmatians

H eaven knows what the outstanding German humanist and poet Conrad Celtis (or Conradus Celtis Protucius, as he preferred being called in the formal humanist style; 1459–1508) expected when he abruptly ended his stay in Rome in 1487, returned to Venice, and traveling thence from Trieste through Hungary, finally reached Cracow about Easter 1489.

Barely thirty, Celtis was at the peak of his career.[1] His treatise on poetry, *Ars versificandi et carminum*—which established his fame—had appeared in 1486 and was followed in 1487 by his edition of two plays by the Roman tragic dramatist Seneca, *Hercules Furens* and *Thyestes*. In recognition of his contributions to the spread of the "new learning" in Germany, the Holy Roman Emperor Frederick III crowned him with the laurel wreath at Nuremberg on April 18, 1487, and conferred the title doctor of philosophy. As the first German so honored, Celtis was full of justifiable pride. Thereafter he always affixed the title "poeta laureatus" to his name and insisted that portraits depict him in his doctor's cap with the laurel wreath around it.

For a non-Italian humanist who had never visited the home of humanism, the trip to Italy on which Celtis embarked after the triumphs of Nuremberg was like a Moslem's pilgrimage to Mecca. Doubtless expecting a warm reception after the distinctions conferred on him by the emperor, Celtis was rudely awakened by the reality of Italian indifference. Instead of capping the triumphs of Nuremberg, his journey to Italy was clearly a disappointment. To Celtis, ever sensitive about the backwardness of German culture compared with the Italian, it must have confirmed his worst fears that it would be a long time before Italian humanists would see Germans as anything but barbarians.

In view of the glories of Italian culture, which in his mind embraced Roman antiquity as well as the Renaissance, Celtis never had any illusions about German culture. In his well-known programmatic poem "Ad Apollinem repertorem poetices ut ab Italis ad Germanos veniat" (To Apollo, the Inventor of Poetry, That He Come to Germany from Italy, 1486) he himself speaks of the German as a "barbarian, of warrior or uncouth origins" (barbarus . . . vel acer / Vel parens hirtus), "ignorant of the beauties of Latin culture" (Latii leporis / nescius).[2] It is to raise German culture, and above all German literary art, to the level of the Italian that Celtis appeals to the classical god of poetry to leave Italy and come now to Germany, "a country still uncultivated by the strings of your lyre" (Tu veni incultam fidibus canoris / Visere terram). Lest his fellow Germans take umbrage at his references to them as barbarians, Celtis indirectly compares Germany to Rome before the impact of Greek culture; just as Rome was transformed by the visit of Phoebus, so now can Germany be transformed if Phoebus will only come there from Italy:

> Tu celer vastum poteras per aequor
> Laetus a Graecis Latium videre,
> Invehens Musas, voluisti gratas
> Pandere et artes.

(You were swift and happy in crossing the vast sea from Greece to Latium, bearing the Muses with you, so desirous were you of making known the arts you hold dear.)

But in the poem's final stanza, Celtis reiterates the "barbarous" state of German culture:

> Sic velis nostras rogitamus oras
> Italas ceu quondam aditare terras;
> Barbarus sermo fugiatque, ut atrum
> Subruat omne.

(We now thus pray you to come to us as once you came to Italy. Let barbarian speech take flight, that all darkness at last may be eliminated.)

A few years later, in his fiercely proud and nationalistic "Public Oration Delivered in the University of Ingolstadt" (Oratio in gymnasio in Ingelstadio publice recitata, 1492), Celtis again exhorted his fellow Germans to "emulate the ancient nobility of Rome" (aemulamini, nobiles viri, priscam nobilitatem Romanam), "shake off [your] repulsive coarseness and acquire Roman culture" (exuta foeda barbarie Romanorum artium affectatores esse debebitis).[3] They should, moreover, "do away with that old disrepute of the German among Greek, Latin, and Hebrew writers who ascribe to us drunkenness, savagery, cruelty, and everything else bordering on bestiality and excess" (Tollite veteram illam apud Graecos, Latinos et Hebraeos scriptores Germanorum infamiam, qua illi nobis temulentiam, immanitatem, crudelitatem et si quid aliud, quod bestiae et insaniae proximum est, ascribunt). The Germans, in fact, were duty-bound to destroy remaining barriers to assimilating Latin culture, since in Celtis's view—as expounded especially in the Ingolstadt address—they were the "survivors of the Roman Empire" (Romani reliquias imperii). What Celtis had in mind, of course, was that the Germanic Holy Roman Empire was the successor of the Roman Empire of yore and that the Germans thus had almost as much right as the Italians to regard Latin culture as their patrimony.

Celtis's upset over his lukewarm reception by the Italians was reflected directly in the Ingolstadt speech and in one of his best-known epigrams, "De puella Romae reperta" (On the Body of a Girl Unearthed in Rome). While praising the Italians for their love of literature and their cultivation of it, which the Germans would do well to emulate, he also excoriates "Italian sensuality" (Italicus luxus) and "fierce cruelty in extracting filthy lucre" (saeva in extorquendo argento pernicioso crudelitas), by which the Germans themselves have been corrupted. The epigram "On the Body of a Girl Unearthed in Rome" speaks for itself: "A thousand years have I lain beneath this stone; now set free from the grave I speak thus unto the Romans: I see no citizens now as Romans used to be, distinguished in justice and sense of duty, but sad of heart I behold only ruins, now merely a monument to men of past ages. If after another hundred years I should see you again, I think that scarcely the name Roman will survive."[4]

The idea of traveling to eastern Europe after his disappointing sojourn in Italy may have come to Celtis during his stay in Rome. A compulsive wanderer since he left home at age seventeen, Celtis needed little encouragement to set off on yet another trip. But why he chose eastern Europe, and especially Poland, after Italy provides interesting material for speculation.

While in Rome, Celtis made a point of visiting the Accademia Romana. It is entirely possible that the founder of the academy, Pomponio Leto, brought up the scandalous affair of a former member,

Filippo Buonaccorsi of San Gimignano, better known as Callimachus Experiens. Though neither the Italian's nor the German's writings say so, in view of Celtis' intellectual curiosity and his fondness for traveling, it seems reasonable that the subject might have arisen.

There were, to be sure, other possible reasons for Celtis's interest in Poland, or more precisely in Cracow. One was certainly the highly regarded University of Cracow, which had become a magnet for students from neighboring countries, above all the German lands and Hungary, where humanism had already sunk roots. Because of the universality of Latin, the humanists regarded themselves as citizens of an international republic of classical letters. Halls of learning, wherever they happened to be, were always open for intellectual stimulation, good conversation, and the opportunity to earn money by lecturing and tutoring. The last consideration was of some consequence to Celtis, since until his appointment by the emperor Maximilian I in 1497 as professor of poetry and eloquence of the University of Vienna, he held no regular academic post and depended on such lecturing and tutoring for an income. The laurel wreath and doctor's cap conferred on him by Frederick III in 1487 may have been prestigious, but they brought small monetary reward.

Another factor in Celtis's decision to travel to Poland could well have been his interest in the Cracow astronomer and mathematician Albert Blar of Brudzewo (or, in the Polish version of the name, Wojciech z Brudzewa or Wojciech Brudzewski).[5] Celtis himself had already become attracted to these sciences as well as to astrology, and he would certainly have been aware of the University of Cracow's prominence in them. Albert Blar, who was Copernicus's teacher, had once been a student of the distinguished German scholars Peuerbach and Regiomontanus and could easily have become known to Celtis when the poet was a student of the no less famous German humanist Rudolf Agricola in Heidelberg. In any case, Celtis was impressed with what he had heard of Blar and wanted to make his acquaintance. He was obviously not disappointed. The two men became close friends during Celtis's stay in Poland from 1489 to 1491 and maintained a correspondence after his departure.

Celtis's typical Renaissance enthusiasm for geography sheds light on yet another possible reason for his visit to Cracow as well as on a demographic aspect of late fifteenth-century Polish humanism.[6] German patriotism, which shaped Celtis's views on art and politics, grew more stridently nationalistic with time. Before his journey to Poland it manifested itself above all in his first publication, the *Ars versificandi et carminum* (A Treatise on Poetry), which established his reputation and earned him his laurel wreath. A guide to the writing of poetry—of course in humanist Latin—the work was intended to hasten the advent of the new learning among the Germans, whose cultural achievements Celtis still held in low regard. Accompanying the manual was his famous ode to Apollo, meant to exemplify the kind of poetry the German genius was capable of creating. Implicit in the appeal for humanizing German culture was a growing sense of national pride and a desire to rival, indeed surpass, Italy.

If we shift our attention from Celtis's crystallizing Germanism to the socioeconomic and ethnic composition of contemporary Cracow, we find a vibrant, prosperous city with a middle class whose upper stratum in particular bore a distinct German character. Polonization and, at least among the wealthy, ennoblement accelerated in the course of the sixteenth century, but in Celtis's time this had not yet happened to any significant extent.

Reflecting the close relations between town and gown, the university community—faculty and students alike—also had a strong German presence. Among the scholars who were to become Celtis's closest acquaintances, for example, were such men as Albert Blar himself; Stanisław Selig, an astronomer, mathematician, and physician who bore the Greco-Roman humanist name Statilius Simonides; and Jan Ursyn (Ursinus), a member of the well-to-do Ber (Bär) family of Cracow, a doctor of medicine and law who also lectured on Sallust and wrote an epistolary handbook first published in Nuremberg in 1495 or 1496 under the title *Modus epistolandi cum epistolis exemplaribus et orationibus annexis* (How to Write Letters, with Model Letters and Speeches Appended).[7] There were also Sigismundus Fusilius, of the Gossingers of Wrocław (Breslau), who lectured on Vergil's *Georgics,* and the Silesians Aesticampianus the Elder (real name Jan Sommerfeld), who lectured on Aristotle and wrote a handbook on epistolography, and Laurentius Corvinus, known in Polish as Wawrzyniec Korwin but born Raab or Raabe.

Whereas the universality of Latin and the cosmopolitanism of humanist learning tended to minimize ethnic differences within academe, social and cultural contacts between the German urban patriciate in Cracow and their ethnic confreres at the University of Cracow if anything reinforced them.

For Celtis, then, Cracow and its distinguished center of learning were perceived as a Germanic island in a Sarmatian sea, since it was as Sarmatia that Poland was known to him. His literary career bears out this contention. Apart from his *Ars versificandi* and important editions of the tragedies of Seneca and the Latin dramas of the tenth-century German nun Hrotswitha, for whose rediscovery he is given credit, Celtis's major works were a volume of *Amores* (1502) and a collection of *Odes* edited posthumously by his students and published in 1513. Acknowledged as his most outstanding literary contribution, the *Amores* recount his four great love affairs with four different women in four cities at four stages in his life. Love and geography are integrally interwoven in the *Amores* and explain the work's quadripartite division.

Not only did each of Celtis's love affairs have its own geographical locus, but each city in the *Amores* represents a point on the compass that marked, in Celtis's conception, the natural boundaries of Germany. The western locus was Mainz, the northern Lübeck, the southern Regensburg, and the eastern—Cracow. That is why the full title of the *Amores* in Latin reads: *Quattuor libri amorum secundum quattuor latera Germaniae* (Four Books of Love According with the Four Borders of Germany). In traveling to Cracow, then, Celtis was headed not just for a highly regarded university with a significant German presence but, in his mind, for a German city.

Celtis's predilection for geography had an ideological as well as a romantic rationale. In staking out the boundaries of Germany as the expanse where his poetry recreates a life of adventure and passion, Celtis demarcates Germany itself as a literary entity. Toward the goal of creating a German literary entity, in a humanist sense, Celtis devoted a great deal of energy to establishing literary academies or, as he called them in Latin, *sodalitates* (sodalities). As a meeting ground for like-minded and like-cultured men (and occasionally women) sharing a passion for classical antiquity as well as good companionship, the academy, or sodality, was a familiar signpost of the humanist landscape. Wherever he set foot for any length of time, Celtis plunged into organizing a sodality and nurturing acolytes. If the sodalities did not correspond perfectly to the points on his literary compass and varied in significance and duration, they still represented the legacy of a German writer and pedagogue whose dream was the emergence of a great German literary culture symbolized by a renowned literary society strategically located at each boundary of the German world. In this spirit, then, Celtis founded the Sodality of the Rhineland (Rhenana) at Heidelberg, the Danubiana at Vienna—these two became the most renowned—the Codonea, or Baltica, at Lübeck, and the Vistulana, whose full name in Latin was Sodalitas Litteraria Vistulana, at Cracow. Celtis's feelings about the sodalities come through clearly in the opening poem of his book of epigrams "Ad quattuor sodalitates litterarias Germaniae, ut sub tutela illarum libri sui evolent" (To the Four Literary Societies of Germany, That My Books May Soar under Their Patronage):

> Quattuor Almannis quicunque habitatis in oris,
>   Jure sodalitio qui mihi fertis opem,
> Seu vos Rhenus alat seu Vistula Danubiusve
>   Sive Codoneis ora lavatis aquis. . . .[8]

(You who inhabit the four shores of Germany, who bring your work to me by right of sodality, whether it be the Rhine, Vistula, or Danube that nourishes you, or shores washed by the waters of the Baltic, I entreat you, behold these little books of ours with calm mind and turn their pages often. It used to be that whenever we looked to German shores we, the learned throng, were amused by these books of ours. They were either jokes or serious only by virtue of their subjects, or something the profane crowd connected to Bacchus. Our written epigrams thus sing, comrades, and I ask that they fly protected by your name.)

Imbued thus with a humanist missionary zeal and a growing German national pride, Celtis struck out for what he regarded as the eastern German city of Cracow, or Croca as he sometimes called it in Latin. The elation that always filled him on the eve of a new journey was mitigated on this occasion, however, by a certain anxiety at the thought of coming among a population still made up predominantly of Sarmatians, whom he looked upon as primitive. If a stay in Germanic Cracow and its distinguished seat of learning was pleasant to contemplate, the surrounding Polish Slavic environment awoke contrary feelings. He recalled his mood at the time in the *Amores*, written after he left Poland: "Then eager to visit foreign lands, I, Celtis, with bad omens, head for eastern realms where the primitive Pole [crudus Sarmata] works the empty plains and inhabits poorly built huts and where the Vistula, which now marks the limit of the Germanic regions, spreads out its waters with its vast branches."[9]

The bad omens accompanying Celtis to Poland seemed to be fulfilled when he beheld Cracow for the first time. As he relates in the same first book of the *Amores* from which the quotation above was taken, hardly had he caught sight of the royal castle on the Wawel Hill and the city "rising proudly within its walls" when a terrible storm arose, obscuring everything. To Celtis, uneasy about the trip from the start, the storm seemed divine punishment for "abandoning" his native country. His description of it—dramatic and hyperbolic—infuses the event with portent and illustrates Celtis's poetic style at its best. I shall quote the first few lines in Latin and add the rest of the passage in translation:

> Vix mihi visa vagum mox cingunt nubila solem
>   Flabraque de variis confremuere plagis:
> Eurus Achaemeniis vertisset flatibus orbem,
>   Ni Caurus rapidis obvius isset equis;
> Frigidus hinc Boreas madidis Notus hinc ruit alis
>   Et gravis effusis decidit imber aquis,
> Murmure quin etiam concussus inhorruit aether,
>   Ruperat ut scissum Iuppiter igne polum. . . . (11:19–36)

(I barely saw it. Soon clouds encircled the moving sun and winds bellowed out of different quarters. The east wind would have overturned the world with gusts from Persia had not the west wind raced to meet him on swift steeds. On this side the cold north wind, on that side the south wind rushes with drenched wings, and the rain falls in a heavy downpour. And even the sky trembled, struck with a roaring when Jove burst the heavens rent with a flame. Soon the complaining birds in the gloomy fields grew silent, while the woods and groves echo with their groaning. But the fatal raven with his ill-omened voice flies about and with his cries prophesies all dreadful things that will happen and now beats my temples with his fluttering wings, tearing my cheeks, which I try to protect from his savage claw. The horse, thrice stunned, reared his saddled back, stamped his hoof on the ground three and four times over, and hurling my limp body over his sleek shoulders, made off in swift flight away from the city.)

Celtis then besought God to understand that he was driven to leave his country and seek out other lands to win glory, renown, and honor— both personal and national—and that if he was now being punished for desertion he asked that his torment be brief. Regaining his composure, he next considered that perhaps he had misread the signs and that the storm might be a favorable omen, that the trip to Cracow would be lucky for him. These thoughts were barely entertained, however, when he was struck senseless by a bolt of lightning. When he was restored to health by the intervention, he says, of Phoebus (the "pater vatum," father of poets), he finally understood that the god wanted him to live so that he might yet sing the four frontiers of his country ("ut patriae fines quattuor ipse canas"), thereby fulfilling his destiny as a German bard. The "sacredness" of his calling rightly merits, in his view, the vigilance of deities. And so it was that Conrad Celtis at last entered Cracow, shaken but inspired.

His activities for the two years he spent in Teutonic Croca, in the land of the Sarmatian heathen, combined the typical pursuits of the touring humanist and the humanistic tourist. Once he discovered he could move about safely, he spent much of his first year in travel, visiting Gdańsk and the Baltic region, exploring the Carpathians, participating in a hunt for the famous Polish bison with which that great lover of hunting, Pope Leo X, was to be so captivated, and visiting the equally famous salt mines of Wieliczka, which he compared to an excursion through Tartarus. All these new sights and adventures found expression in his poetry, above all in the *Amores*, where his brief but realistic description of the bison antedates by some thirty years (and conceivably might have influenced) the Polish Latin poet Nicolaus Hussovianus's *De statura, feritate ac venatione bisontis carmen* (Poem about the Size, Strength, and Hunting of the Bison):[10]

> The rugged earth nourishes shaggy-haired bison and powerful wild oxen, monstrous animals truly worthy of amazement. The huge bison dazzles with its eyes and hooked horns and has a face covered over with black hair. Its hanging dewlaps, which it carries in long fleece, are glands that cause its thick throat to swell out. When an enemy approaches it rushes to meet him with its high horns and tosses limp bodies into the open air. It brandishes the trunks of trees and aged oaks as it tosses its head about wide fields. When a hunter attempts to fell it with a thick mass of spears, he tricks the beast with a clever maneuver: first he provokes it with javelins or drawn bow, thereby infuriating the animal in its wounded muscles. This done, the hunter swiftly takes flight, protecting himself behind an oak tree from the bison's horns aimed at him. Thinking that it has caught the fleeing enemy with its horns, the beast rages, all the while wearing itself out as it races around in a circle attacking the great oak trees. Protected by a tree trunk, the hunter often challenges the beast and pierces its loathsome hide with cruel arrows. Its body thus totally exhausted, the animal loses its energy, while the hunter himself is now exhausted from the savage fight. Soon others standing around in a cordon finish off the great hulk with their spears.[11]

At the university in Cracow, Celtis lost little time seeking out such luminaries as the astronomer Blar and the Italian humanist and expatriate Filippo Buonaccorsi. Dedicated to establishing literary sodalities, possibly on the model of Pomponio Leto's Accademia Romana, Celtis set about creating one in Cracow, with the support and collaboration of Blar and Buonaccorsi. These three humanists formed the nucleus of the Sodalitas Litteraria Vistulana, which soon attracted other friends Celtis had already made in Cracow, both at the university and in town and court. Most prominent were such Cracovian humanists as

Laurentius Corvinus, Jan Ursinus, Statilius Simonides, and Aesticampianus the Elder.

Because of his own reputation as a humanist, Celtis had no trouble teaching and tutoring *extra muros*, chiefly within the student residences, or *bursae*, reserved for foreigners: the "bursa Germanorum" and the "bursa Hungarorum." One formal lecture of which a record exists—perhaps his only one in Cracow—was delivered on July 23, 1489, on the subject of epistolary art, in which Celtis had a considerable interest and on which he published a treatise in Ingolstadt in 1492 titled *De condendis epistolis* (On the Composition of Letters).

Certainly an auditor at university lectures, Celtis officially registered at Cracow only in 1489 during the rectorship of Maciej z Kobylinki (Matthew of Kobylinka).[12] But you will not find the name Celtis on the university rolls. His original name was the quite ordinary craft-related Pickel, meaning "pickaxe" or "stonecutter's chisel," which he had long ago dropped in favor of Celtis or Celtes to imply a more romantic Celtic or Greek origin. Since a latinized name was also de rigueur among the humanists, Celtis translated Pickel into Protucius and so registered at the University of Cracow under the name Conradus Celtis Protucius Johannis de Herbipoli (son of Johannes of Wipfeld).

During his residence in Cracow, Celtis's energies found two main outlets. First, he provided an undeniable impetus to the development of a Renaissance humanist literary tradition in Poland; second, he found in Poland the inspiration for his greatest poetry.

In the literary and intellectual sphere, Celtis's principal contribution was establishing the Literary Society of the Vistula, the first humanist society in Poland in any formal sense. Although it lacked staying power once Celtis left Poland, while he was in Cracow there is every indication that it was successful and had the support not only of the university and town elite but also of members of the royal court and the local nobility. Generally meeting in private residences, the *sodales* came together to discuss literature and humanist learning, to read from their own works, to enjoy urbane conviviality enlivened by good food and drink (for the latter especially, Celtis had a definite propensity) and, in all likelihood, the company of women. Celtis found almost any event an occasion for writing poetry, so it comes as no surprise that several of his odes and epigrams are devoted to members of the Literary Society of the Vistula. In "Ad Georgium Morinum in laudes eloquentiae" (To Georgius Morinus in Praise of Eloquence, *Odarum liber I*, 20) Celtis hails the Cracow town councilman (*rajca*, in Polish) Jerzy Morsztyn as a man of sound mind and civic responsibility, prais-

ing him in particular for his sumptuous dinners and the learned
company encountered at them:

> Saepius lautis epulis honorans
> Convocas doctam, generose, turbam
> Instruens largis tua liberalis
> Munera mensis.[13]

(In frequently honoring people with lavish feasts, you magnanimously
assemble a learned throng, augmenting your duties with bounteous
meals.)

Elegant and witty, Morsztyn enjoyed entertaining his guests by recalling the deeds of the ancients and surveying the warfare of the
Greeks and Romans:

> Comis et doctis salibus facetus
> Gesta priscorum memoras virorum
> Militis Grai et Latii Quiritis
> Arma recensens. (17–20)

(With amiable and learned charm, you wittily recall the deeds of ancient
warriors, reviewing the campaigns of Greeks and Romans.)

In "De cena Miricae" (A Dinner Party at Mirica's, *Odarum liber 1*,
21), addressed to the Cracow town scribe (*notarius*) Jan Heydecke, who
was an enthusiastic humanist and affected the latinized name Mirica,
Celtis recalls how the wine served abundantly at Polish social gatherings (and his fondness for it) made his assimilation of "Sarmatian
customs" no easy task:

> Cum tua Pannonio fuerat, Mirica, Lyaeo
>   Cena parata mihi
> Tractaque Parrhasiae languent ubi plaustra puellae
>   Raraque stella micat,
> Miraris, pedibus surgam male fultus et uncto
>   Lentus eam capite.
> Civibus et cunctis narratur ineptia nostra
>   Iam male nota mihi.
> Sarmaticos volui potando discere mores,
>   Sed mea fata negant. . . .(25)

(After I was treated to Hungarian wine at your dinner party, Mirica, and the drawn wagons of Callisto [that is, the Big Dipper] grow weary and a rare star shines, you wonder that supported badly by my feet and sluggish I take my leave with head well oiled. My foolishness is gossiped about by all and has become to me a bad sign of recognition. In drinking, I wanted to come to know Sarmatian ways, but my fates decreed otherwise. But do invite me back again, paying no heed to yesterday's goblets of wine and the too few clever words that, sober, I may overwhelm your dinner-party guests by regaling them with Socratic turns of phrase. But on the other hand, once Phoebus has completed his orbit in the sky, he cannot be turned back again. If, therefore, your gates are open to such false shame, I shall always shun them.)

A few of the odes are more in the nature of testimonials to prominent members of the Cracow university community who became both personal friends and supporters of Celtis's literary sodality. "Ad Ursum medicum et astronomum de situ Cracoviae" (To Ursus, Doctor and Astronomer, on the Situation of Cracow, *Odarum liber I*, 8) is dedicated to Jan Ursinus (Ber), a humanist physician also interested in astronomy who in 1488 delivered a lecture at the university on the worthiness of the medical profession.[14] In lavishing praise on Ursinus, Celtis was in fact acknowledging the growing importance of the role of Cracow physicians in advancing humanism. Besides practicing medicine, Ursinus also lectured on the Roman historian Sallust.[15] The ode "Ad Statilium Simonidem medicum et philosophum" (To the Physician and Philosopher Statilius Simonides, *Odarum liber I*, 23) was conceived in the same spirit. Celtis praises the medical skill of the Cracow physician, astronomer, and mathematician Stanisław Selig (Statilius Simonides), who also had established his credentials as a humanist by lecturing on Roman authors at the university from 1488 to 1492. It was especially for the latter accomplishment as well as for the many pleasant hours spent in his company that Celtis hails Statilius as his "doctus sodalis" (learned companion). In "Ad Albertum Brutum astronomum" (To Albertus Brutus, Astronomer, *Odarum liber I*, 17) Celtis pays homage to the distinguished Cracow astronomer Albert Blar, who is praised not only for his astronomical knowledge, but also for his prowess in astrology, a strong personal interest of Celtis's reflected in a number of his works: "You know, father, the secret signs of the oblique heaven that change the shapes of things and by their gifts preside over births in the elevated constellation: Aries and Taurus and Gemini, Cancer and Leo, Virgo, Libra and Scorpio, Sagittarius and Capricorn, and the Fishes [Pisces] born in the flowing river. Everything in the heavenly order is known to you."[16]

Of the several odes dedicated to members of his Cracow circle, the most interesting in terms of what Celtis hoped to achieve with his first literary sodality is "Ad Sigismundum Fusilium Vratislaviensem de his, quae futurus philosophus scire debeat" (To Sigismund Fusilius of Breslau on What the Philosopher of the Future Ought to Know, *Odarum liber I,* 11). Fusilius, whose real name was Gossinger, received his bachelor's degree from Cracow in 1486 and his master's in 1489. During the time Celtis was in Poland, Fusilius gave lectures at the university on Vergil's *Georgics,* one of the most important influences on Celtis's own literary development. Fusilius became a member of the Literary Society of the Vistula, and Celtis's ode to him assumes the character of a humanist guide to life and learning, encapsulating those properties of mind and attitude that Celtis regarded as fundamental to the humanist ideal and clearly intended his sodalities to propagate. The ode is not very long and can be quoted in full in translation:

Fusilius, I have known you for two years now. You were among my most sincere friends in the time of my travels in the cold land of the Sarmatians close to the icy sky where the North Pole, carrying with it the radiant wreath of Ariadne, sleeps between the two Bears [the Great and Little Bear, or double constellation], all the while revolving in its slow orbit. Your birth star endowed you with admirable qualities of character and real assurance of a lofty mind.

From the first you, as a person of taste, detested laziness and repulsed crude forms of speech, barbarous expressions, and the ancestral growling of an uncouth language.

Now, in your desire to learn the Roman tongue, you acquire a fine distinction, for you strive after that of which learned men approve whose hearts burn with a noble passion.

Spurn the ravings of the lying throng, flee the ignorant masses, and, happy, you will then come to know the truth revealed to few.

Let the great Molossian hound be an example to you. When puppies annoy him with their loud yapping, he ignores the noise of his inferiors and quietly goes his own way.

Proceed then; learn the three languages that will bring you much honor, along with Hebrew and Latin the writings of the renowned Athenians.

Contemplate the nature of confused chaos, where the elements pour forth in beautiful forms but with discordant goals, agitating the seeds of the world that will eventually return whence they came.

Find out with soaring mind the causes of individual things; give thought to the blowing of the winds and the tides of the raging seas.

Learn why earthquakes cause cities to collapse and mountains to tremble, and why the domain of fire is troubled by floods of water.

Find out why dark hollows of the earth produce sulfur and disgorge precious metals, and why hot springs restore the bodies of the ill.

Discover why lightning crackles with such a loud roar in the clouds, and study the wrath of rainstorms, slow-falling snow, and icy hail.

Know the various planets as they move in different orbits and Apollo's distress when his chariot has been put to flight by the pale-faced moon.

Wonder at the stars that escape from the vaulted sky, and at the twin couch of the sun; think, too, of peoples hidden away on another world.

Learn to tell the nations scattered over the globe, and their languages and customs, and in what climate they occupy this earth suspended in the air.

Read the deeds of bygone men, celebrated on the Tarpeian Hill, and what Greece achieved through the famous triumphs of the Macedonians.

Hold in contempt the favors of unstable fortune, learn to bear adversity, and all your days will pass quickly in happiness.

Ascend nobly the straight and narrow path of virtue; it alone gives you the untroubled life to lead.

Only virtue confers happiness, for it alone can promise quiet rewards in the celestial home and dispel the fear of the hideous shades of the Stygian prison.[17]

Whatever the active support given the Literary Society of the Vistula and the good times its members enjoyed, Celtis remained its driving force. With his abrupt departure from Cracow in 1491 it lost its momentum and soon fell into desuetude despite a noble effort by the ablest of the German humanist's Cracovian "disciples," the Silesian Laurentius Corvinus. Apart from his own contributions to the development of humanism in Poland as a writer and teacher, Corvinus may be remembered for his verse encomium appended as a preface to Copernicus's first published work, a Latin translation of a collection of exemplary letters in Greek by the seventh-century Byzantine writer Theophylactos Simocattes. The importance Corvinus attached to Celtis's mentorship can be judged from the letter Corvinus wrote on March 31, 1500, from Wrocław, where he had become the town writer. Praising Celtis for his teaching, above all, Corvinus expresses regret that when the opportunity existed he did not drink more deeply of the fountain of learning: "Time and again, most illustrious teacher, as I ponder the drinking of those nectars of your instruction that you abundantly poured into my dry throat beneath the Sarmatian sky, I cannot help but groan loudly that I did not quaff more of the precious liquid from your most copious fount of letters."[18]

By far the richest fruit of Celtis's two-year stay in Poland was his major poetic work, *Quattuor libri amorum* (Four Books of Love, 1502).

Although it was composed after he had left Poland and it deals only in part with his stay, it was clearly inspired by that country.

Much of Celtis's time in Poland was spent, as we have seen, visiting different parts of the country, attending lectures at the University of Cracow, making friends both in the academic community and among the town elite, and organizing and directing the first of his literary societies, the Literary Society of the Vistula. As busy as he undoubtedly must have been, Celtis still found time for a torrid love affair with the young wife—whom we know only as Hasilina— of an older aristocrat.

The effect of the romance of Celtis's life and art was considerable, for it was with Hasilina that the poet appears to have first discovered passion. It was out of this love that the idea for the *Amores* grew, and it was to Hasilina that the entire first book of the work, sections of the second, and a number of his elegies, epodes, and epigrams were devoted. If Hasilina was followed in time by Elsula of Regensburg, Ursula of Mainz, and Barbara of Lübeck—to whom the second, third, and fourth books of the *Amores* are dedicated—she remained not only Celtis's strongest female attachment, but the most vivid and real of any of the women who appear in his writings.

Although we have no way of knowing when and in what circumstances Celtis met Hasilina, his poetic account of his travel to Poland suggests that their first encounter occurred not long after he reached Cracow and that its impact on him was immediate and powerful. In the poem "Ad Hasilinam de aborta tempestate, dum Cracoviam Sarmatiae peteret, et signo veris" (To Hasilina of the Storm That Arose While He Was on His Way to Cracow in Poland and of a Sign of Spring), which appears in the first book of his *Amores*, he recalls: "With much on my mind, I set out anxiously for the city [Cracow], soon captured, Hasilina, by your eyes. My heart lies enveloped by gloom and my mind thus unseeing does not exercise its strength. And when it is not thinking of you, embraced by all my heart, the image of your beauty always stands before my eyes" (12:75–80).

The ode "Ad Hasilinam erotice et hodoeporice" (A Love Poem to Hasilina, *Odarum liber I*, 14) leaves no doubt that at least from Celtis's point of view the romance with Hasilina was the most memorable experience of his stay in Cracow:

Called back one day from the city of Romulus I soon climb the cloud-capped Apennine Mountains, from where I left the Rhine as now I leave behind the Po.

From here, by arched skiff, I approach the wide gulf of the Adriatic where the city of the Istrians [Trieste] raises up its famous towers across the Venetian waters.

Then I am swiftly borne from the plains of the Adige across the Alps, again reaching the damp Rhine fallen like an icy fountain.

Next I come to the head of the great Istria where the vast forest of the Bacenis stretches out in wooded pastures, twisting its way among remote hills like a huge tree.

Alone I make my way with rapid steps toward unknown lands where the golden yellow Elbe and the Silesus thrust back sluggish courses by means of a swirling eddy.

I then pursue a direct course to the Vistula, where the land of the Sarmatians opens wide plains and where the high roofs of royal Cracow surge upward.

Here Hasilina, glowing with her flames, begins to ensnare an ardent spirit with alluring games, thereby relieving a body oppressed by fatigue.

Oh thrice and more was I happy that by means of such a love I could cause the fates to stop and the time of an uncertain life that will never return to pass imperceptibly.

Not possessed of the might of great Jove and the gods, I could not change my stars, and even less so confronted by the radiance of a comely face and a beautiful body.

A brilliant flash of lightning glitters from her divine mouth; her face glows, suffused with ruddiness; her eyes flash like two burning constellations. . . .

Possessed by a better life my spirit takes flight on joined lips, suspended prostrate in your mouth as if in blissful death. (17–18)

The passionate, erotic nature of the relationship between Celtis and his Cracovian paramour forms the subject of several of his poems, including the first book of the *Amores*. Typical—and perhaps the best known of these—is "De nocte et osculo Hasilinae, erotice" (On a Night Spent with Hasilina and Her Kisses, an Amatory Poem), which appears as the tenth "carmen" (song, poem) in his first book of odes. I shall quote the poem in full, in Latin and in translation, as the best way to demonstrate Celtis's characteristic combination of lofty humanistic imagery and an earthy realism that in some of his poems about women becomes quite graphic:

> Illa quam fueram beatus hora
> Inter basia et osculationes
> Contrectans teneras Hasae papillas
> Et me nunc gremio inferens venusto,
> Nunc stringens teneris suum lacertis
> Pectus languidolo gemens amore,

Quod me reciproco fovebat aestu
Cogens deinde suos meare in artus,
Dum nostros animos per ora mixtos
Cum vinclis adamantinis ligavit
Diva ex caeruleo creata ponto.
O nox perpetuis decora stellis,
Quae divum facies levas coruscas
Et fessis requiem refers salubrem!
Nunc stes Herculeo velut sub ortu
Aut qualis Suetiis soles sub oris,
Dum Phoebus pluvium revisit austrum,
—Nullam per spatium binestre lucem
Fundit perpetusas ferens tenebras—
Sic fervens satiabitur voluptas! (13–14)

(How happy I was in that hour, among kisses and nuzzlings, feeling Hasa's soft breasts, and now burying myself in her lovely lap, now squeezing her breast in my tender arms, groaning with languid love, for she was fondling me with reciprocal passion, forcing me thereupon to enter her body, while the goddess born of the blue sea tied together with adamantine chains our two souls merging at our mouths. O night adorned with constant stars, who lifts up the glittering faces of the gods and brings healthful rest to the tired. May you now stand still as at the birth of Hercules or as you are wont to do in Swedish regions when Apollo returns to visit the rainy south and for a period of two months brings forth no light, covering everything with constant darkness. Thus will my glowing ardor be satisfied.)

Celtis tended to be yet more explicit in his epigrams, as if the very brevity of the form sanctioned the elimination of most or all of the usual classical mythological apparatus to permit a concentration on basics. The following two examples are typical:

De pacto Hasilinae
Pacta mihi fuerat Hasilina in gaudia (lecti)
    Testaturque suos in mea vota deos.
At postquam sensit, noctem modico aere redemi,
    Praefixit longas femina docta moras,
Scilicet ut gravius miserum torqueret amantem
    Et daret effusa largior aera manus.
Interea quartum Phoebus separaverat ortum,
    Et tulit illa viros quatuor inguinibus.[19]

(On a Pact with Hasilina)
Hasilina made a pact with me about the pleasures of her bed and invoked

her gods to witness my vows. But afterward she determined to redeem the night with small change and, shrewd woman that she was, imposed long delays. You can well imagine how this might torture the wretched lover dreadfully and constrain him to offer more lavish reward. In the meantime, Apollo had sundered the fourth rising, and she [Hasilina] carried off four men by their privates.)

Ad Hasilinam

Non satis est, Hasilina, domi te vendere cunnum,
Dum tuus a tectis forte maritus abest,
Quadriiugis sed rapta volas per rustica tecta,
Ut capiant merces rura beata tuas. (10)

(To Hasilina)

You are not satisfied, Hasilina, to peddle your cunt at home while your husband happens to be away, but led away by a four-horse carriage beneath peasant roofs you also want the blissful countryside to enjoy your beneficence.)

That Hasilina bestowed her favors on men other than her husband and Celtis is obvious from more than one poem. In "De fide Hasilinae" (On Hasilina's Fidelity), for example, Celtis bemoans the fact that in bestowing her "golden kisses on insipid admirers" it is as likely she will add sincerity to the love she proffers him as that a "bent plowshare will plow up a fish" (erutus aut curvo piscis erit, 8).

The first book of the *Amores*, which is devoted mainly to the relationship with Hasilina, is as much a lament about the pain and sorrow of love as an expression of romantic joy. In the third elegy, "Ad Hasilinam de aborta temptestate . . . (To Hasilina, on the Storm That Arose While He Was on His Way to Cracow . . .), he describes the heat of the passion consuming him and his inability to alter his fatal course:

Behold, O cruel woman, the very marrow [of my bones] consumed, and see the bones themselves dissolved by your flames. Behold how my spirit nearly forsakes my weary limbs and proclaims you to be the cause of its death. See, Phoebus has traversed his oblique round one time, and his sister has brought her horns filled twelve times from the moment when you, hardhearted, took possession of my cares and roasted my gentle heart on a fire not easy to bear. Whether the earth sees the sun, or cloudy time drags on, whether the fatal sisters have spun threads for me such as will make me die beneath the yoke of love, or whether harmful lovesickness (a disease my stars just happened to give me) will always hold my heart in its grip, no rest or any limit is near. (12:87–100)

As the book progresses, Celtis excoriates his Polish paramour for mental cruelty, deception, fickleness, and ingratitude in harsher terms, as we see in the seventh elegy, "Ad Hasilinam perfidiam et inconstantiam sibi exprobrat ignemque tectum magis urere" (To Hasilina, in Which He Complains of Perfidy and Inconstancy and Speaks of His Secret Flame Burning Hotter):

> By voice, bearing, and gesture, as well as by the look on your face, you give me clear signals and feign both hope and fear. Alluring, you move me, but, shameless, you flee emotion, O woman like the apples of Tantalus. (16:9–12)

> Inconstant, woman bears a changeable heart: what she sought, she spurns; what she desired, she hates. (17–18)

> Now you reveal to me, as to a confidant, furtive loves, and you report how often this one or that one is with you. And you wish to make me yet a secret accomplice in these intrigues, so that I may suffer more—an adulterer possesses you and another, delighting in her who is mine, is warmed by love while he holds you, my life, in his desires. (23–28)

> Ingrate, tell me, why do you repay nothing and why, cruel one, do you deny me what you have given others? See, my eyes already discharge tears and water moist lips with abundant showers. Just as the sun burns in the spring season and the heat releases snowy waters, so are the Carpathian peaks melted by the torrid sun and the swift Vistula borne by swollen waters. In like manner your blazing fire, as it bears down, detaches the soul from the body, and alluring Amor caresses unfeeling breasts. But, merciless one, you provide my fires no companion, nor do my arrows penetrate your heart. (61–72)

By the time Celtis reached the thirteenth elegy, "Ad Hasilinam cum sacerdote deprensam" (To Hasilina Caught with a Priest), whatever restraints existed previously all but disappear in an outburst of indignation:

> Why at this moment are your eyes lowered and both your bright cheeks drained of their color? Why does your hair stand on end, and why do you not hurl impudent words with your usual garrulousness?
> A mind knowing your crime can hurt you like an unseen wound, and your intrigues torment you in various ways. Well known are the tortures of the Sicilian tyrant [Phalaris, a tyrant of Agrigentum who was known for his cruelty] and the punishments that frightful Rhadamantus [son of Jupiter, brother of Minos, and one of the three judges in the lower world]

has in his possession. Hasa, I have said that you will besmirch your name with guilt and notoriety will drown out your accomplishments, since so often you have dared to disrupt a legitimate wedding by exposing for sale an impudent thigh. Your guilt last night, when your husband had gone off to hostile fields, is written all over your disgusting face. And as for me, I suffered chills the whole night where a shaved man [a priest] was taking his pleasure. But we propose to pardon the secret immorality, inasmuch as your head is turned by holy men, Hasa, who can divert the gods from our crimes and restrain the lightning of ruddy Jove.(P.25)

Of course, much of the anguish Celtis suffered in his relationship with Hasilina was caused by her marital status. As if to justify his affair with her and, more obliquely, her relations with other men in general, Celtis depicts Hasilina's marriage as a vale of tears. In the epigram "De lacrymante Hasilina" (On Hasilina Weeping, 1, 89),[20] her husband is described as "cruel," a wife beater who subdues Hasilina by "dragging her around, bloodied, by the hair." Another epigram, "De smaragdi natura" (On the Nature of the Emerald, 1, 23),[21] brings together Celtis's serious interest in the occult and his loathing for Hasilina's marital status. Inferring an occult bond between the "power of precious stones" (gemmarum vires) and the "secret seeds of the heavens" (occultaque semina coeli), Celtis describes an incident, supposed to have occurred between Hasilina and her husband, that, in his view reveals such a link. His beloved, he states, wore on one finger a Scythian emerald of perfect color and shape. But when she gave herself to her "detested" husband, the precious stone burst in two. Celtis was also unable to resist the temptation to address a poem directly to Hasilina's husband. In the ode "Ad maritum Hasilinae insensatum" (To Hasilina's Husband Grown Old, *Odarum liber I*, 22) the emphasis is no longer on his cruelty but on his decrepitude. He is "blind with his eyes open" and reminds Celtis of "Oedipus, who once, supporting himself with trembling staff, followed his daughter Antigone to prayers." He is also "deaf in both ears" and in fact is "growing old in all his senses." In the poem's parting shot, which spares Hasilina little as well, Celtis berates the husband as a "haughty parent stiffly disdaining the heavenly powers before a noisy brood while your wife sets aflame as many rivals as Vervex yielded lovely violets, as the sky sent down the gnats of Leo, as Libra brought forth opulent fruit, and as Capricorn again stripped bare cold branches."[22]

Celtis's poetry sheds light on other aspects of his Polish romance as well. That Hasilina's marriage was childless, for example, seems clear from the epigram "Ad eundem" (To the Same, 1, 31); "Hasa begs the gods to let her bear a happy offspring, but tell me, by what man can she be made pregnant? She says that her unloved husband is always in a rush and her other gigolos sterile in love."[23]

The question naturally arises at some point what language Celtis and Hasilina used. Celtis, of course, knew no Polish when he came to Cracow, and it seems unlikely that she knew Latin, at least well enough to speak it. The answer is provided by the fourth elegy of the *Amores*, dedicated to "Bernardus Viliscus Roxolanus," whom we know to have been Wilczek z Boczowa (of Boczów), a notary of the king, dean of the cathedral of Przemyśl, and eventually archbishop of Lwów.[24] A member of Celtis's Cracow circle, he often acted as the German poet's interpreter with Hasilina until the lovers found some way to communicate without an intermediary. Bernardus Viliscus's role in the romance is described this way in the elegy:

> Candidus interpres Hasilinae saepe fuisti,
>   Germanam linguam sprevit ut illa meam;
> Tunc ego condidici te praeceptore puellae
>   Sarmaticae linguae barbara verba loqui;
> Sed magis illa rudem potuit mihi flectere linguam,
>   Iunxerat ut labris basia blanda meis
> Ludebantque simul lascivo murmure fauces
> Et mea pugnabant oribus ora suis.[25]

(You were often a sincere interpreter of Hasilina, since she scorned my German tongue. Then, with you as my teacher, I learned to speak the barbarous words of the girl's Sarmatian language. But she was better able to bend the crude language to me as she joined tempting kisses to my lips, at the same time as her throat teased me with impudent murmuring and my mouth did battle with her ears.)

The intensity of Celtis's Polish romance notwithstanding, the affair was fated to end unhappily. The German humanist apparently pursued the object of his affections for the better part of a year but was ultimately rejected when Hasilina refused to leave her husband. That this was at least one of the main reasons for his sudden departure from Cracow in the spring or early summer of 1491 seems highly likely. Celtis went in such haste, moreover, that he left books and papers behind.

Although clearly stung by the outcome of his torrid affair with Hasilina, Celtis had other reasons for feeling frustrated and anxious to move on. His ambition for a university chair, which he desperately wanted and which had so far eluded him, also failed to be realized in

Cracow. His disappointment was more bitter in view of the contacts he had made in the city and at the university, which he had counted on for support. Then there was the matter of the Literary Society of the Vistula, which for all the participants' enthusiasm and Celtis's guidance remained too elitist and never became the type of humanist circle Celtis had in mind.

Celtis's career after leaving Poland is of less concern to us here. But let us briefly consider his subsequent activities before turning to later echoes of his Polish romance. From Cracow he made his way to Wrocław, and from there to Bohemia and Moravia before finally coming to rest in Nuremberg, the city of his first triumph. The foul mood in which he left Poland apparently stayed with him the rest of the trip. If Wrocław made no memorable impression on him, he positively disliked the Czech lands and the Czechs themselves and vented his feelings in a number of malicious epigrams. Celtis found almost no aspect of Czech life redeeming, but he took particular delight in mocking Jan Hus and the entire Hussite movement. Unfortunately, several of the epigrams became known while Celtis was still in Bohemia and caused such outrage that he had to quit the country in haste.

Celtis was not long in Nuremberg before being invited to nearby Ingolstadt, where a new university had been founded in 1472 and a regular teaching position seemed in the offing. The appointment (for only one semester) finally materialized on May 5, 1492. Celtis began with lectures on Cicero's rhetoric, and his teaching proved so successful that he was renewed for another semester. The high point of his stay in Ingolstadt—where he managed to remain, with only a few interruptions, until 1497—was the famous public oration he delivered, probably in August 1492, in conjunction with his lectureship on oratory, the "Oratio in gymnasio in Ingelstadio publice recitata" (Public Oration Delivered in the University of Ingolstadt).[26]

A few days after delivering his oration, Celtis was on the road again, traveling to Regensburg and Nuremberg, where he remained in an atmosphere congenial to humanism until the end of 1493. The outgrowth of his stay in Nuremberg in particular was one of his greatest literary works, a prose description and encomium that he titled simply *Norimberga*. It was begun in 1493 but completed later and published only in 1502.

Celtis's dream of a regular academic position came true at last in early 1494 when he was recalled to Ingolstadt to take over the professorship of humanities vacated by the poet Johannes Riedner. But bigger and better things lay around the corner.

Once Celtis became aware of the great awakening of the arts and learning in Vienna following Maximilian's ascension to the throne of the Holy Roman Empire and of the new prominence accruing to the University of Vienna, he began taking steps to land a position there. His efforts paid off handsomely when in March 1497 he was offered the first full-time regular lectureship in poetry and rhetoric at the university. In a sense, Celtis had at last found a home. The few years of life left to him were among the most productive of his career. Besides his lectures on standard humanist fare, he actively promoted the study of Greek, becoming the first person to teach Homer at a German university; he founded the most illustrious of his humanist circles, the Sodalitas Litteraria Danubiana (Literary Society of the Danube); he issued his immensely influential edition of the Roman historian Tacitus's *Germania,* which was accompanied by his own poetic *Germania generalis* (dedicated to the emperor Maximilian I); he published his major poetic work, the *Quattuor libri amorum,* in 1503; and in 1501, with the emperor's blessing and support, he established a new Collegium Poetarum et Mathematicarum comprising two professors of poetry and oratory and two of mathematics and headed, of course, by Celtis himself, now holding the title *lector ordinarius* in poetry and oratory at the University of Vienna. Although the new college began to wither even before Celtis's own demise in 1508, the joyful occasion of its official inauguration on Celtis's forty-third birthday, February 1, 1502, marked the highest peak of his career since he was crowned *poeta laureatus* by the emperor Frederick III on April 18, 1487.

With academic as well as literary success now well within his grasp, Celtis must surely have relegated thoughts of Hasilina of Cracow to a corner of his mind. After all, he had been away from Poland for several years and had not had any contact with, or heard from, his former Polish paramour in all that time. But nearly a decade after the romance and with its ashes long cold, Celtis's memory of those steamy, stormy days in Cracow was jogged on three occasions. In 1498 and 1499 letters from two of his most devoted Cracow admirers, Aesticampianus the Elder (Jan Sommerfeld) and Laurentius Corvinus, informed him that Hasilina had become a widow and hence was available for marriage, if the *poeta laureatus* was still interested.[27] Alas, he was not. His other encounters with Eros in the intervening years had made the past irretrievable, except as art. And it was, perhaps ironically, because of that art that in 1500 Celtis heard from Hasilina in person, for the very last time. In a letter alternating anger and supplication, she expressed indignation over the circulation of Celtis's poems about her, which gossip from Vienna had brought to her attention, and pleaded with the poet to suppress them.[28] By way of a belated reply,

Celtis saw to the publication of the complete text of the *Amores* in Nuremberg in 1502. On February 4, 1508, in the midst of undiminished pedagogical and literary activity that included, among other things, hymns to the Blessed Virgin, Celtis at last succumbed to the syphilis that for years had wracked his body.

CHAPTER 4

Period of Transition

The hasty departure of Conrad Celtis from Cracow in 1491 and the death of Callimachus in 1496 slowed the momentum of Polish humanism, creating a void of inspiration and leadership that was not easily filled. Members of the Literary Society of the Vistula who had been recruited by Celtis and Callimachus made an effort to keep the society alive, both out of conviction and as a tribute to its illustrious founders, but their absence was keenly felt.

Of the writers who were active in what may be regarded as a period of transition, the most important were Laurentius Corvinus (Raabe, d. 1527), a Silesian, who came to play a role in the early humanist literary activity of Copernicus; Paweł z Krosna (Paul of Krosno, family name Procler, ca. 1470–1517), a prolific if undistinguished poet who was more important as a pedagogue and most interesting for his connections with Hungary; and Jan z Wiślicy (John of Wiślica, ca. 1485–1520), a student of Paul of Krosno and the author of a lengthy poem on the battle of Grunwald of 1410 that ranks as the first work by a Polish Neo-Latin poet based on national history.

Laurentius Corvinus the Silesian

Although it is Corvinus's connections with Copernicus (about which more in the next chapter) that focus attention on him, his importance for fledgling Polish humanism cannot be defined wholly by his place in the history of the great scientist's first published work. Corvinus, son of a Silesian patrician family, and his good friend Zygmunt Gossinger, son of a town councillor of Wrocław, traveled together to enroll at the University of Cracow in 1484. They received their bachelor's degrees in 1486 and their master's degrees in 1489, and both thereafter lectured at the university in the capacity of "extraneus non de facultate," or professors without permanent chairs. Their specialty was Vergil, with Corvinus expounding the *Bucolics* and Gossinger the *Georgics.*

When Celtis established, with Callimachus, the Literary Society of the Vistula, Corvinus and Gossinger (who then assumed the Latin name Sigismundus Fusilius) were quick to become members. The association of Celtis and Gossinger became particularly close, so that when Celtis quit Cracow Gossinger went with him as far as Wrocław, which Celtis recalled in an ode to Gossinger titled "Quibus instituendi sint addescentes" (To Worthy Teachers). Gossinger's subsequent travels to Bologna and Rome, which Corvinus mentions in his poem "Ad Sigismundum Fusilium in Italiam pergentem" (To Sigismundus Fusilius on His Journey to Italy), removed him from the attempts to keep the small humanist circle in Cracow alive after the departure of Celtis and the death of Callimachus.

After his friend's departure, Corvinus remained in Cracow lecturing as before and working on his first publication, a cosmography titled *Cosmographia dans manuductionem in tabulas Ptholomei* (Cosmography, with a Guide to Ptolemy's System), published in Basel about 1496. The other high point of this period was his friendship with Copernicus, who studied in Cracow from 1491 to 1495.

Corvinus's departure from Cracow may have been only slightly less abrupt than that of Celtis and Gossinger, but it was not marked by any bad feelings; much the contrary. Back in his native Silesia, where he became rector of the parochial school in Świdnica, Corvinus reflected warmly on his Cracow experiences and acquaintances and in this spirit dedicated his second published work *Carminum structura* (The Composition of Poems, 1496?), an outline of Latin versification, to the students of the University of Cracow ("augustissimi gimnasii Cracoviensis studentibus"). Further evidence of Corvinus's affection for Cracow, and Poland generally, was his "Hortulus Elegantiarum Magistri Laurentii Corvini Novoforensis partim ex Marci Tullii Ciceronis surculis, partim ex su germine consitus. In cuius fine describitur Cracoviae Poloniae Metropolis carmine saphico" (Little Garden of Delicacies of Master Laurentius Corvinus of Wrocław, Sprung up in Part from Marcus Tullius Cicero and in Part Sown from the Author's Own Seed. Its Borders Contain a Description of Cracow, the Metropolis of Poland, in Sapphic Meter). Preceded by the distich "Has tibi, Sarmati-

cum doctissima Croca, sub axem / Corvinus leto mittit ab orbe notas"
(To You, Most Learned Cracow of the Sarmatians, beneath the Vault
of Heaven, Corvinus Sends These Words from the Land of Abundance"), the "Little Garden" was published by the Cracow printing
office of Haller in 1502.

Corvinus eventually left Świdnica for Wrocław to become rector of
the parochial school of Saint Elizabeth's Church. How meaningful his
Cracow experiences still were to him is evident in his efforts to maintain
a correspondence with Celtis[1] and to win a larger following for humanism by staging classical Roman plays. In 1500 and 1502, for example,
Corvinus arranged for the presentation of Plautus's *Eunuchus* and
Aulularia in the Wrocław town hall, just as Celtis had staged classical
drama in German academic circles and prepared an edition of two
tragedies of Seneca.

From Wrocław Corvinus was transferred in 1503 to Toruń in north-
central Poland. He remained there about two years, during which he
honored the memory of his old friend Gossinger, who died in 1504,
with a short epitaph. From Toruń Corvinus returned to Wrocław,
where he eventually went over to the Reformation and became extremely active in the Protestant cause. Throughout his career, Corvinus maintained close contacts with Cracow and Polish humanism.
Much of his occasional poetry deals with events in Poland, and in 1518
he was part of a Silesian delegation to the nuptials in Cracow of King
Sigismund I and Queen Bona. Along with such promising humanist
poets of the younger generation as Jan Dantyszek (Dantiscus) and
Andrzej Krzycki (Cricius), Corvinus participated in a poetic "tourna-
ment" celebrating the festivities.

Corvinus, like his fellow Silesian Aesticampianus the Younger (Jan
Sommerfeld, Jr.), was not in Cracow long enough after the passing of
Celtis and Callimachus to have more than a marginal role in the
effort to continue the Literary Society of the Vistula and maintain the
momentum of literary humanism in Cracow, despite his spiritual ties
with the university and royal city and his writings about Poland and
Poles.

Paul of Krosno and the Hungarian Connection

The immediate continuation of the work of Celtis and Callimachus
in Poland fell mainly to a poet of lesser talent, Paul of Krosno (in Latin,
Paulus Crosnensis). Son of the mayor of the sub-Carpathian town of
Krosno, Paul came to Cracow about 1500 to pursue his studies after

an academic tour in Greiffenberg in Royal Prussia. He received his master's degree in 1506 and spent the academic year 1507–1508 lecturing on classical literature at the University of Cracow and trying to establish a literary as well as scholarly career. By all accounts he was a conscientious and popular teacher. In print, scholarship preceded poetry; in 1508 the Cracow printer Haller brought out his edition of the satires of Persius. The appearance of plague in Cracow that same year interrupted his career and sent Paul fleeing for refuge to Hungary, thereby beginning one of the more interesting episodes in the history of Polish humanism.

Paul's choice of Hungary as a haven was no whim. Besides safety from plague, he could count on a good reception among the Magyars, thanks to one of his Cracow University students, the Hungarian Sebastyén Magyi (Sebastianus Maghyus, or Magius, d. after 1522). The Pole's relations with Magyi were close, and when the Hungarian returned to his native land in February 1508 Paul wrote a "propempticon," or farewell verse, on the occasion.[2] Largely through the good offices of Sebastyén Magyi's father Pál (Paulus), Paul was introduced to one of the most powerful Hungarian nobles of the period, Gábor Perényi (d. 1526), who became a most hospitable and generous patron while the Polish humanist was among the Magyars. Paul also enjoyed the hospitality of the important Thurzó family and, as befitting a humanist poet, sought to repay their patronage with poems. These panegyrics, especially those to Perényi and the Thurzós, make up a significant part of his poetic canon.

Paul of Krosno's first published poetry, and his only major collection, appeared in Vienna in 1509. The volume contains panegyrics to his Hungarian patrons and some religious and other poetry, written before he went to Hungary. The longest poem in the collection, in a sense its centerpiece, is a 1,114-line panegyric in praise (appropriately) of Ladislaus, king of Hungary, and Stanislaus, patron saint of Poland; the work bears the title "Panegyrici ad divum Ladislaum Pannoniae regem victoriosissimum et sanctum Stanislaum praesulem ac martyrem Poloniae gloriosissimum . . ." (Panegyrics to the Divine Ladislaus, Most Victorious King of Hungary, and to Saint Stanislaus, Most Glorious Bishop and Martyr of Poland).

The prose dedication to Paul's principal Hungarian patron is less interesting for its familiar encomiums than for the few details it affords of Paul's personal life, such as that plague was definitely the reason he left Cracow for Hungary ("Quapropter exinde, ut e gymnasio nostro Cracoviensi pestilentiali saevitia pulsus in Pannonios quaerendae salutis gratia fines me contulissem . . .," Therefore, driven by the plague then ravaging Cracow, I betook myself from my classroom to the Hungarian lands for safety's sake).[3] The panegyric poetry addressed directly to Perényi includes "Epigrammata in insignia magnifici domini Gabrielis de Peren" (Epigrams on the Coats-of-Arms of the Great Lord Gabriel Perényi), "Ad magnificum Gabrielem Pereneum salutatorium" (Greeting to the Noble Gabriel Perényi), "Eucharisticon ad Gabrielem Perenaeum" (Thanksgiving to Gabriel Perényi), "Eucharisticon ad eundem" (Thanksgiving to the Same), "Ad Gabrielem Perenaeum" (To Gabriel Perényi), and "Ode ad magnificum dominum Gabrielem Perenaeum pro novo anno" (Ode to the Great Lord Gabriel Perényi for the New Year).[4] Also dedicated to Perényi are religious poems on Saint Barbara ("Elegiacon ad sanctam Barbaram virginem victoriosissimam extemporaliter lusum apud magnificum dominum Gabrielem Perenaeum . . .," Elegy to Saint Barbara, Most Victorious Maiden, Composed Extemporaneously at the House of the Great Lord Gabriel Perényi) and on the birth of Christ ("In natalem Christianum sub horis matutinis apud magnificum dominum Gabrielem Perenaeum lusum . . .," On the Birth of Christ, Composed in the Early Hours of the Morning at the House of the Great Lord Gabriel Perényi), as well as the poems "Ad Thaliam" (To Thalia [a Muse of comedy or light verse]) and "Ode Pauli Crosnensis Rutheni ad Apollinem" (Ode of Paul of Krosno the Ruthenian to Apollo), the latter generally regarded as the poet's best work.

Other prominent Hungarians he similarly honored in verse include István (Stephen) Báthory ("Elegiacon ad magnificum et generosum dominum Stephanum Bathoriensem," Elegy to the Great and Magnanimous Lord Stephen Báthory), who later became king of Poland; his former Cracow student Sebastyén Magyi ("Propempticon ad Sebastianum Maghyum Pannonium," Farewell to the Hungarian Sebastyén Magyi) and "Ad eundem" (To the Same); and Stanislaus Thurzó, who had also studied in Cracow and in 1488 became bishop of Olomouc ("Ad Stanislaum Thurzo praepositum Varadiniensem," To Stanislaus Thurzó, bishop of Várad, and "In cenam Stanislai Thursii lautissimam ibidem lusum," On a Most Sumptuous Dinner of Stanislaus Thurzó, Composed on that Occasion).

When the danger of plague had subsided and Paul thought of returning to Cracow and resuming his academic career, he decided to fulfill a long-standing desire to visit Vienna on the way. The fame of the university there and the activity of its humanists attracted him; moreover, since the route back made Vienna an easy stop, there was every reason to take advantage of the opportunity.

His Hungarian friendships firm, above all with the Magyis and

Perényis, Paul at last took his leave on January 12, 1509. His departure itself served as the occasion for a poem to the most generous of his patrons, "Thanksgiving to Gabriel Perényi." Hailing Perényi as the "splendor and glory of the Hungarian nation" (136:2), the Pole poetically records the pain of leaving Hungary and everything he had known there in these words:

> Nam nunc, care tuis, Gabriel, subducor ocellis,
> Subducorque aula, care patrone, tua
> Et iam Pannonicas mens est mihi linquere terras
> Austriacasque mihi est ardor adire scholas. (137:27–30)

(Now, dear Gabriel, I am being led away from your eyes and from your court, dear patron, and already my mind is made up to leave the Pannonian [Hungarian] lands and proceed to Austrian learned circles).

Apart from his contacts with Austrian humanists, his attendance at lectures, and his participation in the cultural life of Vienna, Paul's stay was fruitful for his literary career. It was while he was in Vienna that he was able to arrange for the publication of his first book of poetry in 1509 at the printing office of Ioannes Winterburger, to whom Paul later dedicated a laudatory poem titled "In laudem Ioannis Winterburger, impressoris sollertissimi" (In Praise of Ioannes Winterburger, the Most Skillful of Printers).

This Vienna volume of Paul of Krosno's poetry contains most of his more significant work—religious and other poems written before his departure from Cracow and the fruit of his Hungarian sojourn—and provides ample material for assessing his place in the history of the Polish Latin literary tradition.

As a humanist, above all as a teacher of the classics in Cracow at a critical point when Celtis and Callimachus were no longer there, when the forces of Scholasticism had again become emboldened, and when the Literary Society of the Vistula had lost its drive and was fragmenting, Paul of Krosno's contribution was undeniably important. By his enthusiastic propagation of humanism, his encouragement of students, and the personal popularity that attracted people to him, he was able to rekindle the fires of the movement and train dedicated pupils who surpassed their master in talent, particularly such writers as John of Wiślica and Dantiscus.

As a poet, however, Paul of Krosno is among the least engaging of the Polish humanists, except for the poetry of his Hungarian period, which commands attention not primarily for its aesthetic qualities but because it represents an impressive range of Polish-Hungarian cultural relations during the Renaissance.

While acknowledging Paul's mastery of classical meters—he uses a wide variety in his poetry—and his rather good knowledge of classical authors, from whom he borrows extensively, giving a kind of bookishness to much of his verse, Polish scholarship on the Renaissance rightly faults the poet for a formal correctness largely devoid of the individuality so characteristic of the best humanist Neo-Latin poetry, such as Celtis's. With a very few exceptions, the variety of subjects, realism, personal quality, and pungency typical of the best Polish humanist poets—Dantiscus, Hussovianus, Krzycki, Ianicius—are not to be met in Paul's poetry. His copious religious verse is devoted mainly to the Virgin Mary, Christ, and various saints (Anne, Barbara, Catherine, and others) and remains close to the medieval tradition in its abstract hagiographic character despite its adherence to common patterns of humanist verse composition.

Among the more successful poems included in the Vienna edition of 1509 are two devoted to his Hungarian patrons, the "Ode Pauli Crosnensis Rutheni ad Apollinem" (Ode to Apollo of Paul of Krosno the Ruthenian) and "In cenam Stanislai Thursii lautissimam ibidem lusum" (On a Most Sumptuous Dinner of Stanislaus Thurzó, Composed on that Occasion). In the first poem the poet, in a prose subtitle, requests that he be inspired poetically so he can worthily praise the great lord Gábor Perényi. After several stanzas devoted to praise of Phoebus, the poet urges the god to hasten:

> Huc, huc, cincte sacris tempora frondibus
> Ornate et cithara splenditer aurea.
>   Huc, huc, Phoebe, citatis
>   Festines, bone, passibus.
> Huc, huc, Phoebe, veni atque enthea spiritu
> Divino facies pectora, dulcibus
>   Nostrum ut rite patronum
>   Possim dicere versibus. (132:21–28)

(Hither, hither, crown my temples with sacred boughs. Provide me with a brilliant golden cithara. Hither, hither, Phoebus, hasten your steps, my dear fellow. Hither, come hither, Phoebus, and inspire my breast with the divine spirit, so that I may pay fitting homage to my patron in pleasing verses.)

The rest of the poem is a panegyric in honor of Paul's patron, Gábor Perényi, who like the poet himself worships at the altar of the Muses:

> Qui castas niveo pectore Musulas
> Laudat, concelebrat, suscipit et colit
> Et qui numen adorat,
> O Grynee sacer, tuum (29–32)

(He who praises, celebrates, supports and nourishes the pure Muses of snow-white breast, and who worships, divine Phoebus, your divinity.)

In a more earthly vein, Perényi is praised as:

> Qui cunctos proceres, qui quoque principes
> Praestat moribus et consiliis bonis. . . . (37–48)

(He who surpasses in virtues and wise thoughts all nobles and even rulers, those who are and those who are yet to be.

He who is a great pride of the Hungarian people, who is called the pillar of an unconquered army as well as the glory of his fatherland. He who is wise, judicious, bountiful, devoted, loyal, courteous, friendly, god-fearing, illustrious, venerable.)

In a familiar gesture, toward the end of the poem, Paul pleads with Phoebus to intercede with Perényi so that his patron will forgive him his common and rude style: "And beseech him on bended knee and persuade him with skillful words so that he may treat with forbearance my worthless boorishness" (57–59).

"On a Most Sumptuous Dinner of Stanislaus Thurzó" falls into the pattern of the poem recalling a typical humanist soiree of learned discourse conducted in a convivial atmosphere and enlivened by good eating and drinking. I quote the poem in full:

> Vana iam nectar sileat vetustas,
> Et dapes magni taceat Tonantis,
> Dulcis omittat Saliaris atque
>   luscula mensae;
> Mittat et quidquid malefida iactat
> Fama et arguti recinunt poetae,
> Nulla nam nostram superant profecto
>   Fercula cenam.
> Cena quae cunctis graphice referta est
> Gaudiis lautisque cibis repleta,
> Cuique adest curas hilarus repellans
>   Bacchus acerbas,
> Cuique adest laetus pariter virorum
> Ordo, qui comi recreare tristes

Famine et miro valet excitare
　　　　Scommate mentes.
Verum ego demens, quid ego misellus,
Vestra quid vecors remoror poeta
Gaudia, et nostris moror aestuosa
　　　　Pocula nugis?
Iste non vanas locus, iste nugas,
Ista non gerras petit hora ineptas,
Sed merum magno modo promptitandum est
　　　　Vase falernum.
Ergo iam grandem, venerande, scyphum,
Thurso, suscepta propereque tandem
Sicca, pergemus satiare grato
　　　　Labra Lyaeo. (Pp.148–49)

(Let boastful antiquity not discourse on the nectar, and let it hold its tongue concerning the banquets of mighty Jove, and let it pass over in silence the sweet dishes of the tables of the Salii.[5]

And let it discount whatever untrustworthy fame boasts of and artful poets praise in song, for surely no dishes surpass our feast, the feast that is so exquisitely full of all kinds of delights and sumptuous dishes, and at which merry Bacchus drives away grievous cares.

Present also is an equally cheerful circle of men who are able to banish sad thoughts with amiable converse and stimulate the mind with splendid humor.

But why do I, in truth but a poor and foolish poet, frenziedly hinder your amusements and stay your eager goblets with my jests?

This place does not demand these silly jokes nor the hour these awkward trifles. Here one just drains the cup of straight Falernian [wine] in grand measure.

And so, venerable Thurzó, here's a huge goblet! Let us proceed then quickly to quench lips dry from expectation with the pleasant drink of Lyaeus [Bacchus].)

As we can see from a few examples of Paul's better poetry, even when the occasion permitted a more personal note the poet's reticence negated all but the most meager details. His mastery of humanist verse form and his knowledge of antiquity and classical literature, impressive as they may be, are insufficient to make up for a poetry that lacks the color, individuality, and realism of so much of the Latin poetry written in Poland in the fifteenth and sixteenth centuries. There is a technical skill in Paul's verse, an undeniable control of form, but with it a kind of austere academic bookishness that is only rarely overcome. Nevertheless, whatever his failings as a poet, Paul of Krosno was able to make a major contribution to the cause of European humanist poetry within a few years of his return to Cracow.

After his sojourn in Vienna, Paul reached Cracow in late 1511 and by 1512 was back at the university lecturing on Ovid, Persius, Claudian, and Seneca. He took a particular interest in the greatest of Roman tragic dramatists and later (in 1513) published in Vienna an edition of two of Seneca's tragedies.[6] While in Cracow he revised several of his earlier poems and wrote a number of new ones comprising mostly religious poetry (principally an elegy to the Virgin Mary, "Elegiacum . . . ad divam virginem Mariam") and several works on Polish subjects. The latter include a poem in honor of Jan Lubrański, bishop of Płock in 1498 and Poznań in 1499 and founder of an elite academy named after him;[7] a poem dedicated to his pupil and follower as a Latin poet, John of Wiślica,[8] a poem celebrating King Sigismund's return (August 19, 1515) from the Congress of Vienna, where a Jagiellonian-Hapsburg treaty was negotiated, and dedicated to the chancellor of the Polish Crown, Krzysztof Szydłowiecki;[9] and above all, a lengthy epithalamium commemorating the wedding in 1512 of Sigismund I and the Hungarian noblewoman Barbara Zápolya.[10]

The Polish-Hungarian rapprochement symbolized by the union of King Sigismund and Barbara Zápolya would obviously have had great appeal for Paul of Krosno because of his own ties with Hungary. But his poetic talent was unable to rise to the occasion even then. For all his good intentions, he could deliver himself only of 356 lines of fairly lifeless panegyrics heavily laden with classical borrowings, mostly from Ovid and Vergil. Celebration of love and marriage is followed by praise first of King Sigismund and then of Barbara Zápolya, with a chorus of maidens to Juno and one of boys to Hymenaea bringing the work to its finale.

The same year—1512—in which Paul struggled to find the proper poetic voice to honor the nuptials of his king provided an opportunity to make a more noteworthy contribution to humanist letters and, at the same time, to Polish-Hungarian cultural relations. While Paul was in Cracow after his stay in Hungary he maintained a correspondence with Hungarian friends, above all with his greatest patron, Gábor Perényi. Perényi urged him to help publish a volume of poetry by a Hungarian poet who was then beginning to attract attention in his own country—János Csezmicei (1434–72), who eventually became known as Hungary's foremost humanist poet under the latinized name Janus (or Ioannus) Pannonius.[11]

Perényi's desire to find a publisher for Pannonius was rooted in more than just enthusiasm for a promising young poet. Pannonius happened to be the nephew of János Vitéz, archbishop of Esztergom and himself one of the earliest important humanists in Hungary.[12] Pannonius had studied in Ferrara for seven years at the renowned school conducted by Guarino Veronese (1370–1460). He returned to Hungary in 1458, where his distinguished uncle helped establish him at the court of King Matthias Corvinus. In 1459 Pannonius became bishop of Pécs and also entered the royal chancery. He was active in public affairs and returned to Italy on several official visits. When the plot that he and his uncle instigated to unseat Matthias Corvinus and replace him with the Polish prince Casimir aborted, Pannonius fled Hungary, presumably trying to reach safe haven in Italy, but he died before he got there.

Paul of Krosno acceded to Perényi's request and prepared for publication the text of Pannonius's major work, the "Silva panegyrica ad Guarinum Veronensem, praeceptorem suum" (A Panegyric Orchard in Honor of His Teacher Guarino Veronese). After writing a prose dedication to his edition in which he heaped praise on both Perényi and Pannonius, Paul sent the manuscript to his former patron, who in turn forwarded it to the Vienna printing office of Wietor and Singrenius, the publishers in 1513 of Paul's editions of two Seneca plays.[13] The work was carefully gone over by the humanist Adrianus Volphardus (1491–1544), with whom Wietor and Singrenius enjoyed close relations. Once he approved its publication, Volphardus added to it an elegy by Pannonius entitled "De arbore nimium fecunda" (On a Very Abundant Tree) and three small poems of his own composition. The augmented edition, Pannonius's first published collection of poetry, was issued in 1512.[14] Pannonius's literary career and international fame now began in earnest. In 1513 an edition of his poetry edited by Paul of Krosno's former Hungarian student and friend, Sebastyén Magyi, was published in Bologna. Magyi had come to the Italian university town to study in 1509; when the Vienna edition of Pannonius appeared in 1512, a copy was sent to Magyi, and it stimulated him to undertake an Italian edition during his stay there. Like Volphardus, Magyi added other works to his edition, an elegy and two epigrams by Pannonius as well as a poem of his own commending the volume as a whole. Five years after Magyi's Bologna edition, in 1518, Wietor brought out a Cracow edition of Pannonius's epigrams under the title *Epigrammata antea non impressa* (Previously Unpublished Epigrams). That same year, a more comprehensive edition of Pannonius's poetry, prepared by Ioannes Frobenius, the well-known publisher of Erasmus, was issued in Basel.

As to why Paul of Krosno chose to publish the poem to Guarino

Veronese instead of others by Pannonius available to him, several reasonable answers have been suggested.[15] The panegyric to his Italian teacher is, after all, Pannonius's acknowledged masterpiece. Then there is Paul's own preference for longer monumental poems, shown in his lengthy panegyric in honor of King Ladislaus of Hungary and Saint Stanislaus of Poland, his epithalamium on the nuptials of King Sigismund and Barbara Zápolya, and his poem on King Sigismund's return from the Congress of Vienna in 1515. Humanist ideology also helped determine his choice. Paul was a devout enemy of Scholasticism, so much that he accepted a lesser teaching appointment at the University of Cracow rather than a more prestigious one that would have required him to lecture on Aristotle. He may have been influenced by Italian pedagogy, in light of which the passages devoted to Guarino's direction of the academy at Ferrara would have been of particular interest. Paul of Krosno was first a teacher and, as a teacher, a propagator of humanism. In view of Guarino's considerable reputation as an educator—the greatest of Renaissance educators, Vittorino da Feltre (1378–1446), was a pupil of his—Paul would have felt affinities that could only have enhanced his enthusiasm for Pannonius's poem and made it his obvious choice to edit for a first collection of the Hungarian poet's work. Paul also shared with Pannonius an exalted sense of poetry and poets that became another bond between them. In his poem "Carmen laudes poeticae artis continens et quod poemata immortalia sint et incaduca demonstrans" (Poem Containing Praise of the Poetic Art and Demonstrating That Poems Are Immortal and Imperishable), he writes at one point:

> Ergo divinos merito poetas
> Dicimus sacroque Dei repletos
> Spiritu, terras superare et alta
> Sidera coeli. (47).

(We therefore rightly call poets divine and full of the holy spirit of God; indeed do they rise above the earth unto the highest stars of the firmament.)

Finding similar sentiments expressed by Pannonius, in the poem to Guarino in particular, served to confirm the rightness of Paul's choice.

Paul of Krosno's career and presumably his life came to an uncertain end some four years after the successful publication of the Pannonius edition in Vienna in 1512 and the appearance in that same year of his own long commemorative poem on the wedding of King Sigismund.

Whether in connection with a church office that he received when he first went to Hungary or because of a new outbreak of plague in Cracow, Paul is believed to have set out on a second trip to Hungary in 1515 or 1516. What became of him remains a mystery; he was never heard from again.

John of Wiślica and The Prussian War

The year 1516, when Paul of Krosno is presumed to have died either on his way to or perhaps in Hungary, saw the publication of the major work by one of his most devoted Cracow students, John of Wiślica (Ioannes Visliciensis in Latin), another ardent advocate of humanism in Poland in the early sixteenth century. The work is a long poetic account of the famous and decisive victory of a combined Polish-Lithuanian force over the Teutonic Knights of the Cross at the battle of Grunwald in 1410, titled *Bellum Prutenum sive Belli Pruteni libelli tres per Ioannem Visliciensem editi* (The Prussian War, or The Three Books of the Prussian War Composed by Ioannes Visliciensis). It was published by the Cracow printer Jan Haller.

The immediate inspiration for John of Wiślica's *Prussian War* was a contemporary event—the Polish victory over the Muscovites at Orsza in 1514. To the poet, this could be related to another triumph of Polish arms over a dangerous and formidable enemy, the battle of Grunwald just over a hundred years before. The poem was also composed at a time when Polish politics had good cause to be preoccupied with the Prussians. Although an agreement was negotiated in 1515 stating that a five-year peace would be used by both sides to settle the differences between them, events in the previous year were perceived as extremely menacing. Negotiations between the Holy Roman Emperor Maximilian I and the Kremlin raised the specter of an anti-Polish alliance that would include the Teutonic Order, now headed by Albrecht von Hohenzollern, along with the dukes of Saxony, Denmark, and Brandenburg. When combat was finally joined with Muscovy, Poland's downfall was predicted throughout Europe, but Hetman Ostrogski's brilliant victory at Orsza on September 8, 1514, turned the tide at least for the time being.

John of Wiślica's purpose in writing *The Prussian War* had several facets. The victory at Orsza was sufficient cause for celebration, but the Prussian threat had still not been laid to rest, so linking a great Jagiellonian victory in the present with one a hundred years earlier suggested a continuity of Jagiellonian supremacy over Poland's most formidable enemies, the Teutonic Order and Muscovy. By linking the victories of Orsza and Grunwald the poet may also have intended to shore up spirits by implying that Poland could still crush Prussian and Muscovite threats, both individual and collective.

There is also reason to believe that in writing *The Prussian War* John of Wiślica sought to make his mark as a poet by doing something new in Polish letters—composing a great historical epic based on a major event in Polish national history. That this also reflected a growing Renaissance enthusiasm for writing history seems highly likely. Although parts of it began to be printed only in 1614, the historian Jan Długosz's monumental twelve-book *Annales seu cronicae incliti regni Poloniae*, on which he worked during 1455–80, was widely known and did much to arouse an interest in national history. John of Wiślica's *Prussian War* was published in 1516, and three years later there appeared in Cracow the first edition of the first published history of Poland, the *Chronica Polonorum* of Maciej Miechowita, which covers events up to the year 1506. Another major contribution to sixteenth-century Polish historiography, this one intended primarily for Western readers, the *De origine et rebus gestis Polonorum* by Marcin Kromer (ca. 1512–89), would be published in 1555 and, like Miechowita's work, would go only to 1506.

In setting himself the task of composing an epic about the battle of Grunwald, John of Wiślica was also well aware that despite the historical significance of the event and the growth of Polish historiography, little had actually been written about Grunwald either in Latin or in Polish. Except for the thirty-odd pages devoted to it in Długosz's *Annales* and that same historian's *Banderia Prutenorum* (written in 1448, published only in 1850), about the Prussian banners seized at Grunwald, little indeed had been written, even by poets, and that little—again except for Długosz—was of a general and rather rudimentary character.

John of Wiślica's sense of the newness, and importance, of what he was undertaking—as well as of his own inadequacy for the task—is nowhere better expressed than in the letter he wrote to his beloved teacher, Paul of Krosno, whose example and solicitude encouraged him in his literary endeavors. Here are some excerpts from the letter that accompanied the *Bellum Prutenum*:

> I reached the conclusion that poets, those worshipers of the Muses, in whose tracks I have set out from afar ponderously and awkwardly, reach beyond the highest peaks of achievement. Since the great defeat administered happily to the Germans by the Poles in the Prussian region enjoys

wide renown, I began to consider the significance of this extraordinary event. Although it is worthier of greater praise, I, however, born almost in the middle of a barbarous land and as yet insufficiently nourished by the Aonian waters [the Muses], have resolved to publish my work polished to the best of my ability amid the labor of many sleepless nights. And notwithstanding that these are my first efforts undertaken at the very outset of my willing service beneath the banner of the Muses, my great wish has been that the memory of that victory in some way be noted in writing and that young people, inflamed by love of praise of their fatherland, should confront the enemy more threateningly and ferociously. Although that great event will not be accurately presented . . . nevertheless, lest such a magnificent deed, untouched and unpolished by the Muses' song, perish in the darkness of dumb silence on account of the indifference of poets, I have composed this work in part from the writings of chroniclers, and in part from the memory of renowned fame with which the whole of Poland is crowned.[16]

The neglect of the subject by other poets, as well as his own lack of fitness for the undertaking, is also underscored by John in another prefatory poem added to *The Prussian War*, this one addressed to Bishop Piotr Tomicki, whom the poet beseeches to present his composition to the king:

> Sunk in despair by the harsh blows of cruel Nemesis, by adverse fates, and by the unfavorable inclination of the stars, O beneficent and most worthy bishop, I have brought forth a sad song from my troubled breast.[17]

> When poets equal to swans by their song, whom vast Poland nourishes and cherishes, chose to pass over in silence the resplendent glory of that battle, I, then, who compare myself not to the Polish poets, brought forth a song which, if lacking in grace and precision, nevertheless befits a barbarous Sarmatian poet. (107:10–16)

When he received a copy of *The Prussian War* along with John of Wiślica's poem to him, Paul of Krosno wrote an enthusiastic reply in verse under the title "Elegia . . . ad Ioannem Visliciensem, Pieridum cultorem, discipulum non poenitendum" (Elegy . . . to Ioannes Visliciensis, Worshiper of the Muses, Pupil beyond Reproach). Ever the pedagogue, Paul mixes pride in a former student's achievement with further advice on the art of writing:

> Laetor Ioannes, laetor carissime, nosse
> Quod tibi sit sacras maxima cura deas
> Et quod amor celsos tibi sit conscendere colles
> Labraque facundis sicca rigare vadis. (197:1–4)

(I am very glad, very glad, dearest John, that you make every effort to know the sacred goddesses, and that you yearn to climb the lofty peaks and moisten your dry lips in streams of eloquence.

Thanks to the talent, which I inspired, you began with burning heart to approach the nine goddesses [the Muses]. (9–10)

But be mindful, in diligently repudiating small blemishes, that you do not stain your best pages with black spots. As ugly as it is to disfigure a calm brow with small moles, so is it ugly to mark up writings with little notes. Do not be ashamed to count syllables frequently on your fingers and even repeat them ten times over. Disregard the grumbling of the mendacious crowd if it cries aloud that holy men are liars, since it strives to lead the spirit away from splendid undertakings and dissuade it from good enthusiasms. The crowd talks nonsense, but poets sing of divine lessons and truly make wisdom resound with the music of their words. They cover their poems with all sorts of magnificent raiment that the sluggish throng is never able to discern, and they take pleasure in concealing their principles with obscure places lest they lose power in becoming accessible to everyone. Indeed, it is pleasant to find even with great sweat what the boundless earth has locked in a deep cavern. More precious is the gold that comes to light on the gem dug out from ruddy depths. (198:33–52)

Paul of Krosno's advice that his former pupil and now disciple not be embarrassed to count syllables and not stain his text with too many corrections, as well as his remarks about the public, can be viewed as a gentle way of admonishing him that there were lapses in his *Prussian War*. John was definitely a more talented poet than his master, with a richer creative imagination, but his lack of Paul's classical training shows up in occasional errors in an otherwise acceptable Latin, in a certain clumsiness in his handling of Latin metrics (hence Paul's remark about counting syllables), and in often awkward use of Latin syntax. John was also guilty of historical inaccuracies (although the contemporary reader probably would have been unaware of them), and it may well have been these lapses and stylistic infelicities that Paul had in mind when he urged his former pupil to take no heed of the "mendacious crowd."

Yet despite its weaknesses, *The Prussian War* was no small achievement. Its author gives ample evidence of a good grasp of Latin literature and Polish humanist poetry, which he demonstrates both by his use of the conventions of Latin epic composition, with its galaxy of gods and goddesses, its invocations, apostrophes, comparisons, and so on, and by his conscious emulation of Paul of Krosno's panegyric and hyperbolic style, displayed to best advantage in the poetry of his Hungarian and later Cracovian periods.

The Prussian War abounds in vivid, colorful, and lively passages, especially when John is describing battles, but the work fails to achieve an aesthetically satisfying and effective unity. As is often true of the Renaissance epic in general, the whole is not equal to the sum of its parts. Nevertheless, the poem was the first attempt by a Polish Neo-Latin writer to compose a major work of verse on a subject derived from national history and of considerable contemporary significance; it was also the first time a Polish Neo-Latin poet consciously sought to instill in his readers, particularly younger ones, a love of country and a sense of national pride. The following excerpts from John of Wiślica's *Prussian War* will introduce the poem; for the sake of space, quotation from the Latin has been kept to a minimum:

> Et Pegasides ad carmina pigrae
> Prosiliunt, oblitae ingentia facta potentis
> Regis dicere et augustum renovare triumphum,
> Quem tulit auspiciis hostes superando secundis,
> Hostes Sarmatico Prutenos nomini acerbos
> Auxilia et Germanorum validissime regum,
> Proh inimica tuis, Rex, quae generosis Polonis
> Exstiterant. . . .[18]

(The Muses were indolent in taking up their lyres, forgetting to proclaim and revive the king's great deed, that superb triumph achieved beneath a favorable sign over the Prussian enemy invidious to the Sarmatians and over the powerful troops of the German kings who with fearful arrogance stepped forth, O king, against these noble Poles. But the enemy's might fell defeated in battle, struck down by God's help and yours, Saint Stanislaus. Their standards soaked in blood today hang in peace in a holy nave and render you homage.[19] Once upon a time, in the midst of a harsh battle, they were plucked from fierce enemies, the Prussians, slain by the Polish eagle, by the bravery, O Sigismund, of your grandfather. The praiseworthy family [the Jagiellonians], made famous by their defeat, has remained victorious for many long years.)

There is a land celebrated everywhere for its shady forests reaching widely as far as the Scythian borders, green in fruit-bearing meadows and abounding in honey, copious in population and in brave warriors. Lithuania was the name given to this place by its ancient inhabitants, who with hard plowshares cultivated the hard soil of the region. The prince there and your grandfather, of the ever-illustrious name Jagiełło, great of birth is he and the most splendid glory of fierce Mars and his frightful war. Most of immense Europe learned this when hordes of German soldiers, defeated in war, fell in rows into the womb of Prussian soil, which

streams flowing with putrid blood turned red, carrying those slain by
Mars out to the waters of the sea. (Bk. 2:1–15)

> Tempus erat calidum, quo Iulius annua mensis
> Maturat per agros Cerealia dona feraces,
> Pulchrum opus incurvis messoribus agricolisque,
> Quo Mars in campis Prutenis constitit acer
> Arma movens, iamque hos clipeum iam volvit ad illos
> Atque, boans Prussis nec non crudele Polonis
> Bellum, sanguineas mortes et multa profatur
> Salva nimis dictu populis poscentibus arma. . . . (169–80)

(It was the hot season when the heat of July[20] ripens the grain in the soil
of Ceres [thought to be an Italian deity representing the generative power
of nature], making lovely work for bowed reapers and farmers. Then it
was that fierce Mars appeared in Prussian fields and brandishing arms
and thundering proclaims cruel war now to the Prussians and now to the
Poles. To those so desirous of arms he foretells bloody deaths and many
things too horrible to mention. In the meantime, wrath has begun to rage
and newly arisen from the depths of Phlegethon [a river of fire in Hades]
Death has again become master. Racing across fields like a bloodstained
snake, he announces many corpses that will fall into the waters of the Styx
and into a bottomless night.)

The action is furious; defenses have begun to crumble. The king himself,
at the head of his men, shatters the enemy troops in a terrible slaughter,
striking down a countless number by his own hand. Corpses are strewn
all about in heaps, as when the wild Tydeus [Oenides][21] sowed death near
the fearsome cliffs of the Sphinx, or when the bellicose Hector bestrewed
the defensive walls of proud Troy with the corpses of Greek princes.[22]

Thus the king himself, an image of ferocity, was making heaps of the
German troops, happy, happy in victorious battle. Now thousands of
Polish cavalry follow his lead, aroused by the combat of unbridled Mars.
They enter the fray, their sharp lances clasped beneath their arms, their
chests protected by mail gleaming like shields. The number of combatants
increases; they cleave bodies with iron, pierce them with shafts, meet
blows with blows. Arms and men are hacked down, and more German
souls are thrown by the sword beneath the groves of Phlegethon like a
great whirlwind. Thereafter, the stout hearts of men are delivered dead
unto the bedchambers of the Furies. The spirit of Mars rises more fiercely
[in people] and with it the lust for war. Swords glisten and shields clang.
The deafening clamor of cavalry and the neighing of horses resound on
all sides. Hand-to-hand combat is joined, the field soon soaked in blood.
Ditches fill up with the slaughtered, the stained soil trembles from the

bodies of the fallen, and the clear sky flashes with swords. So great is the noise and the din of war raised to the starry heaven that it can scarcely be surpassed by the thundering of the Cyclopes, Steropes, and Brontes in the caverns of Aetna [where, according to legend, they made thunderbolts for Zeus]. (326–47)

> Turbula maesta virum duce sic spoliata superbo,
> Vulneribusque gravata et viribus extenuata,
> Currere tentabat, sed cursus clausus ab omni
> Parte fuit radianti milite Marte feroque.
> Sub iuga pars sua colla dabat, pars cetera tetris
> Intermixta cadaveribus sua membra tegebat. . . . (442–59)

(A small group, saddened by the loss of their distinguished leader and worn down by blows and losses of men, sought to flee, but the way was barred on all sides by soldiers in shining armor and by cruel Mars. Those who were beneath the yoke bent their necks, while others tried to hide among piles of foul corpses. There were still others who with hands raised high begged for mercy, but they spewed vain words from their bosoms. No mercy was shown the entreaties and tears of those begging for mercy, since the memory was fresh of how German arrogance had rent the proud bodies of Poles and of swords bloodied against supplicants.

Then all remaining units of the enemy were cut down to the last man, whereupon the victorious Sarmatian, returning from the terrible battle, bore with him the shields of the enemy's fallen leaders, the arms of his men, and the standards, stained with blood and stiffened by gore, which had been gathered up from the battlefield. Fastened above the tomb in the nave of the cathedral venerating you, Saint Stanislaus, these illustrious standards now flutter in dedication to your praise.)

The immensity of Polish pride in the defeat of the Knights of the Cross at the battle of Grunwald is reflected in John of Wiślica's rhetorical admonishment to Rome and other ancient cities that they not compare their great heroes to mighty Jagiełło:

> Cui, tu Roma, tuos noli annumerare Camillos,
> Marcellum, Fabios et Caesaris optima gesta,
> Hectora, Troia, tuum, fortem, Larissa, et Achillem,
> Hannibalemque tuum, Carthago superba, ferocem. (505–11)

(And you, Rome, do not compare to him the greatest deeds of your Camilluses [Marcus Furius Camillus, a Roman general], Marcelluses [Marcus Claudius Marcellus, a Roman general], Fabiuses [Maximus Fabius, a Roman general], or Caesar; nor you, O Troy, those of your Hector; nor

you, Larissa, your brave Achilles; nor you, proud Carthage, your bold
Hannibal.)

So exuberant does the Polish poet's national pride become at this
point that the mightest rulers of the Persians, Arabs, Parthians, and
Greeks are dismissed as unequal to Jagiełło. With the significance
of the Polish-Lithuanian victory at Grunwald and the glory of the
Jagiellonians elaborated through the first two books of his poem, John
can then proceed to the ideological center of his work—the linkage of
the great Polish victory of the early fifteenth century over the Teutonic
Order with what he presents as the no less brilliant or significant
victory of the Poles over the Muscovites at Orsza in his own time.
History is thus made to repeat itself: the battle of Orsza is described
in much the same terms as the battle of Grunwald, and at the conclusion of the battle the Poles, led by another member of the Jagiellonian
dynasty, have seized a great horde of prisoners and captured the once-
resplendent banners of the enemy, all of which are triumphantly
paraded before the magnificent walls of Wilno in the Lithuanian
homeland of the Jagiellonians.

Although the absence of Celtis and Callimachus was keenly felt in
the tenuous environment of Polish humanism and the collapse of the
movement appeared close at hand, the transitional efforts of such
figures as Paul of Krosno and John of Wiślica successfully relayed the
baton from the trailblazers, domestic and foreign, to the more talented
and self-assured humanists who came after them. Only fitfully impressive as writers, Paul of Krosno and John of Wiślica did more than hold
together the fragile chain of Polish humanism at a time of stress.
Through his Hungarian connections, Paul added further strength to
the links already forged between the two most vigorous expressions
of Renaissance humanism in eastern Europe; with *The Prussian War*
of his most devoted pupil, national history and national pride were
handsomely demonstrated to be fit subjects of humanist Latinity.

CHAPTER 5

Copernicus:
The Scientist as Humanist

During the period of transition marked by the dominance of
such writers as Laurentius Corvinus and Paul of Krosno, an
interesting if not well-known contribution to humanist letters in Poland was made by none other than Nicolaus Copernicus. Because of
it, Copernicus has a definite place in the history of humanism in
Poland only distantly related to his great scientific discoveries. In 1509,
thirty-four years before the publication of his celebrated treatise on
the movements of heavenly bodies, Copernicus published his own
Latin translation of a collection of letters originally composed in Greek
by a seventh-century Egyptian-born Byzantine writer named Theophylactos Simocattes (or Simocatos). The edition, printed by Jan Haller
in Cracow, bore the following title page:

> Theophylacti Simocattae
> Epistolae
> Morales Rurales Amatoriae
> Nicolao Copernico
> Interprete
> Carmen Lavrentij Corvini
> Regiae Urbis Wratislauiae
> Notarij, Quo Valedicit Prutenos Describitque, Quantum Sibi
> Voluptatis Attulerint Sequentes Theophilacti Epistolae Et
> Quam Dulcis Sit A Natali Solo Extorri in Patriam Reditus.

(The Moral, Pastoral, and Amatory Letters of Theophylactos Symocattes.
A Poem to the Translator, Nicolaus Copernicus, by Laurentius Corvinus,
Notary of the Regal City of Wrocław, by Which He Bids Farewell to

Prussia and Describes How Much Delight the Accompanying Letters of
Theophylactos Brought Him and How Pleasant Is the Return to His
Homeland to One Banished from His Native Soil)

Although the modest volume seems to have attracted little attention,
its publication was a first in two respects. The Latin translation of
Simocattes' Greek letters was Copernicus's first published work, thus
marking the future scientist's debut as an author. Then, it happens to
have been the first translation of a Greek literary work to appear in
Poland.

By undertaking a Latin translation of what even in the early sixteenth century might fairly have been regarded as a rather obscure
Greek text, Copernicus gave ample testimony to the diffusion of humanism in Poland and the importance the movement held for him.
If the translation has understandably been dwarfed by Copernicus's
subsequent accomplishments, it is nevertheless a valuable document
in illuminating Copernicus's humanist orientation at the outset of his
career. It also argues convincingly for considering him within the
framework of the development of humanism in Poland, since such a
philological exercise as the "recovery" of an ancient Greek text through
translation (naturally, into Latin) was at the very heart of the humanist
enterprise.

Copernicus's Latin translation of the Simocattes letters was yet another link in the chain binding Renaissance Italy and Poland, for it
was clearly in Italy that Copernicus learned Greek and made the
acquaintance of the original Byzantine work. Now what was the route
that led Copernicus to Simocattes and the eventual translation of the
letters?

Like other Polish university students of the time, Copernicus viewed
a tour of Italy as a natural progression in his studies. But the almost
irresistible lure of the homeland of the Renaissance was not the only
reason for his traveling south. His uncle, the powerful Lucas Watzelrode (Łukasz Waczenrode, in Polish), bishop of Warmia, firmly supported the decision, believing that the advanced training in canon
law of his intellectually promising nephew would be an advantage in
negotiations with the papacy over Polish relations with the Knights of
the Cross, who were nominally within his episcopal jurisdiction.[1] After
applying for a Warmian church benefice, which Uncle Lucas was able
to virtually guarantee him,[2] to provide funds for his journey to Italy,
Copernicus set out for Bologna in the summer of 1496. Except for a
trip back to Poland in 1501, he remained in Italy, primarily Bologna,
for the next eight years.

He returned to Poland for financial reasons. When the funds supporting not only Copernicus but also his brother Andrzej, who had joined him later, were depleted, Copernicus left Bologna for Rome, where he spent the greater part of a year in 1500–1501 trying to earn money by teaching mathematics. The income was much too small, however, for him to resume his studies, and eventually he and his brother were persuaded that their only recourse was to return to Poland and petition the Warmian cathedral chapter for permission and funds for a second Italian stay. Their appearance before the chapter on July 21 was successful, and within a few months they were back in Italy. Copernicus was granted a maximum stay of two years to study medicine; furthermore, he was required to complete his training in canon law and return home with a degree.

He at last acquired the doctorate in canon law in 1503, but not from the University of Bologna. When Copernicus returned to Italy he did not resume his residence in Bologna but settled instead in Padua, where he became close to the philosopher Pietro Pomponazzi (Pomponatius, 1462–1525), and to the physician and poet Girolamo Fracastoro (Hieronymus Fracastorius, 1478–1553)[3] Despite his affiliation with Padua during this second study tour of Italy, it was in Ferrara that Copernicus was finally awarded his doctorate, which has no special significance in view of the humanists' fondness for academic itineration.

On completing his Italian studies Copernicus returned to Poland, bringing with him not only the doctorate in canon law demanded by the Warmian cathedral chapter, but also some preliminary work on his Latin translation of Simocattes' letters.

From the time he settled permanently in Poland until 1512, Copernicus was engaged primarily in the service of his uncle Lucas Watzelrode in Warmia. His routine permitted time for intermittent furtherance of his philological interests, and by the spring of 1508 his translation of Simocattes was finished and ready to be shown to a publisher.

It was at this point that Laurentius Corvinus, Copernicus's old University of Cracow acquaintance and fellow member of the Literary Society of the Vistula, entered the picture. Corvinus was then in Toruń, and they had resumed their friendship when Copernicus returned to Poland and entered the service of Bishop Watzelrode. When the notarius or "town scribe" of Wrocław, Gregory Morenberg, died in January 1508, the largely ceremonial but paid position became open, and Corvinus, eager to return to his native city, applied for it. With a well-established literary reputation to recommend him, he won the appointment and after settling his affairs in Toruń set forth to assume his new position in Wrocław. With him on the trip he had the

Latin translation of the Simocattes letters, which Copernicus must have given to his old friend for his opinion. With no previous personal contact with the Cracow publishers and as yet no reputation as a writer, Copernicus undoubtedly had more in mind than just friendship and constructive criticism when he presented Corvinus with a copy of his translation.

Once established in Wrocław, Corvinus lost little time interceding with the Cracow publisher Haller on Copernicus's behalf. Since Haller had previously published two books by Corvinus (*Epicedium*, 1506; *Hortulus elegentiarum*, 1507), he agreed to consider the translation of Simocattes' letters and finally published it, largely on Corvinus's recommendation. Because of an overload in the printing office, however—Haller turned out fifteen books in 1508, no small number by contemporary standards—publication had to wait until the following year. But before we consider the book itself, let us return to Copernicus's study of Greek and his choice of the Simocattes letters for translation.

The abundant scholarship on Copernicus has established fairly convincingly, albeit without firm documentation, that his serious study of the Greek language began only in Padua, that is, during his second sojourn in Italy after his return from Poland in 1501. Circumstantial evidence argues strongly that his interest in the Greek language and in Greek antiquity was awakened in the earlier Bologna period. When Copernicus arrived in Bologna to pursue his degree in canon law, humanism was already in the ascendancy, and the study of Greek and of Hellenistic literature had by now become popular. Symptomatic of that interest was the publication of Chrestonius's Greek-Latin dictionary[4] and a two-volume collection of Greek epistolographers (*Epistolographi Graeci*). The latter was published by the famous Venetian scholar-printer Aldo Manuzio (Aldus Manutius, ca. 1450–1515),[5] and its second volume was dedicated to Urceo Codro (Codrus, 1446–1500), an Italian authority on Greek language and literature who was lecturing at the time in Bologna.

Within the context of the heightened enthusiasm for Greek studies after the Turkish conquest of Constantinople in 1453 and the resettlement of learned Greek exiles in Italy, the appearance of the *Epistolographi Graeci* in 1499 and the Chrestonius dictionary in 1500—preceded by the Manutius-published Greek grammars of Janus Lascaris and Theodorus Gaza in 1495—were ample stimuli to Copernicus's own interest once he had arrived in Bologna. But though the conditions were ripe for his attraction to Greek, there is no evidence that he began any systematic study of the language until later.[6] Since Chrestonius's dictionary was printed only in the summer of 1500 and Codro (whom Copernicus might have heard lecture on Greek literature at Bologna) died on February 11, 1500, it does not seem likely that time allowed Copernicus to assimilate the new tools for a systematic study of Greek language and letters before leaving Bologna for Rome in March 1500. Rome itself was not yet a center of Greek studies. John (Janus) Argyropulos, who had taught there, died in 1486, and Lascaris, whose Manutius-published grammar was mentioned above, was still teaching in Florence and did not take up a post in Rome until much later. Thus, in the year Copernicus was in Rome there was no chair of Greek at the university, and no regular program of lectures on Greek language and literature was available.

Circumstances were more propitious in Padua, when Copernicus returned to Italy in 1501. Between 1497 and 1507, Niccolò Leonico Tomeo, a professor of philosophy, lectured on the Greek writings of Plato and Aristotle besides translating Ptolemy's treatise on the phases of permanent stars. The Cretan émigré scholar Lorenzo da Camerino taught the Greek language at the university during the academic year 1501–1502. Although the little evidence there is suggests that Copernicus began serious study of Greek in a *bursa,* or student residence, rather than in a university course (possibly because the Greek chair was inactive), the encouragement of Greek studies at Padua may have furthered the interest kindled in Bologna. An important manifestation of that encouragement was the appointment of Marcus Musurus (1470–1517) as Lorenzo da Camerino's successor to the chair of Greek studies on July 27, 1503, though the appointment may have come too late for Copernicus to have attended Musurus's lectures, since he returned to Poland after receiving his canon law doctorate from Ferrara in 1503. But their paths were to cross in a more significant way a little later on. When Copernicus set himself the task of translating the letters of Simocattes, he used the edition of Greek epistolographers prepared by Musurus and published by Musurus's patron, Aldus Manutius.

Establishing a reasonably accurate chronology of Copernicus's study of Greek, while important, seems to me less interesting than considering why he decided first of all to translate anything from Greek and then chose the letters of Theophylactos Simocattes, which he found in the two-volume collection of Greek epistolography published by Manutius.

To a great extent, both decisions—to translate from Greek and in particular to translate the letters of Simocattes—were prompted by the same consideration, Copernicus's desire to establish his credentials as a bona fide humanist and to disseminate humanism as a value system. As his experience of humanism expanded in the environment of Bologna, Rome, and Padua, he became the complete convert, not only convinced himself but eager to spread the gospel to others. The enthusiasm for Greek antiquity that was just blossoming when Copernicus first arrived in Bologna was infectious. And even if it cannot be proved that it was then the future astronomer began his study of Greek, there can be no doubt that he was quickly won over to this popular new dimension of the humanist movement.

Once he resolved to learn the Greek language—as much to read the ancient philosophers and scientists in the original as to follow a fashionable new wave of scholarship (humanism being "progressive" and the old Scholasticism, which still had a great deal of punch, being "conservative" or even "reactionary" by comparison)—the urge to translate a Greek text and thereby enter the mainstream of humanistic philological endeavor was irresistible. In view of the clout the Scholastics still wielded and their unrelenting hostility to humanism in general and to the study of the Greek language and culture in particular, the very act of translation was in itself a statement of identification with the new learning, with the "progressives," and of defiance of the by now outmoded and reactionary Scholasticism of the Middle Ages.

The defiance symbolized by the act of translating from Greek into Latin was unmistakably underscored by the text Copernicus chose to translate. That he did not choose a Greek scientific treatise at this early point in his career should come as no great surprise. By translating a literary work Copernicus was conforming to and thus aligning himself with the mainstream of humanist philological scholarship, which sought above all to recover the "lost" riches of classical Roman and Greek literature. Moreover, the translation of a Greek literary work when the interest in Greek culture was just coming to fruition was bound to be regarded as an auspicious debut for a young scholar eager to place himself in the front rank of contemporary propagators of the humanist movement.

The specific appeal of Simocattes' letters was fourfold, I believe. First, they had just appeared in 1499 in the Manutius edition of the *Epistolographi Graeci* and hence were something new. Second, they had been published in a collection of Greek letters by the respected and admired Aldus Manutius, which in itself was sufficient to attract attention. Third, their appearance was a manifestation of Manutius's own ardor for the Greek language and Greek literature. The Venetian publisher's famous anchor and dolphin imprint on the collection guaranteed interest, which a young Polish scholar with humanistic ambitions, in Italy for the first time, could hardly have resisted. Thus, translating from the Manutius collection was an almost certain way of making a literary debut impossible to ignore. And finally, the particular appeal of the Simocattes letters was their variety, their lightness, and their value both as entertainment and as a type of pedagogy, since they are in different styles and serve as models for different occasions.[7] The eighty-five letters in the Greek collection are also short, which must also have enhanced their appeal to a fledgling translator. The following excerpts illustrate the nature of the collection:

Erasmios to Lysistratos (amatory)

The Cupids play with people, and if painters are to be believed, these winged lads take the inhabitants of the sublunar world into captivity. Ah, if only this enemy were visible! Then the firing Eroses would themselves be the targets of missiles. But as it is now, our losses are greater for our ignorance of the nature of our adversaries. Alas, the most incomprehensible feeling has subjugated me. I am madly in love with Melanippe, whose beauty has been recorded by Diodoros. I love her from afar, for I have never seen this woman even in dream; I only heard from someone else that she sings beautifully. It was in my soul that I was wounded, whereas my eyes brought me no harm. Would that I suffered because of them, Lysistratos, for now my ears have become my eyes. You see what the power of the Cupids is. I don't know if she looks like the Erinyes or if what was told me of her is just pure invention. The testimony of one witness does not make for the whole truth. I suffer, therefore, in my soul, and I love one who remains to me unseen. It seems to me that the madness of Pan has possessed me, for he too did not see the object of his love, and the delusion of those in love remained his entire possession. (#36)[8]

Marathon to Peganon (pastoral)

Fleeing from the political tempests and merciless turmoil of the city, I rented this field and thought that my spirit would change. But I fell into worse trouble. Sometimes I have an enemy in rust, sometimes in locusts, and even hail falls once in a while. Hoarfrost, like an unyielding tyrant, destroys crops, and I, an unfortunate man, must feed my family with wind. Where can I turn in my misery? When I recall the dung heaps of the country, I yearn for life in the city. But then when I consider the crush of urban anxieties, my love for the country returns. What you don't have seems better than what is. The only refuge from annoyances is death, whether natural or voluntary. The noose is medicine to me. It would be stupidity for a wretched man to turn cowardly before death. (#41 [157])

Socrates to Plato (moral)

No one suffers abuse, although everyone abuses others and each person freely abuses himself. We are autocrats of honor and offense. Leonides dispossessed you of a field: that is an external matter, your soul suffered no harm. Stealing a ring, Philip exposed you to loss, but you yourself were not harmed, for every acquired thing is not ours. Barbarians killed your son, but no evil befell you, since you were not given your son forever. Just a while ago you did not have him, then he was born, and now you do not have him once again. People inflict harm but do not suffer harm. I admire Homer's Cyclops who, wounded, said that no one had harmed him. This denial by a shepherd was a confirmation of truth. (#40 [157])

Copernicus's translation of the Simocattes letters is preceded by two prefaces. One, by Copernicus himself, is a prose dedication to his uncle and patron Bishop Lucas Watzelrode ("Ad reverendissimum dominum Lucam Episcopum Warmiensem Nicolai Coppernici epistola"), in which Copernicus explains his choice of translation:

It seems to me, most reverend lord and father of our country, that Theophylactus the Scholastic has quite excellently compiled moral, pastoral, and amatory epistles. Surely he was guided by the consideration that variety delights above all else and that, being dissimilar, the inclinations of men are pleased by things that are themselves dissimilar. Some enjoy weighty thoughts, others light ones, and still others only the serious, while there are also those who are attracted by the play of fancy. That is why Theophylactus alternates the light and the heavy, the frivolous and the serious, so that the reader can choose what pleases him most from among this variety of flowers, just as if he were in a garden. There is such a great utility in all he offers, however, that his epistles appear more like rules and precepts for the conduct of human life. The proof of this is their very brevity, for they were taken from various authors and presented in a most compressed and fruitful form. Surely no one will doubt the value of the moralistic and pastoral letters. The amatory, on the other hand, may seem lascivious in view of their title, but just as the physician is wont to soften the bitterness of medicine with sweet ingredients, to make it more agreeable to patients, so the amatory letters have been added here. They have, however, been chastened to the extent that they could just as easily bear the name moralistic. Matters being as they are, therefore, I deemed it inequitable for the work of Theophylactus to be accessible only to readers of Greek and so have striven to render them in Latin to the best of my ability. (50–51)

The second preface, which precedes Copernicus's dedication to Bishop Watzelrode, is by far the more interesting of the two. It is a 116-line poem by Laurentius Corvinus, to whom, remember, Copernicus gave a copy of his translation to take with him on his return to

Silesia from Toruń and who used his good offices with the printer Haller in Cracow to get the work published.

Characterizing himself as the notarius of Wrocław, Corvinus begins his prefatory poem with a farewell greeting to the city of Toruń, which he has left behind. This is followed by praise of Bishop Watzelrode and then of the translator of Simocattes, Copernicus himself. Particularly noteworthy in the opening of Corvinus's poem is the acknowledgment made at this early stage of Copernicus's career of his interest in astronomy. Corvinus writes of the translator as one who also "follows and describes the swift movement of the moon, of the fraternal sun, the ways of the stars and their course in the immensity of the firmament and can, moreover, explain on principles worthy of amazement the marvelous creation of the universe as well as the causes of phenomena" (46:27–30).

In the intimate style of much humanist writing, Corvinus tells his readers why he left Toruń (mainly the urging of his homesick wife Anna, who was eager to return to Silesia) and describes the hardships of the journey, including a detailed account of a pause en route at the hut of a poor man to refresh themselves and their horses. The arduous journey is used to introduce the motive for his preface, praise for Copernicus's translation. Throughout his long and uncomfortable trip back to Silesia, Corvinus's greatest pleasure was in the letters of Simocattes, which he had with him, and until he and his family reached the borders of the "Sarmatian land" the burden of travel was lightened considerably by his reading ("Ista molesta licat via sit, sed lectio Graij / Sola Simocati perbreue fecit iter, / Donec Sarmaticae venio ad confinia terrae" [43–45]).

Hardly had Corvinus reached the outskirts of Wrocław and offered up a prayer for his safe arrival when, as if in answer, the towers of the city loomed on the horizon like mountain peaks breaking the clouds. In a familiar classical hyperbole, so tall were the buildings that they appeared to reach up to the very "globe of Phoebus." Now safe within the walls of Wrocław, Corvinus concludes his preface with further praise for Simocattes' letters, for their variety and for the moral lessons to be derived from their reading:

> Utque Simocati sapientis epistola in auras
>   Prodeat, impressis est patefacta modis.
> Prima docet mores, rus altera, tertia amores:
>   Sic opus alterna texitur usque vice,
> Unde, velut riguo varios de germine flores,
>   Virtutum poterit lector habere decus. (49:111–16)

(The letters of Simocattes, a wise man, are indeed pleasant reading, enlightened as they are with commendable models. The first set deals with moral conduct, the second with the pastoral life, and the third with love. In this way the work pleases with its variety. Just as various flowers grow from a single stalk, so will the reader of these letters receive instruction in various virtues.)

Publication by Haller of Cracow and a laudatory preface by a poet as well regarded as Laurentius Corvinus would have been enough to ensure Copernicus a sympathetic hearing. That the Latin version of Simocattes' letters was also the first translation of a Greek literary work in Poland probably would not have been lost on contemporary readers. But how these readers, or for that matter the scholarly community at the University of Cracow, for whose students the translation was presumably intended, responded to the work, we have no idea. The lack of documentation makes it difficult to establish what reception the translation received, although given the intellectual climate of the time there is no reason to assume it was anything but favorable. When Copernicus's great scientific work appeared in 1543, a little over three decades later, his much earlier translation of the exemplary epistles of a long-forgotten Byzantine writer named Theophylactos Simocattes became a very dim memory. Even Copernicus seems not to have had any particular concern for the fate of the translation, neither recalling it in any memorable way afterward nor exhibiting an interest in its sale or in the possibility of other editions.

When, in later times, Copernicus's genius was universally recognized, his place in the history of science was firmly established, and complete editions of his works were published, informed assessments of the quality of his Simocattes translation were undertaken. Since a fresh philological examination of his translation is beyond the scope of this book, let me briefly summarize the state of opinion on the matter.[9] Although Copernicus's Latin is accurate, albeit on the prosaic side, and largely humanist in style, his translation from the Greek of Simocattes' original is flawed. Since it appears that Copernicus tended to be more literal than liberal as a translator, the mistakes in Greek cannot be ascribed to his taking liberties with the original for the sake of a more readable translation. The problem was twofold. In the first place, the evidence suggests that Copernicus worked not from a printed edition of the Simocattes letters but from a carelessly or hastily made copy of the type prepared for school use when a printed text is either difficult to come by or too expensive; this may have been the case with the Manutius-published two-volume edition of the *Epistolographi*

Graeci containing the Simocattes letters. It would be a plausible explanation for the inconsistencies in the translation compared with the printed original. Then, Copernicus's Greek was not acquired in a formal, systematic manner over a long enough time to allow a flawless translation. Copernicus's enthusiasm for Greek, coupled with his desire to translate the Simocattes letters as quickly as possible so as to make his mark as a humanist, clearly outstripped his command of the language. Yet despite its weaknesses in terms of both accuracy and polish, his translation is worthy of interest. With a largely informally acquired Greek that was still far from mastery and working with an imperfect copy of the original text, Copernicus succeeded in producing a respectable translation. In doing so he demonstrated his own enthusiasm for humanism at this early stage in his career and at the same time contributed to the development of that movement in Poland by being the first Polish scholar to translate a work from the ancient Greek.

CHAPTER 6

Pope Leo X, the Bison, and Renaissance Cultural Politics

No less a curiosity today than when it was first published in Cracow in 1523, the 1,072-line *De statura, feritate ac venatione bisontis carmen* (Poem about the Size, Strength, and Hunting of the Bison) was written in 1521–22 in response to an interest expressed by Pope Leo X in the bison of the Polish-Lithuanian forests. The author of the poem was a writer of humble and obscure origins known as Mikołaj z Hussowa (Nicholas of Hussów) or Mikołaj Hussowczyk, latinized as Nicolaus Hussovianus.[1]

For Leo X to evince an interest in the Polish bison was hardly unusual. The son of Lorenzo the Magnificent and hence a member of the Medici family, the pope was highly regarded in his own time and by subsequent generations for his patronage of learning and the arts. But Leo had another enthusiasm more germane to the present subject—hunting. The pope made ample use of his favorite game preserve, an immense tract surrounding the Villa Magliana, situated some five miles from Rome on the road to Porto. Together with the neighboring property owned by the related Orsini family, this papal hunting estate stretched from the Tiber on the south into the Campagna as far north as the Isola Farnese. So fond was the pope of hunting that he would spend more than six weeks at a time, in fall and winter, in activity more closely resembling slaughter than sport. Because he was physically frail and had to guard his health, Leo was more an organizer of hunting parties and an enthusiastic onlooker than an actual participant. A great variety of animals were killed by his guests, among whom could be found some of the highest dignitaries of the church. One favorite excursion was to Santa Marinella, on the coast. In his book on

Leo X, *White Robe, Black Robe*, Charles L. Mee, Jr., describes, for example, how the papal party would go to Santa Marinella, "where stags and goats and boars would be stampeded over the cliffs into the water, and the hunters would spear them from boats or leap into the water after them—Leo sitting in a large barge amidst the boiling, bloody surf, following the action eagerly."[2] Lest his pleasure be only vicarious, the pontiff was often escorted to the fallen body of a severely wounded animal so that he might personally administer the death blow and thereby, one supposes, preserve the honor of the Medicis.

The area around the Villa Magliana was not the only place the hunt-loving pope pursued his bloody sport. Each year in October, he took special delight in traveling to Viterbo, to the woods of the Citavecchia, where he also maintained excellent hunting lands.

How did Leo X become interested in the Polish bison? The decisive role was played by one of the outstanding Polish churchmen of the period, Erazm Ciołek (Erasmus Vitellius, 1474–1522). Highly regarded for his diplomatic skills as well as for his devotion to learning and the arts, Ciołek rose rapidly to ecclesiastical prominence. From the humble position of parish priest in Wilno, he first attracted attention as one of King Alexander's secretaries and eventually was named bishop of Płock. As a measure of the esteem he evoked in Lithuania, the king elevated him to the nobility in 1502 and subsequently dispatched him as his envoy to the Vatican. Once established in Rome, Ciołek moved easily in papal circles by virtue of his intelligence, culture, and tact, and in time he won the friendship of popes Alexander VI, Julius II, and Leo X.

The relationship with Leo was particularly close, especially during Ciołek's nearly five-year tour in Rome from 1518 to 1522.[3] Both men shared an interest in the arts and in cultivating talent, Leo at the papal court and Erazm Ciołek at his residence in Rome, which assumed the character of a salon. Participation in Ciołek's learned circle was by no means limited to Poles; indeed, this would have been incompatible with the spirit of humanism. The Greek scholar Constanzo Claretti belonged to the circle, as did the humanist known as Montecinereus. Of the Poles who were a part of it, the most noteworthy were a learned burgher from Poznań named Mikołaj Czepiel, who later became a count of the Lateran palace and was renowned for the size and excellence of his library, and probably also Mikołaj Hussowczyk (or Hussovianus, as I shall call him here), during his stay in Rome from 1518 to the fall of 1523.[4] Although the documentary evidence is scanty, it seems most likely that Hussovianus came to Rome in 1518 as a member of Bishop Ciołek's retinue; in what capacity, we do not know.

It was inevitable that in the many conversations between the Roman pope and the Polish bishop the subject of hunting would sooner or later arise. Coming from one of the most densely wooded regions of the old Polish-Lithuanian commonwealth, an area teeming with wildlife, Ciołek had more than enough stories to arouse Leo's interest. So fascinated was the pope with descriptions of the *żubr*, the massive, shaggy-headed bison of the eastern forests, that Ciołek determined to satisfy Leo's curiosity by having the complete hide of a full-grown bison shipped from Lithuania to Rome, where it would be stuffed and placed on exhibit. To this end Ciołek sought the cooperation of the powerful palatine of Wilno, Mikołaj Radziwiłł (the Black), who lent his enthusiastic support. Probably about the same time that Ciołek turned to Radziwiłł (in 1520), the idea came to him to commission Hussovianus to write a poem about the bison for the pope's enlightenment and pleasure, a poem that would also do justice to the flora and fauna of the Lithuanian region, in which the pope had evinced no small interest. The bishop may also have wanted to impress the pope by presenting him with a poem about hunting by a Slavic writer that would rival works in this vein by such Italian poets as Ercole Strozzi and Guido Postumo Silvestri. Strozzi's much admired *Venatio* (Hunting) was dedicated to Lucrezia Borgia; Silvestri, in fact, composed a Latin elegy about the hunting exploits of Leo himself, but it appeared in 1524, after the publication of Hussovianus's work.

Had the bison hide been transported all the way from Lithuania to Rome, the story of Leo X's Polish connections would have been more interesting yet. Alas, none of the plan was realized save Hussovianus's poem. Death claimed the pope on December 1, 1521, before arrangements for shipping the bison hide were completed and before Hussovianus finished his poem. The palatine Radziwiłł followed the pope in early January 1522, and Bishop Ciołek succumbed the following September to the plague then ravaging Rome.

Once he began his poem Hussovianus was not deterred from completing it by the pope's passing. But when the long work was at last ready for the printer, it bore a dedication not to the pope for whom it was originally commissioned but to the second wife of King Sigismund I, Queen Bona, of the Milanese Sforza family, who extended Hussovianus patronage when he arrived in Cracow in 1523. The dedication begins, in fact, with a brief recitation of the poem's origin: "When I was in Rome, Most Serene Queen, the Most Reverend Lord Erasmus, bishop of Płock, for some time regaled Pope Leo X with stories of the northern hunts and the multitude of beasts in those regions. In my presence, he pointed out in a lengthy digression that a picture of the bison, which we call *żubr*, together with the animal's hide, might be exhibited in Rome. Besides promising that this would be done, in pursuit of which he wrote to Radziwiłł, palatine of Wilno, asking him to obtain as large a hide of this animal as possible, he then ordered me, who was at the time his servant, to write something on the nature and manner of hunting of this beast. His wish was to show its image to the pope in both object and word. But all these plans came to naught because of the sudden death of Leo."[5]

Hussovianus also relates in the poem itself how the work came to be written:

> Nuper ad Italiam nullo mihi tempore visam
>   Venimus et iussi teximus istud opes.
> Si licet, hoc veniens longinquis hospes ab oris
>   Legitima certe cum ratione peto,
> Nullus ut exoptet sublimius ista referri,
>   Ad rem noscendam quam satis esse queat.[6]

(We came recently to Italy, which I had never seen before, and having been so ordered composed this present work. If it may be permitted, this guest coming from far distant shores asks, certainly with just reason, that his poem not be regarded as a very great achievement and that it is enough for him that it makes its subject known.)

Whatever the circumstances of its genesis, Hussovianus's lengthy opus about the fierce bison remains a singular achievement of Polish humanist literature. Writing principally for a foreign audience unfamiliar with the beast the poem deals with or its native habitat, Hussovianus approached his task with mingled humility and pride—humility because the poem was commissioned to satisfy the curiosity of no less a personage than Leo X, and pride in being invited to create a poetic work not only about hunting bison in the forests of Lithuania but in a broader sense about his native land.

Hussovianus acquitted himself admirably. Instead of a dry textbook account of the appearance and characteristics of the bison and the way the animal was hunted, the *De statura, feritate ac venatione bisontis* is a vivid, realistic, often graphic narrative. The following passages are typical:

This most savage of creatures is born in the thick forests of Lithuania and is customarily distinguished by such a huge body that when it inclines its head, vanquished and dying, three men can sit between its horns. But its huge neck seems too small for its body in comparison to its other limbs.

Its beard sticks out, frightful with its thick hanging curls. Burning eyes turn red with a piercing anger; the horrible hair of its mane flows over its shoulders, concealing its knees with its whole chest thrust forward. (51–60)

Surpassing all other animals in ferocity, or at least equal to them, it is not dangerous to man except when wounded. It safeguards its life with the greatest care; no one could do more in this respect. Its eyes dart all about, it gazes on all sides, surveying the farthest limits of the road before it. It can detect the sudden movement of a man's eyelids even though no other part of his body may be moving. Its ears can also pick up the slightest noise behind it, for it guards its rear with the greatest circumspection. So long as arrows or weapons gleam, it can be seen walking along with a serious gait. The beast will hold you for a long time with fixed gaze and will stop in its tracks if ensnared in turn by a man's eyes. But if it should happen that the beast be anxiously leading its young, the sudden clatter of arms will send it into a frenzy, and by a roar frightening to hear it will announce its terrible anger. That will then serve as a sign should someone want to come close. (147–64)

The beast was wounded first by light blows—the tips of arrows sent against it hung from its skin. Enraged, it gazed at all the men, all the while emitting terrible noises through trembling nostrils. Then, after making a sudden turnabout, the beast undertook to flee with rapid steps. The horsemen gave chase, their voices raised. The sound echoed to the highest clouds. But when in its swift course the animal reached a place where its path was blocked by a pile of felled logs, the excited shouts of the crowd stopped it. Driven back, it remained standing as if pondering which way to escape. But then it was wounded anew by an arrow sent screaming at it, so that its anger might erupt still more violently. Now seeing its body pierced by winged iron, it fell into a sudden rage and began roaring madly. It pierced the hunters with a savage gaze, all the time observing where they were concentrated the thickest. First it vented its bloody rage at the pack of barking hounds, leaving them a bloody heap, then turned to attack the men one more time. (523–42)

Hussovianus's literary strategy, pursued with great effectiveness, was essentially twofold. Forswearing any learned knowledge of his subject, he draws his account wholly from his own experiences as an observer and participant in bison hunts. The conviction his narrative carries, therefore, is not bookish but based on firsthand knowledge, a point he makes time and again. This personal, informal tone, which runs through the entire poem and gives it much of its freshness and appeal, is struck from the very beginning, when Hussovianus recalls how a bullfight he and friends happened to see in Rome reminded him of the bison hunts of his native Lithuania and led eventually to his writing the *De statura, feritate ac venatione bisontis*:

> Not long ago, in a crowd of people, I happened to witness a spectacle that was held in Rome. When bulls let loose for the purpose were joining fierce combat, repelling swarms of missiles with their bodies, and anger become sharper among the animals by their goading turned their swift tormentors to more frequent bloodshed, and when I saw in wonderment how much ferocity there was in the rage inflamed by the applause of the crowd and the wounds inflicted on the beasts, friends I was with happened to mention the northern forests. I began to speak openly in response to their many inquiries. I told of various hunts and of the great strength of the animals. But my tongue got me into trouble. Now this task has been given me that I repeat my words in song, and I am ordered to write speedily. (1–14)

Hussovianus's literary strategy serves another purpose as well. It enables him to strike a pose of modesty: he cannot compare himself, of course, to Roman writers (scriptoribus impar / Romanis), but certain of his way with the subject of his poem, he, a Pole (Polonus), will head toward "northern woods," acting as a guide through the forests of Lithuania. Neither early Slavic commentators (he mentions having read "many ancient things in the books of the Ruthenians") nor such figures of classical antiquity as Pliny offer accurate and detailed descriptions of the bison. The terrain through which he will be taking his readers is largely uncharted, therefore, and there is unmistakable pride in his demurral that he cannot familiarize "learned people" (doctis) with books that describe the awesome dimensions of the bison, because there are none. His humility has limits, however; he is quick to point out that he himself has read a great deal but has found nothing to pass on to his readers ("Multa revolventi nihil hac est parte repertum" [109]). Probably as a diplomatic gesture toward Italian readers, he declares that the only author who says anything interesting about the bison is Paulus Diaconus, a Lombard historian who, commenting on its enormous size, stated that he had heard from a reliable oldtimer that the animal's hide was large enough to hold fifteen men ("Scribit enim rigidi fido senis ore relatum / Quindenos una pelle cubasse viros" [113]).

Hussovianus's knowledge of the bison, on the other hand, comes neither from books nor from the accounts of other people. It is all firsthand, for, as he says proudly, "I am not moved by the sight of the hide or the huge horns of beasts, since I have often turned them over in my hands" (Me non visa movet pellis, non ampla ferarum / Cornua vel manibus saepe revulsa meis [115–16]). In assuming the task of writing a great poem on the bison—which no one else has attempted—he is aided not only by his personal knowledge but by years of hunting, beginning with his father's training, and by a life of hardship ("Quidquid erit, longus venandi proferet usus / Et labor ac vitae tempora dura meae. . . . Me pater instituit latebras lustrare ferarum" [117–18, 121]). By speaking often in the first person, Hussovianus maintains a tone that is at once casual and knowledgeable: his experience, which he suggests is vast, lets him write about bison and bison hunting at great length, in great detail, and—most important—with impressive authority.

The narrative progression of the *De statura, feritate ac venatione bisontis* moves from a description of the appearance, characteristics, and habitat of the bison to a lengthy and richly detailed account of the tracking and hunting of the beast, culminating in its killing. The structure of the poem is loose enough, however, to accommodate several digressions, which Hussovianus blends into his narrative so skillfully that they seem an integral part of the poem.

In one of these digressions Hussovianus defines his literary "philosophy," which is based on avoiding bookishness. Since his account of the bison is drawn entirely from personal experience, he is both true to life and free of indebtedness to secondary literary sources, whose value he has already dismissed. This realism and independence—which are hardly common in humanist Neo-Latin poetry—lead Hussovianus not only to dispense with the classical mythology in which humanist literature abounds, but to attack Christian writers who rely excessively on mythological figures and imagery: "Ought I consider what I should say of the huntress Diana or of any of the retinue that accompanies her? It is inappropriate for this writer to admire the curved bow of Apollo and the arrows so often frightful to the beasts struck by them. Not Jove do I revere, nor Juno, but Christ, and it is for the Mother of Christ that my songs are intended" (401–6).

Hussovianus strikes an even bolder note in defense of his own approach to literary creativity in the next few lines when he declares: "I am loath to mix fable and truth. Permit me to say so with simple forthrightness, you who pursue obsolete learning and thereby nourish the errors of ancients in your poetry" (407–10).

Some of the digressions fulfill a major goal of the work, to familiarize foreign readers with the Lithuanian-Belorussian region of the Polish commonwealth that was home both to Hussovianus and to the bison. The longest such digression (663–824) is an extended panegyric to the Lithuanian grand duke Witold (1401–30), Jagiełło's cousin, who initiated the sport of bison hunting as a way of preparing young men for combat: "Such a hunt may, nevertheless, be regarded as foolish, since it is sometimes dangerous to many men, nor can the originator of it, who also now possesses a name of great renown, be entirely absolved of guilt. By such inventions the lofty mind of the hardy Witold restored the exhausted vitality of his country. By means of these exercises he trained young men for war when he was prince of Lithuania" (659–66).

Whatever reservations Hussovianus may have had about hunting bison as a sport, he portrays Witold as a wise ruler who loves peace yet understands the need to prepare for war. So successful are Witold's policies against his adversaries that the "Tatar, out of fear, could offer only feeble blows" (671); the "Muscovite called [Witold] master in servile voice, although great among the powers" (676–77); and the "Turk, though strong, was sending huge amounts of tribute and was on the point of swearing allegiance" (679–80).

In accordance with the emphatic Christian orientation of the *De statura . . . bisontis,* Witold's greatest achievement—his conversion of his people to Christianity—is reserved for praise until the end of the digression, as if his embrace of the Christian faith marked the culmination of his career: "He was the first who received the laws of Christ together with his nation, overthrew the old holy places of the people, erected temples to the greatest god, and with great piety gave his wealth to their servants. He banished all the monstrosities of the old gods and was himself the witness of his former errors" (819–24).

Hussovianus knew only too well how difficult it was to banish the old gods from the grand duchy of Lithuania, the last outpost of paganism in Europe. He makes the tenacity of pagan beliefs and practices in Lithuania the subject of one of his lengthier digressions, devoted to the topography of the Lithuanian-Belorussian region and the mores of its people:

We see such wondrous things in our land. Either God wants everything to be open, or things instead come into being and die by the magical arts. Sometimes thinking about this can disturb the mind. Such great power is always attributed to herbs and words beneath the northern cold, and so many fearful songs can be heard that it all seems to me nothing other than a tale of Medea, although I know it to be almost entirely true. Christians are constrained to forbid such beliefs and practices and usually throw to the flames any person—as soon as the matter is revealed—who entangles himself in such deeds even slightly or who observes these things but does not immediately report them. If someone is branded by an incriminating report of the people, even though the hidden deeds are obscured by shadows, he is seized, at once bound hand and foot, and thrown straightway into the swollen waters. If he is seen to go under, he is revived and declared innocent, but if the opposite happens, he is always believed to be guilty. We have seen people restrained by nooses above a high abyss struggling to sink their heads in the water as thousands of noisy onlookers watched. From that time on deep bewilderment struck me dumb, for I saw with my own eyes how the waves would appear to approach the ill-omened head only to turn away from it at the last moment, and how the water indeed no longer seemed to resemble itself. Fire is a fairer test, always destroying such monsters and punishing the wicked. You may doubt what I am recounting, but you can see these things taking place before your own eyes throughout Lithuania; I followed only what I myself experienced. But nevertheless impressionable people cultivate the traditional arts practiced by evil women. (291–322)

Reading these lines from a sixteenth-century Polish Neo-Latin poem, one is reminded of Czesław Miłosz's remarks in the fictionalized account of his boyhood, *Dolina Issy* (The Issa Valley, 1955), on the pagan vestiges woven into the fabric of rural life in his native Lithuania:

The Issa Valley has the distinction of being inhabited by an unusually large number of devils. It may be that the hollow willows, mills, and thickets lining the riverbanks provide a convenient cover for those creatures who reveal themselves only when it suits them. Those who have seen them say that the devil is rather short, about the size of a nine-year-old; that he wears a green frock coat, a jabot, his hair in a pigtail, white stockings, and tries to conceal his hoofs, which are an embarrassment to him, with high-heeled slippers. Such tales should be treated with a certain caution. It is possible that, knowing the superstitious awe in which the Germans are held—they being people of commerce, inventions, and science—the devils seek to lend themselves an air of gravity by dressing up in the manner of Immanuel Kant of Königsberg. It's no coincidence that along the Issa another name for the Evil Spirit is the "Little German"— implying that the devil is on the side of progress. . . .

There is no predicting whom they might impersonate. A girl lights two candles on St. Andrew's Eve, gazes into the mirror, and her future is revealed: the face of the man with whom her life will be joined, or the face of death. Is this the devil in disguise, or could it be the work of other magical forces? And how is one to tell them apart, those creatures coinciding with the advent of Christianity from those native inhabitants of bygone days, like the forest witch who switches children in their cradles,

or the little people who stray at night from their palaces under the roots
of the elder bushes? . . .

The peasant farmers along the Issa used to place, by the entrance to
their cottages, a bowl of milk for the water snakes, which were not afraid
of humans. In time, the inhabitants became fervent Catholics and the
presence of the devils made them recall the struggle being waged for
dominion over the human soul.[7]

Other digressions in the *De statura . . . bisontis,* perhaps the most
important, are political in nature and inform the work with a meaning
that transcends satisfying papal curiosity about an exotic animal. Hussovianus's emphasis on his own fidelity to Christian tradition and
practice, which we have already observed, insinuates itself as a national
characteristic. Writing as a Pole who is above all a good Christian,
he becomes a representative of his nation, which zealously defends
Christian principles. The confluence of literary strategy and political
purpose in the *De statura . . . bisontis* comes clearly to the fore. Commissioned to write a poem about the bison for Leo X, Hussovianus saw
the literary work as an exceptional opportunity, not to be lost, to make
his distant and exotic homeland more familiar to his Italian readers
and to press the case for Polish political positions among an audience
whose support was of no small importance. The attack on the perpetu-
ators of ancient errors in the passage quoted therefore bridges the
poetic and political credos.

After establishing his credentials as a loyal *Christian,* Hussovianus
goes on to use his Christianity—which is at once individual and national—to indict those antagonists with which the Polish state then had
its hands full: the Turks and the Teutonic Order of the Knights of
the Cross.

As an infidel power menacing not only Poland but European Christendom as a whole, the Turks represented an easy target that could be
named and railed against in a manner calculated to win an immediate
positive response:

> Turcus enim miseram caedit tantummodo plebem,
>   Diripiens arces, oppida, templa, domos,
> Anticipans portus, firmans loca, milite complens,
>   Quae satis, ut cunctos perderet, apta videt. (1011–14)

(For the Turk assaults only an unfortunate people, leveling citadels,
towns, temples, and houses, seizing harbors, and fortifying places by
manning them with soldiers to destroy whatever he sees fit.)

But the Turkish threat is just an excuse to castigate the Christian rulers of Europe, whose energies and resources are diverted from the campaign against the common enemy—the Turk—by conflicts among themselves and by the religious dissension (Hussovianus has in mind principally the Lutheran "heresy") that has newly erupted. When European Christendom and indeed the integrity of the church itself are under siege and the times demand unity among Christian states, what, asks Hussovianus, are the rulers doing?

> Ne quid nunc agitem, terrent atrocia mentem
>   Bella, quibus toto Mars fremit orbe ferus.
> Optima religio Christi turbata vacillat,
>   Debilis in campo, non bene firma domi,
> Ipsa suis in se gladiis dum scinditur, hosti
>   Turpiter in praedam ludibriumque cadit. . . . (985–1001)

(How can I not be anxious now, when terrible wars, with which fierce Mars roars throughout the entire world, frighten the mind? The supreme religion of Christ reels in confusion, lame in the field and not very strong at home. While it tears itself asunder with its own swords, it falls shamefully in booty and derision to the enemy. Long does it beseech heaven for so much help for which our crimes yet forbid us to hope. In the meantime, what are the rulers doing? Are they asleep? Alas, never did they have more cause for anxiety. But what of it? One head of state readies armies against another. They view the slaughter of their own people with eyes defiled by death, and this now has become a pleasure to them. Having perpetrated a great evil, they amuse themselves with our blood.)

Underlying Hussovianus's fulminations was the concern that internecine strife among the Christian states of Europe and widening religious dissension would deny a geographically vulnerable Poland outside assistance in the struggle with the Turks. Counting on the ability of the Holy See to restore a sense of common Christian responsibility in the face of obvious dangers, the Polish poet saw nothing untoward in taking full advantage of his commission to inject an unmistakable appeal that the pope work to achieve Christian unity—in a way, of course, compatible with Polish interests.

Polish interests were also uppermost in Hussovianus's mind in the poem's more oblique appeal for a sympathetic understanding of the Polish position with respect to the Knights of the Cross. By opposing Polish domination over the Prussian region and conspiring with Poland's enemies (meaning the Muscovites and Tatars), the Teutonic Order drains the resources of the Polish state in senseless conflict, thereby weakening it as a Christian bulwark against Tatars and Turks. Support of the papacy had long been a cornerstone of Polish policy toward the Knights, so Hussovianus's interjection of the Polish-Prussian conflict comes as no surprise.

For diplomatic reasons, given the sensitivity of the issue and a Vatican approach not always acceptable to the Poles, Hussovianus is not as overt in dealing with the issue of the Knights as in writing about the Turks. The Knights are never mentioned by name in the poem, but there is no doubt about whom such lines as these refer to: "Wars, alas, can also be conducted by us for some advantage or other, but a people united by the league of baptism does not inflict harm, nor does it threaten our interests from another side. Those whose peace is defended by our zeal attack us and wish our destruction. They prepare an ambush for us by joining their arms to those of our enemies, whom they stir up by secret vows and counsel. By their own motion they oppose passing time, always in order that our ruination may direct it their way" (445–54).

How much importance Hussovianus attached to the Christian political dimension of his poem can be seen from the work's final forty-six-line prayer imploring the Virgin Mary to end the conflicts and dissension tearing the fabric of Christian unity and to restrain the enemies of peace. Since the prayer is one of the finer passages in the poem, I quote it in full:

> Virgo, Dei mater, cuius dum scribere nomen
>   Hic vellem, pavidae contremuere manus,
> Attonitusque diu nequeo comprendere mente,
>   Qua taceam, tecum qua ratione loquar,
> Si taceo, digna es, quam totus clamitet orbis,
>   Cuntaque communi voce creata sonent. . . . (1027–72)

(O Virgin, mother of God, when I wanted to write your name here my hand trembled with anxiety and, stunned, for a long time I was unable to understand whether I should better remain silent or whether I should speak with you. How can I be silent, when you are worthy of the whole world proclaiming you and all creatures singing your praises with one voice? But how ought I to speak when human speech and mind do not know what words are fitting to mention you? Trusting, however, in your goodness, which surpasses everything that is beneath immeasurable God, I approach now with quaking heart, and begging your grace I throw myself, O Virgin Mary, at your feet. Shabby and dirty of dress, and shabbier yet within, all pale I conjure prayers from my bloodless mouth not because I am worthy of uttering even a single word, but because you alone are able to raise us up again. Taking pity on man's fate, God set you atop the lofty peak, and like the power of light or a bird that looks after its featherless young you, O Holy Virgin, keep mankind warm. Just as an attentive mother lifts up an infant boy, so do you raise up those you see have fallen. Now, O celebrated majesty of the maidenly flower, join your prayers to my vows. Look upon the madness of wars and fields soaked by blood, see how greatly fate permits the sword to be used against a people who united by the covenant of your son deserves to live in brotherly peace. I beseech you, instill a sound mind in our princes, that they may see they have betrayed the vows of their office. Since they are guilty of having slackened the reins of the world, are they not guardians only in name, and in fact wolves? Meanwhile, so that they may have a chance to recover their senses, restrain our savage enemies and obstruct their hatred that they may not ensnare an unfortunate people and drag hapless nations into their chains.)

The last ten lines of the prayer, and of the poem, underscore Hussovianus's urgency about the political situation. Forsaking as presumptuous a direct appeal to Leo X's successor—Adrian VI (1459–1523), who was elevated to the papacy on January 11, 1522—Hussovianus instead incorporated an appeal to the new pope within the concluding prayer to the Virgin Mary. Since Adrian (of Utrecht) was serving as cardinal of Tortosa in Spain when he was elected to the papacy,[8] Hussovianus asks that he come to Rome as quickly as possible to initiate a vigorous pontificate that will, needless to say, understand Polish concerns. Addressing the Virgin Mary, the poet declares: "Prepare the way for Adrian VI. Constrained, let him reject any causes or counsel of delay, and outstripping fast winds let him race across the surface of the sea and let him seize the swords now wielded by madness. Let him show himself unto the stupid in whose lands those enemies take up positions, whom it is proper to overthrow lawfully so that he who lawfully receives unbought titles may legitimately direct the arms of his nation. And let Adrian strive to achieve such a pontificate as lacks the hateful dread of time" (1063–72).

Besides having an undeniable poetic gift of considerable power and individuality, Hussovianus was also a patriot in more than one sense. His poem about the bison breathes with a deep love of nature that is reflected everywhere in his work. But this love of nature also has a specific locus: the woods and forests of the former grand duchy of Lithuania. Regionalism, especially Lithuanian and Ukrainian, has played an enormous role in the development of Polish literature down to the present. It thus becomes possible to situate Hussovianus in a particular Polish literary landscape and to see him as a precursor of such great poets of the Polish language as Adam Mickiewicz in the nineteenth century and Czesław Miłosz in the twentieth, who drew inspiration from the same sources. But Hussovianus's patriotism is both regional and national at the same time. His political allegiance is wholly Polish—in terms, that is, of the Polish commonwealth, whose interests he found an opportunity to advance in poetry.

What is remarkable about the *De statura . . . bisontis* is the skill with which Hussovianus has merged the poem's elements in a harmonious whole, much as the regional and national have been reconciled. The description of the bison and bison hunting logically requires the poet to describe the beast's habitat, which in turn rationalizes the lavish display of his love of nature in its universal and specific aspects as well as his familiarity with the customs of the people. He explains bison hunting as a sport while writing proudly about the past greatness of medieval Lithuania. This motivates a portrait of the great ruler Witold that stresses his love of peace and his acceptance of Christianity. The excursion into the past then forms a logical bridge to the concerns of the present. The Polish-Lithuanian state, of which the grand duchy of Lithuania is now a part, is characterized as a bastion of Christianity in need of support at a time when the unity of Christian Europe is being shattered by senseless strife among its rulers while the infidel waits eagerly at the gates.

Hussovianus's own Christian loyalties, emphasized at several points in his poem, link him both to the region that forms the setting of the work and to the Christian peace-loving and peace-promoting policies of the Polish commonwealth. He is an appropriate spokesman, therefore, for both the grand duchy of Lithuania and the Polish commonwealth, whose zealous defense of Christianity inspires pride as deep as his love of nature.

How Christianity, peace, and international politics are made to relate to the subject proper of the poem—bison hunting—illuminates the underlying cleverness of Hussovianus's conception. The poet unobtrusively but unmistakably insinuates a parallel throughout his work between the senseless slaughter of the beasts as sport and the senseless slaughter of men in war. As a faithful Christian who deplores the shedding of blood, Hussovianus finds the most effective moments to steer his reader's thoughts from images of animals being slaughtered in the hunt to those of men dying in combat. Moreover, he arouses revulsion toward bloodshed in general by sparing no detail about the killing of the bison. The rest of the parallel comes together easily. While Christian rulers feud in pursuit of selfish goals, thereby placing all of Christian Europe in jeopardy, the Polish commonwealth remains steadfast in its loyalty to the church and the Christian faith. It thus deserves the support of both the church and a grateful Europe for its heroic defense of Christendom against the common enemy.

To appreciate how smoothly Hussovianus has integrated his digressions with the narrative and has interlocked the main themes of the poem, let us look at a specific instance, that point in the *De statura . . . bisontis* where he first introduces the subject of war, unites it with bison hunting, registers his hatred (as a Christian) of war, and finally pleads the case of Poland as the bulwark of Christendom.

After establishing in lines 401–16 that his poem will venerate not the ancient gods of the Romans and Greeks but Christ and the mother of Christ, he then goes on to advise his readers:

> Dulcia qui sequeris, qui res exquiris amoenas
> Hic nihil horridulus floris agellus habet,
> Et glacie et nivibus passim iacet obrutus altis;
> Hoc opus hiberni temporis esse decet. (417–20)

(Whoever seeks delights or looks for pleasant things will find nothing of beauty in this rather rough little field, which lies buried beneath ice and deep snow. This work belongs more to the season of winter.)

The next few lines (421–26) introduce the theme of war, link combat with hunting, and establish Hussovianus's own repugnance toward war:

> Cogimur assiduis aestatem volvere bellis,
> Otia venandi sola ferebat hiems.
> Hunc quoque praeripuit Martis violentia morem
> Bellaque frigoribus continuata iuvant.
> Par dolor et lacrimas et mea verba rapit.

(Compelled to spend the summer in incessant warfare, we can enjoy the pleasures of hunting only in winter. The violence of Mars also encourages the custom, so that our men enjoy wars waged in the cold of winter. The detestable thing [war] overcomes my ability to remain silent and arouses grief, tears, and anger in me.)

Moved to speak of war despite his detestation of it, Hussovianus next advances the cause of Poland as the last defender of the faith:

> Privato gerimus communia milite bella,
> Ut sacra lex fratrum tutior inde foret. (427–28)

(We wage wars for all with our own army so that the sacred law of brothers [the Christian faith] may be the more secure.)

> Nos sumus extremi, quorum sua tela fatigat
> Corporibus quorum sanguine tardat iter,
> Ne ruat interior saevumque profundius ensem
> Inferat ac sternens obvia quaeque secet.
> Haeret adhuc frendens. (441–45)

(We are the last whose spears weary the enemy and the blood of whose bodies slows his way. Without our opposition, he would overrun those behind us, plunge his fierce sword deeper, knock down everything standing in his way and cut it to pieces. Until now he remains rooted to the spot, gnashing his teeth.)

When the digression has gone far enough and he has made his points, Hussovianus returns to the main subject of bison hunting by first asking the rhetorical question, "Quid iuvat in silvis questus disperdere?" (But what good does it do to lament such things in the woods? [475]). This immediately sets the stage for the resumption of the narrative by reestablishing its locus, the forests of Lithuania and Belorussia. The poet then directs himself as narrator to resume his tale: "Vocem / Hinc refer ad brutas, Hussoviane, feras" (Henceforth, Hussovianus, turn your voice back to the wild beasts [475–76]).

In like manner, after his long digression about Prince Witold of Lithuania, Hussovianus signals the return to his narrative by speaking again in the first person, as a storyteller who has strayed too far from his subject:

> Propositi memor esse mei dum cogor et arti
> Temporis, ante prior conficienda fera est.
> Immodice forsan videor digressus ab illa,
> Sed tamen interea stare necesse fuit,
> Dum longo clamore feram cursuque fatigent. (827–31)

(I am constrained to be mindful of my subject and the passage of time, since there is the matter of the beast's being finished off. I may seem, perhaps, to have strayed excessively from it, but it was necessary to pause while the hunters were wearing the animal down with prolonged shouting and pursuit.)

After regaining the momentum of his narrative, Hussovianus soon launches into one of the most vivid passages in the entire poem:

Once, during a hunt of King Alexander, an awful thing happened that is still talked about and that, were it not for God's intervention, might have enveloped the entire kingdom in grief. A platform was erected on four high columns for the benefit of those observing the hunt. The queen [Yelena, wife of King Alexander of Poland and daughter of the Muscovite prince Ivan III] was seated here together with her assemblage and with her noble ladies and maidens. Below, young men stood in view, delighting in the animals and vying with one another to attract attention and to turn hearts by their skill and strength. Then Cupid shot his arrows from atop the highest tree. How easy for you to play bloodless games whenever you wish! But why here in the forests, dangerous lad? Behold, someone wanting to find favor in a damsel's eyes falls in an absurd and sudden death, led by you, capricious Cupid. And while the beasts ran about and chased their pursuers, and while all of this was of great interest to the onlookers, a radiance lit up the sky from the women's garments in which interwoven white and gold shimmered and red silks of variegated design glowed warmly. Soon this wondrous sight, which caused great excitement, gripped the beasts and for a moment seemed to restrain them. I do not say that this species [women], which is accustomed to delighting men's senses, had power over raging beasts. Thereupon, other bison appeared on the scene with a thunderous roaring and launched an all-out attack on the hunters. One of the great animals, however, wounded and bleeding and surely aware of what was happening to it, stood its ground and began shaking its head as if wondering at the colors of the spectators and trying to discern people's faces. It seemed that, indignant at the spectacle being prepared by its slaughter, it wanted to make its imminent death memorable. It bellowed, therefore, its nostrils all swollen (this was a signal to the herds in the rear) and, taking aim, shook loose one of the columns of the royal platform with a blow from its head. The platform barely remained upright on the remaining three. If the entire structure had slipped and fallen down because of fate, a mind overcome by great dread cannot imagine how soaked the earth would have been by blood and how red the beast's horns from the cruel slaughter that would have taken place. Chased with great effort, the beast overcomes its feelings and dislodges its rage. Its huge mouth fills with foam, its tongue hangs down a long time from its jaws, its tail noisily cleaves the air, and thick clouds of steam pour from its snout. The cold might have hardened its invincible strength if not that it was gushing sweat from all the exertion and its huge body, exuding perspiration on all sides, trembled from heavy breathing. It rushes about, its movements lacking any order and its eyebrows often twitching convulsively. Tufts of shaggy hair fly from its mane from the labored breathing; raging at its own body in the absence of others, it plucks and tears its own hair and, furious, kicks its own belly with its hooves. While gusts of wind shake the dry foliage, the bison rushes into it with a headlong leap. Scattering birds create a trembling shadow as the great beast plunges deeper into the bushes. (887–948)

I shall conclude this chapter on Hussovianus and his poem about the Polish bison with a digression of my own. It concerns the literary rediscovery of Hussovianus's Latin poem in Poland in the late nineteenth century and subsequent efforts to translate it into Polish and other languages.

The name of the great poet of Polish romanticism, Adam Mickiewicz (1798–1855), looms so large in the history of Polish literature that it often seems no study of a Polish literary topic is complete without at least a deferential mention of him. Here, however, he is germane to the rediscovery of Hussovianus's poem.

Mickiewicz died in Constantinople in 1855. Before his ill-fated journey to Turkey to heal rifts among rival Polish mercenary forces organized to fight against the Russians in the Crimean War, he had been living in Paris since 1832, the most celebrated literary figure in the so-called Great Emigration that followed the suppression of the Polish November Insurrection of 1830–31. It was natural, then, that his remains would be returned to Paris, where they were interred in the cemetery of Montmorency, to remain there until a more favorable political climate in Austrian-partitioned Poland toward the end of the nineteenth century permitted their transfer to a crypt in the Wawel Castle in Cracow. Understandably, a number of ceremonies took place in conjunction with this reinterment, which occurred on July 4, 1890.

One of Mickiewicz's greatest admirers in the literary community at the time was a talented poet of peasant origins named Jan Kasprowicz (1860–1926). When Mickiewicz's remains were laid in their resting place among those of Poland's rulers and greatest poets, Kasprowicz composed a poem entitled "U trumny wieszcza. Dwa fragmenty poświęcone pamięci Adama Mickiewicza" (At the Bard's Coffin: Two Fragments Dedicated to the Memory of Adam Mickiewicz). The erection of a statue to Mickiewicz in the old marketplace in the center of Cracow provided the subject for yet another poem, "Przed pomnikiem Mickiewicza" (Before the Statue of Mickiewicz). A few years later, when the centenary of Mickiewicz's birth gave cause for still further celebration, Kasprowicz delivered a public lecture, "Mikołaj Hussowskiego 'Pieśń o żubrze' i 'Pan Tadeusz'" (Mikołaj Hussowski's [*sic*] "Poem about the Bison" and "Pan Tadeusz").[9] In it he sought to draw parallels between Mickiewicz's major poetic work, the twelve-book lyrical epic *Pan Tadeusz* (Master Thaddeus, 1834) and Hussovianus's poem about the bison.

Long regarded as the single greatest achievement of Polish poetry, *Pan Tadeusz* is a nostalgic though not uncritical evocation of the life of the traditional Polish gentry in the Lithuanian region of the former

Polish commonwealth on the eve of the Napoleonic campaign against Russia. In writing the poem, Mickiewicz sought to provide, as an antidote to the frustrations and uncertainties of the émigré existence, a larger-than-life picture of a bygone existence, of the Poland of his own youth now universalized as the collective memory of the Great Emigration. The work brims with the typicality of the world of the old Polish gentry, and on one level it surely can be regarded as a monument to a Polishness now invested with spiritual sustenance.

Among the favorite pursuits of the old gentry was the hunt, to which Mickiewicz devotes an entire canto of the *Pan Tadeusz*. The description is spectacular for its unerring sense of detail, its evocative power, and its manifest love of the forests of the poet's native Lithuania.

The point of Kasprowicz's lecture was not merely appreciation of Mickiewicz's principal poetic achievement—there was hardly a dearth of that even then—but a fresh perspective on Mickiewicz's place in Polish culture. For Kasprowicz, Mickiewicz was above all a *national* poet whose inspiration derived from a deep love of land and nation, without which a work such as *Pan Tadeusz* would have been impossible. Kasprowicz believed that for a Polish poet such inspiration was a requisite for greatness; in its absence there remained the hollow cosmopolitanism of foreign fashion.

Although the idea is not conveyed overtly in his lecture on Mickiewicz, one senses in reading Kasprowicz that he discerned two main currents in the development of Polish literature: the self-consciously cosmopolitan, nurtured from alien sources and unresponsive to native stimuli, and the authentically national. For Kasprowicz, then, Mickiewicz was not an isolated genius, but the highest expression of a truly native Polish poetic creativity whose presence in Polish literary experience revealed itself even before the triumph of the vernacular language in the second half of the sixteenth century—revealed itself, in fact, in Nicolaus Hussovianus's Latin poem of 1521–22.

Kasprowicz was struck by the similarities between Hussovianus's poem and those parts of Mickiewicz's *Pan Tadeusz* set in the forests of Lithuania and devoted to a vivid account of the hunting rituals of the old Polish gentry. Also, in both poems the long and carefully crafted descriptions of nature serve purposes besides art. Landscape in *Pan Tadeusz* becomes a magic carpet by which the Polish émigré of the 1830s in a distant alien city can be transported back to the lost land of his youth, to a homeland of happier times. For Hussovianus, writing in the universal language of Latin about bison hunting in the Lithuanian-Belorussian region of the Polish commonwealth, which had ceased to exist by Mickiewicz's time, was used to familiarize foreign readers with his homeland, in which he took great pride. It was also a way to elicit support for, or at least a better understanding of, Polish political anxieties.

Largely unsympathetic toward the cosmopolitanism of Polish turn-of-the-century modernist literature, Kasprowicz would naturally have chosen in his lecture to emphasize the Polishness of Mickiewicz's *Pan Tadeusz* as well as the love of country it reflects. It also would have been natural for him to want to establish an impressive genealogy for the work—a certain tradition, so to speak, within Polish literature. One might expect, however, that Kasprowicz would seek to relate the author of *Pan Tadeusz* to Poland's foremost Renaissance vernacular poet, Jan Kochanowski (1530–84), rather than to the long-forgotten Latin writer Hussovianus. By thus departing from the anticipated and customary, Kasprowicz was setting Kochanowski outside the tradition he saw as culminating in *Pan Tadeusz*. For all his acknowledged greatness, Kochanowski, from Kasprowicz's point of view, was too cosmopolitan, too European. Hussovianus seemed a more truly national poet whose major work, the *De statura . . . bisontis*, held forth a promise fulfilled over three centuries later in *Pan Tadeusz*. Although Hussovianus wrote in Latin, by virtue of all its other qualities his poem is a splendid example of a truly national Polish literary work. Conversely, Kochanowski's mastery of Polish was no guarantee that his works would be distinctly Polish in anything but language.

Since Latin is a well-established cultural tradition in Poland, it is certainly possible that Kasprowicz happened upon Hussovianus's poem in a quest for the authentic Polish antecedents of a masterpiece such as Mickiewicz's *Pan Tadeusz*. More likely, however, his interest was spurred by the publication in Cracow in 1894 of an edition of Hussovianus's poems (*Carmina*) edited by the scholar Jan Pelczar. Until the Pelczar edition, the original Cracow publication of the *De statura . . . bisontis* existed in only two copies. One belonged to Michał Juszyński, who donated it to the Czartoryski family library in Cracow in 1798, and Mickiewicz probably did not know of it. The other was in the possession of Father Józef Malszewicz of Grodno, who gave it to the Imperial Public Library of Saint Petersburg in 1853. This copy was the basis for a limited edition of one hundred copies of the poem that was published by the library on the fiftieth anniversary of the Moscow Society of the Students of Nature (Moskovskoe Obshchestvo Ispytateley Prirody) on December 28, 1855.

However he came upon Hussovianus's poem, Kasprowicz's enthusiasm led him to translate it into Polish. The translation, which was supposed to appear in Lwów in 1914, never was published, perhaps another casualty of World War I. To this day no complete Polish translation of the *De statura . . . bisontis* exists. All we have are the translated excerpts in Kasprowicz's lecture and in an anthology of Polish Latin poetry first published in Warsaw in 1957 and reprinted in Szczecin in 1985.[10] There are, on the other hand, complete published translations of Hussovianus's poem in both Russian and Belorussian—and therein lies a tale.

The Russian translation of the *De statura . . . bisontis* was published in the literary-social-political journal *Neman* in 1968; it is a new translation and quite literal.[11] The Belorussian translation, which is more poetic but also freer and not without error, is based on the Russian one in *Neman* and appeared the following year in the Belorussian journal *Polymya*, published in Minsk.[12]

The contemporary Soviet Russian and Belorussian interest in Hussovianus's sixteenth-century Latin poem seems unusual only if we are unfamiliar with Soviet cultural politics. Since the end of World War II, Soviet literary and historical scholarship has expended considerable energy to make a convincing case for a Renaissance culture if not in Russia proper, then in Belorussia and Ukraine, or in what the Russians regard historically as western Russia. The reasons are not obscure. After incorporating some sixty thousand square miles of the prewar Polish state into the Soviet Union after the war—territory peopled largely by Lithuanians, Belorussians, and Ukrainians—that is, by the peoples of the medieval grand duchy of Lithuania that united with the kingdom of Poland to form the Polish-Lithuanian commonwealth—the Soviets have been intent on dissociating the achievements of Polish subjects who were not ethnic Poles from the history of the multiethnic commonwealth in order to enhance the Belorussian and Ukrainian cultural heritages. Hussovianus is a case in point.

In newer Soviet scholarship on the Renaissance—from the 1960s and 1970s in particular—Hussovianus is claimed for Belorussian culture and is portrayed as a major figure in the development of a Belorussian Renaissance. In his book (in Russian) *The Neo-Latin Poetry of Belorussia and Lithuania,* published in Minsk in 1979, V. I. Doroshkevich, of the Belorussian Academy of Sciences, argues for the non-Polish content of the poem about the bison and states at one point that Hussovianus's work was actually unpopular in seventeenth- and eighteenth-century Poland because it did not deal with Polish history, did not exude an authentic Polish patriotism, and did not correspond in its orientation to the prevailing ideology of the Polish nobility.[13] Because Hussovianus himself was not a member of the nobility and celebrates a Lithuanian-Belorussian landscape in his poem, Doroshkevich argues, he was all but forgotten until the revival of interest in him in the late nineteenth century, which came in the context of a renewed enthusiasm for Polish antiquity.

At one point in his poem Hussovianus identifies himself as "Polonus" (a Pole), which Doroshkevich correctly, I believe, takes as a reference to a concept of statehood rather than an ethnic affiliation. Copernicus, an ethnic German, might similarly have identified himself as "Polonus" in the sense of a subject of the Polish Crown. But the Belorussian scholar is quick to point out that "many Polish scholars" accept Hussovianus's "Polonus" in the narrow ethnic sense.[14] The Poles, suggests Doroshkevich, are really of two minds about Hussovianus: on one hand, they ignored him for several hundred years because he did not seem Polish enough; on the other hand, because of his acknowledged importance in the development of a Slavic Renaissance, they are eager to claim him as one of their own for the greater glory of Polish culture.

The campaign to claim Hussovianus for Belorussian culture has already produced its share of aberrations, of which even Doroshkevich, a generally respected scholar, has been critical. In his *Neo-Latin Poetry of Belorussia and Lithuania,* for example, he takes issue with another Belorussian scholar, Vladimir Kolesnik, who not only has situated Hussovianus in the "broad historical context of the 'Belorussian Renaissance,' " but has determined that the *De statura . . . bisontis* was influenced by Belorussian folklore. Doroshkevich concedes the possible contribution of folklore but argues as well—without documenting his case—for the importance to Hussovianus of old Russian aesthetics (drevnorusskaya estetika) and the "civic spirit" (grazhdanskii dukh) of Belorussian chronicles, to which he attributes the formation of the poet's patriotic views. Linguistics has also been enlisted in the campaign of Belorussianization; the translator of Hussovianus into Belorussian, Yazep Semyazhon, has written that the poetic lexicon of the bison poem contains a "multitude of Church Slavonic and bookish phrases literally transposed into Latin."[15]

I will forgo any discussion of attempts by Lithuanian scholars to prove the Lithuanian ethnic origins of Hussovianus other than to mention in passing the article by V. Sakavicius that appeared in 1922 under the title "Nicolaus Hussovianus, kaipo pirmasis lietuviu humanistas" (Nicolaus Hussovianus as the First Lithuanian humanist).[16]

Concluding their short introduction to the Russian translation of Hussovianus's poem published in the journal *Neman* in 1968, Yakov Poretsky, one of the translators, and Yu. Prenskaya express the conviction that "The *Poem about the Bison,* on the strengths of its merits, will undoubtedly be esteemed by the Soviet reader as one of the shining moments in the cultural heritage of the Belorussian, Lithuanian, Polish, and Russian peoples."[17] Somehow I doubt this is the kind of fame Hussovianus had in mind when he warily accepted Bishop Ciołek's commission to write a poem about the Polish bison for Giovanni de' Medici, otherwise known as Pope Leo X.

CHAPTER 7

At the Courts of Kings and Emperors: Dantiscus as Diplomat and Poet

Jan Dantyszek (John of Gdańsk or Ioannes Dantiscus, 1485–1543) was no stranger to the circles of the powerful and scholarly when, not long before his death, he composed a poem about his life, *Vita Ioannis Dantisci*. It was with obvious pride that he wrote the following words:

> Principibus magnisque viris, doctisque, probisque
> Convixi fugiens, quos mala vita tenet.
> Hinc et amicitias nactus, socios et amicos,
> Qui me tot scriptis visere saepe solent
> Inter quos procul est magnus Cortesius ille,
> Qui mundi reperit regna tot ampla novi.
> Ultra aequatorem Capricorni sidus adusque
> Imperat estque mei tam procul ille memor.
> Non me fastidire solent regesque, ducesque,
> Doctorum pariter magna caterva virum.[1]

(I lived among princes and great men, among the learned and the virtuous, avoiding only those who led evil lives. It is for this reason that I came to know sincere friendship and acquired many acquaintances who keep in touch with me by frequent letters. Among them, now far away, is the great Cortés, who discovered so many great realms in the New World. He reigns beyond the Tropic of Capricorn and even from there still remembers me. Kings and princes do not disdain me, nor does a large throng of learned men.)

Although only the Spanish conquistador Fernando Cortés is mentioned by name, the list of the mighty and renowned whom Dantiscus

161

knew personally and exchanged correspondence or poetry with is long and impressive. It includes, to mention just a few, the Holy Roman Emperors Maximilian I and Charles V, the Austrian diplomat and historian Baron Sigismund von Herberstein, Erasmus of Rotterdam, Thomas More, Nicolaus Copernicus, Philipp Melanchthon, and George Sabinus (Schüler), first rector of the University of Königsberg.

Dantiscus easily attracted luminaries. He was certainly the best-known and most highly esteemed Polish diplomat of the Renaissance.[2] An affable, polished, and multitalented man, he spent the greater part of his life in diplomatic service both to the kings of Poland and to the Holy Roman Emperors. His professional career carried him throughout Europe and enabled him to develop an extraordinary range of friendships, all reflected in poetry noteworthy for its immediacy, down-to-earth qualities, and cosmopolitanism.

From his assumed name of Dantyszek in Polish and Dantiscus in Latin, it seems clear that he came from the great Baltic port of Gdańsk (German Danzig).[3] His family was German and, despite his later claims to aristocratic origin and a family name of Von Hoeffen (latinized as De Curiis), both humble and impoverished. His father Simon (Szymon in Polish) was probably a merchant, and his paternal grandfather was a ropemaker by trade (hence known as Flachsbinder, "ropemaker," in German) who had settled in Gdańsk, possibly from the Lower Rhine area, because the seaport offered him opportunities to practice his craft. Scorning the name Flachsbinder, Dantiscus preferred to be known either as Von Hoeffen or as Linodesmon, the Greek equivalent of "ropemaker," until finally settling on Dantiscus.

Dantiscus's talents were recognized early; hardly had he enrolled in the University of Cracow in 1500 when, either that same year or in 1501, he was summoned into the court service of King John Albert. As he recalls in his autobiographical *Vita Ioannis Dantisci*: "But then the royal court drew me into literary work [litterulis] / And made me serve three kings" (295:15–16). The "litterulis" (notes, or minor literary activity, in Latin) makes it clear that however precocious he may have been, Dantiscus was expected to work his way up the court ladder by first serving as a secretary. His ascent was both rapid and brilliant, but there were some detours. In 1502 he saw military action in the campaign against the Tatars and Wallachians, then he resumed his studies in Cracow. In 1506, with the equivalent of a royal stipend, he went off on the obligatory Renaissance tour of Italy, not primarily to study, but to broaden his knowledge of the world that mattered and to acquire polish.

When he had been in Italy only a short time, Dantiscus took advantage of an opportunity to travel to Palestine, visiting Corfu, Crete, and Cyprus along the way. The journey was anything but dull. He endured a storm at sea and then, in Jerusalem, the sixteenth-century version of a mugging. Having survived both, Dantiscus was back in Cracow in 1507. The journey was but the first of many he would make throughout his career, and whatever pleasure he derived from traveling, he was always acutely aware of its hardships and hazards. Both facets of the experience of travel are amply articulated in the *Vita Ioannis Dantisci* and represent a recurrent theme in Dantiscus's writing in general:

How many lands and seas I traveled let Jerusalem, Italy, Spain, and others bear witness. I twice visited Hungary and was also in Vienna, where a great congress of kings took place [the Congress of Vienna of 1515]. (295–96:21–24)

What I experienced in the vicinity of the Adige, in the fatherland of the learned Catullus, gives me no pleasure to remember. I pass over what happened to me in the snowy Alps and the many times I found myself surrounded by armed peasants. And then later I was brought to Belgium. (296:29–33)

In the course of twelve years I thrice served as envoy of the king in Spain. I came to know Denmark, France, the king of England, and many German and Italian princes. Oftentimes I was exposed to manifest dangers, oftentimes to secretly prepared ambushes; I had to make my way over mountains and through valleys, across fields, impassable cliffs, swift rivers, shoals, swamps, and lakes, not only in time of peace but during fierce wars, through wedges of horsemen, through swarms of foot soldiers. Whether because of pestilence, heat, cold, or wind, I never willingly deviated from the road on which I had set out. But why recall the many unpleasantnesses of the journeys through heavy downpours or spring floods, or all the different tricks practiced by innkeepers more vicious than snarling wolves? (297:51–66)

And then Dantiscus mentions that since the funds provided him for travel were usually insufficient, he had to take money out of his own pocket: "And at no time was the money provided for travel sufficient, so that when it ran out, I had to go into debt" (67–68).

As Dantiscus's stock at court began to rise, he was entrusted with commissions of ever greater responsibility both within Poland and regarding foreign policy. Domestically, he was often asked to represent the king at provincial diets, and on one such occasion he played a significant role in a dispute with residents of his home city of Gdańsk.

It was in his capacity as a representative of the Polish Crown that he appeared with King Sigismund I at the Congress of Vienna in 1515. This convocation of the two Jagiellonian kings (Sigismund of Poland and Ladislaus of Bohemia and Hungary) and the Holy Roman Emperor Maximilian I had as its primary purpose improving Jagiellonian-Hapsburg relations by marrying Ladislaus's children Ludwik and Anna to Hapsburg candidates. Sigismund also had three other goals in mind: to lessen the emperor's support for the Knights of the Cross in Prussia, to win approval of his policy against the Muscovites, with whom the Hapsburgs were conspiring against the Jagiellonians, and to establish a new "league" against the Turks.

The idea of a great coalition of European states against the Turks—long a popular concept but easier to propose than to realize—enjoyed Dantiscus's wholehearted support, and he lost no opportunity to promote it. Poetry was one avenue of persuasion for which Dantiscus had already demonstrated a particular affinity. His lengthy "silva" (literally "grove" or "forest," but used to mean a large poem) *De nostrorum temporum calamitatibus silva* (On the Calamities of Our Age), which he published in Bologna in 1529 during a five-month diplomatic tour and addressed to Pope Clement VII (1523–34) and the Holy Roman Emperor Charles V, sums up views on the "Turkish question" that he had held as early as the Congress of Vienna in 1515. The poem also reflects a growing urgency since the congress because of the loss of Belgrade and the island of Rhodes to the Ottoman sultan Süleyman I in 1521 and 1522, respectively, the Turkish victory over the Hungarians at Mohács in 1526, and the unsuccessful but costly Turkish siege of Vienna in 1529.

After a detailed review of European defeats at the hands of the Turks, beginning with the death of King Ladislaus III of Poland at Varna in 1444, Dantiscus reiterates the Polish position, which he had presented at the Congress of Vienna fourteen years earlier, that the Turkish conquests were aided by internal strife and a lack of cooperation among the European states. This disharmony weakens Christianity in general and imposes great burdens on the Polish commonwealth in particular because of its exposed geographical position. In support of his argument, Dantiscus cites the Polish defeat in Bukovina in 1497 and the subsequent ravaging of south Polish lands.

Without the cooperation of other European states, which the Poles failed to get—as, for example, in the case of Louis II of Bohemia and Hungary, who eventually lost his life at Mohács—the Poles cannot defeat the Turks by themselves, despite their readiness, even eagerness, to fight. It was in quest of such cooperation, in fact, that Dantiscus was sent on the three missions to Spain that he mentions in his *Vita Ioannis Dantisci*. But with a war in progress between Charles V and Francis I of France, what help could the Poles count on in Europe? The Polish king had no recourse but to conclude a peace with the Turks, which Dantiscus defends while at the same time indicating Polish willingness to break the treaty should an anti-Turkish league come into existence.

After describing the present situation in the bleakest terms, Dantiscus appeals to the pope to do his utmost to end discord in Europe and achieve that harmony among states necessary to eliminate the Turkish threat once and for all. He mentions, moreover, that it was to secure papal cooperation that the emperor Charles V came to Rome: "The emperor is ready; he will go swiftly wherever you order, and for that reason also falls at your feet. Forsaking his own Spain, he has made his way hither, so that in coming he might fulfill your wishes" (151–52:319–21).

Appropriately, Dantiscus urges Clement not to delay, but to empower the emperor to begin organizing the great campaign against the common enemy. To persuade his readers of its feasibility, he enumerates the strengths of individual European nations—including, among others, the Frisians and Batavians (by which he means the Dutch). Not above formulating strategy himself, he also advises that a principal aim ought to be seizing the Bosporus to deny the Turks an escape route: "The Thracian Bosporus should be taken first so that the way might be blocked to the surrounded enemy!" (150:277–78).

The poem ends on the same note of humility it began with. In a short preface, Dantiscus had sought to appeal to his readers' taste for novelty; after all, was not a Sarmatian (that is, Polish) poet publishing his work in "Latium" (Italy) indeed a novelty?

> Cum nova delectent, nova, lector, Sarmata vates
> Edidit in Latio carmina; nonne placent?
> Si re non alia, placeunt novitate, quod ante
> In Latio vates Sarmata rarus erat. (140:1–5)

(When new things are pleasing, dear reader, are not the new songs of a Sarmatian poet published in Italy also pleasing? If for no other reason, they may please by their novelty, for before, a Sarmatian poet was rare in Italy.)

He also apologizes for any crudeness in his Latin style and regrets that his verses may not "exude the liquids of the Castalian spring." But if readers understand the content of his poem, the "words are no matter of concern" to him (13, 16).

In concluding, Dantiscus addresses the emperor directly again, apologizing for any infelicities and begging him not to view the poem contemptuously because it "wears the black mourning garb of the face of our time" or because a "Sarmatian has dared raise his voice among Latin swans" (Sarmata vel Latios quod perstrepit inter olores [158:509–10, 511]).

Faithful to humanist style, Dantiscus peppers his poem with classical imagery—he speaks of his undertaking of *On the Calamities of Our Age* as a "Sophoclean *coturnus*," referring to a high shoe worn by Greek actors that Sophocles is believed to have introduced to the theater, meaning in this context something worthy or dignified. But it remains that Dantiscus's "Turkish" poem, like others he wrote, was inspired less by the Muses than by the desire of an up-and-coming diplomat with literary talent to comment on the politics of the age.

Dantiscus's career as a poet had been launched just a few years before the Congress of Vienna when his first volume of poetry was published in Cracow in 1510. Its title was taken from the longest (534 lines) poem in the collection, *De Virtutis et Fortunae differentia somnium* (A Dream about the Distinction between Virtue and Fortune), in which the narrator (Dantiscus) encounters an allegorical Fortune, who has two faces, happy and sad. The narrator then recounts those powerful people in the past who came to know the fickleness of Fortune. Fortune does not smile upon those who pursue her like ardent lovers but have cast Virtue aside. Unlike Fortune, Virtue is not fickle, but men continue to be lured to Fortune by her superficial beauty. Because of the abandonment of Virtue in the pursuit of Fortune, the poet sees himself surrounded only by deceit and falsehood; everything is in ruins, everything has been turned upside down. The poem now takes on a Polish aspect as the narrator is transported to contemporary Poland, where he is permitted to behold those responsible for the land's being drenched with blood. But the right hand of King Sigismund has overthrown them. The poem closes with the narrator waking from his dream and setting himself the task of transcribing it in verse.

A Dream about . . . Virtue and Fortune is actually an elaborate praise of Dantiscus's patron of the time, Maciej Drzewicki (1467–1535), bishop of Przemyśl (1511), chancellor of the Polish Crown (1513), bishop of Włocławek (1513), primate of Poland (1531), former pupil of Callimachus, humanist, bibliophile, and in Dantiscus's poetry the embodiment of virtue. Dantiscus addressed several other poems to his patron: two epigrams under the title "De Tauro, Drevicii insigni" (On the Bull, the Coat-of-Arms of Drzewicki); "Ad Drevicium strena" (A New Year's Gift to Drzewicki), written in Sapphic strophes; "Ad Drevicium epicedium," a funeral ode to Drzewicki on the death of his brother Walerian (to whom Dantiscus also dedicated two epitaphs), a secretary of the king and canon of Cracow and Poznań; and "Ad Drevicium commendatio" (In Praise of Drzewicki). In the manuscript version, Dantiscus's *Dream* was preceded by an epigram of Copernicus praising Dantiscus and connecting him to his names De Curiis and Linodesmon. This was omitted, however, in the printed version of the poem.

The wedding in 1512 of King Sigismund and Barbara, daughter of István Zápolya, palatine of Transylvania, provided the occasion for Dantiscus's most impressive poem before the Congress of Vienna, and it greatly enhanced his position at the court. The royal nuptials were celebrated with all the appropriate fanfare, which included poems commemorating the event by the leading poets of the day, Dantiscus and Bishop Andrzej Krzycki among them.

A little over three hundred verses long, Dantiscus's *Epithalamium in nuptiis Sigismundi ac principis Barbarae* (In Celebration of the Nuptials of Sigismund and Barbara) formed the core of the poet's second volume of poetry, published in Cracow the same year as the royal wedding.

Written in hexameters except for the first twenty-one verses, which are in elegaic distichs and form a panegyric invocation to the king and his future wife, the poem is a classically florid account of how the gods brought about the royal match. After the invocation, the poet conducts his readers to Mount Olympus, where a council is taking place between Juno, the goddess of marriage, and Venus, the goddess of love. They are concerned about the fate of the Polish king and have come together to choose a mate for him. After reciting the king's virtues (he is morally upright, courageous, and bold in battle, among other things) and his victories, the gods ponder who would be most suitable as his bride. At this point Venus tells Juno that one of her Cupids recently flew in from Pannonia (Hungary) to report a girl whose likes he had never beheld. She is of a famous Hungarian family, the Zápolyas. Flying across the kingdom of Poland, the Cupid also espied a ruler with the countenance of a divinity (Sigismund). Venus relates further that she decided to go with her retinue and see for herself. Sigismund is indeed as handsome as her own husband once was. Concluding that Barbara Zápolya would be the ideal mate for Sigismund, she has one of her Cupids fire an arrow of love at him, after which he yearns for the

Hungarian beauty. She then goes to Barbara and urges her to prepare herself for marriage. The poem ends as the entire nation is summoned to share the happiness of the young couple.

To solidify his position with the royal family and also to gain acknowledgment as King Sigismund's court poet, Dantiscus lost little time following up his verse celebration of the nuptials with a short "deprecatio," or entreaty, to Sigismund ("Ad Sigismundum deprecatio") in which he promises to depart in future poetry from antique subjects and devote himself exclusively to singing of the king and his deeds: "Te solum, rex magne, canam, Sigismunde, tuosque, / Dent modo textrices stamina longa deae" (Of you alone, great King Sigismund, and yours shall I sing. May the divine weavers grant you long threads of life [57:17–18]).

Three other small works by Dantiscus date from this same period. In "Ad iuventutem" (To Youth), the poet urges young people to make the most of their youth by shunning the temptations of Venus and Bacchus and exercising their intellects. His admonishment, like much of his poetry in general, has a distinctly personal character. Holding his own wild youth up as an example, Dantiscus declares: "Exemplar tibi sim, teneros sic perdimus annos, / Lenaeum colerem donec in orbe deum" (Take me as an example, how I wasted the tender years as long as I cultivated only the god Bacchus in the world [37:25–26]). Had he drunk more of the waters of Hippocrene on Mount Helicon instead of wine, his poems would advance with more learned feet, and Apollo would guide his measures. "I am withering away," he states near the end of the poem, and in perishing he exhorts his friends to learn from his example how to be on guard. In advising young people to make the most of their youth, especially by reading the works of learned men such as those the discerning Jan Haller publishes—Haller being the Cracow publisher of Dantiscus's first book of poetry in 1510—Dantiscus manages to praise both his publisher and himself.

Another figure who aided Dantiscus's early career as a poet is praised in the fairly short poem "In laudem Pauli Crosnensis" (In Praise of Paul of Krosno). Paul had been his teacher at the University of Cracow, and Dantiscus regarded him as his master, although he surpassed Paul in poetic talent. Several of Dantiscus's early works were influenced by Paul, among them his panegyrics to Drzewicki and a poem to the god Janus ("Ad Ianum") asking his favors in the new year, above all for King Sigismund and his people. In its own way, "In Praise of Paul of Krosno" is Janus-faced. The poem is, in fact, a panegyric addressed to the magnate and patron of the arts Bishop Jan Lubrański (1456–1520) of Poznań. So virtuous and outstanding a man is Lubrański, states Dantiscus, that he is indeed a fit subject for poets. To be sure, Krzycki, "whom the god Apollo himself taught to weave sweet words into sweet-sounding rhymes" (59:21–22), has sung of him. "I, too," continues Dantiscus with feigned modesty, "have frequently tried to sing of you in song, but my small boat ran aground in shallow waters" (25–26). But now, in acknowledgment of Paul of Krosno's superiority as a poet, Dantiscus declares that "his master" (meus . . . praeceptor), "who will bring here unto you his gifts of talent" (ingenii qui fert haec sua dona tibi [27–28]), will undertake Lubrański's praise for him. The poem closes with Dantiscus beseeching Lubrański, his "second patron" (after Paul), to be favorably inclined to Paul, who like other poets will cause him to live "as long as the earth and the stars in heaven live" (dum tellus astraque celsa manent [40]).

Dantiscus's interest in political poetry, which reached its peak in his *On the Calamities of Our Age,* had manifested itself before the Congress of Vienna in a poem inspired by the victory of the Poles, led by Hetman Konstanty Ostrogski, palatine of Kiev, over the Muscovites at Orsza on September 8, 1514. The poem was titled *Silvula de victoria inclyti Sigismundi regis Poloniae contra Moscos.* It was designated a "silvula," or little "silva," to suggest that the work was almost an improvisation, directly inspired by the event it describes. Dantiscus had models for this type of occasional poetry in the works of the Roman poet Publius Statius (ca A.D. 40–96) and the Italian humanist poet Poliziano. The poem also falls into the tradition of the epinicion, originally a Greek choral ode in honor of a victor in the games. Among Renaissance poets, the genre was popular for celebrating military triumphs. In Dantiscus's poem, the Polish victory at Orsza is presented as a type of divine punishment on Great Prince Vasili of Muscovy who, encouraged by the Holy Roman Emperor Maximilian I, broke the peace concluded with the Poles in 1508; it is God himself who by means of Polish knights has chosen to smite the perfidious and lying Muscovites. Dantiscus's "silvula" was first published as a separate brochure by the Cracow printing office of Florian Ungler on September 23, 1514. It was also included in an anthology of poems about the Polish victory that was compiled on the initiative of Primate Jan Łaski and edited by the historian Bernard Wapowski (d. 1535). Intended chiefly for foreign readers, the anthology was published in Rome in 1515.

Dantiscus's presence at the Congress of Vienna in 1515 proved a great boost to his career as a diplomat and also provided material for a few of his most interesting poems.[4] His eloquent advocacy of the Polish cause at the side of his king and his impassioned pleas for concerted action against the Turks attracted attention in high places

and won him much admiration. When the congress ended he remained in the Austrian capital as the Polish king's personal envoy to
the Holy Roman Emperor Maximilian I. Impressed with Dantiscus
and eager to use his obvious talents as a diplomat, Maximilian drew him
closer to his court and dispatched him on several personal missions,
including three important trips to Venice in 1515 and 1516. Dantiscus
thought enough of these missions to mention them specifically years
later in his *Vita Ioannis Dantisci*: "When the victorious grandfather of
the present emperor [Maximilian I, grandfather of Charles V] waged
war with the haughty Venetians, who rule over three realms, I was
three times in their camps as an envoy and concluded the peace on
fixed terms" (296:25–28).

   As tokens of his esteem for Dantiscus and his service to him, Maximilian in 1516 raised him to the nobility (after which Dantiscus assumed
the Latin version of his putative family name Von Hoeffen—De
Curiis), conferred on him the honorary degree of doctor of both laws,
and made him the first Polish recipient of the wreath of *poeta laureatus*.

   The first literary fruit of Dantiscus's appearance at the Congress of
Vienna was a small poem (fifteen distichs) addressed to King Sigismund I of Poland ("Ad Sigismundum carmen") and hailing the congress itself. The hyperbolic character of the panegyric is evident from
the outset as the poet asks a rhetorical question:

> Quis magno tantos et tot cum caesare reges
>   Convenisse umquam vidit in orbe prius?
> Cuncta revolvamus, quae nunc retroque fuerunt
>   Tempora, conventus nullibi talis erat
> Ante nec ad Priami, magnam nec Agenoris urbem.
>   Quin etiam numquam Martis in urbe fuit! (83:1–6)

(Who ever saw anywhere in the world such a convening of so many kings
together with the great emperor? Let us review all times, past and present,
and still no such congress ever existed, neither in Priam's Troy nor in the
great city of Agenor [Tyre], nor even in the city of Mars [Rome].)

   Of all the rulers in attendance in Vienna, the most welcome guest
of all ("gratissimus hostes") is none other than Sigismund of Poland,
attested by the emperor's poet (Caesaris . . . vates), "who greeted you
first with the esteem of which he was capable, using so many fine words
in praise of you" (Qui te, quo potuit, nuper suscepit honore, / Fecit et
in laudes tot bona verba tuas [84:21–24]). The poet referred to in
Dantiscus's poem was Joachim Watt (Ioachimus Vadianus), a humanist,

"poet laureate," and, at the time Dantiscus knew him, professor at the University of Vienna. Dantiscus's poem was first published, in fact, by Wietor in Vienna in 1515 in a small volume containing Vadianus's welcome to the Polish king Sigismund under the title *Oratio coram inuictissimo Sigismundo Rege Poloniae etc. in conuentu Caesaris et trium regum, nomine Universitatis, Viennae Austriae per Ioachimum Vadianum Poetam Laureatum habita, cum carmine in laudem eiusdem Regis annexo, in quo quaedam de isto conuentu continentur* (Public Address to the Invincible Sigismund, King of Poland, etc., at the Congress of the Emperor and the Three Kings, in the Name of the University of Vienna, Austria, by Ioachimus Vadianus, Poet Laureate, Together with a Poem in Praise of the Same King in Which It Is Related of That Congress).

Besides his fellow poet laureate Vadianus, Dantiscus made other friendships during his stay in Vienna that were similarly reflected in his poetry. One was with the prominent Austrian diplomat Sigismund von Herberstein (1486–1566). An important statesman under the emperors Maximilian I and Charles V, Herberstein also gained renown as a historian, principally for his Latin-language work on Russia, which appeared under the title *Rerum Moscoviticarum commentarii* (Vienna, 1549). As a diplomat, Herberstein's main task was to make peace between Poland and Moscow in the wake of the Polish victory at Orsza. Dantiscus became quite close to Herberstein, having first met him in Cracow, and dedicated a poem of 155 lines to him when Herberstein returned from an important diplomatic mission to Moscow in 1516–17. Published in Cracow in 1518, the poem was called a "soteria" after the title of a collection of "silvae" by the Roman poet Statius (*Soteria Rutili Gallici*). Herberstein is extolled above all as the man uniquely qualified and hence chosen by the emperor to "quiet the bellicose roars of those clamoring for war between the king of Sarmatia and the fierce tyrant of the Muscovites." Of all his knights, Herberstein was "the only one to whom the emperor might entrust such negotiations" (94:51–55).

It was also to Herberstein that Dantiscus addressed an eight-verse epigram as a dedication to the most poetically significant literary work of his Vienna period, the elegy "Ad Gryneam" (To Grynea, printed in 1518), in which he recalls his romance with and eventual departure from an Austrian woman known only as Grynea, so named from Apollo Grynaeus, who had a temple and an oracle dedicated to him in the city of Grynea in Moesia (Aiolis, in Asia Minor). In this respect Dantiscus merely followed the example of Roman poets, who frequently titled love poems with pseudonyms borrowed from nicknames of the god Apollo (hence Tibullus's Delia and Propertius's Cynthia).

In the poem Dantiscus recalls his ardent romance with Grynea and the pain he felt at having to leave her:

> Durior est mea sors, dum desero maestus amatam.
>   Quae me prosquitur meque tenere cupit.
> Avelli amplexu, nudis discedere ab ulnis,
>   Linquere tot risus, basia, furta, iocos.
> Absque dolore quis haec, humano sanguine cretus,
>   Quisque libens umquam, qui ista reliquit, erit? (88:25–30)

(My fate is all the heavier when, sorrowful, I forsake my beloved, who pursues me and desires to restrain me. To tear away from her embrace, to take my leave of her naked shoulders, to abandon so much laughter, so many kisses, love intrigues, and games: who, made of human blood, would ever be able to give up all these things willingly and without grief?)

So great is his sorrow at leaving Grynea that Dantiscus envies the classical Leander, who at least died for love. But because his own fate causes him, as a diplomat, to "roam over land and sea," he does not know where on earth and in what circumstances death will finally overtake him. Enumerating the many places his career takes him and his need to travel for long periods, Dantiscus expresses his conviction that a peaceful homelife such as most people lead is out of the question for him. He must bid farewell, therefore, to his beloved before their love grows any deeper, and he must heed the call to far-off shores. Three times he wanted to turn back to her, he declares, and three times he was prevented from doing so by the affairs of state that keep him so busy. She alone can cure the wound in his heart "with a pleasing glance," and she alone has the power to restore his health "with but a touch of her hand" (91:101–2). But she will quickly disappear, he grieves, and he too will be carried away faster than the wind blows. Nothing thereafter will relieve his pain, not even Apollo, master of the medicinal art.

The last significant literary work by Dantiscus from his Vienna period relates to his friendship with the Italian humanist Riccardo Bartolini (Ricardus Bartholinus or Bartholin, died 1529). In 1515 the printer Wietor in Vienna brought out a volume of occasional poetry whose title derived from a verse account by Bartolini of the journey of Matthias Cardinal Lang of Gurk (a small city in Corinthia, Austria, on the Gurk River) to the Congress of Vienna, *Hodoeporicon id est Itinerarium Reverendissimi . . . Mathei . . . Cardinalis Gurcensis. . . .* The collection also contains two works by Dantiscus: a short poem addressed to the reader of Bartolini's *Hodoeporicon* ("Ad lectorem Hodoeporici") extolling the literary qualities of his friend's work, and a 274-line epic in hexameters entitled *De profectione Sigismundi regis Poloniae in Hungariam* (The Departure of King Sigismund of Poland for Hungary). The subject of *The Departure* is Sigismund's trip from Wilno (Lithuania) to Bratislava (Latin Posonium) on the way to Vienna shortly after the victory of Orsza. After Orsza, Sigismund was summoned by his ailing brother Ladislaus, king of the Czechs and Hungarians, to meet him in Bratislava for preliminary discussions between themselves and with Cardinal Lang, who was acting as the emperor's plenipotentiary. Sigismund's journey took him from Wilno to Cracow, where he left behind his wife, who was then pregnant, and thence to Bratislava. Accompanied by a retinue of some fifteen hundred horsemen,[5] Sigismund arrived in the present-day capital of Slovakia on March 24, 1515. He was greeted by an impressive assemblage made up of King Ladislaus, his children Ludwik and Anna, and a large number of followers. Dantiscus's poem on the occasion is essentially an account of that journey interspersed with a substantial political digression on the subject of the growing Turkish menace, which to Dantiscus's mind was worsened by the dissension among the Christian rulers of Europe. After painting a grim picture of Turkish successes and the danger Christendom now faced, Dantiscus concludes with an appeal to the emperor—who chose not to appear in person at the Bratislava "presummit" meetings—to crown the Vienna congress with the achievement of unity and harmony among its participants for the sake of a strong common front against the Turkish enemy:

> Then come, Roman emperor! The kings joined to you by blood [Elisabeth Hapsburg was the mother of Sigismund and Ladislaus] desire your swift arrival. Not only will they enter into a league with you against the enemy but—if you are not seen idle by delaying unduly—will also enter into nuptial arrangements and wedding celebrations with you. If the ramparts of Austrian Vienna are now to be approached and the swift Danube crossed, if tents are to be pitched in a friendly field along the banks, or wherever it may please the congress, hasten thither to the kings! The time is already ripe, and the occasion demands war against the Muscovites and against the savage Turks, who have recently weakened your Hungarians by a bloody defeat [a reference to the defeat of John Zápolya near Belgrade in 1515]. Come then not sluggishly but eagerly, and present yourself straightway! Thus, if only I may see you, it will not grieve me to have come all the way to the Danube from the icy waves of the Dnieper. (73–74:260–75)

While in Bratislava on May 14, 1515, Dantiscus, who had accompanied King Sigismund, and Bartolini, a member of Cardinal Lang's entourage, met and exchanged views about the difficult and protracted negotiations whose settlement at last seemed at hand. Later that same day Bartolini wrote a poem addressed to the Polish king in which he urged him, for the sake of victory against both the Muscovites and the Turks, to reach an agreement with Emperor Maximilian. Bartolini read his poem to Dantiscus the following day. On May 16 the Pole responded with a lengthy poem of his own addressed to Bartolini ("Ricardo Bartolino"), whom he had referred to in his *Departure of King Sigismund* as a "distinguished poet" (egregius vates) of "Etruscan origin" (since Bartolini was from Perugia, one of the cities of ancient Etruria) who "sang of the great deeds of the [Holy] Roman Emperor" (72–73:243–45). The poem assumed the character of a polemical reply to the Italian. Praising the policies of his ruler, Dantiscus rejects the notion that it is King Sigismund who must be persuaded to a program of peace, since that is the goal the king has been pursuing all along: "Exhort those to peace who lead the whole world into wars! I believe, moreover, that steeds racing swiftly on their own do not need spurs. Surely he needs no admonisher who is a zealous lover of tranquil peace and who demands and wishes peace. For many years Sigismund has been favorably regarded as such" (76:42–47).

To strengthen his argument, Dantiscus reviews Sigismund's campaigns against the Muscovites, Wallachians, and Tatars, down to the victory at Orsza, showing that the conflicts the Poles engaged in were defensive. Only when they were attacked did the Poles fight, but they are always ready for discussions and negotiations. At the end of the poem, after recalling the fall of Constantinople to the Turks, Dantiscus declares: "King Sigismund, an implacable foe of the enemies of the divine name, is arriving. He will enter into alliances against them, if there are those who will honor them, and he will on no occasion refuse to march against the Mohammedan camps over which—God grant!— joined together unanimous in mind the warlike emperor together with the great king will triumph" (82–83:212–17).

Dantiscus returned to Poland in 1517 in time to participate in the festivities surrounding the wedding of King Sigismund and his second wife Bona, of the prominent Sforza family of Milan.[6] Queen Barbara had died in 1515 after the birth of her second daughter, Anna (who herself died a few years later). The date of the wedding was April 18, 1518. The nuptials were the occasion for an even greater outpouring of poetry than Sigismund's first marriage. Dantiscus's contribution, by far the most interesting among those composed by Polish poets, was the nearly 700-hexameter *Epithalamium reginae Bonae*. In it the poet attributes the marriage to the initiative of Venus, who wanted to reward the now widowed King Sigismund for his military victories. Mars is asked, therefore, to interrupt the ongoing war between the Poles and Muscovites and specifically the Polish siege of the fortress of Opoczka so that he may communicate the will of the gods to Sigismund. Venus, meanwhile, travels to Italy to accompany Bona and her entourage on their journey to Poland. Along the way sea, wood, and mountain deities join Bona's retinue. Dantiscus uses the occasion to praise the Italians accompanying the future queen, making a point of how much at home in Poland the Italians seem; indeed, he writes, it is as if all of Italy had moved north. Although the poem abounds in classical imagery, as circumstances demanded, Dantiscus's fondness for concrete descriptions also asserted itself, above all in the section devoted to the Polish siege of Opoczka.

Because he had to leave in October on an important diplomatic assignment to Germany and Spain, Dantiscus was unable to finish the poem and apparently put it out of his mind until 1535. But that year, when a quarrel with the state treasurer of Royal Prussia, Stanisław Kostka, over the issue of taxes imposed on his diocese of Chełm caused him to fall into disfavor at the court, Dantiscus renewed his interest in the poem, believing that its completion and publication might improve his relations with the royal family. He thus augmented it with a second epilogue in which he hoped to remind Queen Bona of his services. But the quarrel with Kostka was smoothed over, Dantiscus again returned to favor at the court, and the poem was once more put aside. Not only was it not printed in the poet's lifetime, but it had to wait until 1950, when the Polish scholar Stanisław Skimina published it for the first time in a collection of Dantiscus's Latin poetry.

At the beginning of 1519, Dantiscus was sent to King Charles I of Spain (the future Holy Roman Emperor Charles V) on a delicate diplomatic mission. Joanna IV, queen of Naples, had died in Italy on August 28, 1518, leaving her considerable estate to her niece, Princess Isabella of Milan and Bari, daughter of the king of Naples Alfonso II, of the Aragon dynasty, and Bona Sforza's mother. The transfer of the inheritance to Isabella required the approval of Charles I, who as the grandson of Ferdinand V (the Catholic), also ruled over the duchy of Naples and had his own eye on at least part of the estate.[7] When legal difficulties threatened to impede Isabella's claim, she appealed to her son-in-law, King Sigismund of Poland, to intervene. Since it was obviously in Sigismund's interest to have the huge estate move smoothly into his wife's hands, he lost no time in dispatching Dantiscus, his most skilled diplomat, to Spain. The death of the emperor Maximilian I on January 12, 1519, and the election of Charles I of Spain as his successor further complicated the matter of Isabella's inheritance. Despite his zealous efforts to resolve things in accordance with the wishes of the Polish rulers, Dantiscus failed to overcome the obstacles thrown up by Spanish courts favoring Charles's interests. Determining that the time had come for a change of envoys, Sigismund recalled Dantiscus and placed Hieronim Łaski (1495–1542), another very able Polish diplomat, in charge of the mission. Łaski succeeded in having the case brought before the highest court of Naples, but even then resolution was delayed for a long time. When it finally came, it cost Queen Bona's mother virtually half her inheritance.

Fascinated by Spain and at the same time frustrated over the outcome of his assignment there, Dantiscus returned to Poland in late 1519 in time to become involved in the new hostilities between the Poles and the Teutonic Knights, which erupted in December of that year and lasted until March 1521. The experience provided the material for a poem titled "In exercitum Germanicum Polonos fugientem" (On the German Army Fleeing the Poles). Although adhering in the main to the tradition of the epinicion, the poem is also satirical in its mockery of the Germans for being so easily put to flight.

When his diplomatic career was renewed after the conclusion of hostilities with the Knights of the Cross, Dantiscus traveled widely in the West as an official envoy of King Sigismund. In addition to further activity regarding the inheritance of Queen Bona, he also bore responsibility for pressing the Polish case against the Teutonic Knights in several European courts and for urging haste in mounting an anti-Turkish campaign in light of the dangers then facing Hungary. Perhaps his most interesting port of call before he returned to Spain for further meetings with Charles V was London. Armed with letters of introduction from the Hapsburg archduke Ferdinand and the queen regent of the Netherlands, the Polish diplomat sailed from Calais to England on September 18, 1522.

After disembarking in Sandwich, Dantiscus made his way to Canterbury and thence to London. A meeting with Cardinal Wolsey provided the opportunity for a strong presentation of the Polish view of the situation in Prussia and the immediacy of the Turkish threat. For Dantiscus the timing was propitious, since an emissary of the Knights named Dietrich von Schönberg was already in England attempting to foment anti-Polish sentiment.[8] The meeting with an apparently sympathetic Wolsey led to an audience with King Henry VIII, during which the author of *Utopia,* Thomas More, translated Dantiscus's

Latin. Although receptive to the Pole's entreaties, More stressed that to the English, France, with whom they were then at war, represented a more serious threat than Turkey. During a private meeting with Henry VIII, who apologized for his awkward Latin, Dantiscus succeeded in convincing the English king of the rightness of the Polish case against the Teutonic Knights. Henry agreed henceforth to regard the matter in a different light, and in a gesture of goodwill to the Poles he denied further audiences to Dietrich von Schönberg. Although satisfied that his relatively brief English visit had been a success, at least with respect to the Polish case against the Knights of the Cross, Dantiscus was not favorably impressed with England. The weather was not to his liking, prices were outrageous, and people were greedier than elsewhere.[9] It was in this mood that he left London for Plymouth on October 13, 1522. On November 18 he set sail for Spain on a Portuguese vessel, but a storm forced the ship to return to port; it was ten days before he could resume his voyage. Dantiscus reached the Spanish coast on December 3 and a fortnight later was in Valladolid, where Charles V then had his residence.

On his return to Poland in late March 1523, a journey that carried him from Spain through the Netherlands and Germany, Dantiscus stopped briefly in Wittenberg, where he met Philipp Melanchthon and, through him, Martin Luther, about whom he had already heard much and who obviously interested him. Although he does not appear to have been noticeably hostile to Luther's proposed reforms of the church at this time, Dantiscus became an implacable foe of the Reformation in his later career as a church dignitary. The first step toward this career was initiated on September 14, 1523, when King Sigismund rewarded his services by nominating him parish priest of the Church of Saint Mary, the largest and financially best situated parsonage in his home city of Gdańsk.

After staying in Poland about eight months, Dantiscus resumed active diplomatic work in 1524 as resident ambassador of the king of Poland at the court of the emperor Charles V in Spain. He remained in this capacity until 1532, in what surely was one of the most interesting periods of his life. Although his diplomatic activities were too broad to chronicle here, let me mention at least his journey to Italy in 1529–30 as a member of Charles V's entourage. Charles made the trip to receive two crowns from the hands of Pope Clement VII: that of Lombardy, which was bestowed upon him in Bologna on February 22, 1530, and that of Holy Roman Emperor, which he now received officially with full ceremony on February 24. It was while he was in Bologna for this twin coronation that Dantiscus thought the occasion favorable, given his proximity to both Holy Roman Emperor and pope, to plead again for a new campaign against the Turks. It was with this aim that he wrote his major political poem *De nostrorum temporum calamitatibus silva* (On the Calamities of Our Age), discussed earlier in this chapter. The poem attracted considerable attention and was published in 1530 in Bologna, Cracow, Cologne, and Antwerp.

It was undoubtedly during his long residence in Spain that Dantiscus's interest in Erasmus deepened. Through Spanish translations of the Dutchman's works in the early 1520s, Erasmian ideas began circulating widely in Spain and won a number of adherents. In the first few years of Dantiscus's service there, the imperial court was already becoming a center of Erasmian thought, and it was in this environment that the Polish diplomat met such translators and admirers of Erasmus as Juan de Valdés (1490–1541) and his brother Alonso. Gratified by the Polish diplomat's interest, some of the Spanish Erasmians wrote to inform their master. Thus began a correspondence and eventually a friendship between Dantiscus and Erasmus. At one point, as a token of his admiration, Dantiscus sent Erasmus a medal bearing the Pole's likeness. Erasmus repaid the kindness in 1532 by dedicating to Dantiscus his translation from the Greek of Basil the Great's *De Spirito Sancto*. In the introduction Erasmus mentions the medal he received from Dantiscus. As we have seen earlier, Dantiscus was by no means Erasmus's sole Polish admirer, but the relationship that developed between them was perhaps the most intimate among Erasmus's growing circle of Polish visitors and correspondents. After he became bishop of Warmia in 1537, Dantiscus hung a portrait of Erasmus painted by Hans Holbein in his official residence in Lidzbark. As a similar expression of friendship and admiration Erasmus kept a plaster bust of Dantiscus in his study in addition to the medal the Pole had sent him.

That Dantiscus's time in Spain was not taken up wholly with matters of state and the cultivation of ties with Erasmus and Erasmian thought is manifest in an affair of the heart that had long-standing consequences. Dantiscus had never been indifferent to women's charms, and he left broken hearts across Europe as he moved from one diplomatic assignment to another. We have already heard of his romance with the mysterious Grynea in Vienna. In Spain the principal object of his romantic attentions was Isabel del Gada, an attractive young widow he met in Valladolid.[10] The relationship produced two children out of wedlock, a boy and a girl. Dantiscus flirted with the idea of taking the children to Poland once his term of service at the court of Charles V came to an end. There is no evidence, however, that his plans included

Isabel del Gada as well. But as he became clearer in his own mind about the desirability of a postdiplomatic career in the church, he abandoned the idea. In any case his son died early, and when Dantiscus finally left Spain, both Isabel and her daughter Joanna (b. 1526) stayed behind. Not much is known about the contacts, if any, that Dantiscus maintained with his Spanish "family," but he was certainly not out of their minds. When Joanna reached marriageable age by local standards (barely eleven), Dantiscus began to receive letters from Isabel asking for financial help and especially for a suitable dowry for the girl.[11] Dantiscus was apparently in no rush to comply, but some of his old friends in Spain began reminding him of his obligations. At a certain point Dantiscus also began receiving letters from a candidate for Joanna's hand, one Dantiscus would have found it uncomfortable to ignore, the respected Spanish humanist and fellow Erasmian Jacobo Gracián de Alderete. To defuse the situation, at least temporarily, Dantiscus used his contacts at the court to arrange a position for Alderete as one of Charles V's secretaries. But Alderete, with the assistance at one point of Dantiscus's old friend from Vienna, Erich Godscal, kept up the pressure on his prospective father-in-law. Eventually Dantiscus yielded. He arranged an annual income for Joanna of some twenty-five ducats (Alderete had been demanding two hundred), and Joanna and Alderete married in Madrid on June 3, 1546. Once married, and with Alderete's prospects improving, they wrote to tell Dantiscus they could get along without further support from him. Given the Pole's grudging transfer of money to Joanna, it was all he needed not only to drop further payments to his daughter but to break contact with both her and her mother in far-off Spain. But the story of Dantiscus's Spanish romance does not end there. Joanna eventually had thirteen children, one of whom became a well-known writer and bore Dantiscus's name: Lucas Gracián Dantisco (1543–87), author of the *Galateo español* (The Spanish Gallant, 1582), a historical account of Spanish gallantry so popular that twenty-six editions had appeared by the end of the eighteenth century.

After further diplomatic work, mostly in Germany in connection with Poland's Prussian policy and in Italy in the matter of properties bequeathed Queen Bona by her mother, Princess Isabella, who died on February 11, 1524, Dantiscus returned to Poland about the middle of 1532. His career as a diplomat was virtually at an end. After delivering a final report to King Sigismund and Queen Bona in Cracow, he settled in his native Gdańsk, where he now actively assumed the responsibilities of a churchman. Besides his parsonage of the Church of Saint Mary in Gdańsk, which he had received from the king in 1523,

Dantiscus acquired other ecclesiastical positions that were immensely important in fulfilling his ambitions of high church office, with all the material and political advantages of a prominent place in the Polish church hierarchy. In early March 1530 he was informed that he would be nominated canon of Warmia after the death of Wojciech Bischoff. A more prestigious nomination, to the bishopric of Chełm, came in May of the same year, when death again created a vacancy. The nomination was confirmed by Clement VII on August 3, 1530. After fulfilling all the requirements, Dantiscus was at last consecrated bishop of Chełm on September 14, 1533.

Although he now had both wealth and power, the sailing was anything but smooth for Dantiscus in his new role as a member of the church hierarchy. He first attempted to relieve his diocese of the burden of taxation but ran afoul of the treasurer of the Prussian lands, Stanisław Kostka, a shrewd authoritarian politician who was not easily intimidated. Eventually, however, Dantiscus pressed his case at court and won both the king and the queen over to his side.

Finances were perhaps the least of Dantiscus's problems in Gdańsk. Anger at the inroads being made among the citizens by Lutheranism, toward which Dantiscus had now developed unequivocal enmity, led him to compose an intemperate response in verse during June 1535 under the title *Ionas propheta* (Jonah the Prophet). Long regarded as one of Dantiscus's major literary accomplishments, the poem was sent to Bishop Tomicki from Starogród in a letter dated June 19, 1535.

One of the earliest anti-Reformation diatribes in Poland, Dantiscus's poem sternly admonishes the people of Gdańsk to be mindful of their obligations toward both church and Crown. Holding before them the prophetic vision of the city's imminent destruction, he reminds them of the calamities that have already befallen them in recent times: the plague of 1529, which killed three thousand in just three days; the great fire of 1534, which burned the Siedlce district of the city; and the flooding of the Vistula and Motława rivers in August 1528 and March 1529. By their very nature—plague, fire, flood—the calamities seemed a divine punishment on Gdańsk for its errant ways. Playing on the social tensions in the city, he also raises the specter of class conflict and argues that the well-being and prosperity of Gdańsk rest on its permanent relationship with the Polish state.

Noteworthy in the work are the changes in style accompanying Dantiscus's new preoccupation with the menace of the Reformation. The more he directed his energies as a churchman in Gdańsk toward curbing the spread of the "contagion," the more he retreated from the ideals and models of the Renaissance, which had influenced most of his previous literary work. He all but dispenses, for example, with his heavy reliance on classical literature, apart from a few minor borrowings from such popular poets as Statius and Vergil. In keeping with the character of *Jonah the Prophet,* Old Testament prophetic elements now take the place of classical borrowings. Although this was hardly strange given the nature of the poem, it did represent something new in Poland and set a precedent to be followed later in the writings of such political and moralistic writers as Stanisław Orzechowski and Piotr Skarga. Dantiscus's *Jonah* was never published in his lifetime. It was first printed in 1577, when it appeared in a brochure by Tomasz Samostrzelicki titled *Oratio ad Gdanenses* (A Sermon to the Townspeople of Gdańsk), published in Poznań by the printing office of Melchior Nering. It was added to the brochure as a literary and historical argument, a formula repeated several times in the course of the sixteenth and seventeenth centuries.

Although Dantiscus's intolerance for other faiths was directed primarily against the Protestants, on at least one occasion he wrote unflatteringly about Jews. This was in his short (twenty-four-verse) "Carmen de Judeis" (Poem about Jews), apparently written in the mid-1530s in conjunction with manifestations of anti-Jewish sentiment in Cracow that Queen Bona is believed to have incited. The slight satirical poem consists almost entirely of a catalog of epithets applied to Jews, beginning with "Barbara, inhumana est, petulans, furiosa, proterva" (Alien, rude, impudent, quarrelsome, brazen). After enumerating as many negative attributes as he could think of, Dantiscus concludes with the following appeal: "If you can think of anything else to add, fair reader, do so, and God will give you fitting rewards" (166–67:1–2, 23–24). The poem was not without a possible model, "De reditu suo" (On His Return) by the fifth-century Latin poet Rutilius Claudius Namatianus, which was published for the first time in Bologna in 1520 and which Dantiscus seems to have known. Like *Jonah the Prophet,* the "Poem about Jews" remained unpublished in Dantiscus's lifetime; it was discovered among other manuscripts in his library in Lidzbark and was published only in 1621. A Polish version of the work went through four editions in the second half of the eighteenth century under the title *Błędy talmudowe* (Errors of the Talmud). The relative popularity of the satire in Enlightenment Poland is easy to understand in light of the campaign by social and political reformers of the time to eradicate obscuratism in the country. They were anticlerical rationalists to whom orthodoxy in any form was repugnant. Holding the Talmud responsible for what they regarded as the backwardness of most Polish Jews and their stubborn resistance to social and cultural polonization, they seized any opportunity to discredit the work. Dantiscus's "Poem about Jews" thus seemed tailor-made for their purposes.

With his *Jonah the Prophet* Dantiscus entered one of his most fertile periods of poetic writing. In 1539, four years after composing *Jonah*, he published in Cracow a major didactic work that was one of his best poems. Based largely on his own experiences and reflections, the *Carmen paraeneticum . . . ad . . . Constantem Alliopagum* (Moralistic Poem to Constans Alliopagus), 591 distichs or 1,182 verses long, originated as a reply to a panegyric written in his honor by one of his closest friends in Warmia, Eustachy Knobelsdorf (1519–71), the son of the burgomaster of Lidzbark and the author principally of a description of the city of Paris, *Lutetiae Parisiorum descriptio* (1547). Their relationship went back some time; it was Knobelsdorf, in fact, who had helped finance Dantiscus's studies in Wittenberg, Frankfurt an der Oder, Louvain, Orléans, and Paris.

Knobelsdorf's panegyric, with its reminiscences, apparently awakened Dantiscus's recollections of his own youth and prompted him to propose precepts for the new generation based on his own experiences. That, essentially, was the purpose of the *Moralistic Poem . . . to Constans Alliopagus* (Alliopagus means "Garlic Village" and is the Latin translation of Knobelsdorf's German name). The personal experiences Dantiscus draws on in the work relate to that period in his life when he had started to serve at court and when his principal interests seemed to be drinking, skirt chasing, and carousing. Replete with familiar classical images as well as a description of a stay in a palace of pleasure reminiscent of the *Zodiacus vitae* (The Zodiac of Life, 1531) of Palingenius (P. A. Manzoli), Dantiscus's *Alliopagus* is an appeal to the youth of his day to heed his advice and remain steadfast in their loyalty to the Roman Catholic faith, to nourish their minds especially through reading, to cultivate the art of poetry, and to avoid religious novelties, by which he meant Protestantism. His purpose explains why the *Alliopagus* contains a strong denunciation of Luther and the Reformation beginning with verse 273—"Non credas fidei, quae non nisi nomine constat" (Do not believe the faith that exists in name only)—and extending as far as verse 552 and the emotional outcry "O mores, o quae tempora! Flere libet!" (What times, what customs! They are enough to drive one to tears).

Several of Dantiscus's shorter works from his later period must also be counted among his best poetry. These include principally the "Hendecasyllabi ad Georgium Sabinum" (Hendecasyllables to Georgius Sabinus) three verse epistles written in 1546–47 to the German scholar and poet George Sabinus (real name Schüler, 1508–60), first rector of the University of Königsberg, whose wife was the daughter of Philipp Melanchthon. The poems, written on May 5 and June 5, 1546, and in March 1547, were responses to verse letters Dantiscus had received from Sabinus.

Largely free of the classical antique and mythological trappings of most of his longer poetic works, the epistles to Sabinus are impressive for their naturalness and lack of pretension. In the first, using the same verse form (Apollonian hendecasyllables) in which Sabinus wrote to him, Dantiscus excuses his inability to write verses as lovely as those his friend composes because of his cares, the calamities of the age, and his responsibilities. In the second, also employing hendecasyllables, he expresses his admiration for the newly published book of poetry by Sabinus (*Poemata,* 1544), which he had received not long before. This is followed by a charming picture of spring at his estate in Lidzbark, and he invites Sabinus and his new wife Anna for a visit. The verse epistle closes with a familiar complaint about the problems and responsibilities that constantly pull him away from his beloved poetry.

The final epistle is full of praise for Sabinus's poetry and expressions of pleasure because the emperor has seen fit to raise Sabinus to the nobility. In ending it, and the three-part cycle, Dantiscus offers Sabinus his condolences for two blows he recently suffered, the premature death of his wife and the death of his friend Cardinal Bembo. All three poems to Sabinus were published in a small volume of Sabinus's own poetry in Leipzig in 1558, ten years after Dantiscus's death.

Dantiscus's last major work of poetry was the most highly regarded. This is a collection of twenty-seven religious hymns preceded by two prefatory poems—one addressed to the reader and a second in which his book is the speaker—and two concluding poems of the same pattern, the first addressed to the reader and the second spoken by his book. The entire collection, *Hymni aliquot ecclesiastici* (Several Religious Hymns), was first published in Cracow by Wietor in 1548, the year Dantiscus died.

Apart from the depth of feeling and conviction they reflect, the hymns are noteworthy as a departure from virtually all of Dantiscus's previous poetic writing. Engaged wholly in church work in his later years, Dantiscus must have given serious thought to the most appropriate form for what he surely regarded as his crowning literary achievement. In view of the religious subject matter of the hymns, the classical apparatus of so much of his previous poetry was discarded as inappropriate, and little of it remains. Anything redolent of the paganism of classical antiquity or the fashionable neopaganism of the secular humanists was clearly out of place; instead, Dantiscus sought inspiration in the religious poetry of the Middle Ages. Striving now for simplicity and the quality of both prayer and homily, he chose both shorter verses (mostly eight syllables) and shorter strophes (four-line stanzas). The first prologic poem, "Ad lectorem" (To the Reader), sets forth the artistic program of the entire cycle: "Not for the nine Muses nor for Apollo do I write these hymns; no stream flows here uncovered by the hoof of a winged steed. This book contains only the bloody punctures of the wounds of Christ, the infamous death of the Passion and the cross that he who was innocent endured. . . . Perhaps by its unwrought character this book will find acceptance among the pious. The author, wishing to please, has concealed his own name out of modesty, not from shyness, nor from apprehension, but from fear lest he be censured for arrogance, for he wished to be seen as nothing else than a peddler of the holy cross" (217–18:1–20).

In "Libellus proloquitur" (The Book Speaks), Dantiscus identifies the source of literary inspiration for his hymns and addresses the subject of meter: "Here, reader, you see short verses in the church manner. Regard them kindly and do not disdain them for their simplicity. They lack paint, they have not been bathed in the spring of the Muses, they do not give off the scent of the grove of poets but rather that of the wounded side of Christ. . . . The spondee that appears more frequently than the iamb will not be displeasing, for it is more appropriate to these dimeters. The pace of this verse advances more softly, the headstrong [iamb] more swiftly; that is why the slower one is more frequently substituted for it. In the heat of a quarrel no one is moved by disturbing rhythms, but that which mitigates brings a burning heart to God" (218–19:1–8, 13–24).

As a collection, the hymns are organized essentially around the church calendar. The first group, beginning with a hymn to the Holy Trinity ("Ad Sanctam Trinitatem"), is set at the start of the Lenten period; it includes also hymns to Christ ("Ad Christum"), to Mother Church ("De matre Ecclesia"), and on the Lenten fast ("De ieiunio Quadragesimae"). The next group comprises hymns to Christ—and one addressed to the church and Christ—connected with the six Sundays of Lent and culminating in Palm Sunday. This is followed by eight hymns to Christ on the events of Good Friday, beginning with the appearance in Gethsemane, progressing through the hours of the Passion, and concluding with the "Passionis epilogus" (The Epilogue to the Passion). The rest of the cycle consists of ten hymns. Five are devoted to the Resurrection ("De Christi gloriosa resurrectione," "De resurrectione," "De eadem resurrectione," "Ad Christum: De ascensione et Spiritus Sancti missione," and "De Christi resurgentis apparitione," which is actually addressed to the Virgin Mary) and show greater metrical variation: the first is written in Alcaic stanzas, the second in hendecasyllables, the third in Asclepiadean meter (a type of choriambic tetrameter), the fourth in catalectic trochaic tetrameter, and the fifth in Sapphic stanzas. Three of the hymns are to the Virgin Mary ("Ad Mariam Virginem, Dei Matrem," "In laudem nominis gloriosissimae Virginis Mariae," "In hostes gloriosissimae Mariae Virginis"); one hymn (no. 22) is addressed to the "faithful of Christ" ("Ad Christi fideles exhortatio"), another to the pious reader ("Ad pium lectorem"), and the last, to Dantiscus's book itself ("Ad libellum," subtitled "De turbatis nostris temporibus" [On Our Turbulent Times]).

The motivation for Dantiscus's writing a hymn cycle lay not only in the devout concerns of a high-ranking churchman in the twilight of his life. Sincerity of belief indeed was a factor in the composition of the poems; so too was a certain regret over the impieties of an anything but cloistered youth. But Dantiscus wrote his hymns at a time when the Reformation seemed a real threat to the stability of the church and its inroads in Poland could no longer be ignored. That the Reformation was not far from the poet's mind is established in the cycle's last two poems, which were clearly intended to convey the meaning of the work as a whole. In "To the Pious Reader" verses such as the following leave no doubt as to the object of Dantiscus's wrath: "I have nothing to say about those who in our perverse time destroy what has been solemnly established by the fathers according to custom, and whose bellies and gullets, given to impieties, sing their Germanic dirges. When Christ wishes it, they will suffer grave punishments" (291:48–53).

The picture painted of the contemporary world in the concluding "To My Book: On Our Turbulent Times" is bleak. Countries and people "are being torn apart by many different sects that the faith of our ancient fathers once tempered ("tot variis qui modo sectis / Inter se lacerant, quae vetus illa / Patrum religio condidit olim?" [292:6–8]). Strife and discord are everywhere; fortified cities are under siege; "many are those who oppose the authority of the emperor, but happily he is at last ending their threat and justly subduing the rebels by the sword" (16–18). The death of kings (Henry VIII and Francis I) has brought turmoil to England and France; Hungary cannot be at rest because of the Turkish menace; all of Italy and Spain is in arms; and in an allusion to the origin and spread of Lutheranism, a "contagious doctrine" (dogma . . . pestifer) has issued forth from the Elbe and cold waters flow from the Rhine (31–32). After enumerating the reasons for fear and anxiety in his own time, Dantiscus engages in national self-congratulation by declaring that the only country in Europe that continues to enjoy a safe peace is Poland, and that is because of her two great rulers, Sigismund I, who died not long before, and Sigismund August, who succeeded him:

> Et turbis nec ab his Sarmatis ora
> Est immunis, et hoc propter utrumque
> Regem, sic et eum, qui modo vita
> Excessit pius et sanctus, eumque,
> Qui vivus superest, rectius ut res
> Regni dirigat et sceptra gubernet. (293:22–27)

(And indeed only the land of the Sarmatian is safe from these upheavals, and that is because of her two kings, he who ended his life recently pious and saintly, and he who remains alive so that he might more justly direct the affairs of state and wield the scepter.)

Dantiscus's last years stand in marked contrast to those spent in diplomatic service. Instead of far-flung travel, the pomp and ceremony of royal and imperial courts, and high-level politics, there were the weighty but relatively less turbulent duties of a leading churchman. The pinnacle of his ecclesiastical career came in 1537. It was on July 1 of that year that the prestigious and powerful bishopric of Warmia opened up after the death of Bishop Maurycy Ferber. Dantiscus was one of four canons recommended to the king as Bishop Ferber's successor; so too was Copernicus. But despite the latter's fame as an astronomer and medical doctor, he had never really involved himself in the affairs of the church and was not regarded as a serious candidate. Besides, he was already sixty-four years old at the time, and his age was held as a liability. The election took place on September 20 in Frombork, with all votes cast in favor of Dantiscus. All that remained was the pope's official confirmation, and that was little more than a formality. It came on January 11, 1538, less than a month after Dantiscus had taken up his bishop's residence in the town of Lidzbark.

As bishop of Warmia Dantiscus enjoyed not only considerable prestige but great authority. He ruled over a diocese that was well endowed with wealth and property; not being subject to the authority of the archbishop of Gniezno, he had considerable political autonomy. Dantiscus used his power in his late years to further two causes to which he was deeply devoted. The first was that of the Counter-Reformation. As bishop of Warmia, he campaigned energetically to curb the inroads of Protestantism in the Prussian area, and this brought him into a close relationship with one of the foremost figures of the Catholic Counter-

Reformation in Poland, Stanisław Hosius (1504–79), bishop of Warmia in 1551 and cardinal in 1561. It was Hosius who introduced the Society of Jesus (Jesuits) to Poland in 1565 and who undertook the publication of Dantiscus's *Hymns* after his death. Dantiscus's other great cause was that of the integration of the two Prussias, Royal Prussia, which was part of the Polish Crown; and Ducal Prussia, which remained under the authority of the Knights of the Cross in accordance with the Treaty of Toruń of 1466. In 1525 the grand master of the order, Albrecht Hohenzollern, converted to Protestantism, secularized the realm of the Knights, and as a secular prince brought what then became known as Ducal Prussia under Polish vassalage.

Dantiscus and Albrecht both shared the vision of an integrated Prussian state, but from that point on their views were essentially incompatible. What Dantiscus had in mind was an integration of Royal and Ducal Prussia within the framework of the Polish state. Albrecht's concept of an integration of the two Prussias stopped short of incorporation into a greater Poland. A combined Royal and Ducal Prussia under Albrecht's own leadership and preferably free of vassalage to Poland was his more likely goal. Although relations between Dantiscus and Albrecht were generally good for a number of years, it was their divergent religious views more than the distance between their political visions that eventually erected an insurmountable barrier between them. Dantiscus's fervent desire and efforts to curtail the inroads of Protestantism in Royal Prussia were paralleled by Albrecht's more strident support of the reform movement. Since the two powerful figures were on an obvious collision course—of which they were both well aware—the relationship was bound to suffer. A noticeable cooling set in particularly from about 1545, and time did not permit any change in the atmosphere before Dantiscus's death in 1548. The dream of an integrated Prussia in their lifetime eluded both men.

In his campaign to add new vigor to the Counter-Reformation in Royal Prussia, Dantiscus placed great emphasis on the need to improve the moral and intellectual life of the Catholic clergy of his bishopric. This brought him into an uncomfortable relationship with, among others, Copernicus. Although relations between the former well-known and worldly diplomat and humanist, now bishop of Warmia, and the celebrated man of science were correct, they were neither close nor warm. The overtures seemed to come mainly from Dantiscus, especially after he became bishop of Warmia, and Copernicus remained singularly unresponsive.

What made matters worse was reports brought to Dantiscus that Copernicus was among the clerics in his diocese who were guilty of violating the law of celibacy.[12] Since this was of greatest concern to Dantiscus in his desire to raise the moral level of his clergy, one can easily appreciate his chagrin at confronting a figure as prominent as Copernicus. Dantiscus tried in several ways—first indirectly, later less diplomatically—to have Copernicus remove his concubine, an attractive married woman named Anna Schilling, from his residence in Frombork. Copernicus was obviously loath to part with his female companion, although he recognized he would have to comply with Bishop Dantiscus's wishes at some point. He tried to stall, arguing that Mrs. Schilling was just his housekeeper and that with good help hard to find he would like to retain her services. Eventually she did leave the Copernicus residence, and for a time Frombork, but that was not enough to placate Dantiscus. Because of her charms and her reputation, the bishop feared that were she permitted to return to Frombork she might continue to be a harmful influence on the clergy there. The matter was further complicated because Mrs. Schilling owned a house in Frombork. Copernicus's death ended the problem of her relationship with him, but when she reappeared in Frombork in September 1543 determined to take up residence there, Dantiscus made a concerted—and finally successful—effort to block the move.

Dantiscus's relationship with Copernicus also had a literary side. When the latter's famous treatise *De revolutionibus orbium coelestium* was being readied for publication, Dantiscus wrote an epigram in praise of the work and sent it to Copernicus in June 1541, with a letter suggesting that the great scientist might use it as a kind of preface. When the *De revolutionibus* appeared in Nuremberg in 1543 it did not contain the epigram, which was subsequently lost. Dantiscus fared better with another epigram he wrote for Copernicus's *De lateribus et angulis triangulorum* (On the Sides and Angles of a Triangle); when the work appeared in print in Wittenberg in 1542 it included Dantiscus's epigram.[13]

Dantiscus's responsibilities as bishop of Warmia from 1538 until his death ten years later did not lower the curtain on his activities as a humanist. Though his literary career moved in other directions, as we have seen, he maintained lively contacts with fellow humanists throughout Europe. He corresponded with them at length, encouraged a few to come to Poland, provided information about Copernicus when international interest in his discoveries was mounting, and in general transformed his residence in Lidzbark into a Renaissance humanist salon in much the same spirit as Gregory of Sanok had done years before in Dunajów. Dantiscus's epistolary circle of foreign humanists included such well-known figures as Jan van der Campen,

Gemma Frisius, Conrad Goclenius, and Rutger Rescius of Louvain, Janus Secundus of the Hague, and Cornelius Schlepper of Brussels.[14] These friends proved of inestimable value when Dantiscus undertook to establish a library at the bishop's residence in Lidzbark. Long an avid bibliophile, Dantiscus assembled an impressive collection of books both in his personal library and in that of the bishopric, aided in no small measure by contributions from his friends in other countries. Sad to say, both collections suffered grave losses in later military campaigns.

Although his duties in Warmia virtually precluded further diplomatic assignments, Dantiscus accepted one last commission in May 1538—arranging the marriage of Sigismund August, son of Sigismund I, to Elizabeth, daughter of Ferdinand I Hapsburg. Accompanied by Janusz Latalski, the palatine of Poznań, Dantiscus traveled from Warmia to Wrocław to negotiate the dynastic union, which took place in 1543. On his way back to Warmia, he paid a last visit to Cracow.

Dantiscus's health had begun to deteriorate in 1538. As his sixty-third birthday approached in 1548 he felt the imminence of death and gave literary form to these premonitions as well as to his outlook on life in his autobiographical *Vita* and in two epitaphs. The concluding dozen lines of the *Vita* express pessimism, disenchantment, and a desire to part company with earthly life: "I do not wish to linger longer here where false pretense is victor, where virtue is vice and shame beyond the law, where the perverse mind of men reigns and where might everywhere triumphs. The wrath of punishing God is near at hand. I wish to die and to you, earth, abandon my rotten body. My soul desires to be with Christ. Let his will, by which all things are done, be done! He holds my fate in his hands. After my death I ask that this inscription by which posterity will come to know me be engraved on my tomb: In bidding you farewell, O earth, I do not speak in sadness, summoned as I am to that life which endures forever" (301:181–92).

In the first of his two epitaphs Dantiscus mentions the approach of his sixty-third birthday and recalls hearing that many men have died at that age. If God should choose to take his life then, he asks now that an inscription be made informing people in brief that he served long at court, was sent among the mighty of the world, and was honored with twin ribbons (referring to his becoming a poet laureate and, later in life, a bishop). The second epitaph exudes the same medievalism of his hymns. Consigning his body to worms, to the ashes whence it came, he commends his soul unto God, from whom it first took life. Ambition, hope, anxiety, labor, splendor, pain, and thought restless in human endeavors are all bid farewell. "In the sixty-third year of my life," he concludes, "I set myself free from those enticements that were a cruel prison to me. Life is uncertain; our destinies are fulfilled when they are furthest from mind and least expected. You who wish to live free from care, die unto this world and in this precarious whirlwind live for God!" (302:7–12).

Dantiscus's premonition about the end of his life was accurate. Death claimed him just four days short of his sixty-third birthday, at six in the morning, on Saturday, October 27, 1548. Eustachy Knobelsdorf, to whom Dantiscus had dedicated the lengthy poem *Alliopagus* and who was perhaps his staunchest admirer, was with him. Diplomat, poet, and bishop, indeed one of the outstanding figures of the Renaissance in Poland, Dantiscus was interred in the same Frombork cathedral where Copernicus had been laid to rest five years before.

CHAPTER 8

The Hell-Raiser Who Became Primate of Poland

One of the stunning achievements of the renovation by Italian artists of the royal compound on the Wawel Hill in Cracow in the time of King Sigismund I was the erection of the Sigismund Chapel. Situated along the southern side of the medieval Wawel cathedral just a short distance from the entrance to the castle compound, and providing a striking contrast to the cathedral, it was planned originally for the king's first wife, Barbara Zápolya, who died in 1515. The project was initiated in 1517, but by the time the foundation was laid two years later, King Sigismund also had in mind its eventual use as his own mausoleum. The chapel arose on the site of an older Gothic one that was razed to provide space for a new edifice of spare exterior and richly ornamented interior conceived wholly in Renaissance style. Finally completed in 1533, the Sigismund Chapel was the work of the Tuscan architect and sculptor Bartolomeo Berrecci, who came to Poland in 1516 and played a vital role in developing a Renaissance art and architecture in that country until his death in 1537.

Prominently placed on an outer wall of the Sigismund Chapel near its entrance is a plaque engraved with the following epigram:

> Ne mirere, hospes, decus hoc sublime sacelli
> Saxaque Phidiaco sculpta magisterio.
> Hoc statuit Sismundus opus qui struxit et arcem,
> Clarior hic recta, sed ratione labor.
> Illum ne credas dum momentanea condit
> Atria perpetuam posthabuisse domum.[1]

(Lest you be amazed, guest, at the lofty beauty of this chapel and its sculptures executed under the guidance of Phidias [famous classical Greek sculptor and friend of Pericles], know then that it was Sigismund who erected this work, as it was he who built this castle. But this is the more brilliant effort, and rightly so. Do not believe that when he constructed these present halls he neglected his eternal home.)

The epigram was written by Andrzej Krzycki (Andreas Cricius, 1482–1537), then bishop of Płock, the best Polish humanist poet after Clemens Ianicius, of whom I have yet to speak, and court poet of the reign of Sigismund I.

Krzycki's enthusiasm for Renaissance art and architecture and for the transformation of royal Cracow begun under the aegis of King Sigismund expressed itself in other epigrams. "In hoc ipsum sacellum" (On the Same [Sigismund] Chapel) strikes a philosophical note absent in the first poem on the subject:

Lest you wonder, guest, at the lofty beauty of the chapel and the tombs prepared well before their time, know then that Sigismund erected this work, realizing that he lives as a great king but not unmindful that he too must die. (80)

The construction of the royal armory on the Wawel in 1533, the same year the Sigismund Chapel was completed, was the occasion for four more epigrams celebrating King Sigismund's commitment to peace and his belief that strength was the best guarantor of it. The wisdom of preparing for war in time of peace is the central theme of the poems. The first, "In armamentarium regis Sigismundi primi" (On the Armory of King Sigismund I), concludes, for example, with the admonition that "arms bear peace, in turn are borne in peace" (Arma ferunt pacem, pace paranda tamen [80]), while the second advises, "If a state is happy that fears war in time of peace, there you will recognize the hand of a wise ruler" (Si felix quae pace timet respublica bellum, / Principis agnosces hoc sapientis opus [80]). The third strikes a similar note: "Thundering cannons produced in rare days of peace demonstrate the great deeds of an invincible ruler" (Bombardae horrisonae quae rara in pace parantur, / Magnifica invicti principis acta probant [81]). When the great bell ordered by the king (and known as the "Sigismund bell") was struck in 1521 in the Nuremberg workshop of the artisan Hans Behem, Krzycki greeted it with a witty two-line epigram that asks the question: "If, traveler, the bell seems too big to you, tell me what work of Sigismund is small?" (81).

Krzycki's approval of the transplantation of Italian Renaissance architectural styles to Poland was not only verbal, as in his epigrams on Sigismund's construction projects on the Wawel and elsewhere. During the period 1531 to 1535, while he was bishop of Płock, he was the moving force behind the building of a Renaissance cathedral in his diocesan capital. The work of Berrecci's closest associates, Giovanni Cini of Siena and Bernardino de Gianotis, it had the distinction of being the first large church in the new style to be built in Poland.

As poet of court and castle Krzycki was in an admirable position to observe life at the Wawel in the reign of King Sigismund and his second wife, Bona Sforza, and his many epigrams—a genre he felt particularly comfortable with—offer a remarkably informative picture of the times.

Krzycki came rather easily by his role at court. He was, to begin with, a member of the nobility, which makes him a rare figure among native Polish humanists, who were mostly of burgher or even peasant origin. Far more important, however, he was the nephew of Piotr Tomicki, one of the most powerful figures in Poland during the reign of Sigismund I. Besides his high ecclesiastical positions as bishop of Przemyśl, bishop of Poznań, and finally bishop of Cracow—themselves important power bases—Tomicki dominated Polish domestic and foreign policy for a good twenty years and thus had to be very close to the king.

The relationship between uncle and nephew (Krzycki was the son of Tomicki's sister) was warm, a friendship that may have first developed when Tomicki happened to be in Bologna at a time when Krzycki was studying there. Unlike Danticus, unfortunately, Krzycki wrote almost nothing autobiographical, making it difficult to reconstruct this period of his life in particular. We do know, however, that his teachers in Bologna included the distinguished humanists Codro and Beroaldo.

When Krzycki returned to Poland armed with the "polish" of an Italian academic sojourn, the intercession of Tomicki immediately assured him a respectable post. Among King Sigismund's closest advisers was Jan Lubrański, then bishop of Poznań, who like Tomicki had been an early supporter of Sigismund's candidacy for the throne against significant opposition from powerful lords in that part of the kingdom of Poland known as Great Poland. Tomicki maintained close relations with Lubrański and asked him to find a place for his sister's son who had just returned home from study in Italy. Lubrański took Krzycki on as his personal secretary in Poznań, and when the young man's talents manifested themselves he spared no effort to further his career.

These early years in Poznań revealed more than a single facet of Krzycki's personality. Having settled on the church as the avenue of greatest career potential, Krzycki fulfilled a number of ecclesiastical assignments in Poznań, acquitting himself well and moving up the ladder one step at a time. The future bishop and poet was a devout Catholic whose religious views tended to become narrower and more uncompromising as the years went by. In his later life as a respected church dignitary and man of letters it seemed natural for him to lash out at what he regarded as the moral laxity of some at court and to spew venom with abandon at the Lutherans. It may thus come as a surprise that as a young man the aspiring churchman belonged to a group of hell-raisers known in Latin as "Bibones et Commedones" (Guzzlers and Gobblers). Perhaps inspired by the Literary Society of the Vistula, which Conrad Celtis had founded in Cracow, as well as by similar humanist salons, the circle may have been the brainchild of a fun-loving courtier named Korybut Koszyrski (d. 1528). Krzycki wrote several poems about Koszyrski, including a mock last will and testament and epitaph (long before his death, of course) that convey the ribald carpe diem atmosphere of the Guzzlers and Gobblers.[2] The testament ("Testamentum Coributo") is cast in the form of a dialogue between the dying Korybut and his fellow Guzzlers and Gobblers. Replying to their question about the disposition of his worldly goods, Korybut tells them that the wise man enjoys everything he has while he is alive and reminds them of the rule of their society to "hoard all acquired goods in a live stomach" (est regula nostra, / Quae partas vivo ventre recondit opes [231:7–8]). After assuring them, however, that he has left something to be used to buy tankards for poor taverns and straw beds and the wherewithal to make fire for prostitutes, he has some suggestions as to what should be done with his body. His nose, for example, can be turned into a lamp for the use of prostitutes, while his phallus should be hung over their doors. When Korybut finally breathes his last, his comrades joyfully raise their hands to the stars in thanksgiving that he merited such a pious death. The epitaph to Korybut, "Hymnus fratrum ganae in funere Coribut" (A Hymn of the Brothers of Korybut's Dive at His Funeral), is another exercise in irreverence, this time a parody of the medieval musical sequences that then enjoyed widespread popularity. In her introduction to a volume of Polish translations of Krzycki's poems, Antonina Jelicz also points out that Krzycki's "hymn" shares undeniable affinities with a similarly humorous hymn in honor of the Society of Homerists composed by the Italian humanist Codro, with whom Krzycki studied in Bologna.[3] In lively tercets of two rhymed eight-syllable lines followed by a nonrhyming seven-syllable line, the "hymn" celebrates Korybut's relentless pursuit of pleasures that set an example for all his fellows. Even a prematurely worn-out body failed to dampen his enthusiasm, and in the end he was warmly received in heaven. The concluding verse expresses the following wish on the part of his comrades:

> Te rogamus, nos clientes,
> Tuas laudes sic canentes,
>   Respice propitius,
> Da priapis sublevamen,
> Ori sitim, ventri famem
>   Da perenne gaudium. (233:58–63)

(We beseech you, we your followers, as we now sing your praises, look upon us favorably, give support to our phalluses, insatiability to our mouths, hunger to our bellies, and pleasure forever.)

As we shall see later, with the development of Krzycki's skills as a satirist, this is not the only time he was to parody a hymn.

Krzycki's membership in the Guzzlers and Gobblers generated a number of other poems besides those dealing with Korybut Koszyrski. Several are dedicated to women, presumably female "associates" of the Guzzlers and Gobblers, and are decidedly bawdy. Two examples, both bearing the name of Gonney Zoffka, or just Zoffka, are representative:

> ### Epitaphium Gonney Zoffka
> Zoffka lupanares inter memoranda sorores,
>   His iaceo sacris non bene grata locis,
> Sed quibus assiduo colitur Venus aurea tectis,
>   Ossa in perpetuum nostra iacere velim.
> Nam stridor vulvae strepitusque testiculorum
>   Et qui lascivum spiritus urget opus,
> Plus me, quam cantus atque organa cuncta iuvabant,
>   Et quidquid sacri templa decoris habent.
> Hoc fuerat teneris studium mihi semper ab annis,
>   Haec est virtutis inclita fama meae,
> Quod simul innumeros poteram sufferre priapos,
>   Victa quibus nunquam nec satiata fui.
> Mortua nunc horum doleo quia copia desit.
>   Heu mors, cur tantum solvis acerba bonum!
> Vos igitur moneo, quibus est nunc vita puellae,
>   Ne tempus tanti perdite delicii.
> Invenitur nullo post mortem aere priapus,
>   Pro quo ego, si possem, nunc bona cuncta darem. (236–37)

(I, Zoffka, memorable among brothel sisters, lie down and wish to rest my bones for all time in these holy places where I am not welcome, but under whose roofs splendid Venus is worshiped regularly. That is because the squealing of cunts and the groaning of balls and whatever else encourages the uninhibited activity of spirits delight me more than all the singing and organ playing and all the holy decorations in which temples abound. The celebrated fame of my talent is that I was able to submit to countless pricks at the same time without ever being conquered—or satisfied—by them. Now that I am deceased, grieve that my supply of hours has run out. Ah, cruel death, why do you deprive a person of so much good? Therefore I warn you who are alive now not to lose the joys of life while you have them. No money on earth will buy you a prick once you're dead. I would now give everything I had, if I could, for one.)

De eadem Zoffka

Dixit Zoffka aliis moriens quaesita puellis,
    Quae fieret vulvae mentula grata magis.
Longa bene attingit, crassa implet, para titillat;
    Quaelibet istarum, sit modo tensa placet. (237)

(As she lay dying, Zoffka explained to other girls which phallus was more welcome to a woman's parts. A long one reaches you way in, a thick one fills you up, a small one tickles you. All of them will please you, so long as they are stiff.)

Similarly attributable to the ambiance of the Guzzlers and Gobblers are the many amatory poems, less licentious than the two above, that Krzycki continued to write virtually throughout his career. Some of these were addressed to his own amorous inclinations, such as "De furore suo" (On His Own Madness) and two poems entitled "De amore suo" (On His Own Passion). The first plays on the contradictions and paradoxes of someone possessed by Eros, in the manner of Petrarch: "What frenzy spins my head? . . . What I desire, I spurn; what pleases me, doesn't please me. Great hatred and great love bear down on my heart at the same time. I don't believe, being certain; I know, and, recognizing, do not know" (237).

In the first poem on his own passion, which begins with the line "Quod dudum immensis ardent mea pectora flammis" (That my heart has long burned with a great fire [211]), he considers that only death may be able to extinguish the flames consuming him, but then he wonders if feeling outlasts death. The second poem on the same theme acknowledges his beloved's victory over him and castigates her for lacking compassion for her victims: "You conquer and gaze upon your victim without mercy. You are not moved by my death, you who are harder than the cliffs of Scylla and more dangerous than a tigress who has lost her young" (212:13–16).

Many of Krzycki's amatory poems appear to be no more than conventional exercises in the genre, such as those on a hardhearted female named Diamanta whose name (Diamond) is perfectly suited to her character. In one, "De duritia Diamantae puellae" (On the Hardness of the Girl Diamanta),[4] the poet bids Venus turn him into a goat, since popular wisdom holds that a goat's blood has the power to break diamonds. The motif of the hard-as-diamond female also appears in one of two short love poems addressed "To the Girl Lydia" (De Lydia puella).[5] Who, asks the poet, would deny that Orpheus's song could charm lynxes and mute stones into following him? But so hard of heart is Lydia, he wonders if even the sweet voice of Krzycki's own lyre would cause her to follow him through desolate plains and fields. The other poem on Lydia[6] is built on a conceit found in Roman poetry and later a Petrarchan commonplace—the paradox of fire in snow. Lydia hits the poet with a snowball, and in disbelief he discovers fire in the snow—meaning, of course, that he has at once fallen in love. He then poses the question, What is colder than snow? And yet his heart is ablaze from snow, and only she who hurled the snowball can put out the fire, not with snow or ice but with the same flame (of passion): "Lydia sola potes nostras exstinguere flammas, / None nive, non glacie, sed potes igne pari" (210:7–8).

That Krzycki was occasionally able to rise above the bawdy and conventional in his amatory verse is evidenced by three small poems inspired by the legend of Lucretia of Rome. A beauty admired for her domestic virtues as well, Lucretia was the wife of Lucius Tarquinius Collatinus. After she was assaulted by Sextus Tarquinius, one of the sons of Tarquinius Superbus, she swore her father and husband to vengeance and then stabbed herself to death. In fulfillment of the oath of vengeance, her husband's cousin, Lucius Junius Brutus, led a popular rising against the Tarquins, toppling them from power and establishing a republic (traditional date, 509 B.C.).

Noteworthy above all in the first two Lucretia poems is their rhetorical structure. Krzycki has cast them in the form of a verse polemic between himself and Jacopo Piso (d. 1527), the envoy of Pope Julius II and of Transylvanian origin, whom Krzycki met either in Cracow, where Piso arrived on January 6, 1510, to encourage renewed hostilities against the Turks, or in Poznań that same year during a meeting of representatives of Poland and the Teutonic Order that Krzycki must have attended together with Jan Lubrański.

The verse polemic is set off by the divergent responses of poet and papal envoy to a portrait of Lucretia that Krzycki had with him at the time. In the first poem, which bears the title "Pisoin imaginem Lucretiae lascivius depictam, apud Cricium inventam" (Piso on a Portrait of Lucretia Licentiously Depicted That He Observed in Cricius's Possession), Piso's vision imposes an almost androgynous character on Lucretia: masculine in her stern visage as she stands poised with a dagger against her breast, yet ultimately—and deceptively—a study not of a wish to die but rather of feminine submissiveness. But Piso sees beyond the obvious subject of the picture and uses it as a pretext for a statement about art—that the power of art is no less than the power of nature itself. This is manifest, moreover, in the way art (here represented by the Greek painter Apelles) has transformed the goddess Flora into Lucretia. So magical are the properties of art that changes in Lucretia's posture in the painting would induce other images and associations. If the dagger is removed from her hands, she would become instead the famous Greek courtesan Thaïs, later the wife of Ptolemy Lagus, king of Egypt; and should she cover her breasts with her gown and take an eagle in her embrace, Lucretia would undergo another transformation, becoming Ganymede, son of the king of Troy, who was abducted by Zeus in the form of an eagle.

In his reply to Piso, in the second poem, Krzycki similarly identifies with Lucretia, as Piso did in the first poem, declaring in the opening line that "Non Flora aut Thais, sed sum Lucretia, Piso" (I am not Flora or Thaïs, Piso, but Lucretia [198]). Again playing with the subjectivity of perception, Krzycki then asserts that Piso's vision of Lucretia as a woman yearning not to die but to submit is no more or less than a projection of Piso's own desire and that in so beholding Lucretia he is, in fact, her ravager Sextus Tarquinius. By the same token, if Krzycki as Lucretia pretended to be Ganymede by covering her bosom, then Piso would want to be Zeus in his role as abductor. If, finally, the subject of the portrait appears masculine (as Piso asserts in the first poem), Krzycki-Lucretia urges Piso not to call him Ganymede but to be Piso to him, and he then will become Socrates ("Sed mihi sis Piso, sim tibi Socration" [199:8]), a possible allusion to the ancient Roman Piso Caesoninus (consul 58 B.C.), whom the poet Catullus mentions as a friendly antagonist of Socrates.[7]

The third poem of the Piso series, "In Lucretiam lascivius depictam" (On Lucretia Lasciviously Depicted), abandons the wit, changes of aspect, and allusiveness of the first two. The speaker now is the portrait's subject, Lucretia herself. Commenting on the alleged lasciviousness of her portrait, which was the original point of departure for the exchanges between Piso and Krzycki, Lucretia declares that if the painting of her seems lascivious to the two men, what better likeness of modesty do they have? She calls on them to desist from their subjective responses to the portrait and accept it on its own terms. Thus admiring Lucretia's noble deed and her defense of honor, they will come to regard her as a true object of reverence.

If Krzycki's earlier bawdy and largely conventional amatory poetry weighs little in the scale of his overall poetic achievement and relates primarily to the boisterous activities of the Guzzlers and Gobblers, it does represent a kind of poetic apprenticeship that proved of inestimable value when he drew close to the court of King Sigismund. Once a member of the court, Krzycki was able to use his powers of observation, his concreteness, his wit and sense of humor, the taste for satire already manifest in his poetic exchange with the papal envoy Piso, and his facile handling of short poetic forms, above all the epigram, to become a chronicler in verse of court life. So numerous and varied are Krzycki's poems about the Wawel and its occupants in the time of King Sigismund I that they have a real historical value, providing details and glimpses unavailable elsewhere.

Although Krzycki's star had been ascending steadily while he was secretary to Jan Lubrański, his breakthrough to the royal court came in 1512 when he became a member of the Polish delegation that was sent to Hungary to arrange the marriage between Sigismund and Barbara Zápolya. Although politically motivated in that Sigismund viewed it as an opportunity to improve relations with Hungary while gaining leverage against the advocates of a pro-Hungary policy, the marriage between the Polish king and his Hungarian bride proved felicitous. They were wed in February 1512, and the queen's death three years later brought deep sorrow to the many, Krzycki among them, who had come to admire her compassion and gentility.

Krzycki's early contact with Barbara Zápolya ripened into a close and sincere friendship, and he was appointed her secretary once she became queen. Now a member of the court, Krzycki consolidated his position with the royal family, rapidly emerging as one of Sigismund's most trusted advisers. Presence at court also opened up a new range of subjects for his poetic talent, which Krzycki lost no time in using to good advantage. His debut as court poet was initiated with several poems celebrating the nuptials of Sigismund and Barbara, published as a small book by Haller of Cracow in 1512. Included in the series are such poems as "De nuptiis Sigismundi regis Poloniae cum Barbara Hungara regina Poloniae" (On the Nuptials of Sigismund, King of Poland, and Barbara of Hungary, Queen of Poland), "Epithalamion

Sigismundi regis et Barbarae reginae Poloniae" (Wedding Song of King Sigismund and Queen Barbara of Poland), "Cantilena in Threncinio cantata" (A Song Sung in Threncinium [Trencseny, Barbara Zápolya's birthplace in Hungary]), "Carmen Sapphicum" (A Sapphic Song), "Cantilena in coronatione reginae Barbarae" (A Song on the Coronation of Queen Barbara), "In insignia reginae Barbarae aquilae coniuncta" (On the Coat of Arms of Queen Barbara Joined with an Eagle), a second poem on the same subject, and "Precatio Cricii ad regem pro quodam promisso, cum esset reginae Barbarae cancellarius" (Supplication of Cricius to the King about a Certain Promise When He Was the Queen's Secretary). The collection offers ample testimony to Krzycki's admirably rapid progress from a writer of bawdy and amatory verses to a court panegyrist firmly in command of the classical mythology-laden idiom of royal flattery. The "Sapphic Song" and "On the Coat of Arms of Queen Barbara Joined with an Eagle" are representative and are short enough to quote in full:

Carmen Sapphicum
Virgo Sismundi nova nupta regis,
Scin Deus qualem tibi dat maritum?
Cuius insignis penetravit atros
    Fama sub Indos.
Cui dedit pulchrum Venus alma vultum
Et caput Pallas pietasque mentem,
Quique victrices agitat secundo
    Marte triumphos.
Iuno sacrarum dea nuptiarum,
Iuno clamosi medicina partus,
Iuno supremi soror atque cara
    Nupta Tonantis,
Tuque plorantem iuveni puellam,
Quae toro sistis violasque zonam,
Clara Cypreae Bromiique proles
    O Hymen, Hymen,
Euge felice properate gressu
Nuptias magni celebrare regis,
Ut bona nobis bonus inde crescat
    Arbore fructus. (27–28)

(Maiden, new bride of King Sigismund, do you know the husband whom God is giving you, whose fame has spread even to the black Indies; the husband to whom Venus gave a beautiful face, Pallas the head, and Piety the mind, and who, with the support of Mars, celebrates triumphs as a victor? Juno, goddess of holy matrimony; Juno, sister and dear bride of

the Supreme Thunderer [Jupiter], and you who place a weeping girl in
a young man's bed and rend her girdle, brilliant progeny of Cypria
[Venus] and Bromius [Bacchus], O Hymen, Hymen, hasten with auspicious step to honor the nuptials of the great king that good fruit may
grow to us from a good tree.)

> In insignia reginae Barbarae aquilae coniuncta
> Ponite nunc miseri vestrum diadema leones,
>   Pannonio cessit gloria vestra lupo.
> Nec tamen hoc satis est. En aquila fertur ad astra
>   Praebeat ut terris regia signa lupus. (28)

(Remove now your crown, poor lions,[8] your glory has yielded to the
Hungarian wolf. But this is not enough. Behold an eagle soars to the stars
so that the wolf may present royal standards to the lands.)

Although we can only speculate on the promise alluded to in the
"Supplication of Cricius to the King about a Certain Promise When
He Was the Queen's Secretary," the poem is interesting for the rare
personal note struck and the ease with which Krzycki was able to
assume the familiar humanist's supplicatory posture before his patron
or benefactor. The promise may, in fact, have involved an ecclesiastical
post in Cracow (Krzycki's appointment to the Cracow canonicate in
July 1512 seems to indicate this) that the poet was eager to obtain both
to fulfill his growing ambition for high ecclesiastical office and for the
financial advantage. The latter appears the weightier consideration in
the poem, since Krzycki pleads that impecuniousness has distracted
him from writing the king's life and celebrating his glory in verse:

> Est mihi magna tuam digne mens scribere vitam,
>   Versiculis laudes et celebrare tuas,
> Sed mea divertunt aliorsum pectora curae
>   Et studium victus occupat omne meum. (30:3–6)

(It is my great desire to write your life in worthy style and to celebrate
your glory in my poor little verses, but cares turn my mind in another
direction, and concern for a livelihood takes up all my energies.)

He goes on to complain that he is being consumed by debt and
to lament that any servant who dispenses household stores or any
court doorman has more advantage from his position than he does
as the queen's secretary. In urging the king now to look with favor
on his request, Krzycki points out that he has the support of none

other than "the most brilliant Juno who is of one body with you and half your soul" (that is, Queen Barbara), of "wise and loyal Achates, the great pride of your court and council" (Achates was the faithful friend of Aeneas; Krzycki is referring here to one of the most powerful men in Cracow at the time, Krzysztof Szydło-wiecki, great chancellor of the Crown [1515] and castellan of Cracow [1527]), and last but not least, of "Bishop Pine Tree" (Jan Lubrański, whose family coat of arms featured a pine tree). With such powerful support, to say nothing of uncle Piotr Tomicki's constant efforts on his behalf, it seems highly unlikely that Krzycki would have been turned down by the king.

The improvement of his financial condition presumably enabled Krzycki to return to writing "official" poetry with renewed vigor. Hetman Ostrogski's victory over the Tatars at Wiśnowiec in 1512, which was the cause of much joy and celebration in Cracow— especially since the victory occurred on the king's name day, May 2—was immortalized in a 128-line panegyric titled "Encomium Sigismundi regis Poloniae post partam de Tataris victoriam" (Encomium after King Sigismund's Victory over the Tatars). The important Polish victory over the Muscovites at Orsza on September 8, 1514, brought forth an appropriately greater poetic response from Krzycki: several short poems in addition to two long panegyrics, "Ad Serenissimum Dominum Sigismundum Primum et magnum Lithuaniae ducem nomine inclitae reginae Barbarae coniugis suae post partam de Moscis victoriam epistula Andreae Cricii cancellarii" (Letter to His Most Serene Lord Sigismund I and Grand Duke of Lithuania Following the Victory over the Muscovites in the Name of Andreas Cricius, Secretary to His Illustrious Wife, Queen Barbara) and "Cantilena de victoria e Moscis parta die natali Sanctae Mariae 1514 rem summarie continens Andreae Cricii inclitae reginae Barbarae Cancellarii" (Song of Victory Seized from the Muscovites on the Birthday of the Virgin Mary 1514, Containing a Summary of the Event by Andreas Cricius, Secretary to the Illustrious Queen Barbara). The most interesting of the poems on Orsza is undoubtedly the last-mentioned 368-verse "Cantilena." Abandoning the traditional hexameters he usually favored for his panegyrics, Krzycki reverted to the medieval sequence he had used in a parodic way in his hymn-epitaph to Korybut Koszyrski of the Guzzlers and Gobblers. The result is indeed curious, a panegyric celebrating a notable military victory and at the same time recapitulating the highlights of the battle, cast in the form of a predominantly rhymed church hymn. A few excerpts will illustrate its style:

Eia chori resurgamus,
Quartam nostri recolamus
Principis victoriam,
Qua nec ullam clariorem
Toto mundo nec maiorem
Sol vidit hoc saeculo.
Ille Moscus celebratus
Tamque potens aestimatus
Quam Xerxes vel Darius,
Qui tot gentes subiugavit
Magnam partem occupavit
Terrarum imperio,
Ecce iacet profligatus
Confusus et spoliatus
Flore sui populi. (42:1–15)

(Come on, let's join in chorus and celebrate the fourth victory of our leader, of which the sun has seen no more brilliant or greater in this world in this age. That Muscovite, renowned and esteemed as powerful as Xerxes or Darius, who subjugated so many peoples and brought such a large part of the world under his rule, behold, now lies defeated, confused, and deprived of the flower of his people.)

Ergo cum nox recessisset
Sacra dies illuxisset
Natalis Deiparae,
Ausi sunt, o mirum dictu,
Structis turmis pro conflictu
Transnatare fluvium,
Et praesertim cum videbat
Stultus hostis et fervebat
Certus de victoria. (47:175–83)

(When night receded and the holy day of the birth of the Mother of God dawned, arranged in battle order they made a bold attempt, O wonderful to relate, to swim across the river in full view of the foolish enemy who was strutting about certain of victory.)

Because of his use of medieval hymn sequence for comic and parodic purposes both during his Guzzlers and Gobblers days and later, Krzycki's preference for it in a panegyric about a military victory obviously comes as a surprise. But it would be wrong to dismiss its use as a lapse of taste or as poor judgment. Throughout his career as a poet, Krzycki employed a variety of meters, and in the "Song" about the battle of Orsza in 1514 he may simply have tried an experiment by writing in a meter not traditionally associated with panegyric or heroic poetry. Then too, it is entirely possible that Krzycki conceived the work as a hymn of thanksgiving for a great victory that could be spoken or sung in the manner of the medieval sequences. If this indeed was his intention he surely miscalculated, given the length of the "Song." While aware of medieval traditions, Krzycki used them only parodically for the most part and not because of any lingering loyalty to them. For this reason it would be best to regard the poem about the battle of Orsza not as an example of medieval vestiges in Krzycki's style but more in the nature of an experiment. Whether it worked is, of course, another matter.

As spontaneous as was the rejoicing over the Orsza victory, so universal was the grief in Poland at the premature death of the very popular Queen Barbara the following year. In view of his close personal relationship with her, Krzycki's sense of loss was both genuine and profound. The most impressive literary expression of his sorrow was the lengthy "Deprecatio immaturae mortis divae Barbarae, reginae Poloniae" (Lament for the Premature Death of the Illustrious Barbara, Queen of Poland). Though an expected gesture given Krzycki's relationship with the queen and his position at court, the elegy still strikes chords of sincerity despite the formalities observed, as in these excerpts:

> Illa Sigismundi coniux dignissima regis
> Barbara, formarum specimen, probitatis imago. . . . (58:6–20)

(That most worthy wife of King Sigismund, Barbara, an ideal of beauty and image of goodness, who came here recently amid the greatest elegance to enter so distinguished a connubial bed and vows, and in so doing raised her own outstanding lineage to the stars, she, of whom no one ever saw anything more gentle or more lofty in so deserving a crown, alas, brought down suddenly by cruel fate before her time, falls groaning in death and abandoning life. Neither strength, nor prayers, nor her youth, nor physicians, nor the great efforts of her husband are of any use. Her cries reach the very heaven, and grave are her tears and sighs. The deities remain deaf, the dreadful law of God can no way be altered, and the Fates break the threads on her distaff.)

> Aspicis ut totam dolor ingens occupat urbem,
> Non cantus citharaeque sonant, stant atria muta. . . .
>   (58–59:29–36)

(You see what mighty grief takes hold of the entire city. Melodies of the lyre no longer sound; houses and public places stand mute, the temples

of God are silent, the joy of life has fled all. Wherever you look, instead
of games, laughter, and festive dances there is only funereal calm, and
the only voice to be heard is that of bitter lamentation. Frightful coffins
are being borne, the air is filled with the smoke of burning candles, and
a long procession accompanies and precedes the funeral train in the
performance of its solemn and unexpected rites.)

Sic nos morte tua maestos hera magna relinquis? . . .
(59:55–61)

(Do you leave us thus grief-stricken, great mistress, by your death? Do
you thus abandon forever the kingdom and the mournful heart of your
beloved husband and this pleasant life? Orphans mourn you; the needy,
whose hardship your right hand greatly alleviated, bewail your passing;
your servants are similarly saddened; your entire court weeps bitterly,
seeing itself deprived of its greatest embellishment.)

After Barbara's death, Krzycki drew closer to Sigismund himself,
becoming his secretary in 1516. In this capacity he not only was privy
to the monarch's plans to take as his second wife the Italian Bona
Sforza, but wrote the speech that Polish emissaries carried with them
for delivery before Princess Isabella, Bona's mother, formally request-
ing her daughter's hand in marriage on behalf of King Sigismund
of Poland. On the Italian side negotiations at the Polish court were
conducted by Cristoforo Colonna (Chrysostomus Columnius, 1460–
1539), secretary of the duke of Calabria, a humanist, a poet of Petrarchan persuasion in Latin and Italian, and an intimate of the Sforza
family. The apparent awkwardness of the Italian emissary's first meeting with Sigismund became the subject of a gracious poem by Krzycki,
who was present at the time. Colonna, it seems, brought a poem to
present before the Polish king. When the formality of the occasion
made it difficult for the Italian to find an appropriate moment to
deliver his poem, Krzycki's previous protector, Bishop Jan Lubrański,
stepped forward, took Colonna by the hand, and whispered something
in his ear, probably encouragement that the moment had come. The
Italian recited his poem, and the king was favorably impressed. Sigismund commiserated with Colonna over his long, hard trip to Poland,
then praised the poem and its author, declaring, "He's one of us!"
Krzycki concludes his poem by exhorting Colonna to go and pine for
his native Italy, after having been received by him "of whom there is
no one more majestic on earth."

Not to be outdone by the Polish court poet, Colonna wrote a flattering, and typically humanist, verse reply to Krzycki. He reiterates the legend dear to Polish humanists that when the Roman poet Ovid was exiled he was sent to lands later incorporated into the Polish-Lithuanian commonwealth. Colonna visited the city of Wilno in 1517 and it was there, he says, that he heard the "Italian Muses singing in the fields" (Ausonias Vilnae in campis cantare Camenas). When he asked them what fate had brought them so far from home, they answered that they came with an exiled poet and have remained there in grief ever since his death. The Muses grieve no longer, however, and when Colonna inquired how they finally overcame their sorrow, they replied that it was because they could constitute the circle around Krzycki, for with him Ovid's poetry has again come to life.

Amid great pomp and ceremony the nuptials of Sigismund and Bona Sforza took place at last in April 1518. Krzycki was expected, of course, to commemorate the event in a wedding poem, and he rose to the occasion magnificently in the most impressive of his "official" works, the "Epithalamium Divi Sigismundi Primi Regis et Inclitae Bonae Reginae Poloniae" (Epithalamium to the Divine King Sigismund I and the Illustrious Queen Bona of Poland), published as a separate brochure in 1518 by Haller in Cracow.

A poem written in celebration of a royal wedding obviously afforded limited opportunity for originality. But Krzycki demonstrated that he was certainly no slavish adherent to convention. Following a prefatory verse puzzle in which the name of the "unknown" author of the wedding poem is spelled out by the first letter of each line, he begins his 351-verse "Epithalamium" by introducing himself into the work as a poet who has come from the faraway frozen north (Lithuania) to Cracow and now appears ruminating on the tumultuous recent history of Poland as he stands on the bank of the Vistula River. Classical mythology and such contemporary events as the campaign against Muscovy come together in the narration, seeming, to Krzycki's credit, neither strained nor merely imitative.

The poet-narrator is distracted from his reveries (which are made part of the fabric of the panegyric by their allusion to Sigismund's military prowess) by the singing and dancing of a procession of mythological deities whose collective presence exudes the sweet scent of flowers. When he asks the Muse Erato the cause of the celebration, she tells him at some length about the two urns by which Zeus controls human destinies. When it appeared that too much of Sigismund's cup of fate had been filled from the urn of good fortune, Zeus added a drop from the other urn to achieve a balance, since life cannot be all joy or all sorrow. The turn in the king's fortunes was signaled by the death of his beloved wife Barbara and by the subsequent passing away of his brother and sister. But when these and other misfortunes seemed to bring him too much suffering, Juno, Venus, and Minerva besought Zeus to relieve his bitterness by giving him a new wife of Latin origin, who would fill his life with delightful love. The bride they have chosen for him, the "adornment of the Sforza family, the rulers of Hesperia [Italy and Spain]" (67:133–34), is described as their own equal in beauty:

> Cuius ad hanc propriam finxit tua Cypria formam,
> Finxit amor, Charites sua numera, cuncta dederunt.
> Fulget in augusta maiestas fronte genaeque
> Virginea probitate rubent, sunt colla decora
> Membraque, sunt oculi pulchro nigrore micantes,
> Aemula labra rosis, fulvo coma concolor auro.
> Sunt artes etiam ingenuae numenque repostum
> Palladis, est lotum Pimplea pectus ab unda. (135–42)

(Venus and love shaped her figure, the Graces gave her all their gifts. Majesty shines on her august forehead, her cheeks glow with a maidenly goodness, her neck is graceful, as are the limbs of her body, her eyes sparkle with a beautiful blackness, her lips rival the rose, her hair is the same color as bright gold. Her native talents and intellect derive from Pallas [Athena], while her bosom is bathed by the waters of Pimpla [a town in Pieria sacred to the Muses].)

Krzycki's comfortable blending of classical mythology and contemporary figures in the panegyric as a whole is well illustrated by this typical passage:

While all the wishes and commands of Zeus were thus being carried out, the divine countenance of the daughter of the Sforzas was being painted by a master whose right hand was guided by Venus, who also blended charm and romantic passion into the paints. Once deliberations and other matters had been settled on both sides, a swift emissary of golden tongue [Cristoforo Colonna, who represented the Sforzas in the prenuptial negotiations], the glory of the bards of the kingdom of Sirena [Naples], was sent to the lands of the Big Bear constellation [the northern lands, Poland and Lithuania]. This emissary well deserved to be the guarantor and patron of so illustrious a marriage, supported as he was by a loyal backer, the bishop [Jan Lubrański] who is the pride of your senate. (68–69:183–92)

After the Muse Erato's account of how the gods arranged the marriage of Sigismund and Bona Sforza, Krzycki resumes his own role as narrator and wonders aloud how he can possibly contribute to the festivities, in view of the wonders he has seen and heard. The remaining 131 lines of the poem constitute a series of exhortations to various groups of people on the way each should participate in the joyous nuptial celebrations. Each exhortation is introduced by the exclamatory "O Hymen Hymen ades, o Hymen Hymenaee" (O Hymen, Hymen, come, O Hymen, God of Marriage). The final three stanzas are addressed, respectively, to Sigismund himself, Bona Sforza, and the heavenly powers. The king is urged to throw open the gates of his palace to all, so that they may better share his pleasure; Bona Sforza is told, once again, of the magnificence of the man she is about to marry ("You will be led to such a husband—a gift of the gods—whose equal [in virtue, genius, and triumphs] nature has not brought forth in our age" [74:332–33]); the powers above are urged to bless the union of Sigismund and Bona with "glorious offspring under a favorable sign."

Although the evidence suggests that Krzycki's relationship with the new queen was neither as close nor as warm as his relationship with Queen Barbara, his position as the king's secretary ensured his place in the royal circle, and it was during this period that his talent as court poet blossomed. Virtually no aspect of life at court escaped his notice or failed to provide material for his pen. Apart from the epigrams on various facets of the renovation of the castle and courtyard on the Wawel, mentioned earlier, there were the usual panegyrics to the royal personages and, as further evidence of Krzycki's specificity and concreteness, epigrams on such subjects as Sigismund's hunting horn and the new judicial code introduced by Sigismund and published in 1524 under the title *Statuta Serenissimi Domini Sigismundi Poloniae regis.* That Krzycki's sense of humor, fondness for parodic mockery, and irreverence were still very much alive is well attested by one of his best-known court poems, "Prosa de Beata Kościelecka virgine in gynaeceo Bonae reginae Poloniae" (On the Maiden Beata Kościelecka of Queen Bona of Poland's Household Entourage). Beata Kościelecka was the daughter of the royal treasurer Andrzej Kościelecki and Katarzyna Telniczanka, a former mistress of Sigismund. She was raised at court and served the royal family primarily as governess to the king's children. Admired for her good looks and much sought after, she was eventually married in 1539 to Prince Eliasz Ostrogski. Krzycki's poem on Beata, which appears to be a panegyric of sorts in praise of her beauty and appeal, is in fact a parody of a church hymn ascribed to

Saint Casimir ("Omni die die Mariae"), of the type the poet had enjoyed writing in his younger days. The opening lines of the poem, "O Beata, decorata rara forma, moribus / O honesta ac modesta vultu, verbis, gestibus" (O Beata, adorned with beauty rare, O virtuous and modest in feature, word, and deed), require little change to retrieve the original celebration of the Virgin Mary. Krzycki's wit elsewhere in the poem comes through particularly in the thinly veiled allusion to Beata's mother's relationship with King Sigismund, when he declares that all the eligible young men are so mad about her they want her for a wife, not just a mistress ("Non amicam sed consortem iuvenes praecipui" [88:6]) and in the last couplet, in which Beata is admonished not to be proud and ungrateful to those who love her but to be friendly and loving in return to those who always praise her, referring also, of course, to Krzycki himself. Besides its tongue-in-cheek humor, the poem appeals by its rhythm, which derives from an earlier hymn tradition. In the following excerpts—the first and last lines—notice the internal as well as end rhymes:

> O Beata, decorata rara forma, moribus,
> O honesta ac modesta vultu, verbis, gestibus! (1–2)

> Ne superbam et ingratam te monstres amantibus,
> Sed comem et redamantem te semper laudantibus. (13–14)

Krzycki's wit, which was often playful, could turn sharp when the mood struck him. A good example of this, and nearly a costly one, involved no less a personage than the queen. The poet's relations with Bona Sforza were correct, if not warm, but they deteriorated rapidly when her refusal cost him the coveted bishopric of Poznań. Krzycki of course wrote his share of panegyrics in honor of the queen, mostly in the form of epigrams such as "De regina Bona" (On Queen Bona) and "In laudem reginae Bonae" (In Praise of Queen Bona). But when the relationship between them cooled, he could not resist the temptation to vent some spleen, which he did in a malicious epigram inspired by the Sforza coat of arms and entitled "In serpentem Bonae reginae Poloniae" (On the Snake of Bona, Queen of Poland):

> Si sub rupe draco conclusus hiante caverna
>   Urbis Cracce tuae magna vorago fuit,
> Quod mirum, quod in arce sedens rerumque potitus
>   Solus inexpleto viscere cuncta voret? (87)

(If a dragon hidden beneath a cliff in a dark cave was the great abyss of your city, Krak [Cracow], is it any wonder that when it seated itself in your castle and made itself master of things its insatiable belly would want to devour everything?)

As if that was not enough, Krzycki followed it with a shorter epigram on the same subject:

Quando sub arce fuit, Cracovia sole peribat,
    Cum sit in arce draco, patria tota perit. (87)

(When the dragon was beneath the castle, only Cracow was ruined. But after it went inside the castle, the whole country was finished.)

The epigrams inevitably reached the queen, who chose to avoid exacerbating the issue by pretending she did not understand their true meaning. Moreover, to express her pleasure, she sent Krzycki a doe that she had taken on a hunt and promised him the support of Zeus, meaning the king.[9] Seeing an opportunity to repair at least some of the damage his malice had caused, Krzycki responded to the queen's gift with one of his best shorter poems, the clever but at the same time charming "Lepus captus in venatione per reginam Bonam de fato suo" (A Hare Caught on a Hunt by Queen Bona, about His Own Fate). The poem is narrated by the hare, who addresses a passerby and asks if he is praising the hare's death or if he is saddened by it. The hare himself cannot entirely make sense of his own passing. There was never a hare on earth faster than he, he declares, yet he was caught. Why? Because the wondrous huntress (Queen Bona) restrained the nimbleness of his legs by her gaze alone. How could he turn his eyes from her beautiful figure, her features worthy of a goddess, the majesty of her bearing, her eyes like stars, her throat like ivory, her lips like roses of Paestum (a town in southern Italy famous in classical times for its roses)? When the queen's hounds finally caught him, the cause of his delight was at the same time the cause of his death ("Interea canis ore petor, comprendor et una / Causa voluptatis fit mihi causa necis" [86:13–14]). If the hare was happy beholding the huntress's beauty, he was certainly unhappy that by doing so he also brought about his own death. His only consolation is that if he had to be caught by someone he is glad that it was by her, since even Zeus would wish to be thus ensnared ("Sic capiendus eram hoc felix qui captus ab ista / A qua se cupiat Iuppiter ipse capi" [87:17–18]).

The malice and acerbic wit evident in Krzycki's epigrams about

Queen Bona characterize a sizable number of his other generally short satirical poems. These were aimed for the most part at court dignitaries and others with whom Krzycki at one time or another had crossed swords, whose political attitudes he opposed, or whom he resented for personal reasons. Collectively this body of works sheds as much light on Krzycki's own personality as it does on the life at court. Consider, for example, his poem on Katarzyna Telniczanka, former mistress of Sigismund I and the mother of Beata Kościelecka, whose beauty and desirability had provided the inspiration for his humorous parody of a church hymn. In the poem about Telniczanka, humor and light-heartedness give way to sheer malice. Krzycki neither liked nor trusted Telniczanka from the time she settled at the court of her son Janusz, bishop of Wilno, after the death of her husband in 1515. He regarded her as a meddlesome intriguer and spared her nothing in his poem "In vetulam hircissantem" (On a Poor Old Goat Who Stinks to High Heaven). The work is a recitation of Telniczanka's physical flaws and her grotesque pretensions to elegance. Her face is full of wrinkles, her hair is like a Gorgon's, her mouth reeks horribly, her nose and red eyes are always running, her withered breasts hang down to her belly button, her stomach and behind are like two large wine jars, and so on and on. No matter what she does or where she goes, looking at her makes one want to vomit. Yet she decks herself out in pearls, fancy clothes, and perfume and thrusts herself in among young women, seeking to join in their amusements and pretend she is one of them. The poem ends with Krzycki warning her not to make any advances to him:

> O larva, o facies, aevo ingratissima nostro,
>   Tene putas spolium cordis habere mei?
> Desine, nam non est mea tam vesana libido,
>   Ut ruat in capuli praecipitata decus. (218:19–22)

(O ghost, O face most unpleasant to one of my age, do you think that you can take my heart in booty? Desist, for my lust has not yet become so wild that it would race after a decoration for a coffin.)

When a former fellow member of the Guzzlers and Gobblers, Jan Zambocki, a courtier, royal secretary, and notorious gossip, expressed sympathy for the Protestant reform movement that was beginning to make inroads in Poland and was absolutely repugnant to Krzycki as a member of the Catholic church hierarchy, he lambasted him in a few poems. Zambocki's enthusiasm for Lutheranism, according to Krzycki,

sprang not from any desire to accept the truth but from his unwilling-
ness to fulfill his religious obligations and from an impulse to heap
malice on churches, priests, and the very heavens ("In Ioannem Zambocki"). The denunciations are still stronger in the lengthier "In eundem Zambocki" (On the Same Zambocki), whose opening line reveals
perhaps the main source of Krzycki's anger. "Behold, he maliciously
keeps track of my deeds with dull arrogance and plucks at my reputation with vile mouth" (124:1–2).

Stung by Zambocki's gossip mongering at least as much as by his
embrace of Luther, Krzycki unleashed a torrent of abuse that for
intemperateness outdistances anything else he wrote in the same vein.
Zambocki is denounced as a "calumniator against God," "of uncertain
origin," "a seducer of young boys," "a bungling, ranting lawyer" who
"prostitutes his tongue in [defense of] unworthy cases," a man who is
"untrustworthy, shifty, and argumentative," and a coward who will
stoop to anything to avoid military service ("ad bellum quando instat
iter, mox causa paratur, / Vel prece vel pretio, quo mimus ire queat"
[13–14]). As proof of his accusations, Krzycki declares that one need
only regard the man's gait, nervously turning head, and gloomy look
and the theatrical shape of his beard. Returning at the end to the point
of departure for the poem as a whole, Krzycki asks, "Should such a
man be able to diminish me and my fame?" (125:26).

Envy, especially of Krzycki's literary reputation, figures again in
the deprecation of Jan Górski of Miłosław, a man with considerable
ambition for a career at court who eventually became a royal secretary
but was forced out of the court because of his intriguing and constant
efforts to gain advancement. In one poem Górski is accused of mocking Krzycki's poetic talent only because he himself would like to write
verse but cannot, since "a lyre spurns crooked hands and songs the
weight of a big belly"[10]—the latter a reference to Górski's large body
and wide girth: "Maior et est magno corpore nemo tibi" (No one
surpasses you in bigness of body), Krzycki writes elsewhere.[11] More
seriously, Górski is accused of making so much money from the fines
he imposed on priests for alleged criminal acts while he was an official
of the Poznań archdiocese that he was able to build the biggest house
in town.[12]

That Krzycki himself could be motivated by envy in aiming his barbs
is only too apparent in his wickedly malicious verse attacks on Stanisław
Tarło, a royal secretary, Cracow canon, and later (from 1537) bishop
of Przemyśl. Tarło was a well-educated humanist with a great fondness
for music and a certain literary talent, all of which caused Krzycki to
view him as a serious rival. Besides unwarranted snobbishness, Krzycki

accused Tarło of lacking any poetic talent and of thinking that poetry was much like yanking money out of someone, a rather nasty allusion to Tarło's appointment as a tax collector. Krzycki's venom is not confined to two or three poems but is spread through eleven works, constituting a cycle in themselves: "In Stanislaum Tarlonem, canonicum Cracoviensem, archidiaconum Lublinensem, S.R." (To Stanisław Tarło, Canon of Cracow, Archdeacon of Lublin, Royal Secretary); "In eundem" (To the Same); "In eundem Tarlonem, qui ob scriptum in se carmen litem struebat" (To the Same Tarło, Who Wanted to Bring Suit Because of a Poem Written about Him); "In eundem" (To the Same); "In carmina Tarlonis satira" (A Satire on Tarło's Poems); "Republica ad poetas suos" (The Republic to Her Poets); "Apollo ad lectorem" (Apollo to the Reader); "Apollo ad vatem stercoreum" (Apollo to a Dung-Filled Poet); "Vates quispiam, querimonia Apollinis et reipublicae permotus, in has operis laudes prorupit" (A Certain Poet, Moved by the Complaints of Apollo and the Republic, Burst Forth in Praise of a Certain Work); "In Stanislaum Tarlonem, canonicum Cracoviensem qui invectivam in se facinori Herostrati, qui Dianae templum incendit, comparabat" (To Stanisław Tarło, Canon of Cracow, Who Compared an Invective Written against Him to the Villainy of Herostratus, Who Burned down the Temple of Diana); and "Dialogus contra Stanislaum Tarlo, canonicum Cracoviensem, secretarium regium" (Dialogue against Stanisław Tarło, Canon of Cracow and Royal Secretary).

The ridicule of Krzycki's "Tarło cycle" pivots on Tarło's tax-collecting duties. Krzycki spares nothing in his effort to portray his victim as a corrupt official who robs whenever he can and also as a would-be poet of no talent whose approach to poetry is that of a ruthless, dishonest collector of taxes. Krzycki contends in "The Republic to Her Poets," for example, that to Tarło counting poetic feet is the same as counting coins ("Condere credit idem versus, quod condere nummos" [138:5]).

Behind much of Krzycki's unscrupulous denigration of Tarło's poetry lay an unsavory albeit curious bit of literary intrigue. Tarło had devoted much energy to writing a Latin poem, which he never succeeded in finishing, about the "Prussian War" waged between Sigismund I and the Knights of the Cross. A servant of Tarło named Wilamowski presumably purloined the manuscript and showed it to Krzycki, who made it the butt of savage mockery and used it as the basis of his withering assault on Tarło's talents as a poet.[13] In "To Stanisław Tarło . . . Who Compared an Invective Written against Him to the Villainy of Herostratus, Who Burned down the Temple of

Diana," which is devoted entirely to the "public exposure" of Tarło's "Prussian War" poem and its author's violent reaction to his critics, Krzycki even brings up the matter of the poem's theft, claiming it was stolen not by a servant bribed by a literary rival but by a girlfriend of Tarło's who was lured by "superior passion."

As if calling Tarło's manhood into question—as he does in this poem—were not enough, Krzycki elsewhere denies his rival any place in the community of poets. This "new poet" (Tarło) did not descend from the heights of Helicon—so the opening line of "Apollo to the Reader" informs us—but sprang from a "filthy stye." For those wanting to follow the old Roman custom of purging their bile to whet their appetites, Krzycki recommends that they just read the "putrid verses of this poet full of dung" (Qui stomachi bilem vis mox facturus orexim, / Hoc putre stercorei perlege vatis opus).[14] And finally, in "The Republic to Her Poets," Krzycki, now speaking in the name of the Republic, exhorts her bards to "banish the disgrace" (meaning, of course, Tarło), admonishing them that just as it is the soldier's duty to expel an invader from the borders of the state, so is it the poet's responsibility to drive monstrosities from the sanctuary of his art.[15]

Rank was no protection against Krzycki's barbs, as is amply attested by his poems on such very prominent personages of the time as Jan Łaski (1456–1531), archbishop of Gniezno, primate of Poland, and great chancellor of the Crown; Jan Latalski (1463–1540), chancellor of Queen Elizabeth of Lithuania, later secretary to King Alexander and archbishop of Gniezno; Krzysztof Szydłowiecki, great chancellor of the Crown and castellan of Cracow; and Erazm Ciołek, bishop of Płock and one of the more able Polish diplomats of the period, whom we met earlier as the man who commissioned Nicolaus Hussovianus's poem about the bison for Pope Leo X.

Krzycki's verse assaults on these notables run the gamut from the amusing to the outrageous. Latalski, for example, who was highly regarded by both Sigismund I and Queen Bona but was equally well known for his fondness for drink, is accused in the same poem, "De Ioanne Latalski, episcopo Cracoviensi" (On Jan Latalski, Bishop of Cracow),[16] both of being a drunkard and of having bribed his way into the church. The emphasis is mostly on Latalski's drinking, and to make his point Krzycki tells how the good bishop once entered the cathedral of the Wawel Castle to celebrate mass at the altar of Saint Stanislaus. Just at the moment Latalski crossed the threshold, the doors closed of themselves, shielding the silver statue of Saint Stanislaus that was a gift from the king. Furthermore, a candle was knocked over and struck the bishop on the head. Krzycki mentions that though there are different explanations of the strange event, his own interpretation is simply that a sober man (Saint Stanislaus) feared a drunkard, lest the drunkard compel him to drink huge goblets of wine.

Great Chancellor Szydłowiecki is taken to task for his alleged greed, which is so great, according to the poet, that he is willing to sell his country down the drain for money.[17] Worse still, like Judas, he is willing to sell out Christ, whose own name he bears, referring to Szydłowiecki's first name Krzysztof (Christopher). Szydłowiecki, in fact, is worse than Judas. While Judas betrayed Christ for silver, the great chancellor was happy to settle for herring ("Argentum Iudas, halecem satrapa pro te / Christe capit").[18]

Krzycki's malice knew no bounds when it came to Primate of Poland Łaski and Bishop Erazm Ciołek of Płock; his poems on the two church dignitaries seem to exceed even the liberal humanist tolerance of just such invective. Fueling Krzycki's dislike of Łaski were the primate's anti-Hapsburg proclivities, which ran counter to the views of both Krzycki and his uncle Piotr Tomicki, and his flagrant nepotism when it came to the career advancement of members of his own family. In "In eundem archiepiscopum" (On the Same Archbishop),[19] Krzycki accuses Łaski of making his way to the top by cleverness, a shrewd tongue, secular drive, treachery, and crocodile tears. Railing against the primate as the "eternal shame of the fatherland and the ruin of the clergy" (Dedecus aeternum patriae clerique ruina [118:5]), Krzycki accuses him of being "an inciter of wickedness and the destroyer of good" (fomes sceleris perniciesque boni [6]). As his fury mounts, Krzycki goes so far as to brand Łaski a "deceiver of king, kingdom, and friends" (Tu regem regnumque, tuos tu prodis amicos [119:13]). For all his intrigues and machinations (including cheating death by feigning illness), the primate is labeled the world's greatest hypocrite, sycophant, and busybody. He is also greedy beyond belief. Finding just the right note on which to end his invective against the foremost Catholic churchman in Poland at the time, Krzycki declares, referring to a church ceremony Łaski initiated, that "it is right that Christ is borne on the cross before you, for everything that you do nails him to the cross" (Recte igitur prae te fertur crucifixus Iesus, / Omne tuum rursus quem crucifigit opus [23–24]).

The mudslinging in the poem on Bishop Ciołek, "In Erasmum Ciolek episcopum Plocensum, qui Romae ageus legationem regis Poloniae Sigismundi primi, cardinalis creari concupivit" (On Erasmus Ciołek, Bishop of Płock, Who While in Rome as the Emissary of Sigismund I, King of Poland, Strove after a Cardinal's Cap), easily rivals that in the work on Łaski. An exceptionally skillful diplomat, highly regarded by King Sigismund and the Holy Roman Emperor, who entrusted him with several important missions, Ciołek was of plebeian origin, which his detractors (Krzycki included) never let him forget, despite his eventual ennoblement. In his poem Krzycki makes much of Ciołek's humble origins, claiming that his father was a shoemaker or, worse yet, a self-taught musician (lyrista). Furthermore, who his father was is uncertain ("Incertum tamen hic parens, an alter" [146:14]). As for his mother, Krzycki has no doubt: she was a tavern wench and a whore ("Caupona et meretrice matre natus" [15]). It was his mother, practiced as she was in harlotry, who helped him take his first steps in murder, slander, and falsehood. The calumny here serves a very specific purpose—the portrayal of Ciołek as eminently unworthy of the cardinal's cap on which his sights were set. Ciołek was decidedly pro-Hapsburg in his sympathies, and while he was in Rome in 1518 he was instrumental in arranging the coronation (in Trent) of Maximilian as Holy Roman Emperor. In exchange for Ciołek's help, Maximilian promised him a cardinalship, which brought angry attacks against Ciołek in the diet of Piotrków in 1519 and was opposed, moreover, by Sigismund himself. Also incensed by Ciołek's ambition for a cardinalship, Krzycki used all the ill-intentioned gossip about Ciołek's humble origins to demonstrate his inappropriateness for high church office. Appealing at one point in the poem directly to Pope Leo X and the emperor Maximilian, Krzycki urges them to know Ciołek's real origins and accuses the bishop of trying to make his case with the pope and the emperor by filling them full of nonsense: "Nugis te Leo teque Caesar implens, / Nostis, quod genus et quod ite stemma / Ducit; non facile est referre verum" (146:8–10).

Krzycki's venomous pen served him well when he diverted his malicious wrath from prominent members of royal court and clergy to the Protestants, whose inroads in Poland at the time, especially in the Prussian region, caused growing alarm among the church hierarchy. Following the practice of much of his other satirical poetry, Krzycki struck at his enemies not with single salvos but with whole verse cycles. The "Lutheran cycle" follows a certain natural progression. Beginning with a denunciation of Luther himself, it proceeds to attacks against his followers, then, because Luther was a German, against the Teutonic Order because it too is German, and finally against the citizens of Gdańsk because they are predominantly German and it was among them that Lutheranism scored its first successes in Poland.

In the first poem in the cycle, "In imaginem Lutheri" (On Luther's Image), Luther himself is the speaker. Describing himself at the outset as that Luther who is known already throughout the world, he goes on to boast of the stupidities and inconsistencies of his "teachings" and the idiots who take them seriously:

> Ideas already damned once I now repeat, as I boast of being the spirit of God. I write contrary to tradition, to the church fathers, to the councils, and often contrary even to myself. I want mysticism in writing when it suits my need, or none at all if the purpose is better so served. Believing in nothing, I propound the teachings of Christ under the pretext of which one is permitted to tear anything apart. No one takes my words for either pious or right, but blaspheming holy things and the saints pleases many. It is to people like these that I am strong, as indeed every madman is strong, but these aside there isn't a grain of sense in me. I rail at popes and kings alike with impure tongue and take pleasure even in befouling my own nest. Now no decent person has anything to do with me unless he has lost his mind. (99–100:3–17)

Because he has done more than anyone else to raise the honor of his country, he concludes, he is revered there more than Christ!

The following poem, "Condiciones boni Lutherani" (Precepts for the Good Lutheran), informed with the same spirit, employs a different rhetorical strategy. Whereas in the first "Lutheran" poem Krzycki has Luther deliver a boastful self-indictment, the second poem takes the form mostly of a set of precepts to which the narrator—a "papist"—admonishes all those who wish to follow Luther to adhere. Needless to say, the "precepts" are what one would imagine coming from the pen of Bishop Krzycki; but they also typify the arguments of the church against Luther's reforms. Here are some of the "precepts":

> Execrate priests, hold the heavens in contempt, disparage approved customs, fasts, and prayers. . . . Make nothing of sacred vows, absent yourself from confession, disdain divine service. . . . Understand holy scriptures as you wish, the more easily by rejecting the time-honored doctors [of the church], laws, and the deeds of the saints. Become a good cheat, make yourself learned in vilification. . . . Act thus if you would be a loyal follower of Luther. Let him who wants call papist—a term he holds humorous—him who preserves rites, laws, and faith, and who follows the holy fathers in the dogma of Christ. (100:1–3, 4–6; 101:9–11, 14–18)

From Krzycki's point of view, the renewal of hostilities with the Knights of the Cross in 1520 and the outbreak of serious civil unrest in Gdańsk in 1525 were all part of a greater Lutheran-Germanic conspiracy against Poland. The threat to the integrity of church and faith in Catholic Poland posed by Luther's demands for change thus had its obvious political corollary in the continued conflict with the Teutonic Order and the turmoil in Gdańsk. Defense of church and defense of state became one in Krzycki's mind, and his response therefore was that of a ranking member of the Catholic church hierarchy in Poland who was at the same time an ardent Polish patriot.

After excoriating Luther and Lutheranism in a few poems, Krzycki augmented his "Lutheran cycle" with several works lambasting the Teutonic Knights and their German allies and predicting all sorts of consequences for the citizens of Gdańsk should they fail to restore civil order and maintain their subservience to the Crown of Poland. The Poles' routing of an army sent by German princes to the aid of a hard-pressed Albrecht, grand master of the Teutonic Order, in September 1520 became the occasion for a short celebratory poem, "De fuga exercitus Germanici a principibus Germaniae Cruciferis in auxilium missit" (On the Flight of the German Army Sent by the Princes of Germany to the Aid of the Knights of the Cross);[20] the work was preceded by a longer prose preface in which Krzycki expands on the rightness of the Polish cause and argues that only the Christian piety of the Polish king prevented the rout from being turned into a greater calamity. As if drawing an object lesson from the defeat of German arms in 1520, Krzycki immediately followed "On the Flight of the German Army" with the epigram "In levitatem Germanorum" (On the Nimbleness of the Germans), in which "levitas" is used sarcastically with reference both to the swiftness of the German retreat before Polish arms and to the ease with which the Germans could change from one set of beliefs to another:

> Germanicum, lector, iam nosti robur in armis,
>   Accipe et in sancta religione fidem.
> Cetera cum mutent una est cum mota cuculla,
>   Pectora non robur dicito, sed folium. (104)

(Reader, you already know what the strength of German arms is. Now learn what their loyalty is in matters of faith: as easily as they change in other ways, so do monks there change their habit. Their hearts are not solid oaks, but just leaves.)

On the Teutonic Order itself Krzycki wrote a few short poems intended to expose the perfidy of the Knights. In "Ad Sigismundem regem Poloniae" (To Sigismund, King of Poland)[21] the king is urged not to accept the assurances of the grand master of the Order, for he never kept his word to anyone—the Holy Roman Emperor, the

Muscovites, the pope, or God himself—and surely cannot be trusted to keep his word to the Polish king. Should the grand master prove loyal to the Polish king, however, which he doubts, then Sigismund surely will be greater than emperor, Muscovite, pope, or God! The point of the satire in "In ordinem militum cruciferorum" (On the Order of the Knights of the Cross)[22] is the standard of the Order, displaying three crosses of different colors. Krzycki states that the men bearing these standards also fall into three categories: the red, who can rightly be said to be "of Jesus," since he stained himself with his blood; the white, corresponding to the thief on the right (of the cross of Jesus), whose crimes were bought with just a few words; and finally the black, the criminal on the left side, and it is he who rightly acknowledged the perfidious Order as his own.

The disturbances in Gdańsk in 1525 were of a sociopolitical as well as religious nature and were eventually viewed with such alarm in Warsaw that the king himself resolved to intervene directly lest the revolt get out of hand and spread to other parts of the Crown.[23] The crux of the problem in predominantly German Gdańsk was the elite makeup of the governing town council, which now found itself challenged by less privileged social strata who demanded a larger voice in the administration of the wealthy port. Exacerbating the tensions were the generally pro-Polish loyalties of the town patriciate, which Lutheran agitators attempted to exploit by fanning the fires of religious as well as social conflict. When the confrontation erupted into open street rioting, the seriousness of the situation could no longer be overlooked, and so in 1526 King Sigismund made a trip to Gdańsk with the express purpose of quelling the uprising as expeditiously as possible. Leaders of the riots were taken into custody and later executed, but to avoid sharpening the tensions by other punitive measures against the city, Sigismund pursued a generally moderate course that included, among other things, a reaffirmation of the city's privileges.

The outrages against the church by Lutheran-provoked rioters as well as the very real threat to internal Polish stability posed by a rebellious Gdańsk—all coming within a few years of the renewal of hostilities with the Knights of the Cross—provoked Bishop Krzycki's wrath in the extreme. In addition to the anti-Lutheran works cited previously, he also wrote a few poems on the Gdańsk situation urging the king to take stern measures against the unruly and ungrateful city. Two of the poems are of particular interest in that they reflect Krzycki's awareness of the importance of the Vistula River and Vistula trade between Gdańsk and the rest of Poland for the continued prosperity of the city. In "Ad Sigismundem Primum regem Poloniae: Qua ratione

Neptunus Vistulam a Gdano divertit" (To Sigismund I, King of Poland, on Why Neptune Diverted the Vistula from Gdańsk)[24] Krzycki uses a natural event—a temporary diversion of the Vistula caused by flooded embankments—to draw a mythological interpretation for the king's benefit:

> Seeing the citizens of Gdańsk sacrilegiously devouring meat at a time when fish was prescribed, Neptune, raging angrily at such contempt for the uncertain fruits of the sea by those who owe their wealth to the sea, diverted the course of the river along which everything flows and directed its swollen waters into another current. So it was that Neptune vented his wrath at those who hold fish in contempt and avenged himself on them. How much more fitting is it to you, great king, to take vengeance by your legal right on those who disdain both you and God. (105–6)

"Ad eundem" (On the Same) completes the picture by now showing the Vistula itself complying with the king's punishment of the city. Seeing "insane rebellion" among the common people of Gdańsk and the breaking of the faith owed both master and God, the river alters its course, thereby bringing pleasure to the king, who was readying his punishment for the miscreants. The poet asks in conclusion: "Who can deny, most illustrious king, that men support you and your just undertakings, when the rivers themselves support them?" (106:7–8).

Two interesting footnotes to Krzycki's literary career grew out of his strong feelings about the events in Gdańsk. One relates to his satirical attacks in verse on Krzysztof Szydłowiecki, who then held the rank of great chancellor of the Crown. In the previous discussion of Krzycki's satires on prominent members of the court, we saw that his greatest complaint about Szydłowiecki concerned the chancellor's greed, which was so great that he was willing to sell out his country for money. The basis of the indictment was the bribe apparently given to Szydłowiecki by citizens of Gdańsk who were aware of his very close relations with the king and eager that he use his influence to temper Sigismund's judgment on the city after the suppression of the disturbances of 1525.

The second footnote concerns Krzycki's relations with Erasmus, mentioned in the Introduction to this book. The Polish bishop, as we saw, was a great admirer of the Dutch humanist and corresponded with him, sending his own works for comment and at one point warmly inviting Erasmus to Poland. The Dutchman never took advantage of the invitation, but did develop a real esteem for Krzycki. In the wake of the Gdańsk episode it came to Krzycki's attention that his writings about the Gdańsk riots and the Lutherans had been given to Erasmus by a mutual friend, the diplomat Hieronim Łaski. Fearful lest his intemperance change Erasmus's opinion of him and jeopardize their relationship, Krzycki lost no time writing to Erasmus and expressing embarrassment that such foolish things, dashed off under the impress of the events, had reached his great hands. He claims, moreover, that he was virtually compelled to write as he did about the Lutherans because his too obvious sympathies toward them brought down a host of detractions upon him and he had to silence the mounting chorus of abuse.[25]

How important Krzycki considered his relationship with Erasmus can be easily gauged from the reverence informing his poem on Erasmus titled "Andreas Cricius episcopus Desiderio Erasmo Rotterdamo" (Bishop Andreas Cricius to Desiderius Erasmus of Rotterdam). Each day, writes Krzycki, brings new testimony of how far the glory of Erasmus reaches, for even the stern Sarmatians and the untamed Scythians already possess his numerous books. Although Ovid was esteemed when he lived among the Goths, it never occurred to him to entertain them with Latin verse. But Erasmus is widely read in far northern lands beyond the Don, though he himself is not there. Krzycki then goes on to praise Erasmus for the worthiness of his writings and for his editions of the works of ancient authors, both Greek and Latin. Special praise is lavished on the Greek text of the New Testament that the Dutch humanist published in 1516 with the addition of his own Latin version. "Sour Sophists" (tetricis . . . sophistis [257:17]) at first besmirched it, but now "this brilliant jewel sparkles as if from gold ("Nunc velut ex auro lucida gemma micat" [18]). That Krzycki must have written this poem in praise of Erasmus sometime before the Gdańsk episode of 1525–26 seems obvious from the last six lines, where Luther (who is not mentioned by name) is indicated as the man who has now come to undo all of Erasmus's great work:

> Ecce inimicus homo zizania sparsit ubique,
>   Infecit segetes herba maligna tuas.
> Excide infelix lolium loliique satorem
>   Confice; si facies, Hercule maior eris.
> Ille homines tantum laedentia monstra peremit,
>   Per te etiam superis quae nocet hydra cadet. (21–26)

(Behold a hostile man strews chaff everywhere, spoiling your crops with harmful weeds. Extirpate the wretched darnel and destroy him who sowed it. In doing so, you will be greater than Hercules. He only killed

monsters menacing men; you, however, will fell the hydra threatening
the very heavens.)

Long interested in and involved with affairs of state—an inevitable
consequence of his position as well as of his relationship with his uncle,
Piotr Tomicki—Krzycki felt a need as time went on for more public
utterances on political matters. This need culminated in three of his
most important literary works, written in the years immediately pre-
ceding and following the Gdańsk disturbances. The first of these was
the *Religionis et reipublicae querimonia* (The Complaint of Religion and
the Commonwealth), published in 1522 by Wietor in Cracow. The
second was the *Threnodia Valachiae* (The Lament of Wallachia), also
published by Wietor in 1531, and the last was the *Dialogus de Asiana
Diaeta* (Dialogue about the Asian Diet), which Krzycki wrote not long
after becoming primate of Poland following the death of his predecessor, Maciej Drzewicki, toward the end of 1535.

Although composed in different styles and addressed for the most
part to different issues, these three political works of Krzycki's were
inspired by anxiety over the future well-being of the Polish state,
primarily aroused by the growing arrogance and selfishness of the
nobility. Only through universal moral improvement would it be possible to alter course before it was too late; hence it was a *moral* transformation that Krzycki came to advocate—in an interesting reflection of
Erasmian thought—rather than any concrete program of political or
other change aimed above all at curbing the gentry's privileges.

Consisting of a lengthy verse dialogue between Religion and the
Commonwealth over the current sad state of affairs in the country,
The Complaint of Religion and Commonwealth combines medieval and
Renaissance elements—medieval in its personifications of "Religion"
and "Commonwealth," and Renaissance in its preference for the dialogue form (which Krzycki also favored for his more clever satirical
Dialogue about the Asian Diet). Speaking first, Commonwealth laments
that widespread pettiness and greed make a mockery of her name,
since so many of her citizens are busy pursuing private interests to the
detriment of the common weal. Krzycki is careful in his short prose
preface to the dialogue and in the main body of the work not to indict
any single class of society or institution but to place the blame for the
plight of the state on a decline of moral standards manifest in the
contempt everywhere for honor, virtue, tradition, and piety. The
spread of dissension by clashes of conflicting selfish interests only
weakens the state and makes it a tempting prey for its covetous neigh-
bors, who gleefully observe its disintegration. Only in religion and in

a handful of worthy people (whom Krzycki does not identify) does Commonwealth have her true defenders.

But hardly are these words spoken when Commonwealth espies Religion, apparently also on the verge of abandoning her. This is a cue for the appearance of Religion, who has her own lament to voice. Despised and maltreated no less than Commonwealth, Religion especially grieves over the abuses of those within the church, whose misconduct also brings scorn on her many loyal servants. Painting a gloomy picture of spreading lawlessness and disdain for any moral authority, Religion bemoans the misfortunes that have overtaken church and state alike, misfortunes so calamitous that even king and Senate seem powerless before them. The work closes, however, on an optimistic note as Commonwealth reassures Religion that they both will survive the adverse winds now buffeting them, for a "pious ruler" together with a "small number of supporters" and "great efforts being undertaken in Parliament" are upholding their common cause and endeavoring to save them. After all, "Christ never torments or abandons those who remain steadfast in their loyalty to him."[26]

The *Lament of Wallachia* resembles the *Complaint of Religion and Commonwealth* in verse structure and the use of personification. There is, however, just one speaker—Wallachia—and the generalities of *The Complaint* give way to a specific political topic, the Wallachian *hospodar* Petrylo's breaking of a treaty with Poland and his defeat at Obertyn in 1531 at the hands of the great hetman of the Polish Crown, Jan Tarnowski. Krzycki's poem is, in fact, dedicated to Tarnowski. In a prose preface, the poet tells the hetman that once while he was sick abed with a toothache Wallachia appeared to him to bemoan her own misfortunes, thus diverting Krzycki's attention from his pain. In parting Wallachia left behind the *Lament*, which Krzycki is now sending to Tarnowski.

The purpose of Wallachia's lament—and Krzycki's political argument—is to convince the Polish king that he should take the defeated principality under the protection of the Crown of Poland, thereby freeing her from the Turkish domination to which her ruler has led her. Ultimately, the appeal was to no avail, however. The victory at Obertyn and the return to the Poles of territory seized by *hospodar* Petrylo did not change the status of Wallachia. The Turkish sultan insisted that the principality was subordinate to the Ottoman Empire, and King Sigismund did not regard it as in the best interests of the Polish state to go to war to challenge that claim.

Krzycki's strategy in the poem is to emphasize Wallachia's proud military past and her Christianity, thereby suggesting that she is worthy of Polish protection against the Turks by virtue of both her heroism and her desire to remain loyal to her Christian faith. This strategy accounts for the basic division of the *Lament*'s ninety verses into two almost equal parts. In the first Wallachia recounts her victories over her foes, including the Poles, from the time she was first founded as a Roman colony:

> I am that celebrated colony of Roman origin founded along the shores of the Black Sea in a place where we were always threatened with destruction by our Scythian enemies. (113:1–3)

The rest of the poem is taken up with Wallachia's lament over her present plight: once the proud conqueror of Turks, Poles, Hungarians, and Germans, she has been humbled by one man, Tarnowski, and now begs that she not be punished unduly for the treachery of her leader. The basis of the appeal for the protection of the Polish Crown appears especially in the following passage:

> Nunc mihi quid superest, tantum si pergis atroci
> Milite me miseram diris et perdere flammis,
> Quam genus in Turcos nostrum nostrosque penates
> Mutare et priscum Moldavi exstinguere nomen
> Vicinumque tibi peiori sorte locare. (115:55–59)

(What will remain to me now if you abandon me, wretched, to perish at the hands of fierce soldiers or in cruel flames or if our people and our home are forced to become Turkish and the ancient name of Moldavia is extinguished, with the result that in the end we will become a worse neighbor of yours?)

By far the best of Krzycki's political works is the prose *Dialogue about the Asian Diet.* Inspired by the Piotrków diet of 1535, held in the absence of the king, who was in Lithuania at the time, the *Dialogue* is a well-written satire aimed chiefly at the nobility as represented in the diet but containing admonishments for the whole of Polish society. The dialogue takes place between three speakers—Commonwealth or State, Nobody, and Everyman—with Nobody representing a typical delegate of the nobility and Everyman the polity. After the last two denounce each other for hypocrisy, insincerity, and selfishness toward the state, Commonwealth delivers a lengthy satirical sermon on civic responsibility. To begin with, Commonwealth admonishes, it is not for either Nobody or Everyman to discourse or deliberate on her well-being; that is the obligation of her ruler and the Senate. Since every soul is subservient to higher authorities, Everyman must also be obedient to their commands. This means revering God, then the civic rulers, and finally any more immediate superiors that he may happen to have. The "mysteries" of court and diet are not for Everyman to know, although Nobody is free to know them if he so desires. Everyman is further enjoined to abide by and defend the institutions and traditions of his forebears, while Nobody has the right to hold them in contempt. Everyman must refrain from unrest and upheaval, but Nobody can storm as he chooses. There then follow more specific prescriptions for various sectors of society—the clergy, judges, magistrates, lawyers, notaries, provincial administrators, customs officials, merchants, courtiers, physicians, and even poets and astrologers. Among the gentry, the older members are advised to look after their estates and the younger ones to "pursue military service instead of pillage, and to exercise themselves in the art of war, not in the acquisition of profit, in military camps rather than in bathhouses" (militam citra rapinam colant, Marteque non Mercurio, in castris, non in vaporariis se exerceant [295]). Plebeians, on the other hand, are warned not to regard themselves as the equals of princes and noblemen. In short, Everyman must heed the words of the apostle about paying respect to whom respect is due and tribute to whom tribute is due (Romans 13:6). Only Nobody is free not to give anyone his due.

After Commonwealth speaks, Nobody promises that he will carry out everything asked of him. Everyman declares, however, that while everything pertaining to him is just, he is not sure he can abide by every injunction and must therefore deliberate all the issues. Or better yet, perhaps he will leave the entire matter to his delegates to the diet. Commonwealth loses no time in replying that if matters are left to the kind of representatives who have been sent to the diet, who have served only their own interests, then Everyman and the state are doomed. When Nobody declares that he is the only person—as the one who points out the proper road to follow—to whom Everyman is obedient, Everyman promises to be concerned that future diets be wiser and more useful to society as a whole. Commonwealth concludes the dialogue by expressing the hope that God will grant it.

The *Dialogue about the Asian Diet* was Krzycki's last work. He died less than two years later, in May 1537. A hell-raiser in his youth, Andrzej Krzycki, or Andreas Cricius as he was known among humanists throughout Europe, became one of the truly outstanding figures of the Renaissance in Poland. A keen observer of life around him, a passionate defender of whatever he believed in, a malicious wit, Krzycki embellished his career as a vigorous member of the church hierarchy with an impressive and richly varied literary output in a Latin that he wielded with undeniable mastery. Although he was one of Poland's most gifted Latinists, he himself regarded his literary activity as marginal, something subordinate to his ecclesiastical and political interests. His relentless opposition to Lutheranism in Poland and his rapierlike pen notwithstanding, he enjoyed cordial relations with some of Europe's foremost humanists, Erasmus included, who held him in high esteem. His protégé and the most talented of any of Poland's Latin-language Renaissance poets, Clemens Ianicius—whom we will meet in the next chapter—left an indelible portrait of him in several of his elegies and epigrams. The German humanist and rector of the University of Königsberg, George Sabinus, whom we encountered in the context of his relationship with Jan Dantyszek (Dantiscus), met Krzycki once during a visit to Cracow. Upon learning of Krzycki's becoming bishop of Gniezno, he wrote an elegy to him ("Ad Andream Critium [*sic*] Archiepiscopum Gnesnensem"), praising his accomplishment and also informing him of the great loss of Erasmus. The elegy opens with Sabinus recalling the hospitable reception accorded him by Krzycki when he visited Cracow: "Tempore Sarmatici quo regis in urbe Sabinus . . . Ianua noticiae Praesul aperta tuae" (When I, Sabinus, arrived in the city of the Sarmatian king . . . the gates were thrown open, Bishop, by the kindness of your friendship with me).[27] Sabinus further recalls Krzycki's wishes for his visitor's future happiness in his impending marriage to the daughter of the illustrious German humanist and Protestant thinker Philipp Melanchthon and his promise to be a guest at the wedding. Now that the nuptials are approaching, Sabinus reminds Krzycki of his promise and hopes that he will attend despite his heavy responsibilities. In closing, Sabinus congratulates Krzycki on his high church office, declaring that "there was no one worthier of the honor" and "nothing greater than your genius." Even allowing for the exaggeration of humanist panegyrics, Sabinus's elegy conveys a sincere admiration for Krzycki's gifts that was hardly unique.

CHAPTER 9

Clemens Ianicius, the
Fragile Blossom of Polish Latinity

Clemens Ianicius,[1] the last of the Polish humanist poets who wrote only in Latin, lived but twenty-seven years; he was born in 1516 and died in 1543. In that short life, however, he succeeded in raising Polish Latin poetry to its highest level. None of the Polish Latinists before him and perhaps only Maciej Sarbiewski (Sarbevius), a seventeenth-century Baroque poet who also wrote exclusively in Latin, possessed his talent.

No finer introduction to Ianicius's life and work exists than an elegy written by the poet in late 1541 and included in his major work, *Tristium liber* (Book of Elegies), a collection of ten elegies inspired by the *Tristia* of his favorite Roman poet, Ovid, and first published in 1542 by the widow of the well-known Cracow printer Florian Ungler. Ianicius's elegy is deeply personal and a splendid example of his poetic style at its best; I shall offer here a fair portion of its 184 lines in translation, followed by a few lines in the original to illustrate the simplicity and elegance of its style.

Chronically ill for a number of years with a degenerative disease of the liver and spleen, Ianicius must have sensed the nearness of his death when he wrote the seventh elegy, despite his temporary recovery from the acute illness that gave rise to the poem. In making himself the subject of the elegy, Ianicius was giving serious thought to the meaning of his life and how he wanted posterity to regard him. The elegy is titled "De se ipso ad posteritatem, cum in summo vitae discrimine versaretur, quod tamen evaserat" (About Himself to Posterity, Written during a Most Severe Illness from Which, Nevertheless, He

Recovered) and recalls the tenth elegy in book 4 of Ovid's *Tristia,* which the Roman poet wrote while in exile.

You who would think of me and might wish sometime to know my life better, read these verses dictated hastily when dropsy was plunging me into the depths of Lethe [the river of oblivion in Hades].

High above the marshes of Żnin lay the village of Januszkowo, named for a certain Januszek. . . . For years, my father used to plow the fields there. He was a man proud and unbent in his poverty. When he was bemoaning the loss of children to the plague then ravaging our land, he beheld my birth through his grief; so it was that he was childless for only ten months. The light shone for me on the fourth day after the Ides of November [November 17], on a Sunday afternoon, on the very same day that our king doffed the mourning garb he had worn for an entire year following the death of his wife Barbara. . . . Her death deeply saddened everyone.

I was scarcely five years old when my schooling began and I stood upon the threshold of the Muses. My father loved me so greatly that he did not want the hard plow to injure my frail hands or the hot sun to burn my face. After I obtained the rudiments of learning from unskilled masters . . . I then entered the academy which [Bishop Jan] Lubrański had founded above the currents of the Warta River. There I happened upon a man [the humanist Krzysztof Hegendorf] who splendidly taught the wisdom of the Latins and the Greeks. Taking a special interest in the young shoot, he undertook to nurture it carefully and tenderly until at last your name, Vergil, and yours, beloved Ovid, resounded in my ears! Reading, I came to worship, for poets became for me gods. How many tear-drenched entreaties I raised to Apollo, their patron, that he accept me into his chorus and into his retinue, if only as a lowly camp follower. He gave an assenting nod, I ran toward him, he stretched out a hand and proferred me a lyre. How I fondled it, ran my fingers up and down it, tenaciously, happily—not a day or night passed without my lyre. I begrudged not the effort—I remember even now—that I devoted to achieving what mastery my years permitted.

When I read my verses for the first time in public, I was three months shy of my sixteenth year. The subject was Lubrański himself, for it seemed fitting that my fledgling efforts be dedicated to him. People applauded me not for the merits of what I had done, but because of the hopes they placed in a lad. From that moment I was first among my contemporaries, and my master showed me greater love. Having tasted this moment of fame, which had long been pleasing to me, I worshiped it in the very depths of my soul, and each day I fancied ever greater undertakings and then hurled myself along whatever roads seemed to lead to them. But frightful poverty stood before me on my path, hobbling my feet. My father told me there was no more money to be spent on furthering my studies. When I was just about to take my leave of the Muses, fate unexpectedly came to my rescue. Krzycki was then bishop, dearer to Phoebus than almost anyone. He opened the splendid gates of his court before me, promising good fortune to my Muses, and he would surely have kept his promises had not premature death claimed his life. After this loss, which was so painful to me, [Piotr] Kmita took me into his home. Making up for the loss of my first lord, it was he who sent me, sparing no expense, where I had longed to go, to the land of the Latins.

Like a merchant after jewels, I hurried off to the Euganeian Pallas [Padua] to acquire her priceless wisdom. But Fortune envied me and constrained me by illness to return to my family hearth sooner than I wanted and Kmita desired. What was there to do—we are all creatures in the hands of fate. I shall die then at home, my one comfort being that the soil of a foreign land will not cover me. You who will be lamenting a deceased friend . . . inscribe in large letters on the stone that may stand above the grave the following words: "Here I rest without Hope and without Fear Yet Truly Alive. Farewell, Dead Life!" That will suffice.

Now, dear reader, I shall return to you, to spin further the tale of my life. I was sickly, and the smallest labors exhausted me. Yet I was fair to behold and cheerful of disposition (though one could detect a certain shyness in my eyes). Articulate, I had a firm voice, a fair complexion, and a tall, good figure. Easily antagonized, quick to anger, I could often nurse a grievance for days on end. I never concealed animosity, but at the same time tried to make certain that I was never the cause of any. I was selective and constant in friendship, knowing there is no greater treasure than friendship. If fate had endowed me with great wealth, I do think that nobody would live more splendidly than I or be more generous. . . . I have always had a compassionate heart, and the tears that come easily to my eyes are full of anxiety, like those of a deer. I have had only contempt for armaments and have been an enemy of bellicose Pallas. I have been too much enamored of refined manners, dress, and food, as if I had been born into the female sex. From childhood until the twenties, I drank only water, and it was from that time, I believe, that my liver began to suffer. That water, of which I imbibed frequently, is now strangling my life. Many people, mistakenly judging from false appearances, believed I am given to licentiousness just because I like songs and jokes or because my earliest verses were devoted to the subject of love. . . .

And now you ask, what became of those works? Like other unripe fruits of my creative imagination, they were tossed into the flames, as worthy of a short life as anything else undertaken in the rush of youthful ambition. But now, with my twenty-fifth year behind me and the time ripe for greater things, I must leave this earth, dying prematurely, unable to glorify you, O motherland, as I wanted by singing of your past deeds and kings or of what today is worthy of celebration,

especially the nuptials that his father—our king—and Ferdinand of
Austria are arranging for Sigismund August. Alas, others will celebrate
these after I have gone. I do only what I can, and that is to pray that
he live and rule in triumph. . . .

If beholding the phantom of my body some shade should ask how
with that murderous water in my body, with a sick liver and spleen, I
could live longer than normally would be expected of a person suffering
from such an illness, I shall reply that I had a doctor whose power
surpassed that of the son of Apollo [Asclepius]. He summoned Hippoly-
tus but once from the abyss [death], while my doctor [Jan Antonin,
Ioannes Antoninus (1499–1543), a Hungarian who studied in Cracow
and Padua and was the court physician of Sigismund I] extricated me
from the grave many times and deceived the Fates, delaying my
designated hour by many a day.

If he was unable, however, to return me my former health, it was
not his fault but that of the incurable poison of my illness. Such sickness
as well as others can often be cured, but who except Christ can conquer
dropsy? Montanus [Giovanni Baptista Montanus, a famous Italian
doctor] and Cassianus [Francesco Cassianus, another distinguished
Italian physician], whose fame brightened the Italian land, each an
unsurpassable master of his art, were unable to tame the poison of this
serpent, although it had barely penetrated my body at the time. . . .
Be that as it may, this was my family lot; my father died of it before
me. No wonder then that in the face of such opponents the physicians'
hands lost their strength.

And yet more will I say, O my life, for what other name can I give
you who has returned life to me so often? You will hear it all yourself
when after many years have run their course you come to join me. All
of you whom I am leaving behind me here now, you too will be there.
. . . the Fates never gave any person an eternal home here on earth.[2]

> (Si quis eris olim nostri studiosus, ob idque
>   Nosse voles vitae fata peracta meae,
> Perlege, quae propere dictavi carmina, cum me
>   Hydrops Lethaeis iam dare vellet aquis. . . .)

The poverty Ianicius speaks of in the elegy above did not preclude
his receiving a fine education. His first serious training in classical
studies came in the renowned collegium established in Poznań by
Bishop Jan Lubrański. It was while he was a student at the collegium
that Ianicius enjoyed his first literary success, when he read publicly his
poem dedicated to Bishop Lubrański. This favorable public exposure
brought the young poet to the attention to Andrzej Krzycki, who
happened to be a good friend of Lubrański's; Krzycki, in fact, had
accompanied Lubrański to Hungary to arrange the nuptials of Sigis-

mund I and Barbara Zápolya. Krzycki had by now become a very high-ranking member of the Roman Catholic church in Poland and a prominent—and powerful—statesman.

Krzycki's interest in Ianicius became patronage when the poet's father could no longer support his son's studies. Krzycki invited the young man to his court about 1536, probably as a librarian. It was while he was at Krzycki's court and upon his patron's recommendation that Ianicius worked on his first cycle of poems, forty-three short, epigrammatic lives of the archbishops of Gniezno, *Vitae archiepiscoporum gnesnensium*. The last of the poems in the cycle is dedicated to Krzycki, commemorating his death on May 10, 1537, and his entombment in Gniezno on July 8 of that year.

Ianicius's close and by all accounts warm relationship with Krzycki, who did much to further his education and career, is reflected in several of his works. In one epigram (26) he not only compares Krzycki to the patrons of such great Roman writers as Vergil, Tibullus, and Horace, but exalts him as superior in piety to his ancient predecessors. Then, lest his epigram be understood as implying he feels equal to the Roman poets, Ianicius hastens to assert that by the same degree to which Krzycki exceeds their patrons in piety, those writers exceed Ianicius in talent and in poetry.[3] The first elegy in Ianicius's *Variarum elegiarum liber* (Book of Elegies on Other Subjects) recalls the occasion when the poet first saw Krzycki, then archbishop of Gniezno, and spoke with him. Hailing Krzycki as the "greatest man in the Sarmatian nation" (Sarmaticaque virum . . . in gente supremum [82–90]) and extolling his virtues by several mythological parallels, Ianicius exhorts his fellow Poles to take pride in themselves as a nation and to understand that their glory is growing thanks to this man alone. In the past, he argues, the Poles were esteemed only for their prowess in war, but now because of Krzycki they are beginning to earn fame in the "peaceful arts of the Muses"; moreover, Polish youths, following Krzycki's example, are learning how to expel barbarism from their land. Again alluding to Krzycki's patronage of him, as in the epigram above, Ianicius goes on to say that Polish youths are attaining previously unimaginable cultural heights not only because of Krzycki's example, but also because of his zealous patronage. The relevant verses in Latin read as follows:

> Bello clarus eras tantum studiumque Gradivi
> Inter vicinos laus tua tota fuit.
> Iam nunc pacificis Musarum ex artibus amplum
> Incipis a Cricio nomen habere tuo.

Cuius ab exemplis condiscit multa iuventus,
Barbariem patrio pellere posse solo.
Nec tantum exemplis; accenditur illa favore
Et patrocinii sedulitate sui. (88:103–10)

With Krzycki as inspiration and cause, there are springing up those, Ianicius declares, whose great talent will spread the glory of Poland throughout the entire world. Again Ianicius first insinuates a sense of his own self-esteem as a poet, then judiciously dispels an atmosphere of hubris by assuming great modesty, as in the epigram, or by stating, as here, that his remarks have been prompted not just by Krzycki himself but by the many proofs that he has received from Krzycki of how those inspired by him are disseminating a new Polish glory.

In other poems devoted to Krzycki Ianicius celebrates his birthday (*Book of Elegies on Other Subjects*, 2), curses spring because that is the time of the year when his patron fell ill (*Book of Elegies*, 3), recalls a trip to Cracow Krzycki once took at the beginning of winter that was so favored by the gods that they sent spring days instead of the usual snows of the season (*Epigrams*, 27), and of course mourns the primate's passing (*Epigrams*, 28, 29, 30). In the first of these last three epigrams, Ianicius berates himself for being a false prophet in that the signs in nature he interpreted as boding well for Krzycki's trip to Cracow proved malevolent, for the rigors of the journey contributed to his patron's demise. In the second of the epigrams, Ianicius notes that Krzycki died during the outbreak of war, for when he saw war erupt again, as a lover of peace all his life, he preferred to die together with a dying peace than continue living ("Pacis amans Cricius cum surgere bella videret, / Pace simul voluit cum moriente mori").[4] The last of these epigrams, "De se ipso, post mortem Cricii" (About Himself, after Krzycki's Death), speaks of the "drying up of Krzycki's field" (following his death) that his "Calliope [the Muse of epic poetry] cultivated" and how she is now sailing on Kmita's river; the epigram closes with the poet's conviction that if the "master of the river" favors him, he will find in water the harvest that he once enjoyed on land ("Quas habui in campo messes, has quaero per undam; / Si faveat dominus fluminis, inveniam").[5]

The Kmita referred to in Ianicius's epigram was Piotr Kmita (1477–1553), palatine of Cracow from 1535 and an exceptionally influential figure in Polish politics. Kmita was also the patron of a few of the most prominent representatives of the Polish Renaissance, among them the historian Marcin Bielski (1495–1575) and the vigorous pro-gentry and anti-Reformation polemicist Stanisław Orzechowski (1513–66). When

Ianicius became "orphaned" by Krzycki's death, Kmita took him under his wing. Relations eventually soured between the poet and his new patron, who was well known for his tempestuous and combative personality, but Kmita played an important role in Ianicius's life.

Although Ianicius was always sensitive to the world around him, especially to its beauties, it was principally owing to Kmita's influence that he came to take an interest in politics. It was Kmita, for example, who persuaded the poet to write a new cycle of historical epigrams on the lives of the Polish kings along the same lines as his Krzycki-inspired *Lives of the Archbishops of Gniezno*. Beginning with the legendary founders of the Polish state, Lech and Krak, Ianicius's fourty-four-epigram cycle, *Vitae Polonorum principum*, covers every Polish ruler down to Sigismund I. It was also to the influence of Kmita's environment that Ianicius's major political poems—*Querela Reipublicae Regni Poloniae anno MDXXXVIII conscripta* (Lament of the Commonwealth of the Kingdom of Poland Written in the Year 1538) and *Ad polonos proceres* (To the Polish Nobles)—have to be ascribed. Let us take a closer look at these two works.

In the *Lament of the Commonwealth*, Ianicius addresses the growing lawlessness of the Polish gentry, who in their pursuit of selfish interests are ignoring the needs of the state as a whole and thus placing it in great jeopardy. Appealing to the gentry (nobilitas) as "alone in their passion and zeal for my salvation" (Sola meae superes cupida et studiosa salutis [4:27]), Ianicius's Commonwealth exhorts them above all to overcome their avarice and their disregard for the concerns of the state and to recognize that their very existence is bound up with her well-being:

> Omnia parva putas, quae sunt mea, maxima cum sint,
>   In quibus et vitae est summa caputque tuae. (83–84)

(Everything that is mine you hold to be small, though they may be the greatest in which are to be found the very source of your own life as well.)

Virtue, laws, and freedoms, instead of being upheld by the gentry, are now gravely threatened by their disharmony, and their actions cannot be excused solely on the grounds of the contrariness of a hostile Senate (with reference to the magnate-dominated upper house of the bicameral Polish diet). Truth is unpalatable to them, and those who dare speak the truth are threatened with the loss of their titles and possessions. Even the Commonwealth fears speaking the truth, lest she bring down on herself greater calamities. At the end of the *Lament,* speaking through his Commonwealth, Ianicius pleads with the gentry to "adhere to the judgments of the king and the decisions of the Senate and to restore to health the sundered minds of a people" (Consilium Regis moderare et vota senatus / Et sanos scissi fac animos populi! [101–2]). In "To the Polish Nobles" Ianicius, speaking for himself, passionately pleads for harmony among the magnates and reminds them of the fate of ancient Sparta, once a lawgiving (legifera) nation, destroyed by the same disease of disharmony. The magnates, as a class, are accused of so weakening the fatherland by their madness (furor) that they are forcing the neck of a distressed freedom beneath a new yoke (Libertasque novo colla dat aegra iugo [12:86]). Sadly, they fail to understand that when the state falls because of their selfishness and misdeeds, they too will fall beneath the ruins.

Undoubtedly, the greatest single benefit of Kmita's patronage to Ianicius was the opportunity to travel to Italy to further his studies. The poet had long dreamed of such a trip, but it was only with Kmita's backing that in the spring of 1538 it became a reality. Ianicius, in fact, requested such backing in the sixth elegy in his *Book of Elegies on Other Subjects*. The poem is worth a closer look for what it reveals of the sycophantic yet clever acrobatics humanists frequently employed in their quest for favors from their patrons. Without mentioning directly that he wants Kmita's support for a period of study in Italy, at least in his poem, Ianicius argues that from the time he entered Kmita's service he has been so burdened by cares both because of his beloved Krzycki's death and because of his own illness that his pen has run dry. All he wants now is to sing the glory of Kmita and his clan, but he is so depressed that he cannot rise to the task. Furthermore, assuming a posture of false modesty, he claims that his talents leave much to be desired and that Apollo "plays an unrefined lyre" (Et meus incultam pulsat Apollo chelyn [114:62]). Kmita, however, has it in his power to "give me talent, to give zeal and inspiration, such as Calliope has been accustomed to giving to those who worship her; you have the power to transform me in the course of not many years and to change him who was a goose into a swan" (Tu potes ingenium mihi, tu dare pectus et ignem, / Quem dare cultori Calliopea solet, / Tu potes haud multos me transformare per annos / Et facere, ut fiat, qui fuit anser, olor [63–66]). Ianicius closes his verse entreaty by saying that his request is a mere trifle to Kmita but of great importance to him.

Ianicius's powers of persuasion accomplished their purpose, and with Kmita's support and blessings he set out in the spring of 1538 on the arduous journey to Italy, accompanied by other young Poles going there to study. Once settled in the university town of Padua, the poet spent most of his time attending lectures by the distinguished humanist Lazzaro Bonamico. That Ianicius knew Bonamico's reputation as an outstanding scholar of Latin culture before he left Poland and chose Padua for that reason seems clear from the eighth elegy in his *Book of Elegies on Other Subjects*. The work is addressed to Bonamico and carries the title "Ad Lazarum Bonamicum scribit, cum primum Patavium venit" (In Which He Writes to Bonamico Soon After Reaching Padua). In it, Ianicius informs Bonamico that he is the reason for his journey, that it was because of him he crossed the Alps ("Causa viae, Bonamice, mihi es; te propter in Alpes / Ivimus [120:9–10]). It has been a month since he came to Padua, declares Ianicius, and until writing his elegy he has been reluctant to engage Bonamico in conversation. Because of a peasant suspiciousness of which he is ashamed, he fears that his "barbarisms and tongue conscious of its own undisciplined sound might offend your Latin ears" (Ne mea barbaries Latias offenderet aures / Et sibi discincti conscia lingua soni [13–14]). Further on in the elegy, which brims with fulsome praise for Bonamico and his scholarly achievements, Ianicius mentions that before leaving Poland he had shared his enthusiasm for the Italian scholar with an older friend who was also to study in Padua and who may have been Ianicius's first source of knowledge about Bonamico. "Do you believe me," he asks Bonamico, "that while I was still in my homeland my heart, of its own accord, was already burning with a great love for you who was so far away? I often spoke about you with yours, for he is yours, with Hosius, and many times did I celebrate your name" (37–40). The Hosius Ianicius is speaking of here was, of course, Stanisław Cardinal Hosius (1504–79], the outstanding representative of the Counter-Reformation in Poland.

Once Ianicius overcame his trepidation about establishing personal contact with Bonamico, he and his Italian mentor eventually became good friends. The friendship survived the poet's departure from Padua and return to Poland. In the sixth elegy in his *Tristia,* written back in his own country, Ianicius, addressing Bonamico directly, recalls the Italian's many kindnesses toward him when he was in Padua and mourns the hopelessness of his ever repaying them. In the kind of image he could conjure up with such facility, Ianicius speaks of reckoning Bonamico's kindnesses toward him as a "greater task than counting the flakes of snow that, released from a heavy cloud by a puff of Boreas, fall to earth like so many strands of wool" (42:7–10). A line such as "That I exist, that I live, that I see my own country and those close to me and everything that is mine, all of that is—after the gods— your gift" (Quod sum, quod vivo, patriam quod cerno meosque / Et

mea, post superos muneris omne tui est [27–28]) may seem no more
than typical humanist panegyric effusion, but Ianicius makes it quite
clear in subsequent verses that he indeed owed his life to Bonamico.
At one point during his stay in Padua he fell very ill with the sickness
that was eventually to fell him, and he recalls that but for his mentor's
swift action he might indeed not have survived:

> Nuper enim vestra (reminisci est dulce malorum)
>   Cum variis essem fractus in urbe malis
> Meque unum febres et peior febribus hydrops
>   Sub miseram traherent et sacer ignis humum
> (Adde omni gravius leto dextram ulcus ad aurem,
>   Ex quo non parvo tempore surdus eram)
> Cumque Charon cumba iam me exspectaret in atra
>   Et ferruginea posceret aera manu,
> Tu subitam mihi primus opem, Bonamice, tulisti,
>   Sum raptus manibus de Phlegethonte tuis,
> Tu summos aegro medicos, tu cuncta dedisti,
>   Quorumcumque illud tempus habebat opus. (29–40)

(When not long ago—how sweet it is to recall calamities once past—I lay
broken by various woes in your town and when fever and, worse than
fever, dropsy and the accursed fire burning in me were dragging me to
a wretched grave (add to all that a sore on my right ear more painful than
death, on account of which I was deaf for a long time), and when Charon
was already awaiting me in a black boat and held out a dark hand to me
for the fare, you were the first, Bonamico, to come to my help without
delay, and it was by your hands that I was snatched from Phlegethon [one
of the five rivers in Hades]. You sent the sick person the best doctors, you
provided everything that was necessary at the time.)

When his health obliged Ianicius to change climates and leave Padua
as soon as possible, it was Bonamico who not only provided the funds
for the trip but interceded with the university authorities so that Ianicius could receive his degrees and titles without actually completing
his studies. The poet recalls this in his elegy when he writes: "You send
me forth, but beforehand you see to the matter of my titles, which
now have no small weight among people" (51–52). What Bonamico in
fact arranged for Ianicius—possibly with the help of Pietro Cardinal
Bembo (1470–1547), an important writer in both Italian and Latin—
was for the young Pole to appear before an extrauniversity commission
that was to examine his qualifications for a degree. After the examination, Ianicius was granted the title "doctor of liberal arts and philoso-

phy." Among the notables present was the *podestà* of Padua and future cardinal Gasparo Contarini (1483–1542), who stepped forward after the degree was conferred to place on Ianicius's head the laurel wreath symbolic of poetic glory. Even though he was compelled to leave Padua early because of his poor health, Ianicius at least had the satisfaction of returning to Poland not only with a doctorate from a distinguished Italian seat of learning but with the additional title "poeta laureatus."[6]

Ianicius wrote of his illness in Padua and the necessity of his premature return to Poland in two other elegies in his *Tristia* collection. Elegy 2 is, in fact, an extended prayer to the Virgin Mary to grant him the patience and courage to endure the fever and pain wracking his frail body. Of particular interest is the very concrete picture the poet paints of his own condition: "I am now pale and thin, like the phantoms of the dead that people claim to have seen often at night. My eyes have become hidden, as if buried, in two pits and are much weaker now in sharpness. I am no longer able to turn my head, and it is the same with other members of my body, for they are no less weak. My hands and my feet, now indolent, have abandoned the service they once performed properly. Fastened to a bed, I lie for days on end like a newborn and helpless babe."[7]

One of the other Poles who studied in Padua at the same time as Ianicius was Piotr Myszkowski, who later became a bishop and royal chancellor and earned a place in Polish literary history as the patron of Poland's greatest Renaissance poet, Jan Kochanowski. Myszkowski remained in Padua after Ianicius left, and in his fifth elegy (in the *Tristia*) the poet informs his friend of the state of his health and the rigors of the journey back to Poland. Although he regrets having to leave Padua so soon, Ianicius can report that while he is still ill he has at least parted company with the sickness that obliged him to leave Italy. He describes his trip back home as a nightmare. At the outset, riding a miserable nag, he endured twelve days of uninterrupted rain mixed with hail and snow. Adding to the discomforts of the journey through the Alps were the heavy, odoriferous clouds of sulfur he encountered. Worst of all, however, was traveling through inhospitable Styrian (Austrian) cities and towns. Ianicius's account of these is graphic:

No one is more barbaric or wilder than this Alpine people, unless perhaps the wolves themselves. The newcomer is held in contempt by all, a guest is regarded as an enemy, and no more so than when he is wearing clothes of Italian cut. Imagine the comforts that awaited me, drenched to the skin, in these barbarous homes. And add in the fact that, ignorant of their language, I was constrained to indicate by various signs what it was I needed in my illness. Although they understood these signs almost at once, there wasn't a single soul who wanted to be of any service. Indeed, when I asked them for anything, a drunken crowd just laughed at me and acted as though they didn't understand my entreaties. Although it was certain poison for me, I was often compelled, out of sheer hunger, to eat dishes that were prohibited to me. (40:27–40)

Whatever the setbacks his poor health cost him in Padua and his disappointment at returning home early, Ianicius loved Italy and the Italians and wrote of them glowingly in his poetry. Not long after arriving in Padua, for example, he wrote an elegy addressed to his friend Stanisław Sprowski, the young palatine of Podolia, that typifies his views. The elegy (the seventh in his *Book of Elegies on Other Subjects*) begins with a very brief summary of current European political events as seen from Ianicius's perspective in Italy, about which Sprowski had inquired. But this is not what truly interests the poet, and he passes on to praise of the natural beauties surrounding him: "The whole year was a continuous blossoming of flowers so that one could not tell if it was spring or another season. Twice during the course of the year bunches of grapes swelled on full vines, and branches of trees were always heavy with fruit. Without the farmer's sweat the earth furnished abundant crops from its compliant soil" (116:35–40).

Ianicius's enthusiasm for the Italians is almost boundless. "When I behold the customs of men," he writes Sprowski in the same elegy, "I think that among so many peoples there is none pleasanter than they are. There is nothing of pride in them or stupid haughty words or the raising of eyebrows in speech. Their gentle words convey a sense of mutual esteem; I do not know if it is sincere, but it is accompanied, nevertheless, by affection. Everything is commended by a certain pleasant gracefulness, affability, and charm mixed with seriousness. There is much elegance here, but without any of the wasteful extravagance of things that unwisely squanders resources. Moderation is carefully observed in their refined way of life; they attire themselves with modest charm and are modest in their consumption of food" (47–58). Ianicius is especially impressed with the relative tranquillity of Italy. "If even here there is no peace," he observes, "there is at least the image of peace everywhere; the law prohibits everyone from bearing arms. No one girds himself, therefore, with a proscribed sword except when he is setting out from his town on some far journey" (67–70). It is no wonder, then, that Italy has been so favored in the arts and eloquence. How happy he would be to have been born Italian, he exclaims rapturously toward the end of his elegy to Sprowski; but fate decreed otherwise. Nevertheless, he is not unhappy being a Pole; he admires Italy ("Italiam miror") but reveres his fatherland ("patriam veneror"); one country (Italy) induces wonder in him, the other love ("Afficit illius me stupor, huius amor" [85–86]).

Another person with whom Ianicius shared his love for Italy was none other than Cardinal Bembo. Writing to him shortly after Bembo's elevation to the College of Cardinals, Ianicius could barely contain his joy at being in Padua:

> One thing I am certain of, that from the time I took up residence in Padua, I seem to be living almost in heaven, and so long as this continues to be my fate, I shall regard myself as excessively fortunate and excessively happy. Who would not be delighted by the beauty of the Euganean sky, the very location [of Padua], the moderate climate of the region, the wondrous plan of the walls, which Apollo would choose for his own were he to rebuild Troy. . . . Wherever you look, this city has the delights of the country and the kind of beauty that reigns in fertile fields, the kind of beauty that is pleasing to the divine dances of the Muses, who for this reason have established this very place as the citadel of their arts, or for the reason that such a truly splendid peace flourishes here and these goddesses are friends of peace and seek refuge in safe places. (124:15–22; 126:27–32)

From praise of the land Ianicius passes to praise of the people, assuring Cardinal Bembo that as a "son of the Sarmatian sphere" (Sarmaticae qui sum regionis alumnus) he will always bear opulent testimony to the virtues of the Italian people, of which the whole world should be made aware. "With you as an example, Bembo," he declares, "I will show what Italian sincerity, charm, and ready goodwill are all about, for hardly had I seen you when you allowed me what I myself feared even to wish for, and that is that I might worship you." With further praise for Bembo's modesty and accessibility despite his elevation to a cardinalship and the other great honors heaped on him, Ianicius closes his elegy with the assertion that no one will outdo him in praying for the cardinal's long life: "I do not know if your fellow countrymen pray for it, but for certain a multitude of foreigners do, and among them I am the first to so pray."[8]

Although Piotr Kmita enthusiastically assumed patronage of Ianicius after the death of Bishop Krzycki and made possible his trip to Italy, the relations between poet and patron were neither as close nor as warm as those between Ianicius and Krzycki. Eventually they deteriorated until they were beyond repair. A vain as well as an ambitious man, Kmita apparently expected that his patronage would result, among other things, in an outpouring of poetry attesting his generosity as well as in panegyrics addressed to him and his family, past and present. Ianicius obliged to an extent, but his production of such poetry was neither as plentiful nor as rapid as Kmita desired, leading to pressure by patron and resistance by poet. Kmita was impulsive and rather insensitive and was not above berating Ianicius for what he assumed to be laziness and self-indulgence. Further contributing to the deterioration of their relationship was the gossipy meddling of the fiery, combative gentry polemicist and anticelibate church canon Stanisław Orzechowski, who also enjoyed Kmita's patronage and, like Ianicius, studied in Italy at Kmita's expense; Orzechowski and Ianicius were in Padua at the same time in 1538 and early 1539. Similarity of temperament as well as political outlook brought Kmita and Orzechowski closer; obviously envious of Ianicius and of Kmita's support of the talented young poet, Orzechowski sought to undermine their relationship by encouraging Kmita to see Ianicius as lazy and indifferent.

Probably the first literary evidence of the storm gathering between patron and poet is Ianicius's longish third elegy in the *Tristia*, written during his stay in Padua. While copious in the conventional praise of a patron that one might expect from a humanist poet or scholar at this time, the elegy is an attempt to explain why Ianicius was out of touch with Kmita for some nine months. The elegy makes it quite clear that the work arose as a response to complaints Kmita registered while Ianicius was in Padua. These complaints were directed not only to Ianicius himself, but also to his Italian mentor Lazzaro Bonamico, who defended the poet in correspondence with Kmita.[9] The elegy also makes clear that Kmita was put out not so much because he had not heard from his young charge since he left Poland as because promised or at least anticipated literary works by Ianicius were so slow in reaching him. This, one can assume, was proof to Kmita of his protégé's laziness. At the very beginning of his elegy, Ianicius mentions the complaints he has received from Kmita and his patron's imputation of indolence:

> Ecquid ais, postquam data sunt tibi carmina tandem
> A me post menses vix quoque missa novem?
> Scilicet accusas ignavum pectus et istam
> Forte putas animi desidis esse moram.
> Di mihi sunt testes, tam longa quod otia nobis
> Nulla, satisfacerent quae tibi, prorsus erant.

Est opus ad carmen, quod te dignum sit, et amplo
Tempore et internis morsibus esse procul. (26:3–10)

(Are you saying that it is only after nine months that you at last received
the poems I sent you? You are accusing me, no doubt, of having a lazy
character, and perhaps you believe that this delay was caused by my
indolence. The gods are my witnesses that I had far too little peace and
quiet in which to render you your due. To create a poem truly worthy of
you, it is essential to have both sufficient time and as much freedom as
possible from inner cares.)

Ianicius then explains that he has not had a single happy day in the
year then coming to an end. Although he has had the strength to
pursue the studies for which he came to Italy, he has lacked that
spiritual tranquillity necessary for the composition of poetry. Now, to
make matters worse, he is deeply disquieted by Kmita's suspicions
about him and by his enemy's (a reference obviously to Stanisław
Orzechowski) encouraging and affirming them. The real reason for
his seeming neglect of his lyre, he avers, is his scholarly pursuits,
above all philosophy, and he tells Kmita, as a defense, that "no one
simultaneously honored the temples of the great Phoebus [meaning
the arts] and plumbed the mysterious ways of nature. . . . And I too,
when I marvel at the innermost secrets of Sophia [wisdom] lack the
time to return to the worship of the god of Claros [Apollo]" (39–
40, 49–50). In a lengthy apostrophe to the goddess of wisdom that
continues almost to the end of the elegy, Ianicius exults in his submission to her will and, in an interesting maneuver, attributes Kmita's
patronage of him ultimately to the good fortune of which she is the
architect. Again alluding to Orzechowski's attempts to undermine his
position with Kmita, the poet challenges envy "to intrude as much as
it wants so as to be able to win to itself that one thing of which in the
future it may be ashamed" (Impediat livor, quantum libet, ut sibi id
unum, / Quod pudeat posthac, conciliare queat [111–12]). At the end
of his verse apologia (to call the elegy what it really is), Ianicius attempts
to ingratiate himself anew with his patron by courting Kmita's vanity.
He tells him, for example, that the consolation he derives from Kmita's
wisdom is like the consolation he finds in his studies, which perhaps
he will be able to prove to his patron if fate and God allow him to
return home. He recalls the walls of Kmita's residence at Wiśnicz and
his thoughts of how they might rise to the very heavens—which means,
one can assume, how he might best extol them in his poetry. The
walls of the Kmita family residence are high enough of themselves,

continues Ianicius, and "great with the glory of your ancestors, without my daring to say anything of you yourself" (magnique tuorum, / Audeo nil de te dicere, laude patrum [121–22]). Flattering comparisons are then drawn between the Kmitas and ancient Rome and between the Kmitas and the gods, as the poet suggests that the very greatness of his patron makes it difficult to find the means to celebrate him and his clan in song. But drawing on the examples of Rome and the gods, he points out that "Rome was the greatest, and yet this greatest Rome deemed her poets worthy of using her as the subject matter of their works. The gods, also—who since they are gods, nothing is more worthy of praise than they are—offer themselves and their temples as subjects of worshipful meters" (123–25). With the notion of the immortal greatness of Kmita and his family thus firmly insinuated, Ianicius closes his elegy by asking his patron to allow him (like Rome and the gods) to sing his praises sometime and by telling Kmita that he can help the poet in his work by just treating him kindly ("placida . . . fronte," literally, if Kmita shows him a kind face). Since the obstacle to Ianicius's immortalizing Kmita in song was less the greatness of his patron and his illustrious forebears than the poet's fear of a further erosion of his position, especially in view of Orzechowski's intriguing, his appeal to Kmita to continue to look upon him with favor is rather poignant.

When Ianicius's literary strategy for placating his patron and restoring his goodwill proved for the most part to no avail, the poignancy became desperation. We see this, for example, in Ianicius's epigram 63, addressed directly to Kmita ("Ad Petrum Cmitam"). It is short enough to quote in full in translation and needs no commentary:

> Kmita, you come to others, but not to me. You are near to all, but are absent from me. Although you are near in body, you are far in spirit. I see that I have incurred your disfavor, but I do not know what gave cause and substance to so much wrath. Perhaps I transgressed in something. But you who so often forgive many people the greatest crimes, forgive me as well! Forgive me, I beseech you! It is enough that unjust fate torments me; do not add more wounds to the wounds I already bear. God is God above all because he pardons, pities, raises one up, and causes one to become greater. Imitate him, and you will do it, for your noble spirit learned to follow the path indicated by him. (172)

Throughout his short life friendship mattered a great deal to Ianicius (undoubtedly at least in part because of his weak health, his dependence on patronage, and later his tempestuous relationship with

Piotr Kmita), and he made it an important theme in his writing. For obvious reasons, physicians also played a vital role in his life, and of those who treated him two in particular—both foreigners—are warmly recalled in his poetry. The first was the Veronese doctor who taught medicine at the University of Padua while Ianicius was a student there; he is known by his latinized name, Ioannes Baptista Montanus. Ianicius's fourth elegy in the *Tristia*, composed in Padua in the spring of 1540, is devoted to him. Although it has its share of familiar mythological allusions, the elegy strikes sympathetic chords in the reader by its very personal character and its expression of the understandable grief of a very young and talented man whose plans are thwarted by illness and who already realizes his life will be short. "Oh, my vain hopes!" he cries out early in the work. "I have wasted all the time I was supposed to have spent on my studies. I weep over my books already gnawed by worms, and I can almost hear how they too lament over me in silence" (34:11–14). Nature, to which he is ever responsive, fills him with some hope, for he sees signs of approaching spring. Even though "violent death lies in wait just outside [his] doors with menacing scythe in hand," his hopes seem fulfilled when Dr. Montanus undertakes his treatment, for he is the only person who can help him now. After all, the poet recalls, he is the physician who treated Pope Clement VII (1523–34), of the Medicis, and the same physician of whom that pope's dissolute nephew, Ippolito Cardinal de' Medici, who died at the age of twenty-four (possibly of poison), is supposed to have said on his deathbed: "Death, you would have no such fast claim on me if even the shadow of my Montanus were here!" ("Tam cito nil in me"—clamabat—"iuris haberes, / Mors, hic Montani si foret umbra mei" [45–46]). Ianicius obviously felt a kinship with Montanus. Recalling that the physician came to teach at Padua at the request of Venetian senators (who exercised political control over Padua at the time), he notes that Montanus accepted the prestigious invitation reluctantly, preferring instead "to live with friends in his native land [Verona] and pass his days there in tranquillity." But it was not only their attitudes toward friendship and quietude that brought the young Polish poet and the Italian physician close together. There was also the fact, as Ianicius notes near the end of his elegy, that apart from the burden of his work Montanus was denied the peace and quiet he loved by the "madness of envy whose assaults celebrated men always ignore and have no fear of. . . . As you know, she [envy] tolerates the small but attacks the very highest, just as thunderbolts more often strike at high mountains, but in vain; I say in vain because the summit of a mountain struck so many times by the bolts of Jove remains unmoved and will abide forever" (63–64, 67–70). Even when writing of the noted Italian doctor who treated him in Padua and became his friend, Ianicius clearly had the difficulties with his patron and the malice of Orzechowski on his mind.

An even closer bond of friendship was forged between Ianicius and the other doctor who figured prominently in his life, Jan Antonin (Ioannes Antoninus). A Hungarian from the town of Košice in present-day Slovakia, Antonin received his bachelor's degree from the University of Cracow in 1517 and studied medicine in Tübingen and Padua. On the way back to Poland from Italy, he successfully treated the ailing Erasmus in Basel, beginning a friendship that also included correspondence; Antonin, in fact, lived in Erasmus's home from July to November 1524. After his return to Poland in 1526, Antonin settled in Cracow; he became an official resident of the city in 1536 and soon held the position of royal physician.[10] Antonin also treated patients other than the royal family; these included some of the most prominent people in Cracow at the time, Ianicius among them. A warm relationship developed between the poet and the doctor, and Antonin was with Ianicius when he died.

Antonin figures in several of Ianicius's poems—epigrams 13, 64, and 65, and the eighth elegy in his *Tristia* collection. In the first epigram the poet expresses his gratitude to Antonin for returning him to health, saying that he owes him much but, since he has little to give, will render himself entirely ("sed ipsum, / Totus ut est, totum do tibi Ianicium" [144:3–4]). Moreover, he promises that his Apollo (as the god of poetry) will forever celebrate Antonin's Apollo (as the god of medicine) in song and will "for all time serve him even with his harsh-sounding lyre." Epigram 64 expresses the poet's agreement to compose an epitaph for Antonin. Ianicius tells the physician that since he is alive and in all respects healthy he can forget about death. However, since Antonin asked him, he will write his epitaph, but he hopes that he will not need one sooner than ten centuries ("ante decem saecula"; Antonin, however, died, like Ianicius, in 1543). The last epigram is, in fact, the promised epitaph; it reads as follows:

> Dum medeor multis, succumbo laboribus hancque
> Sic reperi requiem. Cura laborque, vale! (172)

(Healing many, I succumb to my labors and have thus found this repose. Farewell, cares and labors!)

The longest literary work inspired by his friendship with Antonin, elegy 8, is 170 lines—one of Ianicius's longest poems in general. Much of the elegy is taken up in commiserating with Antonin over the Turkish capture of Buda, the ancient capital of the Hungarian kings, on September 2, 1541. The elegy was probably written toward the end of that year. The fall of Buda to the forces of Sultan Süleyman I (the Magnificent), which ended Hungarian independence, occasioned widespread dismay and fear throughout Europe. This explains the emotion of Ianicius's poem and its recitation of the cities and states already conquered by the Turks. The following passage is typical:

> They lead in the unfortunate [Hungaria], fettered by heavy chains, no longer able to return to her own home, in mourning garb, filthy, poor, exciting pity by her tangled hair, her head, trembling and bloodied, lowered. Neither sickness, nor sex, nor age spares captivity; the enemy mows down everything before him in insatiable rage. A person vainly calls out to a son, another vainly to a parent, a young girl, bound, vainly implores a soldier. Children are murdered at their mothers' breasts; there is no place free of groaning, slaughter, and bloodshed. Burnt houses fall to ruin, and the property and sweat of the farmer and all species of animals are plundered. In short that land, so long happy, all gold, now lies all in chains, in slaughter, in fire. Feast on our blood, cruel Süleyman, feast, drink your beloved goblets to the bottom! Your wishes are fulfilled: the peoples against whom you wage war, bathed from the fountain of the blood of Christ, lie now beneath your feet. (66:127–44)

Not long before his death in 1543, Ianicius wrote two works of a political nature, which may seem surprising in view of his rapidly deteriorating health and the very private character of much of his writing. The first of these is similar in spirit, if not in form, to his earlier *Lament of the Commonwealth* and *To the Polish Nobles*. Inspired by concerns over the Turkish threat raised at a meeting of the Polish diet in Piotrków in early 1542, the work, which bears the title *In polonici vestitus varietatem et inconstantiam dialogus* (Dialogue against the Variety and Changeability of Polish Dress), reflects the poet's concern that the nobility's affectation and faddishness in costuming may represent a dangerous loss of manly vigor. The speakers in the dialogue are the long-deceased King Jagiełło and the famous court jester of King Sigismund I, Stańczyk, who was still alive at the time. In essence, the dead king plays straight man to the witty and sharp-tongued jester. Seeing the dangers to Poland posed by the rampaging Turks who have already overrun Wallachia and Hungary, the dead king has arisen from the grave to ask if he can help his nation in its time of need. Since he is not bound by any later treaties with the Turks, Jagiełło is set to lead a campaign against them. When Stańczyk asks where he will get the men for his campaign, Jagiełło replies that he will recruit the sons of the men who helped him conquer the Prussians. The jester offers to show Jagiełło what these sons look like today and then summons a parade of Polish nobles for the king to behold. Of course to the old king they are unrecognizable as Poles. In his time, Jagiełło laments, his warriors all dressed the same, but now they are all decked out like birds of different plumage. Worst of all, much of their finery seems of Turkish inspiration. (Eventually this Turkish style of dress became fashionable among the Polish nobility and remained so for a very long time.) As a crowning touch, the jester then offers Jagiełło a glimpse of the Polish Senate. The variety of dress is enough to drive the king to tears. "The Venetian Senate," he exclaims in disgust, "does not vary its dress. Long purple robes cover all of them the same. That is why their republic never changes and will always remain the same" (252:73–76). Stańczyk's defense of the different items of dress Jagiełło deplores is nothing more than a satirical ploy to set the self-indulgent extravagance and silliness of many of them in bolder relief. As the dialogue nears its end, Jagiełło asks Stańczyk who he is. "A soldier," replies the jester. When Jagiełło says he cannot tell that from Stańczyk's dress, the jester retorts that the king does not look like one, dressed as he is in an old sheepskin coat. Jagiełło registers surprise that he cannot be recognized as a king just because he is modestly attired, then asks the jester to explain his dress, particularly a large sack stuffed with wool or hay that he sees hanging from Stańczyk's neck. The jester explains that it is a shield to protect his back. In a parting shot at the arrogant intolerance of criticism among the nobility, who bristled at suggestions that their growing taste for opulence compromised their manliness and ability to defend the state, Ianicius has Jagiełło reply with the rhetorical question: "Is it now the custom among you to reward with the rod those who speak the truth?" (254:102). The danger to the state posed by the nobility's acquisitiveness and seemingly unappeasable appetite for luxury generated great concern among reform-minded statesmen and political writers in sixteenth- and seventeenth-century Poland. Not surprisingly, Ianicius's clever dialogue became one of the weapons in their arsenal.

Ianicius's last literary work, completed, in fact, on his deathbed, was a two-part epithalamium in honor of the impending nuptials of King Sigismund August and Elizabeth of Austria, daughter of Ferdinand, king of Bohemia and Hungary and later Holy Roman Emperor. Since he died in January 1543, Ianicius did not live to participate in the celebration, which took place on May 6 of that year. The poems were discovered among his papers by his heirs, his two closest friends, the physician Jan Antonin and the Wilno humanist and jurist Augustyn Mielecki (better known by his latinized name, Augustinus Rotundus). In deciding to make the work public Antonin and Rotundus declare, in an interesting prose preface, that they were motivated above all by the unusual nature of the epithalamium. Instead of following the usual conventions governing this kind of "official" poem, Ianicius dispensed with the familiar mythological figures, descriptions of the many virtues of bride and groom, and lengthy accounts of the traditional processions and festivities (which he knew he would not live to see) and approached his subject from a different angle. It is this difference in literary strategy, obviously dictated by the poet's awareness of approaching death, that makes his epithalamium on the nuptials of Sigismund August and Elizabeth worth looking at.

One notices first that the epithalamium has two parts. The first is dedicated to the groom's father, Sigismund I, and the second to the groom himself, Sigismund II August. This generational division is also the key to Ianicius's strategy. The first poem, to the old king, will address the achievements of Sigismund I and the greatness of his family; the second, to the son, the present king of Poland, will celebrate the rule of the new king as a continuation of the beneficent rule of his father and the marriage with Elizabeth of Austria as a guarantee of sons who will carry the wise policies of the first two Sigismunds far into the future, to the greater glory of the Polish state.

In the poem to the elder Sigismund, Ianicius does away almost completely with classical antique or mythological imagery. The poem recites the old king's achievements, beginning with his great victories over the Wallachians, Turks, and especially Muscovites. Because of these victories Poland is a more prosperous land, and this prosperity and abundance are reaching layers of the population hitherto virtually untouched by economic advantage. In both parts of the epithalamium, Ianicius personalizes his work by injecting himself directly into the texts. In the first part, for example, the poet interrupts his praise of Poland's abundance to assure his addressee, the old king, that in so speaking he does not wish to convey the impression that he regards wealth as worthiest of praise or places it on the same level as the highest virtues. "We have earned our name with iron, not gold," he declares, "and it is just because of this iron that we now preserve this gold" (190:155–56). Ianicius also praises Sigismund I for bringing about beneficial changes in the old ways. The barbarism of the past "has been driven far from your borders and has returned to the Goths, to whom it is more natural. Once upon a time, in war, the Sarmatian knew only how to strike the enemy by cutting and stabbing, to vanquish him, and to chase him in hot pursuit. He still can do these things and do them well, but he can also do others things that one can regard as more appropriate to a civilized way of life" (165–70). Among these "other things," Ianicius mentions the knowledge of other languages and the cultivation of the "great arts," which demand the efforts of either mind or hand. The wise policies of Sigismund I have also brought a change in the Poles' outward appearance. In the past they wore their hair twisted and hanging down to their shoulders, and the longer their locks, the more handsome they were considered. Scythe-shaped clogs with long pointed toes were also regarded as attractive footwear, but these have gone the way of twisted, shoulder-length hair. After enumerating the advantages to the church and religion in Poland brought by King Sigismund's reign, Ianicius concludes his panegyric with praise of other members of the royal family.

The second part of the epithalamium, addressed to Sigismund August, is somewhat more conventional. There are far more classical and mythological allusions (hardly any appear in the first poem), and both bride and groom are praised, expectedly, for their beauty and wisdom. As in the first poem, the poet steps forward at a certain point to speak directly to his readers. The poem begins with praise of the lineage and beauty of Sigismund II's intended, Elizabeth of Austria. In describing her beauty, which few queens equal and none can exceed, Ianicius strikes a personal note when he assures his readers that he is not merely repeating the words of others ("Nec narrata loquor") but is relying on his own observation of Elizabeth, whom he beheld once in Vienna, where as a "poor man" he happened to be the guest of some wealthy person. There is no reason not to take the poet at his word, and he is probably speaking of the time he stopped off in Vienna (in 1540) on his return trip to Poland from Padua. Ianicius recalls further that he espied the princess when she was entering the "ancient church of Saint Stephen" just ahead of her mother, as was the custom then.[11]

Ianicius's praise of the young Sigismund II August as the fulfillment of his father's dreams and the continuer of his admirable policies carries with it certain precepts that the poet believes will help him achieve his goals. The most interesting of these clearly reflect the outlook and concerns of a Renaissance humanist poet-scholar dependent on patronage. "Be loving in your guardianship of learned men," counsels the poet, who then, invoking the name of the revered Jagiełło, goes on to declare that "he was a great admirer of them. Because of them, the fame of your accomplishments will grow and live; because of them, your name will live through all eternity."[12] By bringing learned men beneath the beneficent custodianship of his patronage, Sigismund August will ensure his own immortality; these men will write of his deeds, and his fame will spread throughout the world and will live forever. Among the examples of heroes and rulers, both ancient and more recent, who became immortal because of what was written about them, Ianicius mentions King Matthias Corvinus of Hungary, who was a great patron of learning and the arts, and the Holy Roman Emperor Sigismund (1410–37), grandfather of Sigismund August's grandmother (Elizabeth, wife of King Casimir the Jagellonian). So great was the emperor Sigismund's attachment to learned men, writes Ianicius, that it was considered "his only fault in life, in the opinion of all" (Cuius id unum / In vita, vulgo iudice, crimen erat). "He took them unto himself with as much love," continues the poet, "as an anxious father shows his children. He always counted them among his special friends and always wanted to have them at his side." This incurred the wrath of the emperor's nobles, who proclaimed that it was shameful for the great emperor to be so devoted to "such people, most of whom come from insignificant homes and whom a poor mother nursed in some unknown place" (Quales parva domus gignit plerumque parensque / Lactat in obscuro non opulenta loco). To this the emperor replied, quoting Ianicius: "These people to whom nature and God gave a genius greater than mine and yours I place above all others. I esteem them according to their virtues. Why do I have to know where they were born?" The poet closes his admonishment to the young king, and virtually the epithalamium itself, with the exhortation, "You are King Sigismund August by name; since these are the names by which you are known, honor those whose names you bear by your deeds. Be unto poets what he [the emperor Sigismund] was once upon a time, and do not think shameful what was so seemly to him!" How truly appropriate it was that this most talented of Poland's Renaissance Latin poets, for whom poetry was the essence and meaning of his very short life, would have poets and poetry uppermost in his mind as he lay composing his last work on his deathbed.

CHAPTER 10

Epilogue: Jan Kochanowski and the Twilight of Polish Humanism

The year 1543 has long been regarded as a watershed in the history of Polish culture. This was the year, for example, when Poland's best humanist poet, Clemens Ianicius, died. Although poetry continued to be written in Latin in Poland well into the seventeenth century, as well as scientific, historical, political, and other types of expository literature, Ianicius's death marks the end of the *exclusive* use of Latin by Polish Renaissance poets. In this respect the humanist phase of the Renaissance in Poland had also reached its end. Further enhancing the watershed status of 1543 in Polish culture, this was the year when Copernicus's most famous and influential treatise, *De revolutionibus orbium coelestium* (On the Movements of Heavenly Bodies), was published and when the great scientist, whose outlook was patently shaped by humanism, himself died. It is no coincidence that humanism as an intellectual movement peaked in Poland with the appearance of this greatest product of Polish Renaissance scientific thought.

It was also in 1543 that Andrzej Frycz Modrzewski's first two treatises appeared, proposing the most far-reaching program of political reform in Poland between the Renaissance and the Enlightenment. In the first, *Oratio Philaletis Peripatetici* . . . (Discourse of a Peripatetic Truth-Sayer), Modrzewski addressed the social and moral wrong of restricting the right of burghers to acquire rural property, while in the second, *Lascius, sive de poena homicidii* (Lascius, or On the Punishment for Murder), the great reformer pleaded for stiffening the punishment for murder and urged the equality of all citizens, peasants included, before the law. This year also saw the appearance of the first major literary work in the Polish vernacular. Bearing the title *Krótka rozprawa między trzema osobami: Panem, wójtem i plebanem* (A Short Discourse between Three Persons: A Squire, a Bailiff, and a Parson), it was written by Mikołaj Rej (1505–69), who is traditionally accorded the distinction of being, to use the well-worn cliché, the "father of Polish [vernacular] literature." The first of many works in prose and verse, mostly of a social and moralistic character, *A Short Discourse* is a satire directed mainly against the gentry and the clergy by a writer who was, significantly, a Calvinist and who, though he knew some Latin, wrote exclusively in Polish.

After his groundbreaking *Short Discourse*, Rej wrote the biblically inspired *Żywot Józefa z pokolenia żydowskiego* (The Life of Joseph of the Jewish Tribe, 1545); *Kupiec* (The Merchant, 1549), an anti-Catholic morality play in verse; a folksy prose exposition of Protestantism entitled *Postilla* (1557); a prose adaptation from the Latin of the psalms of David (*Psałterz Dawidów*, 1546); a didactic work about how a young man should conduct himself in order to live a happy and virtuous life (*Wizerunek własny żywota człowieka poczciwego*, [A Faithful Image of an Honest Man, 1558]); and his immensely popular *Zwierciadło* (The Mirror, 1568), a loosely structured consideration of the constituent features of a good life, written in a combination of prose and verse. Rej's advice, in brief, emphasizes choosing a proper wife and shunning court service and public office in favor of the traditional pursuits of a provincial squire.

Although Rej was the first *major* writer in the Polish language, he was not the initiator of a Polish vernacular literary tradition. That distinction belongs to a figure who has attracted a fair amount of attention in Polish scholarly circles in recent years, Biernat z Lublina (Biernat of Lublin, ca. 1465 to after 1529).[1]

A burgher by origin and a priest, whose works were placed on the Index because of his suspected Hussitism, Biernat is best remembered for two works in particular, both written in the vernacular; *Raj duszny* (Paradise of the Soul, published in 1513), a prayerbook adapted from Latin (which Biernat knew) and often reprinted, and *Żywot Aesopa Fryga, Mędrca obyczajnego, wraz z przypowieściami jego* (The Life of Aesop the Frygian, a Virtuous Sage, Together with His Proverbs), published originally, it is believed, in 1522 and consisting of a life of Aesop adapted from a work by the Italian humanist Ranuccio d'Arezzo together with fables traditionally attributed to Aesop. Biernat's status as a burgher (unlike Rej, who belonged to the gentry) is important in understanding the emergence of a vigorous vernacular literature in Poland between 1513 and 1543.

The introduction of printing in Poland dates from the year 1503, when the first regular printing house in the country was founded in Cracow by a wine dealer and bookseller named Jan Haller, who brought in a German artisan, Gaspar Hochfeder, to print the books he published.[2] After two years of cooperation between the two men, Haller took complete charge of the printing establishment, and in the course of some twenty years he published about 260 items.

Other Cracow printers soon came to prominence following Haller's lead. One was Florian Ungler, whose edition of Biernat of Lublin's *Paradise of the Soul* in 1513 was the first book to be printed in the Polish language bearing an author's name (it had been preceded at least by one anonymous book printed in 1508). Another was Hieronim Wietor (or Vietor, as his name often appears in his Vienna publications), who opened a printing office in Cracow in 1517 and became particularly active in publishing books promoting the study and teaching of the Polish language. Wietor's firm was taken over in 1550 by Łazarz Andrysowicz, who greatly extended its range and fame. Two other major Cracow printing houses of the Renaissance were Marek Szarffenberg's, founded in 1543, and Maciej Wirzbięta's, which opened in 1554 and printed the works of such outstanding Polish Renaissance writers as Rej and Kochanowski.

Since Latin was the universal language of humanism, those who wrote in it did not have to rely on domestic printers and could in principle place their works with any publishing house in Europe. Once printing was established in Poland, the earliest printers, in Cracow, mindful of the competition for books in Latin, lost no time developing a new domestic market. Their earliest works were church and state books as well as school texts. But the growth of Polish town life in the late fifteenth and early sixteenth centuries created a market for works of imaginative literature in the vernacular. It was to accommodate as well as expand this new market that the Cracow printers provided the impetus to create just such a literature.

As a growing, prosperous, and increasingly literate urban society (particularly, of course, in Cracow at the outset) began to take shape, the Cracow publishers—beginning with Jan Haller—were quick to recognize and respond to the emergence of a different readership. Lacking the learning and cosmopolitanism of humanist circles, these burgher, or middle-class, readers would not have taken much interest in Latin publications. It was precisely for this new burgher readership—literate, but culturally and spiritually closer to the Middle Ages than to the Renaissance—that Biernat of Lublin wrote in the vernacular. Once the Cracow publishers saw the popularity of his *Paradise of the Soul*, they realized the potential of the market for imaginative vernacular literature and undertook an active campaign to develop a profitable business in Polish-language books.

The campaign began in earnest in the early 1520's—recall that Biernat's hugely popular *Life of Aesop* was published about 1522—and brought to prominence a group of burgher writers who, with the encouragement of the Cracow printers, flooded the market with books in Polish, creating an entirely new market. Besides Biernat of Lublin, this group included such figures as Leonard z Bończy (Leonard of Bończa), Andrzej Glaber z Kobylina (of Kobylin), Baltazar Opeć, Jan Sandecki, Jeronim z Wielunia (of Wieluń), and Jan z Koszyczek (of Koszyczki), the author of a rather polished verse work (one of the few he wrote) titled *Pokorne wspomnienie żywota Pana Jezusowego* (A Humble Recollection of the Life of Jesus, 1522) and, in prose, *Rozmowy, które miał król Salomon mądry z Marchołtem grubym a sprośnym* (Conversations between the Wise King Solomon and the Coarse and Lewd Marcholt), based on Jewish legends about King Solomon, which Wietor published in 1521.

The steady cultivation of Polish as a literary language, which owed much to the emergence of a Polish middle class and the activities of aggressive Cracow publishers of German origin, received further impetus from the great impact in Poland of the vernacular-oriented Protestant Reformation as well as from the emergence of a popular culture in posthumanist Renaissance Europe in general.

It was from the confluence of these currents that there arose Jan Kochanowski (in Latin Johannes Cochanovius, 1530–84), the first great poet of the Polish language and the greatest Polish poet before Adam Mickiewicz (1798–1855). Not only a splendid artist of the word in Polish and the first to demonstrate what could be done with the vernacular in poetry, Kochanowski was also the first major reformer of Polish versification, and his innovations have stood the test of time down to the present.

Kochanowski's impressive oeuvre includes a remarkable verse adaptation of the Psalms (*Psałterz Dawidów*, 1579) that was his first published collection of poems; a humorous mock epic about chess (*Szachy*, [The Game of Chess], published about 1564), modeled on the *Scacchia ludus* (about 1513; definitive edition published in 1527) of Marco Girolamo (Marcus Hieronymus) Vida (d. 1566); political poetry including *Zgoda* (Harmony, 1564), *Satyr albo Dziki mąż* (The Satyr, or The Wild Man, 1564), and *Proporzec albo Hołd pruski* (The Banner, or The Prussian Tribute, 1569); a collection of short occasional poems, mostly humorous or anecdotal (*Fraszki*, Trifles, 1584; the Polish term for a poem of this type, *fraszka,* derives from the Italian name for the genre at the time, *frasca*); a large number of songs on different subjects first collected and published in book form only in 1586, two years after the poet's death; a Senecan tragedy in verse, *Odprawa posłów greckich* (The Dismissal of the Greek Envoys), which was performed in the presence of the king in 1578 at a feast celebrating the wedding of Jan Zamoyski, vice-chancellor and later chancellor and royal hetman of Poland, at Jazdów near Warsaw and was his acknowledged masterpiece; and a cycle of nineteen moving and philosophically engaging threnodies or laments (*Treny,* published in 1580) occasioned by the death of his thirty-month-old daughter, Urszula.

Kochanowski's undeniably great achievement as a poet in the vernacular set an example that later Polish poets could only struggle vainly to equal until the nineteenth century produced the poetry above all of Mickiewicz, Juliusz Słowacki (1809–49), and Cyprian Kamil Norwid (1821–83). Furthermore, Kochanowski provided such an extraordinary boost to the cultivation of the vernacular that except for the seventeenth-century Baroque poet Maciej Kazimierz Sarbiewski (1595–1640), a Jesuit who chose to write only in Latin (under the name of Sarbevius), he ended the hegemony of Latin among Polish poets. Seeing what could be achieved in their native tongue, writers found less and less reason to exercise their talents in Latin. But Kochanowski is still interesting to students of Renaissance humanism in Poland because he also wrote abundant verse in Latin.

Of middle gentry background, Kochanowski was enrolled at the University of Cracow at the age of fourteen (1544). After a few years there, where he easily assimilated the humanist tradition and acquired a solid grounding in Latin, he lived for a year in Königsberg at the court of Duke Albrecht of Prussia. Probably in 1552, like other Polish students before him, he traveled to Padua, where for the next three years he immersed himself in classical philology at the university. Among the well-known scholars he studied with was Francesco Robortello, a highly esteemed commentator and publisher of the *Poetics* of Aristotle who in 1552 became professor of rhetoric. Besides advancing his knowledge of Latin language and literature, during this period Kochanowski learned Greek well enough to attempt to reconstruct Cicero's translation of the Greek writer Aratos's *Phainomena.* After a return to Poland, Kochanowski was again in Padua in 1556, but this second sojourn was interrupted by the death of his mother. He returned to Italy for the third time in 1557 and remained there until no later than the beginning of 1559. When he finally left Italy, Kochanowski went to France, visiting Marseilles and Paris. In 1559 he left France for Germany and thence returned to Poland.

Polish literary historiography has long speculated on whether Kochanowski met Ronsard and perhaps other members of the Pléiade while in Paris, stimulating his interest in vernacular poetry. There is little hard evidence, but that the Pole met Ronsard and other French poets seems reasonable. Since one of the things that would have drawn them together was a growing interest in creating a vernacular literary tradition in their cultures, it seems less likely that Ronsard and the Pléiade were the immediate or principal source of Kochanowski's changing attitude toward the vernacular. The Polish poet, we may imagine, was already developing a different perspective on Polish as a literary language, partly because of experiences in Italy and partly as a result of the diffusion of Reformation ideas in Poland, and so, hearing of the views of Ronsard and his colleagues, he sought them out during his stay in France.

After returning to Poland, Kochanowski began his life at the courts of lay and ecclesiastical magnates. For a time he also was secretary to King Sigismund August. Although attractive church benefices were offered him, he chose to remain a layman. Not long after his fortieth birthday he took a wife and retired from court service to his hereditary estate of Czarnolas (Blackwood) near the city of Lublin, east of Warsaw. Until his death, he devoted most of his time to literary pursuits; it was at Blackwood that his finest works were written.

Nearly as much at home in Latin as in Polish, Kochanowski began his literary career, in Italy in fact, as a Latin-language poet in the best humanist tradition and continued to write in Latin virtually to his death in 1584.[3] Although impressive in number, his Latin poems are for the most part capable but conventional exercises in humanist poetics; in terms of originality, boldness, and sincerity not only do they not compare with his works in Polish, but they also fall well below the works of such Polish Latin poets as Hussovianus, Dantiscus, Krzycki, and Ianicius.

Kochanowski's Latin oeuvre comprises four books of elegies (consisting of forty-six poems of different lengths); an entertaining collection of 123 *foricoenia* (the Latin term for the Polish *fraszki*—short, often humorous occasional poems);[4] twelve odes; an epinicion, or poem of victory, celebrating the Polish king Stephen Batory's successful conclusion of the war with Muscovy and the regaining of Livonia in 1582; an epithalamium on the wedding of Chancellor Jan Zamoyski and Gryzelda Batorówna (sung to lyre accompaniment by the royal musician, Krzysztof Klabon, on June 12, 1583, at the royal castle in Cracow); and a reply to the French poet Philippe Desportes's caustic "Adieu à la Poloigne," which he wrote as a member of the group of Frenchmen that joined Henry Valois in his flight to France after his brief occupancy of the Polish throne in 1574; and a few other small poems on various subjects.

Most of Kochanowski's elegies fall into two major categories: conventional love poems, some addressed to a young woman identified only as Lydia, who was probably the poet's principal romantic interest while he was in Italy, and poems, largely panegyric, addressed to prominent Poles from whom Kochanowski had received patronage at one time or another or at whose courts he had served. This second group of elegies is addressed to such well-known figures as Mikołaj Mielecki (d. 1585), palatine of Podolia and great hetman of the Crown; Piotr Myszkowski (1505–91), bishop of Płock and later Cracow, a senator, humanist, and one of Kochanowski's major patrons; Andrzej Patrycy Nidecki (Patricius, 1527–86), a learned humanist, Latin writer, philologist, and authority on Cicero, and the author of several anti-Reformation treatises; Hieronim Ossoliński (d. 1576), castellan of Sandomierz and a prominent magnate; Filip Padniewski (d. 1572), bishop of Cracow, vice-chancellor of the Polish Crown and a distinguished orator; Mikołaj Radziwiłł (the Black, 1515–65), marshal of the Grand Duchy of Lithuania; Jan Tarnowski (1488–1561), a powerful magnate and an outstanding military leader, and his son Jan Krzysztof Tarnowski (d. 1567); Jan Tęczyński (d. 1562), a magnate, state dignitary, and diplomat who died in Danish captivity after being seized on his way to marry a Swedish princess; and Stanisław Vogelweder (or Fogelweder, 1525–1603), a royal secretary and a member of a Swiss family that had settled in Poland.

For the foreign student of Polish Renaissance humanism, probably the most interesting of Kochanowski's Latin poems are those related to the brief kingship in Poland of Henry Valois (Henryk Walezy in Polish, 1551–89), son of the French king Henry II de Valors d'Anjou and Catherine de' Medici. The first elective king of Poland in 1573, Henry arrived there in late January 1574 to assume the throne. However, when he heard of the death of his brother, Charles IX, he left Poland voluntarily, but secretly, in June to try to seat himself on the French throne. The official act of his dethronement was proclaimed in Poland in May 1575.

Like many other (although certainly not all) Poles, Kochanowski was at first enthusiastic about the kingship of Henry Valois. Two of his Latin *foricoenia*, or occasional poems—numbers 100 and 101 ("In aqui-

lam" [To the Eagle] and "Ad Henr. Valesium Regem Cracoviam ven-
ientem" [To King Henry Valois on His Arrival in Cracow])[5]—express
great hope for what Poland's new French king will mean to the country.
In the first poem the poet declares that all portents indicate that "when
Henry becomes king of Poland, the land will blossom like a lily."[6] The
second poem describes the tumultuous greeting of Henry in Cracow
by the townspeople, the Senate, and the nobility; even the "fiery Sun,
pleased with this view, restrained in their flight the golden-maned
steeds racing across the heavenly expanses, while night, tolerating no
delay, poured forth from pure Olympus so that she herself might
behold you with a thousand eyes" (241–42).

Kochanowski's Latin oeuvre also includes a dozen odes, the first
dedicated to Henry Valois. Titled "Ad Henricum Valesium Regem in
Gallus morantem" (To King Henry Valois, Who Is Still in France), the
ode was obviously written sometime between Henry's election as king
of Poland on May 14, 1573, and his departure from France in December of the same year. As in his two occasional poems to the Frenchman,
Kochanowski looks forward eagerly to Valois's kingship and the great
things it portends for Poland and voices impatience over the new
king's tardy departure from France:

> Quis casus obstat? quis deus invidet?
> Henrice, regum maxime, quominus
> Pulcherrimum ad regnum vocatus
> Sarmaticis videare campis
>   Equo feroci conspicuus vehi,
> Plaudente matrum cum pueris choro,
> Vulgoque densis confluente
> Agminibus studio videndi
>   Novi monarchae? (257–58)

(What circumstance hinders you, what god forbids you, Henry, greatest
of kings, summoned unto the loveliest kingdom, from showing yourself
on a mighty steed in the Sarmatian plains, surrounded by an applauding
throng of mothers with their children and the common people flowing
together in dense crowds, all burning with desire to see their new king?)

The rest of the poem brims with flattery of the new king. At the
very mention of his name, for example, the "defiant Muscovite has
put aside his bombastic threats, and the rapacious Scythians [Tatars]
have ceased trampling Podolian fields with their horses" (258–59).
The poet's greatest wish is that the fates will let him see the day when
"after our enemies have been conquered and the tyrants of the sea

punished, I shall behold you riding magnificently in a chariot drawn by four white horses, displaying conquered leaders bound together in chains, captured cities and standards of war, and wagons weighted down with copious spoils" (259).

The fates, however, decreed differently. Hardly had Henry Valois accepted the throne of Poland and taken up residence in the royal castle than he abandoned his new kingdom to claim the vacated throne of France. The reaction in Poland to the new king's flight was disbelief followed quickly by a sense of rejection, hurt pride, and anger. Kochanowski's enthusiasm for Henry Valois—like that of the many other Poles who had favored the election of the Frenchman—was short-lived. He vented his resentment in his third ode ("In conventu Stesicensi" [On the Diet in Stężyca]), which was addressed to the Polish diet convened to decide what course to pursue in the wake of Valois's defection. No longer an object of fulsome praise, Valois is characterized in the poem as "fickle" (levis); the Polish nation indeed has been "deceived by his departure, or rather flight" (abitu an fuga decepta). Attributing the Frenchman's swift departure from Poland to the unrest and calamities in his native land (we can assume Kochanowski was referring to the disturbances related to the Saint Bartholomew's Day massacre of 1572), the poet pleads with the "great father of the gods" to instill in Valois the desire to return to Poland once he has set the affairs of France in order. If, however, he refuses to resume his kingship in Poland, and if it is "impossible to steer two ships in deep waters with a single helm," then before a "frightful storm erupts" the "abandoned Sarmatians" should be permitted to seek another helmsman for the "aimless ship." The rest of the poem becomes an admonishment by Kochanowski to his fellow Poles—sounding chords struck more frequently and emphatically in his Polish works with respect to the arrogance of the nobility—that in choosing a new king, if they must have a king at all, the Poles should learn to become obedient and to renounce their desire for unbridled authority. "Of what use are good laws," he asks, "if no one obeys them and if all are free to rule the republic and to enact useless laws according to their own judgment?" (263:37–40). "Fear not the threats of the mad barbarian," the poet cautions further in closing," but do not take them too lightly either; take up your arms and accomplish the great deeds that are proper for you. Are we to voluntarily offer our free necks to the barbarian yoke, the way the conquered do, before the bloody judgments of fierce Mars have been rendered and an uncertain contest has run its course?" (263–64:41–48).

Henry Valois's decision to remain in France after his flight from

Poland and the election of the Hungarian Stephen Batory (1533–86) as king of Poland in 1576 might seem sufficient to end Kochanowski's interest in the Valois episode. Ordinarily that would no doubt have been true. But included in the entourage that accompanied Henry Valois to Poland and again back to France was the French poet Philippe Desportes (1546–1606), who upon leaving Poland wrote a rather nasty poem about the country under the title "Adieu à la Poloigne." Referring to Poland in the opening stanza as a land of "empty fields always covered with snow and ice" (plaines désertes / Tousjours de neige et de glace couvertes), the poet vows never to return there at any price; the people, the customs, and the very air of the country are repugnant to him.[7] Ironically saluting Polish houses and huts, Deportes declares that they remind him of the golden age, because people and animals all live in them together. Lambasting the Poles for their heavy drinking, for their barbarousness and arrogance, he says they seek renown throughout the world for their military prowess, but in vain. He goes on to say that if they have so far escaped being conquered it is not because of their manliness but because of their poverty ("Vos bras charnus n' y vos traits redoutables, / Lourds Polonnois, qui vous sont indomptables; / La pauvreté seulement vous defend"). If Poland had a better climate, desirable goods, enough wine, rivers, ports, and mines, she would not have lasted so long. The Turks, for example, prefer to acquire "gentle Cyprus or lovely Candia than your wildernesses, which are almost always covered with ice" (Les Othomans . . . / Aiment mieux Cypre ou la belle Candie, / Que vos déserts presque tousjours glacez). Knowing the impoverishment of the Poles, the Germans prefer to wage war against the Flemish lands, where their labors are better compensated. "For nine months," Desportes declares near the end of his diatribe in verse, "for the sake of my master, the great Henry, I abandoned France for this wasteland, exhausting my poor injured soul, without any comfort save that of seeing him." In the last few lines, he expresses the hope that Henry may become king of some richer land, and that the poet himself may never have to return to Poland.

When Desportes's poem came to his attention, Kochanowski wasted little time writing a reply, also in verse. This was the poem, in Latin (a language Desportes knew), titled "Gallo crocitante" (To the Croaking Cock-Frenchman, the title obviously being a play on words, since "gallus" in Latin can mean both a cock and a Frenchman). If the cold and frosts of Poland are the reason the French left a country that is the safest for guests, Kochanowski asks, how can that be? Born of noble Trojan blood, the Frenchman (Henry Valois) not long before had boasted that as soon as he was summoned to the throne he would set off to destroy the Muscovites and drive the Tatar hordes beyond the Ural Mountains and the frozen seas. But before he reaches Moscow, and before he smashes tents in Scythia, Kochanowski reminds the Frenchman that he first must cross huge lakes and uncultivated fields, deep snows, ice, and great rivers, and that he must have with him numerous divisions, because he will have to contend not only with the Muscovites and Tatars but also with fierce winter and strong winds. It is better that the French leave, declares Kochanowski, because his country needs men who are not afraid of cold and winter. Before they go, however, he invites them to warm themselves in those same huts on which Desportes heaped so much abuse, since they can accommodate even cocks (or Frenchmen); if not, the harsh winter will destroy those who are lightly dressed. Kochanowski next takes up the charge that the Poles suffer from pride and lightheadedness. Since these weaknesses belong to the French and are proper to them "like the color black to a raven and white to a swan," the charge was made deliberately out of a desire "to share and thereby be relieved in part of the odium of such traits, as if indeed another people had been found similar in customs to you. But many years and centuries will pass and the Tiber will carry the immense power of swift water into the Etruscan Sea before a Frenchman will convince a Pole of what the whole world has known for a very long time about the French."[8] Berating Valois, Desportes, and the rest of the French retinue for their abuse of sincere Polish hospitality and referring to them by such epithets as "ingratus fugitivus" (ungrateful runaway) and "barbarus" (barbarian), Kochanowski expresses relief at one point that if he ever drank too much—recalling Desportes's charge that the Poles wallow in drunkenness—he did so in Poland and not in France, where excessive wine could have cost him his life. Moreover, he adds, had he dozed off at a royal banquet in France, so barbarous are the customs that his bloody corpse would have been tossed unceremoniously from a window. Henry Valois and company spent so little time in Poland, the poet continues, that they had no time to see the wealth and abundance of the country, and so they spread false rumors of its poverty. "Why," he asks, "did we seem so poor to you? When Henry was summoned to the throne of Poland the French were convinced that whatever Frenchman comes to our northern land with the king, even if he were only a cockerel, he would certainly enrich himself, and his fate thus changed he would possess much gold, he would be revered second after the king, he would be admired as some sort of hero by the Sarmatians, and gold would be strewn in his path" (360:104–12). After expressing satisfaction that he has repaid Desportes's malicious verses in kind, Kochanowski concludes his "Gallo crocitante" with the wish that he may never hear that the Frenchman has returned to Poland. Since it was also Desportes's wish that he never come back, the Polish poet prays that both their wishes may be fulfilled. If Valois and his circle are still obsessed by the desire to rule, Kochanowski suggests it would be better for "great Germany" (magna . . . Germania) to give them her kingdom; that way the Rhine would see those honored by the crown and scepter fleeing secretly back to their own country bearing transient titles, just as the Vistula did.

Although generally much less intimate and supple a poet in Latin than in Polish, Kochanowski did choose Latin to announce his irrevocable break with court life and his retirement to his family estate of Blackwood. The poem is the fifteenth in his third book of elegies and is believed to have been written in 1570, when he was forty years old. After nine years in court service the poet had had his fill of its pomp and ceremony, its artificiality, its gossip and intrigues and was only too happy when Blackwood became his and he could freely leave court and city and retire to the country and the pursuits of a typical provincial squire. His loathing for court life comes through clearly in the first line of the poem, in which the court is characterized as "deceitful" (fallax).[9] No longer concerned about the (apparently) unfulfilled promises of the court, the poet declares that freedom is dearer to him than jewels, dearer than "the sand that the Lidian river brings him in gold-bearing currents" (137:3–4). The freedom he now enjoys in the country is that of naturalness; freedom from having to heed another's glance, from having to watch his step, freedom to eat when he is hungry rather than when his lord deigns to eat, to organize his life as he himself wants and not according to someone else's plan; in sum, to do whatever he wants whenever he wants. Among the pleasures the poet can now pursue at will are the study of Socrates and the writing of poetry compatible with the Latin Muses, which "his Sarmatian will sing with soft voice" (137:11–14). While filled, expectedly, with classical imagery, Kochanowski's elegy is still a sincere expression of joy in bucolic life. "I am not ashamed," he confesses, "to cultivate fertile fields; the greater shame, I believe, is to be regarded as a servant" (15–16). There were villages long before there were walled cities, he declares, and without the villages the cities would starve; it was from the village that there came the soldier capable of enduring the heat of summer and the cold of winter and the stern consul who rose to power. After enumerating the gods and goddesses who look with favor upon rural life and agriculture, Kochanowski summons the farmer to begin harvesting the grain and, while the rivers are still frozen, to haul wood from the forests to build ships for transporting the grain. The poet's obvious love and knowledge of country routine manifest themselves in his detailed description of the vessel the farmer should build for the safe transport of grain. From lines thirty-seven to fifty-four the elegy reads like a how-to manual. The poem closes with the poet's advice to the farmer that when the Vistula River—which was the principal route by which grain was shipped in Poland—is swollen by its tributaries and "crushes the bridge made of ice, then is the time to lower the shapeless craft into the clear waters so that, loaded with its cargo, it may make for the shores of the Baltic Sea. There is no thought of it returning; it is sufficient that the boatman return home on foot after receiving fair recompense for his goods" (139:55–60).

Although Kochanowski was truly a bilingual poet who wrote Latin verse over a long period and was by no means uninteresting in the classical language, it is significant that he is thought of primarily as the first great poet in the Polish vernacular and the first codifier of Polish metrics. His Latin works tend to be regarded as a phase he underwent on his passage from a studied Renaissance humanism in the twilight of that movement in Poland to a full-blown and vigorous Renaissance vernacular culture, of which he became one of the great architects. With the appearance of Polish-language writers of the talent and appeal of Rej and above all Kochanowski, the ascendancy of the vernacular in Poland was beyond denying. The legacy of humanism was impressive, Latin was still important in Polish cultural life, and the works of the humanist poets acted as a kind of literary school through which the best of the Polish vernacular writers of the sixteenth century passed, transferring to the indigenous language the genres and techniques of verbal art acquired from the Neo-Latin literary tradition. But humanism, with its primacy of Latin, now belonged to the past. It had created the first great period in the history of Polish culture and in so doing brought Poland into the mainstream of European achievement during the Renaissance. It is there that she will remain, whatever the temporary dislocations of political origin.

Notes

The literature on humanism and Renaissance Neo-Latin literature in Poland is not considerable. It is almost entirely in Polish and consists mainly of articles and essays, a few monographs on individual figures, and very well edited collections of primary source materials in Latin, often accompanied by Polish translations. The literature on the Renaissance in Poland in general, however, is so vast that I have considered it of no particular advantage to attempt either a representative bibliography or a bibliographical essay. The following chapter notes cite the materials I consulted in writing this book and, where relevant, additional references to secondary literature that may interest informed readers. Many of the studies listed in the notes contain bibliographical information of use to the specialist wishing to pursue a particular topic in greater depth. For an exceptionally comprehensive bibliography on the Renaissance in Poland, readers who know Polish are advised to consult Jerzy Ziomek's survey *Renesans* (Warsaw, 1973), 381–422. Excellent material related to the art and architecture of Renaissance Poland can be found in Jan Białostocki, *The Art of the Renaissance in Eastern Europe: Hungary, Bohemia, Poland* (Ithaca, N.Y., 1976), and in Helena and Stefan Kozakiewiczowie, *The Renaissance in Poland* (Warsaw, 1976).

After the initial reference in the chapter notes, page and line numbers of works cited are usually placed in the text. Where both page and line numbers are given, they are separated by a colon. Numbers standing alone refer either to pages or to lines that follow an initial page reference. To avoid ambiguity in a few instances, p. or pp. for pages, bk. for book, and l. or ll. for lines appear before the numbers.

Introduction

1. For a good general history of Poland in English, see Norman Davies, *God's Playground: A History of Poland*, 2 vols. (New York, 1972).

2. On the history of the University of Cracow in the period of humanism, see especially Henryk Barycz, *Historja Uniwersytetu Jagiellońskiego* (Cracow, 1935). The same author's *Z dziejów Uniwersytetu Jagiellońskiego* (Cracow, 1955) also has interesting material related to the university, mostly in the second half of the sixteenth century. For a very comprehensive history of the university in the Middle Ages and the Renaissance in a Western language, see Casimir Morawski, *Histoire de l'Université de Cracovie*, trans. P. Rongier (vol. 1, Paris, 1900; vol. 2, Paris, 1903; vol. 3, Paris, 1905). This is a French translation of Kazimierz Morawski's *Historia Uniwersytetu Jagiellońskiego* (Cracow, 1900).

3. In her article "Bonet, Gower and Polish Jurists on the Rights of Non-believers," in *Mélanges de littérature comparée et de philologie offerts à Mieczysław Brahmer* (Warsaw, 1967, 467–73), Margaret Schlauch offers a comparative perspective on the Polish contributions on the issue.

4. On Polish-Italian cultural ties in the late Middle Ages and during the Renaissance and Baroque periods, see Mieczysław Brahmer, *Powinowactwa polsko-włoskie: Z dziejów wzajemnych stosunków kulturalnych* (Warsaw, 1980), and Tadeusz Ulewicz, "Związki kulturalno-literackie Polski z Włochami w wiekach średnich i w renesansie," in *Literatura staropolska w kontekście europejskim* (Wrocław, 1977). Polish-Italian cultural relations are also the subject of a brief but interesting essay by Stanisław Łempicki in his *Renesans i humanizm w Polsce: Materiały do studiów* (Cracow, 1952), 101–7.

5. The Latin original of Jan z Ludziska's lecture and information about him (in Latin) can be found in Ioannes de Ludzisko, *Orationes,* ed. Hyacinthus Stanislaus Bojarski (Wrocław, 1971). A Polish translation of the lecture and additional information on Jan z Ludziska appear in an anthology of old Polish speeches, *Wybór mów staropolskich,* ed. Bronisław Nadolski (Wrocław, 1961).

6. The best introductory studies on Frycz Modrzewski are by Waldemar Voisé: *Frycza Modrzewskiego nauka o państwie i prawie* (Warsaw, 1956) and *Andrzej Frycz Modrzewski, 1503–1572* (Wrocław, 1975). See also the collective work edited by Tadeusz Bieńkowski, *Andrzej Frycz Modrzewski i problemy kultury polskiego odrodzenia* (Wrocław, 1974).

7. The literature on the Reformation and Counter-Reformation in Poland is vast. For reasons of space, therefore, I shall cite only several of the more important studies: Aleksander Brückner, *Różnowiercy polscy: Szkice obyczajowe i literackie* (Warsaw, 1962); Henryk Barycz, *Z epoki renesansu, reformacji i baroku* (Warsaw, 1971); Marceli Kosman, *Reformacja i kontrreformacja w Wielkim Księstwie Litewskim w świetle propagandy wyznaniowej* (Wrocław, 1973) and *Protestanci*

i kontrreformacja: Z dziejów tolerancji w Rzeczypospolitej XVI–XVIII wieku (Wrocław, 1978); Stanisław Kot, *Socinianism in Poland: The Social and Political Ideas of the Polish Anti-Trinitarians in the Sixteenth and Seventeenth Centuries* (Boston, 1975); Gottfried Schramm, *Der polnische Adel und die Reformation, 1548–1607* (Wiesbaden, 1965); Janusz Tazbir, *Historia Kościoła Katolickiego w Polsce* (Warsaw, 1966), *Państwo bez stosów: Szkice z dziejów tolerancji w Polsce XVI i XVII w.* (Warsaw, 1967; also available in English translation under the title *State without Stakes: Polish Religious Toleration in the Sixteenth and Seventeenth Centuries* [New York, 1972]), *Arianie i katolicy* (Warsaw, 1971), *Dzieje polskiej tolerancji* (Warsaw, 1973), "Społeczeństwo wobec reformacji," in *Polska w epoce Odrodzenia: Państwo, społeczeństwo, kultura*, ed. Andrzej Wyczański (Warsaw, 1986), 331–56, and *Szlaki kultury polskiej* (Warsaw, 1986). See also the series of annuals published since 1956 by the Institute of History of the Polish Academy of Sciences under the title *Odrodzenie i Reformacja*.

8. On Jan Łaski, or John à Lasco, see Oskar Bartel, *Jan Łaski: Część I, 1499–1556* (Warsaw, 1955), and Halina Kowalska, *Działalność reformatorska Jana Łaskiego w Polsce, 1556–1560* (Wrocław, 1969). Bartel's book is also useful for its extensive bibliography.

9. In his essay "Society and the Reformation" (Społeczeństwo wobec reformacji), in *Polska w epoce Odrodzenia*, ed. Andrzej Wyczański (Warsaw, 1986), 355, Janusz Tazbir, a leading authority on the Renaissance and Reformation in Poland, makes the statement that Jan Łaski was the only outstanding theologian produced by the Protestant Reformation in Poland, but that his European fame was earned not by his writings but by his activities in Frisia and England.

10. For a short popular introduction to Hosius's life and career, see Józef Umiński, *Kardynał Stanisław Hozjusz: Biskup Warmiński, 1504–1579*, 2d. ed. (Opole, 1948).

11. On this see, for example, Stefan Zabłocki, "Poezja polsko-łacińska wczesnego renesansu," in *Problemy literatury staropolskiej: Seria druga*, ed. Janusz Pelc (Wrocław, 1973), 68–72.

12. On Coxe and Poland, see Henryk Zins, "Leonard Coxe i erazmiańskie koła w Polsce i Anglii," in *Odrodzenie i Reformacja w Polsce*, vol. 17 (Wrocław, 1972), 27–62, and this same author's *Polska w oczach anglików XIV–XVI w.* (Warsaw, 1974), 56–69. On the subject of Erasmus in Poland in general, see Claude Backvis, "La fortune d'Erasme en Pologne," in *Colloquium Erasmianum: Actes du Colloque International réuni à Mons du 26 au 29 octobre 1967 à l'occasion du cinquième centenaire de la naissance d'Erasme* (Mons, 1968), 173–202, and Henryk Barycz, "Śladami Erazma z Rotterdamu w Polsce: W 500-lecie urodzin wielkiego humanisty," in *Z epoki renesansu, reformacji i baroku* (Warsaw, 1971), 7–41. For a collection in Polish translation of Erasmus's correspondence with Poles, see Maria Cytowska, ed. and trans., *Korespondencja Erazma z Rotterdamu z Polakami* (Warsaw, 1965).

13. *Opus epistolarum Des. Erasmi Roterodami*, ed. P. S. Allen and H. M. Allen, vol. 5 (Oxford, 1924), 344–45. The letter in question is number 1393.

14. Letter no. 1915 in *Opus epistolarum Des. Erasmi Roterodami*.

Chapter 1. *Gregory of Sanok*

1. Andrzej Nowicki, *Grzegorz z Sanoka, 1406–1477* (Warsaw, 1958).
2. Philippus Callimachus, *Vita et mores Gregorii Sanocei*, ed. and trans. Irmina Lichońska (Warsaw, 1963).
3. Nowicki, *Grzegorz z Sanoka*, 146.
4. Ibid., 149, n. 84.
5. Nowicki, ibid., points out that the *Doctrinale* was in use even longer in western Europe, until 1506 in Wittenberg and until at least 1522 in Cologne.
6. On humanism in Hungary, see especially Marianna D. Birnbaum, *Humanists in a Shattered World: Croatian and Hungarian Latinity in the Sixteenth Century* (Columbus, Ohio, 1986).
7. Callimachus, *Vita*, 44.
8. Joannes Długosz Senior Canonicus Cracoviensis, *Opera omnia*, ed. Alexander Przezdziecki, vol. 13 (Cracow, 1857), 530–33. The elegy is included in the entry for the year A.D. 1434. In his anthology of Polish-Latin poetry, *Najstarsza poezja polsko-łacińska (do połowy XVI wieku)* (Wrocław, 1952), li, Marian Plezia mentions the same epitaph but characterizes it as boring and inflated and "giving off still the moldy odor of the Middle Ages."
9. On the confiscation of the original edition of Miechowita's *Chronica* and the emendations incorporated in the edition of 1521, see Ludmila Krakowiecka, *Maciej z Miechowa: Lekarz i uczony Odrodzenia* (Warsaw, 1956), 209–27. The Special Collections division of Columbia University's Butler Library has a copy of the 1521 edition of Miechowita's *Chronica*, in which I could verify the absence of any reference to Gregory of Sanok.
10. Quoted by Nowicki, *Grzegorz z Sanoka*, 106.
11. Ibid., 146, n. 79.
12. Callimachus, *Vita*, 60.
13. Ibid., 24.

Chapter 2. *From San Gimignano to Cracow*

1. My two principal sources for Buonaccorsi's biography are Gioacchino Paparelli, *Callimacho Esperiente (Filippo Buonaccorsi)* (Salerno, 1971), and Joanna Olkiewicz, *Kallimach Doświadczony* (Warsaw, 1981).
2. On Greek studies in Venice, see especially Deno John Geanakoplos, *Greek Scholars in Venice: Studies in the Dissemination of Greek Learning from Byzantium to Western Europe* (Cambridge, Mass., 1962).
3. On George of Trebizond, see John Monfasani, *George of Trebizond: A Biography and a Study of His Rhetoric* (Leiden, 1976).
4. The principal study of Pomponio Leto and the Accademia Romana is Vladimiro Zabughin's *Giulio Pomponio Leto: Saggio Critico*, 2 vols. (Rome, 1909–10).
5. The first edition of the *Liber* was published in Venice in 1479. An

English translation, under the title B. Platina, *Lives of the Popes,* edited by W. Benham, was published in London in two parts in 1888.

6. Io. Antonius Campanus, *Epistolae et poemata* (Lipsiae, 1707), 155.

7. Paparelli, *Callimacho Esperiente,* 65.

8. On Buonaccorsi's role in the conspiracy, see especially Zabughin, *Giulio Pomponio Leto,* 1:99–132.

9. In his authoritative *Giulio Pomponio Leto,* 1:98–99, Zabughin takes the position that the conspiracy was primarily Buonaccorsi's doing and on several occasions speaks of the "congiura di Callimacho" (Callimachus's conspiracy). See also 119–20. Giorgio Agosti, in his *Un politico Italiano alla Corte polacca nel secolo XV* (Il "Consilium Callimachi") (Turin, 1930), 10–11, points out that contemporary sources attribute most of the responsibility for the conspiracy to Buonaccorsi.

10. Quoted by Zabughin, *Giulio Pomponio Leto,* 1:121, and also by Agosti, *Politico Italiano,* 10, n. 3.

11. Quoted by Zabughin, *Giulio Pomponio Leto,* 129.

12. Ibid., 130.

13. Platina, *De vitis ac gestis summorum pontificum . . . liber* (Cologne, 1551), 302.

14. A marble bust of him, by Bartolomeo Bellano, can still be seen in Rome in the Palazzo Venezia, which was Paul II's principal residence from 1466 on.

15. Although an Italian study of him by Roberto Weiss bears the title *Un umanista veneziano: Papa Paolo II* (Venice, 1958).

16. Niccolò Macchiavelli, *The Discourses,* trans. Leslie J. Walker, S.J., ed. and rev. Brian Richardson, with an intro. by Bernard Crick (Penguin Books, 1981), 135–36.

17. Philippus Callimachus, *Epistulae selectae* (Wrocław, 1967), 24.

18. Joanna Olkiewicz, *Kallimach Doświadczony* (Warsaw, 1981), 47.

19. For the Latin text of the work, see Iulius Domański, ed., "Philippi Callimachi 'Ad Fanniam Swentocham Carmen,' " *Eos: Commentarii Societatis Philologiae Polonorum* 46 (1954 [1952–53]): 131–54. A Polish translation of the poem appears in Atonina Jelicz, ed., *Antologia poezji polsko-łacińskiej, 1470–1543* (Szczecin, 1985), 47–53. This anthology is a second revised edition of the anthology originally published in Warsaw in 1956. All references are to the later edition.

20. For a Polish translation, see Jelicz, *Antologia,* 56–58.

21. See the above-mentioned article by Domański in *Eos.*

22. Ibid., 153: 201–2.

23. Ibid., 147–49: 82–104.

24. Ibid., 152–53: 183–93.

25. The Latin text of the work exists only in manuscript form; for a Polish translation, see Jelicz, *Antologia,* 56–58.

26. For the Latin text of the work and accompanying Polish translation, see Philippis Callimachus, *De his quae a Venetis tentata sunt Persis ac Tartaris contra Turcos movendis,* trans. Maria Cytowska, ed. Andreas Kempfi, with commentary by Thaddeus Kowalewski (Warsaw, 1962).

27. Agosti, *Politico italiano*, 14, n. 2.

28. For the Latin text of the work and accompanying Polish translation, see Philippus Callimachus, *Historia de rege Vladislao*, ed. Irmina Lichońska, trans. Anna Komornicka, historical commentary by Thaddeus Kowalewski (Warsaw, 1961).

29. For the original Latin text and Polish translation, see *Attila*, ed. and trans. Thaddeus Kowalewski (Warsaw, 1962).

30. For the Latin text of the work and accompanying Polish translation, see Philippus Callimachus, *Vita et mores Sbignei Cardinalis*, ed. Irmina Lichońska (Warsaw, 1962).

31. Paparelli, *Callimacho Esperiente*, 161.

32. Ibid.

33. For the Latin text of the treatise, see Philippus Callimachus, *Ad Innocentiam VIII De bello Turcis inferendo oratio*, ed. Irmina Lichońska, commentary by Thaddeus Kowalewski (Warsaw, 1964). Kowalewski doubts that Callimachus did, in fact, deliver the oration in the presence of the pope on the presumed date, June 3, 1490, which was the very last day of the conference.

34. Frederick received his cardinalship only on September 20, 1493, from Pope Alexander VI, some five months after his election as archbishop of Gniezno on April 23 of that same year.

35. Paparelli, *Callimacho Esperiente*, 181.

36. Quoted in Agosti, *Politico Italiano*, 17, n. 3.

37. The letter has been preserved in the Archivo di Stato di Venezia. A text of it appears in Callimachus, *Epistulae selectae*, 144–47.

38. The text of the letter was reproduced in G. V. Coppi, *Annali, memorie et huomini ilustri de San Gimignano* (Florence, 1695).

39. Giorgio Agosti reproduced the text of the *Consilia* from the Cracow edition of 1887 and provided it with an Italian translation in *Politico italiano*, 37–44.

40. On Polish opinion of Callimachus, see Jerzy Zathey, "Z dziejów staropolskich opinii o Kallimachu," in *Kultura i literatura dawnej Polski*, ed. Jan Zygmunt Jakubowski, Zdzisław Libera, and Janina Kulczycka-Saloni (Warsaw, 1968), 32–48.

41. On Callimachus's (and Copernicus's) Italian friends, see Jerzy Zathey, "Włoscy przyjaciele Filipa Kallimacha i Mikołaja Kopernika," *Renesans: Sztuka i ideologia*, ed. Tadeusz S. Jaroszewski (Warsaw, 1976), 125–33.

42. Callimachus, *Epistulae selectae*, 90.

43. On Callimachus's polemic with Ficino over this issue, see also Giorgio Radetti, "Demoni i sogni nella critica di Callimacho Esperiente al Ficino," in *Umanesimo e esoterismo* (Padua, 1960), 111–21.

44. Callimachus, *Epistulae selectae*, 96.

45. The volume came out on December 12, 1486.

46. See Giorgio Radetti, "Il problema del peccato in Giovanni Pico della Mirandola e in Filippo Buonaccorsi detto Callimacho Esperiente," in *L'opera e il pensiero di Giovanni Pico della Mirandola nella storia dell'umanesimo: Convegno Internazionale (Mirandola: 15–18 Settembre 1963)*, vol. 2 (Florence, 1963), 103–

17, and Giorgio Zathey, "Recherches sur le milieu de Callimaque Experiens et de Jean Pico: Trilogus in rebus futuris annorum XX proximorum," in ibid., 119–47, especially 124.

47. Callimachus, *Epistulae selectae*, 126.

48. This and the following quotation are from Callimachus, *Epistulae selectae*, 90.

49. Ibid., 6.

50. Ibid., 124.

Chapter 3. *The Humanist a-Touring*

1. On Celtis's life and career, see Lewis W. Spitz, *Conrad Celtis: The German Arch-Humanist* (Cambridge, 1957); Leonard Forster, ed. and trans., *Selections from Conrad Celtis, 1459–1508* (Cambridge, 1948), 1–19; Kurt Adel, ed. and trans., *Konrad Celtis: Poeta laureatus*, (Graz, 1960), 5–23; Eckhard Bernstein, *German Humanism* (Boston, 1983), 56–67; and Fred J. Nichols, ed. and trans., *An Anthology of Neo-Latin Poetry* (New Haven, 1979), 62–63, 693–95. On Celtis in Poland, see Antonina Jelicz's booklet *Konrad Celtis: Na tle wczesnego renesansu w Polsce* (Warsaw, 1956). In his article "Twórczość Celtisa jako źródło niektórych motywów poezji polsko-łacińskiej pierwszej połowy XVI wieku," in *Od prerenesansu do Oświecenia: Z dziejów inspiracji klasycznych w literaturze polskiej* (Warsaw, 1976), 118–22, Stefan Zabłocki examines Celtis's influence on Polish-Latin poetry of the first half of the sixteenth century by tracing the movement of certain motifs found in his work, particularly the image of Poland as a northern land of terrible frost and snow.

2. Latin text in Forster, *Selections*, 20. Succeeding quotations are from the same page.

3. For the Latin text of the work, see Iohannes Rupprich, ed., *Conradus Celtis Protucius: Oratio in gymnasio in Ingelstadio publice recitata cum carminibus ad orationem pertinentibus* (Leipzig, 1932). Rupprich's slightly corrected edition of the text, together with an English translation, appear in Forster, *Selections*, 36–65. My own translations are based on the text as it appears in Forster.

4. Latin text in Forster, *Selections*, 34.

5. Antonina Jelicz, *Konrad Celtis*, 42–43. In his monumental *Historia Uniwersytetu Jagiellońskiego w epoce humanizmu* (Cracow, 1935), 259, Henryk Barycz states that it was specifically for the study of mathematics that Celtis came to Cracow.

6. Fred J. Nichols has some interesting remarks about this in his *Anthology of Neo-Latin Poetry*, 62–63.

7. Ursinus was one of several physicians who became prominent in Polish Renaissance humanism. For a collection of his works in Latin, see Jan Ursyn z Krakowa, *Modus Epistolandi cum epistolis exemplaribus et orationibus annexis*, ed. and trans. and with intro. by Lidia Winniczuk (Warsaw, 1957).

8. Text in Karl Hartfelder, ed., *Fünf Bücher Epigramme von Conrad Celtes* (Hildesheim, 1963), 1.

9. Conradus Celtis Protucius, *Quattuor libri amorum,* ed. Felicitas Pindter (Leipzig, 1934), 10–11:11–16.

10. Celtis's brief description of the Carpathian Mountains, which appears in the fifth elegy of the *Quattuor libri amorum,* is titled "Ad Hasilinam cum descriptione Carpathi seu Suevi montis" (To Hasilina, with a Description of the Carpathian or Suebian Mountains). His account of a visit to the salt mines of Wieliczka appears in the sixth elegy, "Ad Ianum Terinum de salifodinis Sarmatiae, quas per funem immissus lustraverat" (To Ianus Terinus on the Salt Mines of Sarmatia, Which He Inspected Suspended by a Rope). The description of the bison and bison hunting comes in the final elegy of the first book of the *Amores,* which is addressed to the Vistula River ("Ad Vistulam fluvium ortum et exitum eius describens et de visontibus et eorum venationibus").

11. *Quattuor libri amorum,* 29–30:9–32.

12. Jelicz, *Konrad Celtis,* 33.

13. Conradus Celtis Protucius, *Libri odarum quattuor,* ed. Felicitas Pindter (Leipzig, 1937), 23:13–16.

14. Jelicz, *Konrad Celtis,* 14. For the Latin text of the lecture, see Jan Ursyn z Krakowa, *Modus epistolandi* (Wrocław, 1957).

15. Ursyn, *Modus epistolandi.*

16. *Libri odarum quattuor,* 20:33–41.

17. For the complete Latin text of the ode, see ibid., 14–15. The text, with accompanying English translation, also appears in Forster, *Selections,* 28–33. For additional commentary on the same poem, see Forster, 84–90.

18. Hans Rupprich, ed., *Der Briefwechsel des Konrad Celtis* (Munich, 1934), 393.

19. Karl Hartfelder, ed., *Fünf Bücher Epigramme von Konrad Celtis* (Hildesheim, 1963), 7.

20. Ibid., 5.

21. Ibid., 7.

22. *Libri odarum quattuor,* 25–26.

23. Latin original in Hartfelder, *Fünf Bücher Epigramme,* 9.

24. For the identification of Bernardus Viliscus, I am indebted to Jelicz, *Konrad Celtis,* 46.

25. *Quattuor libri amorum,* 13:29–36.

26. For the Latin text of the work, with accompanying English translation, see Forster, *Selections,* 36–65. Commentary on the "Oration" appears on 96–111.

27. The texts of the letters appear in Rupprich, *Briefwechsel des Konrad Celtis,* 336–38, 361–62.

28. For the text of the letter in German translation, see ibid., 434–35.

Chapter 4. *Period of Transition*

1. Letters of June 26, 1499, March 3, 1500, June 30, 1500, October 26, 1502, and January 20, 1503.

2. "Propempticon . . . ad . . . Sebastianum Maghyum Pannonium" (February 15, 1508).

3. Paulus Crosnensis Ruthenus, *Carmina,* ed. Maria Cytowska (Warsaw, 1962), 75.

4. The texts of these poems, and all others of Paul of Krosno, can be found in the Cytowska edition of the *Carmina.*

5. A college of twelve priests of Mars Gradivus, instituted by Numa, that made solemn processions through Rome on the Calends of March. They had the custom of holding sumptuous feasts after their processions.

6. *Tragoedia secunda Thyestes* and *Tragoedia sexta Troas.*

7. "Reverendissimo in Christo patri et domino, domine Ioanni Lubrantio," in *Carmina,* 162–67.

8. "Elegia ad Ioannem Vislicium," *Carmina,* 197–99.

9. "Carmina magistri Pauli Crosnensis Rutheni de felicissimo reditu ex Vienna Austriaca illustrissimi . . . Sigismundi regis Poloniae . . ." in *Carmina,* 189–96.

10. "Epithalamion" in *Carmina,* 151–62.

11. For a study of Pannonius in English, see Marianna Birnbaum, *Janus Pannonius: Poet and Politician* (Zagreb, 1981).

12. For a good article on Vitéz in English, see Leslie S. Domokos, "János Vitéz, the Father of Hungarian Humanism (1408–1472)," *New Hungarian Quarterly* 20 (Summer 1979): 142–50.

13. Janusz Pelc, *Literatura staropolska i jej związki europiejskie: Prace poświęcone VII Międzynarodowemu Kongresowi Slawistów w roku 1973* (Wrocław, 1973), 159.

14. There had been earlier efforts to publish Pannonius. In 1505 István Brodárics (1471–1539) negotiated with the distinguished Venetian printer Aldus Manutius concerning a Pannonius edition, but nothing came of it. He tried again, also unsuccessfully, in 1512, when the volume prepared by Paul of Krosno made its appearance.

15. These are discussed by Pelc, *Literatura,* 161–62.

16. Ioannes Visliciensis, *Bellum Prutenum,* ed. Ioannes Smereka (Lwów, 1932), 41–42. The entire letter to Paul of Krosno ("Epistula ad Magistrum Paulem de Crosna") appears on 41–44. A complete Polish translation of *The Prussian War* appears in Jan z Wiślicy, *Wojna pruska,* trans. and ed. Jan Smereka, *Zbiór pisarzy polsko-łacińskich* (Lwów, 1932).

17. "Ad . . . Petrum Tomiczki Dei gratia Episcopum Premisliensem ac vice Cancellarium Regni Poloniae meritissimum Ioannis Visliciensis iambicum trimetrum Archilochicum pro commendatione libellorum suorum Regiae maestati," in *Bellum Prutenum,* 106:1–4. The "iambicum trimetrum Archilochicum" of the title refers to the verse meter derived from the Greek poet Archilochos (7th–6th century, B.C.), who introduced it to literature.

18. *Bellum Prutenum,* bk. 1:44–60.

19. A reference to the fifty-six standards of the Knights of the Cross hung above the sarcophagus of Saint Stanislaus in the chapel of the Wawel Castle in Cracow.

20. The battle of Grunwald was fought on July 15, 1410.

21. The father of Diomedes, who took part in the expedition of the Seven against Thebes, near the mountains of Sphinx.

22. Literally the princes, or kings, of Danaus, who was a king of Argos. The selection is from the *Bellum Prutenum*, bk. 2:320–26.

Chapter 5. *Copernicus*

1. On this see, for example, Andrzej Nowicki, *Kopernik człowiek Odrodzenia* (Warsaw, 1953), 34–35.

2. Copernicus became a canon of Frambork (Frauenburg) in Warmia in 1497, the year after he left for Italy.

3. Fracastoro's major work was *Syphilis sive Morbi Gallicus* (1530), a verse treatise on the venereal disease. This was presumably the first use of the term syphilis.

4. Copernicus's own copy of the dictionary has been preserved and is housed in the Uppsala University Library in Sweden. Teofilakt Symokatta, *Listy*, trans. Nicholas Copernicus, ed. with an intro. by Ryszard Gansiniec (Wrocław, 1953), xi.

5. For the best introduction in English to Manutius's life and work, see Martin Lowry, *The World of Aldus Manutius* (Ithaca, 1979). On the connections between the Manuzio family and Poland, see Stanisław Łempicki, *Renesans i Humanizm w Polsce: Materiały do studiów* (Warsaw, 1952), 33–99 ("Polskie koneksje dynastii Manucjuszów"). For a very detailed study of the Manuzio printing office and its effect on Poland, see Mieczysław Rokosz, *Wenecka oficyna Alda Manucjusza i Polska w orbicie jej wpływów* (Wrocław, 1982).

6. On the chronology of Copernicus's Greek studies, see Simokatta, *Listy*, xi–xiii.

7. The letters are typologically distinguished in Copernicus's Latin as "amatoria," "moralis," and "ruralis," the last referring to those of a pastoral character.

8. Symokatta, *Listy*, 68–69.

9. I am following here the discussion of the matter by Ryszard Gansiniec in his introduction to Symokatta, *Listy*, xvi–xix.

Chapter 6. *Pope Leo X, the Bison, and Renaissance Cultural Politics*

1. For an interesting discussion of Hussovianus and his poem about the bison, see also the Belgian scholar Claude Backvis's article, "Nicholas de Hussów," in *Literatura—komparatystyka—folklor: Księga poświęcona Julianowi Krzyżanowskiemu* (Warsaw, 1968), 40–72.

2. Charles L. Mee, Jr., *White Robe, Black Robe* (New York, 1972), 146–48. On Leo X's fondness for the hunt, see also Herbert M. Vaughan, *The Medici Popes (Leo X and Clement VII)* (New York, 1908), 192–214.

3. On Ciołek's reception in Rome in 1518, see Bronisław Biliński, "Polskie tradycje naukowe w Rzymie," *Przegląd Humanistyczyny* 3 (1963): 36.

4. These are the dates suggested by the Soviet scholar V. I. Doroshkevich in his book *Novolatinskaya poeziya Belorussii i Litvy: Pervaya polovina XVI v.* (Minsk, 1979), 135. The Polish historian W. Pociecha, "Królowa Bona (1494–1557)," in *Czasy i ludzie Odrodzenia*, vol. 4 (Poznań, 1958), 230, places Hussovianus's arrival in Rome only in 1521.

5. Nicolaus Hussovianus, *Carmina*, ed. Ioannes Pelczar, Corpus Antiquissimorum Poetarum Poloniae Latinorum usque ad Ioannem Cochanovium 4 (Cracow, 1894), 4–5.

6. *De statura, feritate ac venatione bisontis carmen*, 10:29–34.

7. Czesław Miłosz, *The Issa Valley*, trans. Louis Iribarne (New York, 1981), 6–7.

8. On Adrian VI and his pontificate, see Johann Posner, *Der deutsche Papst Adrian VI* (Recklinghausen, 1962).

9. The text of Kasprowicz's lecture, which includes excerpts from his translation of Hussovianus's poem, can be found in Jan Kasprowicz, *Dzieła wybrane*, vol. 4 (Cracow, 1958), 381–403.

10. *Antologia poezji polsko-łacińskiej, 1470–1543*, ed. and with an intro. by Antonina Jelicz (Warsaw, 1957; reprinted Szczecin, 1985).

11. Nikolai Gussovsky, *Pesn o zubre*. A translation from the Latin by Yakov Poretsky and Iosif Semezhon, *Neman* 7 (1968): 47–70.

12. The Belorussian translation, by Yazep Semyazhon (the Belorussian version of Semezhon's name), appears in *Polymya* 6 (1969): 69–103.

13. Doroshkevich, *Novolatinskaya poeziya Belorussii i Litvy*, 76–77.

14. Ibid., 77.

15. Ibid., 86.

16. This is discussed briefly in ibid., 84–85.

17. *Neman* 7 (1968): 50.

Chapter 7. *At the Courts of Kings and Emperors*

1. Ioannes Dantiscus Poeta Laureatus, *Carmina*, ed. Stanislaus Skimina (Cracow, 1950), 298:83–92. This is the standard edition of Dantiscus's poetry in Latin.

2. Interesting information on Dantiscus as a diplomat, in the context of the sixteenth-century Polish diplomatic service, can be found in *Polska służba dyplomatyczna XVI–XVII wieku*, ed. Zbigniew Wójcik (Warsaw, 1966).

3. For the best biography of Dantiscus to date, see Zbigniew Nowak, *Jan Dantyszek: Potret renesansowego humanisty* (Wrocław, 1982).

4. On the Congress of Vienna of 1515 in general, see Krzysztof Baczkowski, *Zjazd Wiedeński 1515* (Warsaw, 1975). There is also some useful material in the older study of Xawery Liske, *Studia z dziejów wieku XVI* (Poznań, 1867).

5. Baczkowski, *Zjazd Wiedeński*, 179.

6. A good popular biography of Queen Bona is Marceli Kosman's *Królowa Bona* (Warsaw, 1971).

7. I am following the account of the matter in Nowak, *Jan Dantyszek*, 112–16.

8. Ibid., 119. There is also a more detailed account of Dantiscus's English trip, with translated excerpts from his correspondence about it with King Sigismund and Vice-Chancellor Tomicki, in H. Świderska, "Jan Dantyszek, a Polish Diplomat in England in 1522," *Oxford Slavonic Papers* 10 (1962): 38–45.

9. Świderska, "Jan Dantyszek," 44.

10. Nowak, *Jan Dantyszek*, 138.

11. Ibid., 200–202.

12. Dantyszek's relationship with Copernicus is discussed by Nowak, *Jan Dantyszek*, 195–98.

13. Ibid., 199.

14. For further information on Dantiscus and humanists in the Netherlands especially, see Henry de Vocht, *John Dantiscus and His Netherlandish Friends as Revealed by Their Correspondence, 1522–1546* (Louvain, 1961).

Chapter 8. *The Hell-Raiser Who Became Primate of Poland*

1. Andreas Cricius, *Carmina*, ed. Casimirus Morawski (Cracow, 1888), 79–80.

2. Krzycki's other poems on Koszyrski include "Ad Coributum" (229–30), "Lamentatio Coributi patris ganeae ad se ipsum" (230), "Epitaphium Coributi patris ganeae" (233–34), "Aliud" (234–35), "Aliud" (235), "Apothegmata" (235), "Aliud" (235–36), and "Aliud" (236). Page numbers refer to the collection Cricius, *Carmina*.

3. Andrzej Krzycki, *Poezje*, trans. Edwin Jędrkiewicz, ed. Antonina Jelicz (Warsaw, 1962), 9.

4. Latin text, *Carmina*, 206.

5. Ibid., 210, xx.

6. Latin text, *Carmina*, 210, xix.

7. Ibid., 199, n.1. The relevant passage from Catullus (47, 1) is "Porci et Socration, duae sinistrae / Pisonis. . . ." The "Porci" probably refers to a member of the Porcius family. Porcius Cato Uticensis was a leading opponent of Julius Caesar, and Porcius Licinus (about 100 B.C.) was a poet.

8. The "poor lions" signify the coat of arms of the duchess of Meklenburg, who had sought a marriage with Sigismund of Poland. The "Hungarian wolf," in the same line, refers to Barbara Zápolya's coat of arms, while the "eagle" is, of course, the Polish standard.

9. Antonina Jelicz, ed., *Antologia poezji-łacińskiej, 1470–1543* (Warsaw, 1956), 35.

10. "In eundem," *Carmina*, 131:3–4, xxviii.

11. "In Ioannem Górski de Miłosław," in *Carmina*, 130:2.

12. Ibid., 130:4.

13. *Carmina*, 133, n. 2.
14. "Apollo ad lectorem," in *Carmina*, 139:15–16.
15. "Republica ad poetas suos," in *Carmina*, 138:15–16.
16. For the Latin text, see *Carmina*, 161–62.
17. See the poem "In Christophorum de Szydlowiec, castellanum et capitaneum Cracoviensem," in *Carmina*, 150.
18. "In eundem Christophorum," in *Carmina*, 151.
19. Latin text in *Carmina*, 150.
20. For the Latin text, see ibid., 102–4.
21. Ibid.
22. Ibid., 105.
23. The Gdańsk revolt of 1525–26 is discussed briefly by Antonina Jelicz in her introductions to *Antologia poezji polsko-łacińskiej*, 36, and Andrzej Krzycki, *Poezje* (Warsaw, 1962), 15–16. For a more detailed account of the episode and the background to it, see Zygmunt Wojciechowski, *Zygmunt Stary (1506–1548)* (Warsaw, 1979), 218–63.
24. Latin text in *Carmina*, 105–6.
25. Krzycki's letter to Erasmus was published, with commentary, by Maria Cytowska in *Meander*, vol. 9 (Warsaw, 1954), 97. See also Krzycki, *Poezje*, 16.
26. Quotations in this paragraph from *Carmina*, 96:156.
27. Georgius Sabinus, "Elegia IIII, Liber III," in *Poemata et numero librorum aucta, et emendatius impresa, quam antea fuerunt* (Leipzig, 1558), pages unnumbered. For a Polish translation of the Sabinus elegy, see Krzycki, *Poezje*, 126–27. Sabinus wrote several other poems (in Latin) to Poles, which are contained in the Leipzig collection of his works. These include elegies to Eustachy Knobelsdorf ("Eustachius A. Knobelsdorf, Canonicum Varmiensem, Poëtam clarissimum," elegy 10, book 6), to Stanisław Hosius ("Ad Episcopum Varmiensem Stanislaum Hosium," elegy 14, book 6), and on the nuptials of Sigismund August and Elizabeth of Austria ("De nuptiis inclyti Regis Poloniae Sigismundi Augusti, et Elissae Caesaris Ferdinandi filiae"), and several poems in his "Liber Hendecasyllaborum" (Book of Hendecasyllables) to Jan Dantyszek and one to Jan Przerębski (1514–62), archbishop of Gniezno and vice-chancellor of the Polish Crown.

Chapter 9. *Clemens Ianicius*

1. He is usually referred to in Polish as Klemens Janicki, although this is surely inaccurate. The -cki ending of a Polish family name indicates noble origin. Since the likelihood seems great that Ianicius was of peasant origin, the form Janicki would be inappropriate. Lack of evidence, however, makes it difficult to determine precisely what the poet's original name may have been; Janik or Januszek have been suggested. Most Polish scholars now refer to him either by his Latin name Ianicius or by the Polish form of this, Janicjusz.
2. Latin text in Klemens Janicki, *Carmina*, trans. Edwin Jędrkiewicz, ed. and with an introd. by Jerzy Krókowski (Wrocław, 1966), 48–58. This edition

also includes parallel Polish translations of all the poems. All further quotations will be from this edition, which will be identified in the notes as *Carmina*. For a good selection of Ianicius's poetry in Polish translation (without the Latin texts), see Klemens Janicjusz, *Poezje wybrane*, trans. and ed. Zygmunt Kubiak (Warsaw, 1975).

3. For the Latin text of the epigram, see *Carmina*, 148.

4. Ibid., 150 ("De morte Cri[cii] sub bellum Leopolitanum").

5. Ibid.

6. For a rather interesting account of the doctor's degree and laurel wreath presented to Ianicius in Italy, see Ludwik Ćwikliński, *O wawrzynie doktorskim i poetyckim Klemensa Janickiego* (Cracow, 1919). Ćwikliński was also the author of the first Polish monograph on Janicki, *Klemens Janicki: Poeta uwieńczony (1516–1543)* (Cracow, 1893).

7. *Carmina*, 22:23–32.

8. The quotations in this paragraph are from *Carmina*, 126 and 128:41–47 and 73–74. Ianicius also speaks of his impressions of the gardens of Cardinal Bembo's residence in Padua in an epigram to his patron, Piotr Kmita. See "*Epigrammata*," 52, "Ad Petrum Cmitam," in *Carmina*, 164–66.

9. *Carmina*, 371 in the commentary on elegy 21.

10. My information on Antonin is based on the note on him in *Carmina*, 435.

11. The quotations in this paragraph are from *Carmina*, 196:9–12.

12. Quotations in this passage are from *Carmina*, 206–7:175–80 and 199–212.

Chapter 10. *Epilogue*

1. On Biernat of Lublin's life and work, see Jerzy Ziomek's introduction to Biernat z Lublina, *Wybór pism* (Warsaw, 1954), and the discussion of Biernat's *Aesop* in the same author's *Renesans* (Warsaw, 1973), 108–13. Although considerably longer and more comprehensive, Ziomek's essay on Biernat in the *Wybór pism* edition is in some respects outdated and marred by an obvious socialist-realist bias.

2. For a good account of Polish printing from the fifteenth through eighteenth centuries, see Helena Szwejkowska, *Książka drukowana XV–XVII wieku: Zarys historyczny* (Warsaw, 1987).

3. On Kochanowski as both a Polish and a Latin writer, see the excellent essay by Wiktor Weintraub, "The Latin and the Polish Kochanowski: The Two Faces of a Poet," in *Actes du Vᵉ Congrès de l'Association de Littérature Comparée* (Amsterdam, 1969), 663–70.

4. For very good Polish translations of Kochanowski's *foricoenia*, see Kochanowski, *Foricoenia czyli fraszki łacińskie*, trans. Leopold Staff (Warsaw, 1956). Like Julian Ejsmond, Staff was also a twentieth-century Polish poet strongly attracted to the challenge of translating Kochanowski's Latin works into Polish.

5. All citations from Kochanowski's Latin poems refer to the edition Jo-

annes Cochanovius, *Carmina Latina*, ed. Josephus Przyborowski (Warsaw, 1884). This edition also contains Polish translations of the works. For other Polish translations of Kochanowski's Latin poetry, see Jan Kochanowski, *Utwory łacińskie*, trans. Julian Ejsmond (Warsaw, 1953). A twentieth-century poet with a great fondness for Kochanowski, Ejsmond aimed primarily at poetic translations of Kochanowski's works, which he achieved with some success; as translations, however, they are quite free.

6. Cochanovius, *Carmina Latina*, 241.

7. Quotations from Desportes's "Adieu à la Poloigne" are from his *Oeuvres*, ed. Alfred Michiels (Paris, 1858). The text of the poem appears on 424–25.

8. Cochanovius, *Carmina Latina*, 357:48–59.

9. The text of the elegy appears in Cochanovius, *Carmina Latina*, 136–39.

Index

Library of Congress Cataloging-in-Publication Data

Segel, Harold B., 1930–
    Renaissance culture in Poland : the rise of humanism, 1470–1543 /
Harold B. Segel.
        p.   cm.
    Includes index.
    ISBN 0-8014-2286-8 (alk. paper)
    1. Poland—Civilization—to 1795.   2. Humanism—Poland.
3. Humanists—Poland—Biography.   4. Renaissance—Poland.
I. Title.
DK4252.S44   1989
943.8'02—dc19   89-30788
                                                              CIP